FROM FEAR TO FAITH

Living in the Presence and Power of God

JANELLE TEMPLETON

Copyright © 2016, 2017 Janelle Templeton.

All rights reserved. No part of this book may be used or reproduced by any means, graphic, electronic, or mechanical, including photocopying, recording, taping or by any information storage retrieval system without the written permission of the author except in the case of brief quotations embodied in critical articles and reviews.

WestBow Press books may be ordered through booksellers or by contacting:

WestBow Press
A Division of Thomas Nelson & Zondervan
1663 Liberty Drive
Bloomington, IN 47403
www.westbowpress.com
1 (866) 928-1240

Because of the dynamic nature of the Internet, any web addresses or links contained in this book may have changed since publication and may no longer be valid. The views expressed in this work are solely those of the author and do not necessarily reflect the views of the publisher, and the publisher hereby disclaims any responsibility for them.

Any people depicted in stock imagery provided by Thinkstock are models, and such images are being used for illustrative purposes only. Certain stock imagery © Thinkstock.

Cover image by John Ishee Photography.

Unless otherwise noted, scriptures are taken from the New King James Version. Copyright © 1982 by Thomas Nelson, Inc. Used by permission. All rights reserved.

Scripture quotations marked NLT are taken from the Holy Bible, New Living Translation, copyright 1996, 2004, 2007. Used by permission of Tyndale House Publishers, Inc. Carol Stream, Illinois 60188. All rights reserved.

Scripture quotations marked NIV are taken from the Holy Bible, New International Version. NIV. Copyright 1973, 1978, 1984 by International Bible Society. Used by permission of Zondervan. All rights reserved.

Scripture quotations marked NASB are taken from the New American Standard Bible, Copyright 1960, 1962, 1963, 1968, 1971, 1972, 1973, 1975, 1977, 1995 by The Lockman Foundation. Used by permission.

ISBN: 978-1-5127-7922-6 (sc)
ISBN: 978-1-5127-7923-3 (hc)
ISBN: 978-1-5127-7921-9 (e)

Library of Congress Control Number: 2017903628

Print information available on the last page.

WestBow Press rev. date: 4/14/2017

In honor of my parents, who gave me their
persevering and eternal prayer covering.
In gratitude to my husband, Mitch, and sons Caleb and Josh, for
their patience and love through my journey from fear to faith.

Contents

Preface ix
Introduction: The Faith of a Mustard Seed xv
Introduction to Growing Faith: Peace in the Midst of Fear xx

1. **The Power of Fear** 1
    Exposing the Root of Fear 1
    The Danger of Doubt 7
    The Problem of Presumption 13
    Fear Arouses Anger 21
    The Fear of the Lord 27
    Growing Faith 1: The Unraveling of Fear and the Revival of Faith .33

2. **The Power of a Hardened Heart** 55
    What Is a Hardened Heart? 55
    Why a Hardened Heart? 61
    Hardened to Understanding 70
    Hardened By Unbelief 78
    "I Believe, Help My Unbelief" 85
    Growing Faith 2: An Immediate Test of Faith 91

3. **The Power of Knowing God** 101
    To Know Christ as the Way 101
    To Seek His Face 106
    To Know His Glory 114
    To Know God's Fullness 124

    Empowered to Know Him 131
    Growing Faith 3: Knowing God versus Knowing Religion 141

4. **The Power of Hearing God** 155
    "Can You Hear Me Now?" 155
    Set Your Mind to Hear 165
    Focused to Hear 174
    Hearing Empowers Holiness 182
    Hear What the Spirit Says 193
    Growing Faith 4: "This is My Beloved Son, Hear Him!" 202

5. **The Power of Understanding** 217
    Hear and Understand 217
    Prepared for Understanding 233
    The Gift of Understanding 244
    God's Presence Opens Understanding 252
    Understanding God's Ways 266
    Growing Faith 5: Unity and the Power of Understanding 276
    The Spirit of Understanding—We'll Understand It All By and By 289

6. **The Faith of a "Mustard Tree"** 297
    The Seed of Faith—His Word 297
    Faith that Believes—His Will 307
    Faith That Surrenders—His Power 322
    Faith that Obeys His Ways 330
    A Tree of Life 347
    Growing Faith 6: Sheltered by Faith 358

Leaders' Answer Guide 373

Preface

There are many things God calls us to do and many ways He may ask us to serve. His call is not always into vocational ministry for we are a body with many purposes and talents. As Christians, He desires us to serve Him in *every* vocation. While there is a unique purpose for the entirety of our existence, life is also a series of many small moments that often leave an impact in ways we may not notice. God wants to be a part of each. As we study, we learn how God will use each moment to grow faith and provide peace when we respond to Him. Sometimes, the difficulty is realizing His presence and power is an available provision. The difficulty often is living and reflecting His presence.

Most of us are familiar with the phrase "God does not call the qualified but qualifies those He calls." This is a true statement intended to help us realize God's plans for us often exceed how we perceive ourselves. While it is intended to encourage fulfillment of an unimaginable purpose, it still can leave us somewhat in a quandary. "So, how does He qualify me? Will I recognize the process? How do I work with it or surrender to it when the path seems unclear? What am I supposed to do?"

After I became a Christian at a young age, I sensed God speaking to me. I had a deep hunger to know and talk to Him. My relationship with God sustained me through struggles of youth and mercifully drew me back to Him when I wandered.

When I was a young mother, one path led me into a wilderness of difficulty on many levels—marriage, health, and ministry. The intensity of these struggles was physically distressing at times, but I sensed God preparing the way for something. Satan's attacks intensified and came at me from all levels almost destroying everything precious including close friendships, leadership, and purpose. In the midst of it, I knew God was calling me to an equipping ministry, but every circumstance seemed to undermine it and obscure the path to follow. As a CPA, I was not certain what form or level this ministry would take. During this confusion, I found myself asking the questions above.

On July 4, 2000, I experienced an intense time of conviction, cleansing, and closeness to God so powerful that it was also unsettling. On this Independence Day, I was convicted of my need for greater dependence on God to experience freedom from fear. I didn't know how to explain it as I didn't fully understand it then. Afterward, God began to reveal Himself in remarkable ways through intercession. However, I still wasn't sure what I was supposed to do.

A short time later, I made a public profession at church. My father and pastor prayed a prayer of ministry consecration over me. So did a leader of an International Women's Ministry. But now what? Seminary? No leading in that direction. For a time, I was a leader in my church's women's ministry, but what I sensed God birthing in me was not consistent with ministry in the church at the time. As I continued to sort out God's leading, this word began to resonate loudly: "Be still and know that I am God."

Through obstacles, fear, failure, and detours of confusion and self-focus, God reiterated: "My 'child-with-a-Martha-heart,' stop trying to do something. Come, spend time with Me." The hunger God gave me as a child to know Him deeply now intersected His calling to equip me for an equipping ministry. To qualify me for His purpose didn't require seminary, exhaustive service, or working in missions at the ends of the earth. Those are the most obvious and God-ordained paths for some, but it wasn't His leading for me. This uncertainty resulted in a tough battle doubting His calling and my worthiness for it. I didn't fit the mold and could see no obvious place to fit in.

While God encourages, many others remind us of how unfit we may be to fulfill God's purpose. This intensifies the battle within between fear and faith. To overcome requires solitude in the prayer closet—the God-given source for intimacy and empowerment. Given prayer's power, Satan will and did seek to undermine and attack it intensely. As a result, solitude required time away from the crowds, rest as a leader for a season, and seclusion sometimes even from other leaders. Solitude in prayer is intimacy with the all-powerful, all-knowing, loving, forgiving, cleansing, empowering God of redemption and empowerment.

It was during this time of solitude that God began to unfold the role fear played in undermining my purpose. As God began unraveling strongholds of fear through His Word and by facing fearful situations, He also began revealing Himself in miraculous, personal ways. Following His baptism, Jesus spent forty days in the wilderness in prayer and in testing. My journey required meditating and regurgitating one particular chapter in His Word—learning how to appropriate its greatest and tiniest details.

More important, I discovered the need to understand His ways. Early in life, I had a hunger for intimacy with God that fueled study of scripture. But this quiet, still journey with God revealed Christ's example to live one's purpose in a fresh way. I began to see the life of Jesus, the Son of Man, set before me in scripture as a Man God groomed for leadership who equipped the disciples in similar fashion. Through Judges 6 and Christ's New Testament example of intimacy with God—and His equipping of the disciples—God equipped me. God revealed how the most important preparation is not limited to learning a skill or a method. It is not limited to perfecting a work or striving in exhaustive fashion to execute a ministry, *but to grow in faith.* His qualifying work in the disciples, in Gideon, and in us is to help us surrender to faith's growth.

This path is different for everyone according to God's unique design, purpose, and vocation. For some it may be on-the-job-training only; for others, it may require short or long seasons of wilderness training and refining. Even through these differences, there are similar parallels for equipping revealed in both the Old and New Testaments. It is these similarities we want to identify and apply.

When a gardener prunes his garden, he must understand the master plan for his garden design. To bring that plan to life, he must understand each plant, the season it blooms or produces fruit, when and how it needs to be pruned, and how much or how little water and fertilizer is necessary. In southern states at least, February is the prime month for pruning roses. For most types of roses, the further back they are pruned, the more they will flourish. February, however, is the worst time for pruning azaleas, and one should never cut azaleas back. Instead, a careful shaping is needed. If they were pruned in February, immature azalea blooms would be cut off preventing a beautiful showcase of spring color.

Christ is our Master Gardener. Through Him, all life is created. He knows every intricate part of us and how we fit into God's eternal plan. Christ knows our strengths and weaknesses—what needs pruning and what needs feeding to display God's glory in due season.

As the Master Gardner, Christ has a plan for pruning us so we experience peace and work with, not against, His Spirit. This is God's process of sanctification or molding us into the image of Christ. We hinder growth when we live more under the influence of fear than faith, which causes unnecessary strife and internal conflict, the opposite of peace and rest.

This process is different for each Christian. Some of us are roses while others are azaleas with different needs and purposes. Yet there are general principles to learn about gardening among all. God's ways we seek to observe in this study are the universal, general truths God unfolds through Christ and the Spirit. Our goal is to learn enough of the Gardner's techniques so that one trusts the pruning process. It is to recognize that painful events occur to enhance beauty in the next season of life. It is to face these events with faith, not fear.

Regardless of one's calling, Christians have been given a seed of faith that God intends to grow. It is a process that equips us to be godly spouses, parents, friends, neighbors, coworkers, siblings, children, or servants! Growing faith strengthens us on every level and helps us live the abundant life. It helps us live in His presence and to reveal His power. This is not a silent or blind process of growth that just happens; it is a process God intends us to seek, embrace, and see with spiritual eyes. We come to know Him more fully through this process. The by-product is empowerment and equipping to understand and fulfill our purpose.

From Fear to Faith uses Judges 6 and Mark's gospel as the core text framing the ways of God to grow faith. Through these examples and many other scriptures, we learn the ways of God to strengthen faith through everyday encounters, great difficulties, and great needs. We study how fear, doubt, and unbelief strive against this process of growth.

We all have areas of our lives we would love to enhance. The battle between fear and faith exhausts our dreams from becoming reality. As long as we are frustrated and distracted with this important dilemma, we perhaps fail to positively impact our wider sphere of influence. Our light can be obscured or hidden by difficulty. Our nation is in serious need of good people sharing God's goodness and love. I know many are praying for revival in our nation. For it to be revived, the church must also make a difference. For a church to make a difference, its people must be renewed and empowered to reveal God's love.

In October 1999, through a study of Ezra, God led me to the intercessory prayer in Ezra 9, and particularly the following from Ezra 9:9:

> For we were slaves. Yet our God did not forsake us in our bondage; but He extended mercy to us in the sight of the kings of Persia, to revive us, to repair the house of our God, to rebuild its ruins, and to give us a wall in Judah and Jerusalem.

As I continued to pray and meditate on this verse, God revealed His ways for revival in it:

"God did not forsake us, but extended mercy to revive us"—God *revives His people.*

"God repairs His house"—God *repairs the church.*

"God rebuilds" Jerusalem—God *rebuilds a nation.*

"God gives a wall"—a nation under God *receives His protection.*

Revive. Repair. Rebuild. Protect. Through this study, I pray you will join in, or intensify, intercession for revival. More important, I pray God will use this study to remove fear, whether obvious or subtle, by empowering faith. God does not leave us struggling to fulfill our purpose alone. His Word, His presence, and His power will guide us through each moment as we train spiritual senses to focus on Him more than what we fear. God will use our journeys from fear to faith to encourage others. As our faith grows, God will be lifted up in His church and in our nation.

Introduction

The Faith of a Mustard Seed

Read and meditate on these verses and answer the following questions.

> Matthew 17:20: "So Jesus said to them, 'Because of your unbelief; assuredly I say to you, if you have faith as a mustard seed, you will say to this mountain, 'Move from here to there,' and it will move; and nothing will be impossible for you.'"

> Matthew 13:31–32: "The kingdom of heaven is like a mustard seed, which a man took and sowed in his field, which indeed is the least of all the seeds; but when it is grown, it is greater than the herbs and becomes a tree, so that the birds of the air come and nest in its branches."

What keeps us from "moving mountains?"

How great must our faith be to have power over the impossible?

Describe what happens to the mustard seed that is planted.

Read Mark 4:35–41. In verse 40, how does Jesus describe the state of the disciples?

In these passages, God gives great insight to the power of faith. First, He teaches that the smallest amount of faith is more powerful than imaginable. It accomplishes the impossible. Second, He speaks of the planting of the seed and its growth into a tree. A mustard seed, the smallest of all seeds, is an *herb* that becomes greater than an herb when it grows into a *tree*! This, God says, is like the kingdom of heaven. Christ planted the seed: "He who sows the good seed is the Son of Man. The field is the world, the good seeds are the sons of the kingdom" (Matthew 13:37–38). When grown, the seed becomes greater and more powerful; it changes drastically from that small seed.[1] It is steadfast, strong, and unshakeable. It thrives under the care of the Master Gardener.

As Christians, the King of heaven lives in us. He is the Word, the source of faith planted in our hearts. We are of the small seed (the church) that will grow into a tree (the kingdom of heaven). He is transforming us into His image. We grow spiritually in proportion to the growth of faith. This increased faith conquers fear. Our strength is a stabilizing factor and protection for those God brings near. God intends to do more in and through our life than we can imagine!

More than discussing fear, this study helps us surrender to and embrace the growth of faith beyond a seed. Yes, Christ says we need only a little faith to experience the power of God, but He came so we could experience His abundance. God's Word tells us He is the author and finisher of faith (Hebrews 12:2). This is a promise to plant the seed and nurture it to maturity. In this study, we will explore how we hinder and further this growth process by the ways we recognize and respond to the Living Word.

Fear interrupts and thwarts the growth of faith. Fear and unbelief are obstacles to trusting God. We will see how God's chosen leaders feared greatly, failed to trust God to prevail, and misunderstood His ways for accomplishing His will. We will study how God grew these leaders' faith so we too become more sensitive to His ways for strengthening it. Let us be

---

[1] See also John 14:12.

encouraged as we learn how the faith leaders of the early church learned to surrender fear to faith.

Whenever you read the word *Flesh* capitalized, it refers to our uncrucified sin nature God is still cleansing. It refers to the self-life that thinks and acts in ways contrary to God's ways, and hinders faith's growth. This study's style is unique to the way God has gifted me. I am an analytical person; I see things as a series of processes. I believe God is using these gifts to help me identify and learn His ways for growing faith throughout His Word and how to appropriate them.

While this study is the product of my journey from fear to faith, there are universal principles I trust God to apply in your life. My journey bears similarities to the journeys we will study in God's Word. Your journey from fear to faith though unique will also bear similarities. Even if fear is not a difficult or obvious battle for you, I pray you continue through the study to glean how God intends to grow your faith and how you can intensify your partnership with God in its growth.

Except for chapter 5, each chapter is segmented into 5 sessions requiring study and reflective questions followed by a "Growing Faith" extension of the chapter's focus. Each session begins with meditation, scriptures, and prayer. These prayers are not intended to substitute for personal prayer the Spirit may breathe in you; these are the prayers God birthed in my heart in intercession for each segment of study. I share them so you can join in intercession with God's work through this study and see Him as the source of the answered prayer. I encourage using each session of each chapter as daily study, allowing the Spirit time and opportunity to appropriate that session's focus in your faith journey before proceeding to the next.

There is a "glove" illustration often used to depict the concept of surrendering to God's work through us—we are the glove, and He is the hand. This study looks at how fear, doubt, and unbelief undermine this surrender, but more important, we look at the ways God empowers surrender through revelations of His Word, His will, and His power. We will discuss familiar scriptures and passages sometimes repeatedly.

As you are asked to read and meditate on these truths, you will be challenged to do so from the perspective of identifying God's ways that reveal His fullness. In God's Word and in the Old Testament particularly, God gave promises to Israel through times of rebellion and closeness to

Him. While these promises may or may not be specific to our lives, they teach us about His character, love, and faithfulness. As we highlight these, we want to better understand the God who gives them. As we look at popular and favored verses in scripture, we will identify how these are God's ways for living in faith over fear and how our biblical heroes model appropriating God's Word.

Satan uses fear to shift focus from God to self. Therefore, we focus less on fear's practical, day-to-day issues and more on subtle or general fear and its spiritual consequences. There are protective forms of fear, but we address destructive fear. The danger of fear is that what starts out as protective fear can easily devolve into destructive fear and unhealthy self-protection. A fear of being burned should not deter us from using fire to keep us warm or to prepare food. While this may be obvious, this study looks at those less-obvious ways fear is destructive. Particularly, we look at how Satan uses destructive fear to rob intimacy with God, of embracing His fullness, of minimizing our full potential, and of short-changing the abundant life of peace.

I pray for a focus that empowers us to see things from God's perspective. Only in the reflection questions do we examine fear's devastating, personal impact. These are designed for personal time with God, not for group discussion if completing this study in a group setting. As fear is exposed, it is not intended that we dwell on it or the severity of personal issues but instead expose the damaging, destructive role fear plays. Most of this study focuses on God's ways for growing faith. I pray God uses it to elevate us as the victor, not the victim, of fear.

As we begin, reflect on people, situations, or circumstances that cause you to fear, worry, or become anxious. Briefly summarize these fears.

Honestly answer the following (generally speaking) regarding the fears listed above. Later reflection on the below responses will be key to growing faith.

Describe your understanding of what God *can do* in these situations.

Describe any understanding of what God *will do* in these situations.

Why is receiving this understanding difficult or confusing?

Describe your willingness to *trust* what He *will* do (His will that is known or unknown).

Why is trusting God with these situations often difficult? List obstacles in your heart and mind that hinder trust.

The Master Gardener plants seeds of faith. He also works to remove fear choking its growth. Let us further work with Him to cultivate "good ground" to nurture faith. His presence is near to reveal His power. Let us open our hearts to hear and understand.

> When anyone hears the word of the kingdom, and does not understand it, then the wicked one comes and snatches away what was sown in his heart. This is he who received seed by the wayside. But he who received the seed on stony places, this is he who hears the word and receives it with joy; yet he has no root in himself, but endures only for a while. For when tribulations or persecution arises because of the word, immediately he stumbles. Now he who received seed among the thorns is he who hears the word, and the cares of this world and the deceitfulness of riches choke the word, and he becomes unfruitful. But he who received seed on the good ground is he who hears the word and understands it, who indeed bears fruit and produces: some a hundredfold, some sixty, some thirty.
> —Matthew 13:19–23

Introduction to Growing Faith

Peace in the Midst of Fear

This section reveals sources of fear, the devastating effects of fear, and the hope we find even in fear. Through Gideon's experiences, we will examine how strongholds of fear begin, how those strongholds begin breaking down, and how faith revives. Chapter 1 of this study helps us examine how fear, doubt, presumption, and unbelief undermine abundant living. For this reason, we must be willing to allow the Spirit to examine hearts intimately in the reflective and introspective study. In Growing Faith 1, we continue exploring Gideon's revival of faith and how it applies today.

As we study Jesus's preparation of the disciples' faith in subsequent chapters, recall the correlating similarities from this Old Testament passage. Allow God to reveal the consistencies throughout His Word for finishing faith. Identify the steps of God's faith-growth process. Allow subsequent chapters to restore and replace what the Spirit exposes in chapter 1. Allow repetitions of God's faithfulness to increase faith and trust in Him.

Our story begins with the circumstances that have caused Gideon to live life in fear, the Midianites' oppression of Israel in Judges 6:1-10.

> Then the children of Israel did evil in the sight of the LORD. So the LORD delivered them into the hand of Midian for seven years, and the hand of Midian prevailed against Israel. Because of the Midianites, the children of Israel made for themselves the dens, the caves, and the strongholds which are in the mountains. So it was, whenever Israel had sown, Midianites would come up; also Amalekites and the people of the East would come up against them. Then they would encamp against them and destroy the produce of the earth as far as Gaza, and leave no sustenance for Israel, neither sheep nor ox nor donkey. For they would come up with their livestock and their tents, coming in as numerous as locusts; both they and their camels were without number; and they would enter the land to destroy it. So Israel was greatly impoverished because of the Midianites, and the

children of Israel cried out to the Lord. And it came to pass, when the children of Israel cried out to the Lord because of the Midianites, that the Lord sent a prophet to the children of Israel, who said to them, "Thus says the Lord God of Israel: 'I brought you up from Egypt and brought you out of the house of bondage; and I delivered you out of the hand of the Egyptians and out of the hand of all who oppressed you, and drove them out before you and gave you their land. Also I said to you, "I am the Lord your God; do not fear the gods of the Amorites, in whose land you dwell. But you have not obeyed My voice."'

The Israelites have rebelled. They have done evil in the sight of the Lord, and consequently, judgment falls because of their sin. However, even as this historical account unfolds, scripture foretells its completion. God's judgment *will* end. In seven years, they are delivered from the evil they recognize fully—the hand of the Midianites—and from the evil they have failed to acknowledge—their sinful rebellion. God is preparing the heart of one He will use for both deliverances; but for Gideon to become a deliverer, he himself must be delivered.

My hope is that we too will come to understand our own need for deliverance so we reach our full faith potential. No single instantaneous transformation from fear to faith turned Gideon, the deliverer, into that mighty man of valor. While he received one tremendous empowerment from the presence of the Lord, he also needed strengthening moment by moment to conquer fear. God's transformation was progressive as Gideon paused to surrender in worship. Each faith-building encounter with God reveals how Gideon was empowered to obey. While some may rightly caution against living with doubt and insecurity as Gideon, we would serve well to follow his example of continual worship in the midst of doubt.

The Midianites, the Amalekites, and people from the East were a real and imminent threat to the Israelites for seven years. They raided the Israelites' crops and cattle descending upon them like locusts. They left the Israelites with little sustenance and with the burden of beginning again with whatever they hid. The only refuge from the plunder was to hide in dens, caves, or strongholds in the mountains. This was not the place or the way God intended them to live, but because of their rebellion, this is the life they knew for seven years.

They cried out to the Lord, not out of conviction of their rebellion, but because of their misery. God heard their misplaced cry and graciously responded with opportunity for repentance and deliverance. Through the words of a prophet, God reminded them of past deliverances. He brought them out of slavery, delivered them from the Egyptians, and drove out their enemies including the inhabitants God used to prepare the Promise Land. He settled them and gave them one primary instruction above all: "Have no other Gods before Me. Do not fear the pagan gods in your midst, fear Me." Yet they disobeyed.

As destructive fear escalates, worship of God diminishes. When we allow fear of worldly things and events consume us, we lose fear of the Lord. He loses first place in the focus of our hearts and minds. When fear of the Lord diminishes, so does protection and freedom. We become vulnerable to Satan's further temptations that enslave us to thoughts and actions contrary to God's will. We make wrong decisions desperately trying to prevent the very thing making us fearful. We are more consumed with stopping the fear—or what we perceive as its source—than acting in ways that result in peace.

The root of fear we need to expose is the fear of anything or anyone above a fear of the Lord. To have no other gods before God is to have no other fears before a fear of the Lord. To put it simply, what we fear is what we worship! Whom we fear is whom we worship! This is true no matter what or whom we fear. Fear steals emotional and spiritual energy to the point of becoming an all-consuming idol. Look at the progressive destruction fear has on faith.

1. Fear restricts worship and focus on God.
2. Diminished worship prohibits intimate fellowship.
3. A lack of fellowship lessens dependence on God and increases self-sufficiency.
4. Self-sufficiency destroys His strength within for obeying (even those things we still know we should).
5. Disobedience blinds us to the deeper truths of God's Word, thwarting faith's growth.

The Israelites' fear fuels retreat into the mountains. Past deliverances by God evidenced His ability to give them victory despite the odds, yet they are not seeking Him fully. There is no bold stand against this affliction, only further retreat into the solace of fear that has become their comfort.

Like the Israelites, we often find places of refuge that provide some measure of safety until God restores us to the place He intends. We may settle into a routine of comfort and complacency, yet that is not how God fully intends us to live. It could be a role we fulfill as parent or provider, it could be a hobby or form of recreation, it could be social retreat, or it could even be in religious activity. We continue to reside in a stronghold of fear, doubt, and unbelief until God strengthens faith. While this stronghold of fear is not where God intends us to be—nor what we desire—we find some sense of safety there. Therefore, as time continues and our fearful focus is not recognized, it becomes harder to acknowledge we are living outside our true purpose. We adjust to the presence of fear and live with a pretense of security. It is a way of life that becomes our place of comfort and peace, a necessary existence but greatly lacking in abundance. There is no understanding that repentance would result in God's deliverance and protection.

The Israelites are not seeking God and they do not seek understanding. They remain oppressed by their misplaced fear and the consequence of this sin. God, however, does not leave them in their rebellion. The Israelites as a whole may have neglected God's call to repentance, but God has found one who will listen.

God can use one person's journey from fear to faith to change the lives of many. We begin by looking at Gideon's encounter with the Lord, paying close attention to how "well" Gideon listened to God in the beginning. Try to imagine yourself in the place of Gideon as we study Judges 6:11-24.

> Now the Angel of the Lord came and sat under the terebinth tree which was in Ophrah, which belonged to Joash the Abiezrite, while his son Gideon threshed wheat in the winepress, in order to hide it from the Midianites. And the Angel of the Lord appeared to him, and said to him, "The Lord is with you, you mighty man of valor!" Gideon said to Him, "O my lord, if the Lord is with us,

why then has all this happened to us? And where are all His miracles which our fathers told us about, saying, 'Did not the Lord bring us up from Egypt?' But now the Lord has forsaken us and delivered us into the hands of the Midianites."

Then the Lord turned to him and said, "Go in this might of yours, and you shall save Israel from the hand of the Midianites. Have I not sent you?" So he said to Him, "O my Lord, how can I save Israel? Indeed my clan is the weakest in Manasseh, and I am the least in my father's house."

And the Lord said to him, "Surely I will be with you, and you shall defeat the Midianites as one man."

Then he said to Him, "If now I have found favor in Your sight, then show me a sign that it is You who talk with me. Do not depart from here, I pray, until I come to You and bring out my offering and set it before You." And He said, "I will wait until you come back."

So Gideon went in and prepared a young goat, and unleavened bread from an ephah of flour. The meat he put in a basket, and he put the broth in a pot; and he brought them out to Him under the terebinth tree and presented them. The Angel of God said to him, "Take the meat and the unleavened bread and lay them on this rock, and pour out the broth." And he did so. Then the Angel of the Lord put out the end of the staff that was in His hand, and touched the meat and the unleavened bread; and fire rose out of the rock and consumed the meat and the unleavened bread. And the Angel of the Lord departed out of his sight.

Now Gideon perceived that He was the Angel of the Lord. So Gideon said, "Alas, O Lord God! For I have seen the Angel of the Lord face to face." Then the Lord said to him, "Peace be with you; do not fear, you shall not die." So Gideon built an altar there to the Lord, and called it The-Lord-Is-Peace. To this day it is still in Ophrah of the Abiezrites.

Gideon's need for protection makes completion of normal duties more difficult and less productive. Gideon is threshing *wheat in a winepress*. Normally, threshing floors are flat and exposed to the air currents so the chaff can blow away easily separating it from the wheat. A winepress, however, is a pit carved in the ground. This makes Gideon's task of separating the wheat more difficult. Fearful Gideon threshes wheat in the winepress to hide from the Midianites, yet the Angel of the Lord refers to him as a "mighty man of valor."[2]

God destined Gideon to become a bold military leader. However, Gideon is not leading anyone as this chapter begins. Gideon's heart is fuel of fear. God sends The Angel of the Lord, God's Surrendered Servant, to adjust Gideon's focus and transform his fear to faith.

This chapter reveals a few interesting facts about Gideon. He has a houseful of servants, indicating he is a man of position; yet he himself is threshing the wheat. He is not idle or so given over to fear and discouragement that he ceases work. It is in his solitude of work that the Angel of the Lord meets with him. The Angel tells Gideon, "The Lord is with you." This announcement has many meanings. First, the Lord, the pre-incarnate Christ,[3] is physically in the presence of Gideon. Second, the Lord is with Gideon in power to restore Israel. Third, the Lord is with the Israelites. God has not forsaken them in the midst of their rebellion and oppression as they suspect.

Gideon, however, lacks understanding of God's purpose and His presence. In verse 13, Gideon responds, "O my *lord*," using a general, respectful address but not recognizing the almighty Lord. He disputes the Lord's announcement, "the Lord is with you." Gideon focuses on outward

---

[2] At the end of this study, we will quickly revisit this portion of scripture. Until then, reflect or meditate on the quality of the wheat Gideon is threshing. Think about how his circumstances (fear) and surroundings (winepress not a threshing floor) are distorting the purity of the wheat and therefore the quality of the taste. Meditate on this as an analogy for life.

[3] Most scholars agree that the Angel of the Lord was the pre-incarnate Jesus. The Angel of the Lord appeared to many Old Testament men of faith, including Abraham and Jacob (whom he wrestled) to name a few. Gideon's and God's responses to the sacrifice later confirm this is the pre-incarnate Christ (v. 22; see Gideon's fear for his life when the sacrifice is consumed and God's response).

appearances. He realizes their oppression results from separation with God. However, Gideon states that the *Lord* has forsaken *them*. He realizes that God delivered them to their enemies but does not understand why. He does not acknowledge the rebellion of forsaking God. Gideon asks all the right questions, but presumes the wrong answers. Notice how fear blinds any perception of truth, perhaps even from seeking it initially.

The Angel of the Lord does not attempt to answer Gideon's questions or correct his misguided understanding. He continues to respond in ways contrary to Gideon's appearance. Gideon is fearful. He is discouraged. He complains with frustration that the God with the power to save them instead abandoned them. Yet in this frightened, confused, state he speaks with boldness to this lord in his presence. The Angel of the Lord replies, "Go in this might of yours, have I not sent you?" Some commentators speculate that prior to this mind frame Gideon was in fact a man of great boldness, yet fear of his circumstances caused his insecurity. If this is true, the Angel's interaction with Gideon is understandable. God knows the true nature of Gideon's heart, which is masked by consuming fear. The Angel does not dwell on his apparent fear, but appeals to his seed of faith.

In verse 15, Gideon does not display might, only more insecurity. He listens to the Angel but cannot accept His revelation. This is the first time Gideon appears to recognize this "person" was sent by God. Gideon responds with more confusion: "How can I save Israel when I am from the weakest clan, and the least in the house of the weakest." Gideon's father and his household continued to worship Baal. Perhaps Gideon is the least in his father's house because he refuses to participate in this pagan worship. If Gideon does not worship Baal, this would also serve to explain why God chose him as a deliverer. A man whose heart is not devoted to false gods is a man through which God's glory would be evident.

The Angel responds by restating his first proclamation: "Surely *I* am with you, and you *shall* defeat the Midianites as one man." Again, note how the Angel does not dwell on who Gideon outwardly appears to be. Instead, He focuses on helping Gideon become the person God intends him to become. The Angel meets with a fearful, insecure, defeated man, yet continually addresses him only as a person already transformed to obey God! The Angel exhorts Gideon with confidence, courage, and hope to be something more than he conceives—a mighty man of valor who will defeat a numerous enemy as if they are one man. There is no question about the outcome; the Midianites will be defeated, because the Lord is with Gideon and knows Gideon will surrender to Him.

However, Gideon is still uncertain. He doubts whether this is truly a messenger of God and doubts God will empower him to fulfill his calling. He asks for a sign; he offers to prepare meat and bread. Gideon's offer would reveal something about this Lord. If this were a prophet or angel, the meat would not be eaten but taken as a meat offering. This evidence would reveal the credibility of the messenger. Gideon was willing to sacrifice what probably was to be used for his own meal. Food was scarce, yet Gideon offers what he has to verify God's will.

Not only did the Lord not eat the offering, He consumed it with a holy fire and vanished.[4] Gideon received more evidence than expected. Gideon realized this was not an angel or prophet but the Lord Himself and responds in worship. In verse 22, Gideon's response reveals his fear of the Lord, "Alas, O Lord GOD! For I have seen the Angel of the LORD face to face." The deliverer God would use to restore a fear of the Lord to His people now reveals his own reverent fear of the Lord.

Imagine how this fear of God builds in Gideon. Imagine how the recorder in his mind recalls all the things he just said to the Lord—the bemoaning manner in which he complained about God's abandonment and failure to intervene, the frustration over his circumstances, the argumentative questioning of God's mission. As Gideon comprehends the undeserved presence of the Lord, he awakens to the insignificance of his problems. There is most likely a remembrance of God's teachings through Moses's encounters with the face of God: "No man shall see My face and live." This recognition is humbling. This truly compels one to worship.

God properly focuses Gideon's fear and begins reviving his faith as He does with us! Notice how Gideon's faith growth begins with God substituting fear. God replaces Gideon's fear of his circumstances with a fear of God. God then says, "Peace be with you, do not fear, you shall not

---

[4] This consuming sacrifice is similar to the instruction God gave Elijah to repeatedly soak the altar with water; a fire from heaven burns the water-soaked wood and dried up the water. This consuming sacrifice was done in the presence of the prophets of Baal (1 Kings 18:18–46).

die." Fear of God is not intended to drive us away from God, but to draw us closer. God's presence was for Gideon's preparation, not punishment.

Nothing about Gideon's situation changes; the threat of the adversary is still strong. The battle with the enemy has not begun. Still, in the middle of this fearful set of circumstances, God changes the focus and heart of Gideon granting peace.

This experience was significant to strengthen Gideon's faith. He was in fear, yet he cried out to the Lord. The Lord revealed *Himself, the Word*, as the Angel of the Lord; *His will* to use Gideon as a deliverer; and *His power* to consume the offering. This is a pattern consistently revealed in God's Word and one we will see Jesus repeat with the disciples beginning in chapter 2. As we read all gospel scripture observe this pattern of God's ways to reveal *His word, His will, and His power* so that we learn more about *who God is*.

As we grow in faith, the importance of understanding God's Word and will intensifies. But correlating God's revealed power to His revealed Word and will is often more difficult to understand and much more of a process. We read, study, and memorize God's Word to guide us in life and to understand His will. But when we experience or witness God's power, most likely we perceive it as a stand-alone event, not as the culmination of His Word and will revealing more of who He is through His power.

As we study the disciples' response to Jesus's power, we will more readily learn how easy it is to know God's Word and to be fulfilling His will yet fail to expect or understand His power. As did the disciples, we often miss the spiritual purpose for it in the beginning, which can fuel fear and undermine faith in the near future. Our goal is to learn from these biblical examples and expand spiritual sensitivities to the same process in our lives.

Similar to the seeking Christian, Gideon wanted the presence of God but found Him in an unsuspecting yet personal and overpowering way. This experience did not fuel pride in Gideon as God's chosen man of valor, the great deliverer of his people. There is no inner exuberating when confirmed as God's chosen leader. There is no haughty advertisement of this great gift from God. Instead, Gideon is humbled in reverent fear of the almighty God. Gideon worships God.

Even before Gideon takes one step to build an army and engage in battle, he builds a lasting monument to God's provision. He calls it the Lord-Shalom, meaning the God of peace. However, this monument is not a tribute for what

Gideon trusted God to do through him in the near future. Through this monument of peace, Gideon gives testimony of what God has *already* done. God, this day, delivers his deliverer from fear to faith in a way that changed his focus from *physical visibilities* to *spiritual realities*. His strengthened faith results in peace. His peace was the catalyst for others to experience God's peace as well. Remember the parable of the mustard seed, an herb becomes greater than an herb growing into a tree and providing shelter for others.

Only when Gideon's heart is settled, only when reverence to God focuses faith, is his heart prepared to receive instruction to complete his purpose! The Angel of the Lord *generally* revealed Gideon's ultimate purpose to deliver his people, but when Gideon worshipped—when he responded to the presence of God and His power—he was prepared to listen and receive God's *specific* instruction. God has Gideon's undivided attention. This is a most critical distinction in God's ways for growing faith.

Focusing on the present crisis left Gideon's heart susceptible to further fear and doubt. Fear and doubt continues to surface in his heart for a time, but God's presence and provision of peace reassures him of His nearness and His faithfulness. No longer does Gideon feel abandoned by God. Every time Gideon realizes the presence and provision of God, he worships. Even in this weak faith, he continues to turn to God in the midst of uncertainty, trusting God to further strengthen and empower him.

Gideon teaches that worship is to be a response to the awareness of who God is, of His nearness and presence, and of His faithfulness. This principle demonstrates why worship is just as important in our quiet time with God as it is corporately. It is more than a part of Sunday morning service, and it is accomplished in ways that far surpass singing praises. Worship is more than an act; it is a state of mind that perpetually depends on God. Worship is necessary to keep us postured in humble fear of God. This reverence positions us to hear His specific will and ways for completing His will. Worship prepares us to fulfill our purpose!

Praise God, He meets us where we are! More important, He meets us as we are with a promise of hope. The fellowship we share with Him calms our fears, focuses our faith, and postures us to hear His specific plan for today. God inhabits the praise of His people (Psalm 22:3). As we worship, He reveals Himself in a personal yet humbling way. Worship of God compels us to refocus fear to faith.

What do we learn about God in Judges 6? This is just one passage we study that reveals God wants us to recognize Him in our midst and receive the blessing of His fellowship, but He also desires that it be a lasting testimony of His greatness. How God settles our heart, how we receive peace even in the midst of great fear, and how we allow God to strengthen faith should encourage others to pursue God.

Be still before Him now, and know He is our everlasting, ever-present, almighty, faithful Prince of Peace.

Chapter 1

The Power of Fear

*Fear not, for I am with you. Be not dismayed, for I am
your God. I will strengthen you, Yes, I will help you, I
will uphold you with My righteous right hand.*
—Isaiah 41:10

Exposing the Root of Fear

Begin with worship, meditation, and prayer:

> Be anxious for nothing, but in everything by prayer and
> supplication, with thanksgiving, let your requests be made
> known to God; and the peace of God, which surpasses all
> understanding, will guard your hearts and minds through
> Christ Jesus. (Philippians 4:6–7)

> "Lord, increase my desire to seek Your face. Help me focus
> on You and Your purpose for today. Allow me to see how
> fear causes me to idolize cares and concerns of this world
> above You. Set my heart on You, I pray in Christ's name."

Fear! Sometimes the sound of the word itself is enough to cause anxiety. When reflecting on things I fear, I become overwhelmed and depressed.

One can expend great emotional energy tormented by fear. Fear results from reality or our perception of reality. We fear what we do not know, and we often fear what we think we know. Regardless of the source, a fearful focus causes one to react in ways contrary to God's best. When it is the destructive form, fear is a very real obstacle to God's rest, peace, and blessings.

As I pondered the grip of fear in my life, God began to reveal faith as my path of deliverance. This is a simple and common principle in the Christian life. If we trust God, we realize there is little to fear. In God's sovereign love, we know He is working all things together for good (Romans 8:28). However, how many of us can say this is how we live each moment? We fear being alone. We fear having children or not having them. We fear for our safety or that of our loved ones. We fear the trappings of an unfulfilling marriage. We worry about finances. We may fear death or the death of those dear to us. We fear powers out of our control—the power of nature, the power of governments, and the power of terrorists. We fear consequences of bad choices. We fear balancing priorities of family and work. We fear the pain, suffering, or unknown issues with our health. We fear living life without meaning. We fear rejection from those we respect. We even fear failing to please God. We fear failure in every sense of the word.

We know we should not be ruled by fear, but it always seems to surface in some way. We know we need to be strong, courageous, trusting, and focused in faith, but this knowledge does not bring the peace we cry for. We need focus. We desire understanding, wisdom, and the power to conquer fear. Sometimes, just maybe we find it, sometimes not.

The constancy of the struggle to live in faith over fear plays tug-of-war with our hearts and minds. We may surrender to walk by faith, not by sight, but fear, worry, and doubt resurge the anxiety and consume us with the very evident, difficult circumstances of life. By faith, we refocus on God's unseen purposes long enough to suppress fear's onslaught. The tug-of-war continues. Can we ever be victorious over fear? How can we have the unshakeable peace in the midst of crisis and chaos like Daniel, like Christ?

Faith is the key to victory, but the continual struggle to live in faith often seems difficult if not impossible. To live in faith, we must live in the power of God day by day, moment by moment. Living free of fear is the blessing of faith.

My father's family has a stronghold of fear that is traceable through known histories for the past 150 years. I grew up under the effects of a fearful mind-set. However, my father also was a bivocational minister. My mother was a woman of great faith with a cheerful resolve to trust and obey God wholeheartedly. From an early age, I had an intense hunger to know God. Even in the presence of these generational sins, God put me in an environment to find His ways for deliverance.

I began to deal with my issues with fear as I completed Beth Moore's "Breaking Free" study. As my journey unfolded, I began to learn how intensely fear, doubt, and unbelief strive to undermine faith. But more important, I began to realize how Christ came to show us God's plan for strengthening faith. Raised in the church, I was aware that it took only a small seed of faith to experience the miraculous, but I remained unaware of the extent God intended it to grow and how my own Flesh damaged that growth. I learned that sometimes for faith to grow, it requires walking through your greatest fear.

David also expresses the emotional distress brought on by fear as well as the deep need for deliverance in Psalm 55:4–8.

> My heart is severely pained within me, and the terrors of death have fallen upon me. Fearfulness and trembling have come upon me, and horror has overwhelmed me. And I said, "Oh that I had wings like a dove! For then I would fly away and be at rest. Indeed, I would wander far off, and remain in the wilderness. I would hasten my escape from the windy storm and tempest."

How many times have you shared David's desire to escape circumstances that birth anxiety and stress? How many times have you expressed your prescription for relief to God? Fear has a way of completely consuming our emotions, thoughts, and desires. Just scan the many chapters of Psalms and notice how many of them record David's plea for peace, rest, and deliverance from fearful circumstances. Though our situations may not exactly parallel those of David, fear is nevertheless just as real. When we are in a state of fear, it is hard to focus on even routine, mundane activities. We become preoccupied with the source of fear and its most expedient remedy. Before we delve into faith's growth, we should:

- identify the fear we now face,
- recognize it in its infancy,
- uncover the deceitfulness of fear,
- honestly realize the power it holds over us, and
- discover the tools for its defeat.

The Bible reveals several causes of fear. Some of these include disobedience, persecution, spiritual warfare, acts of nature, presumption and suspicion, doubting others' maturity, death, and the presence of God.[5] When we are faced with an important decision or life-altering event, fear often surfaces in our thought life fueling doubt, worry, and confusion. Consumed with these thoughts, our focus on God's presence diminishes. If we learn to recognize how fear manifests in its infancy, we are postured to deal with it before it takes a deeper hold over us.

Randomly throughout my yard, several azalea bushes have a thorny vine growing up through the azalea's shallow root system. When the vine is young, it appears to be just another annoying but harmless weed. But the mature vine has a very deep, intricate, knotty root system and long thorns. It sprawls easily through the yard making it difficult to detect and hard to remove. I have found it difficult to destroy the mature vine without destroying the azalea. Pruning the vine to the ground and carefully treating it with chemicals proved unsuccessful. Had I understood the danger of the mature vine and how to recognize it early, it would have been easier to completely remove without damaging the azalea when the vine was young, before the vine's roots were deeply intertwined with the azalea's.

This is also how fear affects faith. The danger of fear is that its harm is often hard to recognize in its infancy. Yet even when we recognize it, we fail to know how to destroy its harmful effects. Or perhaps we don't know how harmful it is until it becomes very difficult and painful to remove. Take a few moments to reflect on sin in your life. If you peel back its many layers, the source of that sin includes the fear of something happening or the fear of something not happening. This reveals the root of fear embedded in a need

---

[5] Genesis 3:10; John 20:19; Acts 27:13–29, 9:26; 2 Corinthians 11:3; Hebrews 2:15; Judges 6:21–23.

for self-protection. It is a defense mechanism that attempts to anticipate and protect us from potential harm or disappointment.

When the uncertainty surrounding God's plan conflicts with our expectations, desires, and remedy for a situation, we become anxious. Self attempts to control or manipulate the situation. With self in control, there is no apparent need for God, His power, or His protection. We walk by sight, not by faith. Yet as Franklin D. Roosevelt stated, "The only thing we have to fear is fear itself!" Fear—the emotion we rely on to prepare us for danger—is the real danger. Christ did not come so we would live in fear but in the power of a sound mind. God does not intend us to be guided by emotion but with spiritual strength—*His* strength planted in us as a seed of faith.

Fear is devastating to faith because it obstructs hearing, relating to, and obeying God. Yet too often, we justify a fearful focus because our concerns are rooted in what is good. This is one of fear's many deceitful aspects. We worry about pleasing others such as a spouse, employer, family, and friends. We fear making mistakes parenting children. We worry about pleasing God with our service. These ultimate concerns are noble, but God asks His children to allow Him to "guide them with His eye" so they will fulfill these goals with His power, not Flesh, through faith in Him, not fear of failure (Psalm 32:8–9).

Most of the study looks at the ways God grows faith, but in this chapter, we must recognize the way Satan uses the destructive emotion of fear to undermine God's best. Fear is a destructive and dangerous emotion at the root of pride and all other anxious emotions. Philippians 4:6–7 gives instruction for responding to fear in a way that brings true protection. Periodically, we revisit key elements of this verse.

- We can choose not to be anxious.
- We should confess fear to God and express our needs to Him not in anxiousness, anger, or resentment but with thankfulness for His eternal purpose.
- We should realize He causes us to walk in peace in the midst of chaos protecting us from the internal onslaughts of Satan's schemes.

Proverbs twice states, "There is a way that seems right to man, but its end is the way of death" (14:12, 16:25). This is a warning not to be ruled by emotions of the Flesh as its end is contrary to the peace and rest desired. Fear, and everything it spawns, fuels destructive thoughts, emotions, and actions. Fear elevates everything in our Flesh while only faith embraces God's Spirit and power within.

Philippians 4:6–7 instructs how to wage war against destructive fear. God says David was a man after God's own heart (1 Samuel 13:14). However, he was also a man who feared greatly. Above, we read of David's anxious expression to God. As a man of war, as the anointed future king fleeing Saul's death threats, David had great reason to fear. However, throughout the majority of David's situations, he reacted appropriately to fear. Much of David's early life is a witness to the truth of Philippians 4:6–7. David expressed fear to God and waited for God to act on his behalf. In Psalm 25:4–5, David teaches how to "make our request known to God" with a heart of faith and trust: "Show me Your ways, O Lord, Teach me Your paths. Lead me in Your truth and teach me, for You are the God of my salvation; on You I wait all the day."

Let this also be the meditation and focus of your heart today.

How is fear an idol? Write your understanding.

In Genesis 3:1–5, what truth did Satan say to Eve?

What truth did Satan distort, and what was an outright lie?

From verse 5, what is the "fear of something withheld" that Satan implies God is keeping from Adam and Eve?

Read James 1:13. Learning from Eve's failure and this verse in James, ask God to reveal how your own fears can lead to deception and destruction.

What "protection" do you need (it may be emotional, physical, mental, financial, or spiritual)?

How is this need affecting your thoughts, actions, and reactions?

What recent or past blessings has God given in your life personally?

Reflect on the fears recorded in the Introduction session. Using David's prayer (Psalm 25:4–5) as a guide, surrender your specific need to the Holy Spirit and record a similar prayer for your situation.

The Danger of Doubt

Begin with worship, mediation, and prayer.

> Trust in the Lord with all your heart, and lean not on your own understanding; in all your ways acknowledge Him, and He shall direct your paths. Do not be wise in your own eyes; fear the Lord and depart from evil. It will be health to your flesh, and strength to your bones. (Proverbs 3:5–8)

> "Lord, empower me to overcome doubt that mistrusts Your promises. Focus my faith on Your truth. Open my eyes to understanding and empower surrender to the path You have for me today. Strengthen me to take the next step."

Doubt is a strategic tool Satan uses to eradicate focus on truth. Eve succumbed to Satan's temptation and willingly traded the blessing of knowing God freely for the knowledge of good and evil. It is hard to imagine what it must have been like to experience the goodness of God and earth without the knowledge of sin and evil. God gave His instruction for protection, not from selfishness or to lord it over humanity. But the seeds of doubt continued fueling pride and fear in her heart causing her to lose sight of the blessings already given.

Eve's fear of not having God's best led to disobedience and resulted in fear of God's judgment: "Then the Lord God called to Adam and said to him, 'Where are you?' So he said, 'I heard Your voice in the garden, and I was afraid because I was naked, and I hid myself,'" (Genesis 3:9–10). This verse illustrates a fact we will continue to explore: Fear perpetuates fear; but faith perpetuates faith!

To live a victorious life over fear, we must beware of doubt. Doubt and fear are two sides of the same coin; one does not exist without the other. Where there is fear, there is doubt that disbelieves God's truth or power over the circumstance or in us. Doubt focuses us on the appearance of truth or its lack. Faith focuses on God's truth—what is true regardless of appearance. God's truth enables us to distinguish between human knowledge and godly wisdom. *Faith reveals the difference between earthly visibilities and spiritual realities.* This is another key element of God's ways to observe as scripture is studied so that we learn how to recognize it in our lives.

Fear may result from the difficulty of circumstance as was the case with David or from internal conflict and temptation in Eve's case. However fear manifests, Proverbs admonishes us not to rely on human understanding as human wisdom and intellect is inferior to God's wisdom. In later chapters, we will learn how to put away human understanding to glean understanding imparted by God.

Doubting God's Promises

Numbers 13 reveals another example of doubt's power and how the appearance of circumstances distracts us from absorbing God's revealed truth. As you read, notice how doubt and fear are inseparable in the minds of those weak in faith.

> And the Lord spoke to Moses, saying, "Send men to spy out the land of Canaan, *which I am giving to the children of Israel*; from each tribe of their fathers you shall send a man, everyone a leader among them" ... Then they told him, and

said, "We went to the land where you sent us. It truly flows with milk and honey, and this is its fruit. Nevertheless the people who dwell in the land are strong; the cities are fortified and very large; moreover we saw the descendants of Anak there" ... Then Caleb quieted the people before Moses, and said, "Let us go up at once and take possession, for we are well able to overcome it." But the men who had gone up with him said, "We are not able to go up against the people, for they are stronger than we." And they gave the children of Israel a bad report of the land which they had spied out saying, "The land through which we have gone as spies is a land that devours its inhabitants, and all the people whom we saw in it are men of great stature" ... And all the children of Israel murmured against Moses and Aaron, and the whole congregation said to them, "If only we had died in the land of Egypt! Or if only we had died in this wilderness! Why has the Lord brought us to this land to fall by the sword, that our wives and children should become victims? Would it not be better for us to return to Egypt?" ... and they [Joshua and Caleb] spoke to all the congregation of the children of Israel, saying, "the land we passed through to spy out is an exceedingly good land. If the Lord delights in us, then He will bring us into this land and give it to us, a land which flows with milk and honey. Only *do not rebel against the Lord, nor fear the people of the land, for they are our bread; their protection has departed from them, and the Lord is with us. Do not fear them.*" And all the congregation said to stone them with stones. Now the glory of the Lord appeared in the tabernacle of meeting before all the children of Israel. And the Lord said to Moses, "How long will these people reject Me? And how long will they not believe Me, with all the signs which I have performed among them?" (emphasis added)

God sent leaders to spy the land He had revealed as theirs. God did not send them to determine if they would possess the land, but to see the greatness of His provision. God faithfully and gracefully preserved Israel from slavery, hunger, thirst, enemies, and from their own ignorance and rebellion to give them *this* land. God has a plan. God made all the arrangements. During the 400 years of slavery in Egypt, God richly cultivated this land into a bountiful harvest that He will deliver to Israel. This is the *Promised* Land.

Instead of celebrating God's gift and worshipping Him for His provision, ten of the twelve leaders panic. They doubt God's promise to turn the land over from its current inhabitants to Israel without great cost of life. They presume God intends this gift to come as the result of their own ability. They recognize their inadequacy, but they doubt God's ability to work through their inadequacy with His power. They fail to comprehend the partnership God intends. (This is a pattern of doubt we will see repeated throughout God's Word.)

Fearfully, they believe God provided for them all the way from Egypt only to leave them on the edge of the Promised Land with their own inability to conquer the mighty inhabitants and still live. Doubt, fear, and self-protection quenched faith and silenced God's promised truth. They allowed earthly visibilities to supersede kingdom realities. If they had died to self and trusted God, they physically would have lived. Instead, their lack of faith, their fear, and their need for self-protection resulted in wandering in the wilderness for years until they did die physically without ever receiving God's promise. The real danger was their fear, not the mighty inhabitants of the Promised Land.

Caleb and Joshua were the two faithful leaders who trusted God to fulfill His promise. Yet those who feared were so intimidated by their boldness and confidence in God that they wanted to kill Caleb and Joshua to silence them. God preserved Caleb and Joshua through the forty years of wilderness wandering, and Caleb was as strong forty years later as when he spied the land. Caleb's life demonstrates the truth of Proverbs 3:5–6.

Why does doubt damage faith? How do fear and doubt disrupt our partnership with God's purposes? A familiar acrostic gives an explanation. Fear is False Evidence Appearing Real. Most often, false evidences are the very evident, physical visibilities. All our human faculties validate the evidence. We see, hear, feel, sense, or know the danger. Our concern is validated by those we respect or the circumstances. These appearances cause us to doubt God's control, ability, or willingness to work this situation for our good. Only faith empowers us to discern God's perspective. As we will learn more fully, faith is believing what God *can do* and trusting what He *will do* or in what *He allows.*

Like Caleb and Joshua, knowing God and remembering His faithfulness is vital to fueling faith. Learning and recalling His ways in the past teaches who He is so we are sensitive to His presence today.

Doubt causes us to lose sight of God's faithfulness. We know God is power and has power, but our experiences with God's power may appear inadequate for the current issues. Remember that God's plan is to grow faith. He allows circumstances that in fact will stretch understanding of Him—times that call for us to more fully realize His greatness and power. With familiarity comes complacency and self-reliance, a place that blinds us from knowing God fully.

God delivers the ten spies from slavery in the prosperous Egyptian land. They know God intends them to live freely in a more abundant land prepared for them. Imagine their doubt: "Why would a God who left us in slavery for 400 years really intend such a blessing or care to intervene to make it happen?" The false evidence appearing real suggests, "God didn't intervene for 400 years. Why should I think He will now?" Perhaps they focus more on God's presumed inaction in the past than His obvious intervention in the present. What God could do, would do, was too great for them to comprehend. Fear led to death. Faith led to life.

Focus on His Faithfulness

In the Old Testament, we see Israel's pattern of losing a godly focus. When they rebel, they ceased to worship God. As God used prophets or leaders to call for repentance, the prophets would begin by recalling God's faithfulness. This sent the message that God is dependable. He is trustworthy and is worthy of our trust because of His faithful provision. As God's faithfulness is remembered, His people are compelled to worship. As God is genuinely worshipped, His Spirit gently and lovingly fuels a desire for repentance.

Philippians 4:6 instructs us to be thankful in all things. We are admonished to focus on God, not the inadequacy or difficulty of the circumstance. Gideon's example reveals that worship is a catalyst for peace in the midst of chaos and fear. Therefore, this verse is not a command to subject ourselves in difficulty to an overbearing God. This is the revealed way for walking in faith over fear. This is the path to freedom though it may require the sacrifice of our pride and our desire to complain, and to control circumstances.

God knows our weakness and His power. God requests worship for His glory, but we need worship for the strengthening of faith. God brings the power of heaven to earth but asks for our partnership in that process. As we worship, as we honor His faithfulness, we partner with Him in the release of His power.

Read Lamentations 3.

Write Lamentations 3:22–25.

Write Lamentations 3:40–41.

Write Lamentations 3:57–58.

Note ways God brought deliverance from fear in your past.

Meditate on the following personalized paraphrase from Psalm 46 and record some of the personal demonstrations of God's faithfulness in your life. If you have difficulty recalling them or have not yet consciously experienced them, record a prayer asking God to reveal His great faithfulness to you.

God is your refuge and strength, a very present help in times of trouble. Therefore, you will not fear, though the earth be removed, and though the mountains be carried into the sea, though its waters roar and be troubled, though the mountains shake with its swelling. God is in your midst; therefore, you shall not be moved by any circumstance or trial. He remains your refuge through the darkest of the night. He never leaves you. Do not lose hope for God will help you just at the break of dawn. Come, behold the works of the Lord who has the power to overcome all things. Do not be anxious for anything. Cease striving in your darkness. Be still and know that He is God. Know the One to be exalted among the nations and on all the earth is the One that is your God. The Lord of hosts is with you and continues to be your refuge.

My ever-present God is worthy of my praise for His ways are faithful in all my life as follows:

God, receive the glory for the great things You have done and continue to do!

The Problem of Presumption

Begin with worship, mediation, and prayer.

> However, when He, the Spirit of Truth, has come, He will guide you into all truth; for He will not speak on His own authority, but whatever He hears He will speak; and He will tell you things to come. He will glorify Me, for He will take what is Mine and declare it to you. All things that the Father has are Mine. Therefore I said that He will take of Mine and declare it to you. (John 16:13–15)

> "Heavenly Father, focus my faith on understanding truth. Set my heart to please You. Teach me to surrender to the leading of Your Spirit. Give me wisdom not to presume understanding of my circumstances or Your provision. Help me identify things in my heart that grieve Your Spirit and that keep me from the flow of Your Spirit in me."

When fear and doubt remain unchecked, those false evidences appearing real lead to presumptuous conclusions. Presumption occurs when we assume an intent, outcome, or attitude and act based on that assumption without verifying its validity with truth and spiritual discernment versus human understanding. Presumptuous actions do great harm as they breed fear and mistrust in the lives affected by our actions. These actions perpetuate falsehoods and misrepresentations that often cause irreparable pain.

Some years ago, I took a continuing education course on the effectiveness of the rumor mill in an office environment. The course concluded that the greater the uncertainty and importance of the information, the more intense rumors became. It surmised that fears of unknowns fuel these rumors that have the potential to influence us greatly. The other interesting statistic was that 75 percent of a rumor's content was usually true but the remaining 25 percent usually comprised false and perhaps significantly damaging misrepresentations or falsehoods.

God's Word reveals these inequities between truth and falsehood. In Judges 6, Gideon presumes God abandoned His people because their adversity is unending. The truth is that God has limited the protection of His people because of their sin, but He has also limited the length of the adversity. There is a separation from God, not because of His unfaithfulness, but because of His people's rebellion and complacency toward Him. This presumptuous belief that their problems are the fault of God and not their own sin paralyzes the people from responding rightly to God and ending their troubles. Notice how Satan used anger and insecurity over a fear of God's judgment and His abandonment to prevent restoration and an end to suffering.

People trapped in fear struggle to see things truthfully. This blindness further perpetuates insecurity and paranoia. With paranoia, there can be little trust in God and often no trust in anyone else. Self is exalted to protect self. This response closes the door to intimacy with God. Without intimacy with God, even good intentions and actions happen because of Flesh, not God's way.

Presumption Is Deceptive

The problem with presumption is the deception that it is truth. The longer truth remains hidden the greater presumption becomes a comfort zone.

Just like God's people in Judges 6, we may know this is not how God intends us to live, but this is our current reality. Instead of seeking truth and understanding how repentance would result in freedom, we resign to live with the circumstances as they are with us as we are. We also may hide in the caves for self-protection as they have become the only place we feel free from harm. As long as we continue to feel safe or happy in our self-focused cave, we become complacent to the severity of the problem. As long as we remain safe, we rationalize that it must not be harmful yet alone the wrong way to live. Our hearts become blind and hardened to any other "reality."

I once saw a movie made in the 1950s about a man working for a company involved in a corporate merger. Rumors were raging about employee terminations and promotions. The main character became convinced he was to be dismissed based on series of events all of which were true but harmless except one. Someone made a critical mistake, accidentally leaving him off a promotional corporate luncheon among the new leaders of the merged entity. That one mistake (the 25 percent falsehood) so greatly fueled presumptuous conclusions in his mind that all conversations and actions convinced him he was unappreciated, not a valued employee, and would be terminated.

In reality, an important promotion was pending. Never once did he attempt to validate his presumptions with his supervisor. As resentment built in his mind, he continued to act and react in ways detrimental to his success culminating in the drafting of a scathing letter to company bosses. Fortunately, before he sent the letter, truth was revealed and his fears eradicated.

If we are honest, we probably have been in similar situations where presumptions led us down an unhealthy path. Fear fuels presumptuous conclusions causing us to compromise values or wise actions. We presume *this* relationship is the only way to be happy even when other indicators warn otherwise. We presume divorce is the only way to find happiness again. We presume compromising ethics professionally is the only way to achieve success, recognition, or financial security. We presume God's ways lack joy and contentment so we resist surrender to them. Parental or godly guidance and correction is not designed to deprive one of joy or happiness; it is designed to correct behavior that is dangerous to health, longevity, and peace.

Let us continue to reflect on how presumptuous attitudes toward God, His will, and His ways are detrimental to our lives and those closest to us. When we act on presumptions without a commitment to pursue God's truth, our hearts harden toward God. Hardened hearts make God's truth that much harder to comprehend. Though God's truth ultimately prevails, our presumptions can cause unnecessary harm, and perhaps like the ten spies of the Promised Land, we miss His blessing in the situation. Our presumptuous actions cause us to fear God's ways, putting self and self's need for protection above trusting God. Let's continue to explore how presumption hinders fellowship with God and understanding of truth.

Can you recall situations in which inaccurate presumptions resulted in wrong actions or relational turmoil? Briefly summarize the presumption.

What portion of the presumption was based on truth, and what portion was false or inaccurate?

Ask God to reveal the specific fear that led you to act on the presumption.

Presumption Leads to Grieving the Holy Spirit

In our relationship with God, presumption and comfort zones can lead us into a form of cookie-cutter religious tradition or habit to the neglect of growing with God. Obedience should never be limited to the fulfillment of worthy religious routines or practice. Obedience constitutes listening to and following God's voice. Do we study the Bible because it is what Christians are expected to do, or do we study the Bible because we hunger for how God will speak to us through His Word? Do we study just to teach, or do we study to learn and be transformed? Do we study the Bible for its history, or is its history studied so we will be empowered not to repeat its mistakes?

Failing to obey God grieves the Holy Spirit. Failing to comprehend God's truth because of Flesh also grieves the Holy Spirit. Ephesians 4 admonishes us to "be renewed in the Spirit of our mind" so we put away the things of the Flesh. In verse 30, we are told "not to grieve the Holy Spirit of God, by whom you were sealed for the day of redemption." Christians are sealed by the Holy Spirit, who works to transform us into Christ's image. However, scripture is clear that Flesh influences how little or much we surrender to the Holy Spirit's work (1 John 2:20, 27–29, John 15:4–5, 10). When we grieve the Holy Spirit, He is not completely removed from our lives (because we are sealed), but our awareness of His presence and the power of His presence is not fully available or apparent.

Grieving the Holy Spirit occurs when we actively sin or disobey God diminishing the fellowship with the Spirit. *Quenching* the Holy Spirit occurs when we reject or fail to surrender to His presence, His leading, also diminishing the fellowship with the Spirit. In either instance, we will not be in intimate fellowship with the Spirit. When we repent, the fullness of His presence eventually returns.

In the remainder of the study, we will revisit principles of not grieving the Holy Spirit. For now, let's focus our awareness on presumption, and the danger it wields on faith with this final illustration. In his book *The Sensitivity of the Spirit*, R. T. Kendall focuses on the correlation of disobedience with grieving the Holy Spirit. He defines and expounds on the principles of grieving and quenching the Holy Spirit. The circumstances surrounding adolescent Jesus teaching in the temple in Luke 2 is the scripture God first used to formulate Kendall's understanding of the Spirit's sensitivity, and it highlights the problem with presumption.

In Luke 2, Mary and Joseph are returning to Nazareth from paying taxes in Jerusalem. They presume Jesus is among the crowd traveling home. Luke 2:44 says, "But *supposing* Him to have been in their company, they went a day's journey, and sought Him among their relatives" (emphasis added). Kendall is quick to acknowledge this passage is referring to Jesus, not the Holy Spirit. However, the nature of Christ, the Spirit, and God are one as all are part of the Trinity. Furthermore, Mary and Joseph's failure to recognize what God was doing through Jesus parallels our failures to recognize the work of God through Christ and the Spirit.

When Mary and Joseph realize Jesus is not with them, they return to where they last knew Him to be. Jesus had been apart from them for one day, yet it took three days for them to find Him. They did not expect to find Jesus in the temple.

Perhaps the real reason taxes had been assessed were part of God's design to have young Jesus introduced publicly to the world. Jesus's presence in the temple revealed the Word in flesh to the leaders of God's people. Mary and Joseph did not know of this plan; they were focused on taking care of their day-to-day affairs. They were doing what they were supposed to be doing but they presumed Jesus was with them. Kendall states, "They sincerely thought Jesus was right there with them. Why? They *presumed* He would adjust to *their* thinking and plans. After all, it was, as far as they were concerned, time to go home. *They did not see a need of adjusting to Him*"[6] (emphasis added).

They did not see the need of adjusting to Him, *just as we often fail to see the need to adjust to the Holy Spirit*. It is easy to have empathy for Mary and Joseph, the earthly parents of the Son of God. Unlike others, they know this truth. God has entrusted His Son to them, and He is lost. This is any parent's nightmare, but I can only imagine how much more so it was for Mary and Joseph. Mary and Joseph became momentarily so focused on their responsibility to God that they failed to comprehend God also had plans for Jesus to fulfill. It was no longer just about their plans; it was about God's eternal plan. This is God's Son come to do God's work. The virtuous parental sense of duty actually became an obstacle to understanding God at work in their midst. They were understandably so concerned with Jesus's *physical* welfare and protection that they lost sight of any *spiritual* purpose. Once again we observe how earthly visibilities supersede spiritual realities.

In the end, God's purpose was fulfilled and Jesus safely returned to His family. But Mary and Joseph missed it. They were not there to see it. They heard great accounts of this young Man so learned in God's scriptures, but they missed the blessing of fellowshipping with Jesus in this early work.

Kendall points out that we also make this same mistake and fail to recognize our need to adjust to the Spirit. While we are focused on earthly visibilities and duties, we can miss a spiritual purpose. We take the Spirit for granted. We assume because we are sealed by Him that He is right here with us. We take His gifts for granted by trying to use gifts empowered with Flesh instead of surrendered to His purpose. Like Mary and Joseph,

---

[6] R. T. Kendall, *The Sensitivity of the Spirit* (Lake Mary, FL: Charisma House, 2002), 7.

our Flesh actions may be honorable; our actions may involve the fulfilling of necessary duties, but they can be miles away from God's purpose. God may intend much more than we comprehend. His ways are greater than ours, and His purposes are higher than ours.

Kendall continues to reveal that to restore the intimacy lost, we have to turn back to that place in our lives where we knew the Spirit to be. We have to repent. We have to recognize why we became lost and separated from His presence, so fellowship will be restored.

Perhaps this separation from His family was for Jesus's continued growth in a way God did not want Mary and Joseph to witness firsthand. It was possibly for Jesus's or His family's relational protection. Regardless, I pray that this illustration opens your heart to this concept: presumption blinds us from understanding God at work in our midst.

This truth will gradually unfold and deepen throughout this study as we delve into scripture and witness the difficulty Jesus sometimes had instructing His disciples. If you have a desire to know God, to be in His presence, you have a passion to see His work in our midst. This study introduces us to the ways, even the "right" religious ways, we circumvent this experience.

God's purposes will be fulfilled in spite of our shortcomings. But our presumption, our failing to adjust, our failure to understand, may prevent us from participating in God's blessing for that moment.

If you are experiencing restlessness over a situation, God may want you to adjust to the leading of the Spirit. Pray for Him to lead you. Don't presume you know the way. Be still before Him and allow His guidance to bring peace even in the midst of uncertainty. Ask Him to reveal presumptions that hinder His leading. Ask Him to help you recognize spiritual realities at work through the physical visibilities.

> Who can understand his errors? Cleanse me from secret faults. Keep back thy servant also from presumptuous sins; let them not have dominion over me: then shall I be upright, and I shall be innocent from the great transgression. Let the words of my mouth, and the meditation of my heart, be acceptable in thy sight, O LORD, my strength, and my redeemer. (Psalm 19:12–14)

Can you recall a time in your service to God when you perhaps carried on, as Mary and Joseph did, in your obligations with human understanding, strength, and natural abilities? If so, briefly summarize this experience.

Describe how this experience affected your efforts.

Describe how this affected your intimacy with God; did it bring you closer to Him, further away, or were there any noticeable changes?

Describe how this affected your relationship with those who participated in this endeavor or were the recipients of this service.

Reflect on how this situation may have changed or what you may have done differently had you had clearer understanding of the Spirit's nearness or distance. Journal what the Spirit reveals.

In the routine activities of your day—with family, friends, on your job, in His service—ask God to increase your awareness of things you fear great or small. Take notice of what causes anxiety. As God brings these things to your attention, spiritually, mentally and emotionally work through the following.

1. Surrender: Choose not to be ruled and controlled emotionally by anxiety.
2. Confess: Express anxiety to God in prayer. Tell Him briefly and simply your need. Do not give Him any instructions for how to remedy the problem.
3. Praise: Ask Him to protect you from doubting His ability to provide. Thank Him for His continued faithfulness in your life.
4. Cleanse: Ask Him to reveal any presumption in your heart. Ask Him to reveal how you think or expect your situation to be

resolved that is not in line with His truth. Ask Him to reveal how fear and presumptuous conclusions result in jealousy, envy, insecurity, accusations, and paranoia. (Remember the heart is deceitful above all things. Recognize a need to be more objective and introspective so you may discern how fear and presumptions affect those around you.)

5. **Seek:** Ask Him to reveal His truth for your situation. Listen and watch how He reveals more of who He is through this need.
6. **Wait:** Wait for His leading before you act or react. Let His peace guide you as He leads. Meditate on even small details He reveals, trusting Him to later reveal its part in His full provision.

Fear Arouses Anger

Begin with worship, mediation, and prayer.

> Rest in the Lord, and wait patiently for Him; Do not fret because of him who prospers in his way, because of the man who brings wicked schemes to pass. Cease from anger, and forsake wrath; do not fret, it only causes harm. For evildoers shall be cut off; but those who wait on the Lord, they shall inherit the earth. (Psalm 37:7–9)

> "Heavenly Father, I release my anger to you. Replace my anger with intercession. Replace my strife with peace."

Through this psalm, David teaches that fear is no justification for anger and bitterness. David faced fear continually but trusted God to be his deliverer. Even when David expressed great anger and wrath toward his enemies, he ultimately surrendered that anger to God trusting God to intervene with His protection. Above, David reminds us that anger is not the correct response to injustice.

When fear reigns, the natural result is anger and resentment of the circumstances, those who caused them, or both. Often we even become angry with God for allowing it or failing to prevent it. Unfettered fear leads to expressions of anger and ultimately roots of bitterness. These expressions are Flesh attempts to control or manipulate circumstances or people. Angry outbursts are attempts to maintain control when everything seems to be out of control. Silent "in-bursts" are unhealthy suppressions of anger. There may be no lashing out in anger, but others around perceive the angry heart nevertheless and are affected by it. Anger is a rebellious refusal to surrender. Fear, doubt, and presumptions lead us to conclude that surrender means accepting what we believe to be wrong—an endorsement of what is harmful and hurtful without mounting a defense.

When God calls for surrender in difficulty, it is not to agree with or accept injustice. Surrender does not always require inaction in response to circumstances. Surrender means to *partner with* God so His purposes for us and for others involved will prevail. Surrender means to focus on the spiritual realties more than earthly visibilities. Surrender may involve waiting for God to intervene on our behalf before we take action. This should comfort us, not fuel greater anger and manipulative behavior. God's goodness is greater than ours and thus so is His wrath! God asks us to surrender to His power to deliver us through the injustice. "Vengeance is mine says the Lord. I will repay evil for evil" (Romans 12:19).

When we become angry with God, we fail to trust Him and His plan. Because we do not know His plan, we resist surrender and refuse to trust. Romans 8:28 says, "All things work together for good to those who *love God* and are called *according to His purpose*, (emphasis added)." Surrender to God frees us from the anger that grieves the Holy Spirit and hinders revelation of His purpose. Like David, Job was a man with many reasons to be angry. Job models the surrender God desires. Job refused to curse God. Though Job at times questioned why God allowed great affliction, he still remained a faithful, trusting servant. He surrendered to God's unrevealed purpose and allowed God to deliver him through the trials even though God chose not to deliver him from them.

Perhaps the most modern witness I have of this deep trust is my mother. Romans 8:28 was her life verse, and "Trust and Obey" was a favorite hymn. At times, I thought her graciousness was misplaced or the result of naïveté. But the more I mature in faith and the more I learn of her trials, the more I appreciate how deeply she trusted this verse. She once told my sister that God graced her with the ability to forgive easily. My observation is that this ability was beyond measure for most. Forgiveness was empowered by her willingness to trust God completely. She relied on the higher purpose God had for her difficulties and the eternal goodness that would result from her obedient surrender.

In marriage, we often fear unmet needs. We may also resent our spouse for failing to meet those needs. I have fought this battle in my own heart. As Christians, we know God has a plan for spiritual intimacy in marriage, yet it seems to evade us; our reality appears to exist contrary to His plan. Somewhere we detoured or ran ahead and became lost. It appears there is no hope for peaceful unity. Left unsurrendered, anger is directed toward God if only subconsciously.

Unresolved anger leads to resentment and bitterness. Bitterness builds both an emotional and spiritual barrier. With this barrier—this wall of protection—erected, restoration is impossible to find. With no promise of restoration, we have little hope of peace and happiness. Ironically, with the wall of protection in place, very little can get over or penetrate it especially from those who have hurt us and let us down. The wall originated from needing deeper love, yet with it built, love has greater difficulty reaching us. We are receptive of love only from those with whom we have no history of hurt, leaving the relationship open for affairs, deception, inappropriate friendships, or emotional affairs.

God does not want either spouse to feel trapped by an unfulfilling marriage. Neither does He intend for the difficulty to end what He has joined together. Marriage is to be an intimate union between man and woman that gives witness to the relationship between Christ and the church. Just as Christ unconditionally and sacrificially committed to us while we were still sinners and imperfect, so does God ask us to honor our marriages—our own unconditional commitment to imperfect persons—a sacrifice of our own welfare for the sake of the spouses and the marriages. We commit to love our spouses for better or worse. Perhaps one of the best definitions I have ever heard of marriage or unconditional love is this: "We are to love one another in light of who God intends us to become without becoming bitter or complacent about whom we are."[7]

---

[7] Dan B. Allender and Tremper Longman, *Intimate Allies* (Wheaton, IL: Tyndale House, 1995).

This truly describes Christ's love for us. God calls us to emulate this love in life but especially in marriage. Marriage more than any other relationship save that of parent and child, is the place where we truly glimpse the others' weaknesses. Yet even this level of knowledge cannot fully grasp one's deep inadequacies that only God knows, and it most certainly cannot fully comprehend all the wondrous gifts and goals God has for our spouses. So if we are to love our spouses as God loves them, we must "lean not on our own understanding, but in all ways acknowledge Him, and He will direct our paths." We have to seek spiritual realities in the face of physical visibilities.

In marriage, God asks us to surrender our Flesh ways of reacting and responding to difficulties. He calls us to draw closer to Him so we see His unique purpose for marriage. As we learn to look through His eternal lens of life, we glean how He uses both partners' weaknesses to refine and polish our strengths. Resentment and bitterness restricts intimacy with God and thus diminishes the ability to see His perspective. Instead, we remain trapped in hurt, disappointment, pain, and resentment.

The walls we erect keep even God out, not because God is inadequate, but because He is holy. His holiness cannot fellowship with bitterness and resentment. His holy nature mandates separation from sin and unrighteousness. He does not abandon us, but He also does not demand our love. He patiently waits until we are ready to receive His love and to surrender to His demolition of the walls.

Read and fill in the blanks from the Word of God first in Ephesians 4:30–32, then in 1 Peter 3:8–12.

"And do not _____ the _____ _____ of God, by whom you were sealed for the day of redemption. Let all _____, wrath, _____, clamor, and evil speaking be _____ from you, with all malice. And be _____ one to another, just as God in Christ _____ you."

"Finally, all of you be of one mind, having _____ for one another; love as brothers, be _____, be courteous; not returning _____ for _____ or reviling for reviling, but on the contrary _____, knowing that you were _____ to this, that you may _____ a blessing.

For 'He who would love life and see good day, let him _____his _____ from evil, and his lips from speaking guile; let him turn away from evil and do good; let him seek _____and _____ it. For the _____ of the Lord are on the _____, and his _____ are _____ to their prayers; but the _____ of the Lord is _____those who do evil.'"

Bitterness grieves the Holy Spirit. Bitterness is sin that prohibits the filling of the Spirit. A lack of fellowship with the Spirit impairs strength to obey. It hinders our desire to persevere through difficulty for it quenches hope. When fellowship with God is strained, we are not postured to hear His instructions, let alone motivated to obey those things we know are right.

We may pray unceasingly for relationships, but if we are not first confessing *and* turning away from bitterness, our prayers are hindered. To move forward with the belief that because we have prayed and "given it to God" our actions are justified, is a false sense of security that can lead to further pain and sin. Without sacrificially laying our need for justice, our need for happiness, our need for intimacy, and our need for peace all on the altar, we are in danger of continuing through life in the Flesh. God has not abandoned us; we have separated from Him. "Apart from Him, we can do nothing" that will bring true happiness, peace, and contentment. God is the One who cleanses, but we must submit to that process. Many times in my life, I presume God's cleansing process is complete in a certain area only to have Him shortly reveal another layer of dirt. Each time, I must choose to be cleansed, or continue operating in the filth of my Flesh.

What relationship(s) in your life need healing?

Ask God to reveal any ways you may have "returned evil for evil, or reviling for reviling" in these relationships.

Ask God to reveal ways you can bring blessings to this relationship.

Someone may sin against us, but reacting to that with anger, resentment, or bitterness is equally if not more damaging to the relationship. As the saying goes, "Hurt people hurt people." What bitter seeds of hurt hinder happiness today? The people who hurt us can never do enough to heal the hurt; only the Healer can. In the interim, choose not to repay evil for evil or pain for pain. Choose to be tenderhearted and forgiving as Christ is with us even when they reopen the emotional wounds God is still in the process of healing. God knows our hurt and despair. He carries hope even when we cannot or will not. Do not push Him away for He knows the path for victory. He may continue to allow the circumstances to exhaust our stubborn refusal to turn to Him.

> Therefore, behold, I will allure her, will bring her into the wilderness, and speak comfort to her … And it shall be, in that day, says the Lord, That you will call Me "My Husband", and no longer call Me "My Master" … I will betroth you to Me forever; yes, I will betroth you to Me in righteousness and justice. In lovingkindness and mercy; I will betroth you to Me in faithfulness, and you shall know the Lord. (Hosea 2:14, 16, 19–20)

You may feel as if you are in a wilderness. You may have been there so long you have little or no hope of coming out. God wants to meet with you there! He is speaking comfort to you. He wants the walls to come down so you go beyond perceiving Him as the sovereign God relegating you to a life of suffering. He wants to show you the depth of His tender, affectionate love. Reflect on the things mentioned in these verses that precede "knowing the Lord," paying close attention to the drawing power of God's love.

- God allures me.
- He brings me into the wilderness not to punish but to speak comfort.
- He causes me to know Him as a tender, compassionate, protective saviour, not a demanding master.
- He binds me to Him forever in His righteousness (goodness), justice, lovingkindness, mercy, and faithfulness—He will be all I need!

The Fear of the Lord

Begin with worship, mediation, and prayer.

> So that you incline your ear to wisdom, and apply your heart to understanding; yes, if you cry out for discernment, and lift up your voice for understanding, if you seek her as silver, and search for her as for hidden treasures; then you will understand the fear of the Lord, and find the knowledge of God. (Proverbs 2:2–5)

> "Lord, teach me *how* to recognize You in the circumstances of my life. Give me a deeper hunger for Your word, and a desire for understanding. Teach me how to mine the treasures of wisdom in Your word. Help me know You more, I pray."

Another important acronym for fear represents a fear of the Lord resulting in faith. Fear of the Lord is a protective form of fear. That acronym is Face Everything And Rise. Let us see a few ways a fear of the Lord develops in scripture.

Look up the following scriptures and briefly summarize what caused a fear of the Lord, paying close attention to the importance of the presence of God in each passage. Meditate on the similarities.

Genesis 22:8–12
Genesis 28:16–17
Exodus 3:3–5
Judges 6:21–23
Daniel 3:25–30
Daniel 8:15–17
Luke 1:11–13, 28–30
1 Kings 18:37–39

To whom did God demonstrate His power or reveal His presence in the above passages? List not the names but the characteristics or natures of their hearts.

Read Exodus 20:4–5 and 34:14. From these verses and the passages above, why do you think God wanted to reveal Himself?

    These passages reveal just a portion of scripture in which God's presence or manifestation of power resulted in fear. Fear of God results in worship of God, which draws us closer to Him and invites His presence among us in fellowship. Intimate fellowship strengthens and empowers faith for we hear and understand His Word when we commune with Him.

    Do you see the process? Fear of God does not drive us away from Him; it draws us closer. Fear of the Lord empowers us to "Face Everything And Rise." Worship of God is an expression of surrender to God and the expression of our need for Him. Perhaps this is why God's first four Commandments involve worship and reverence of Him above all other gods. Once again, God's magnificent wisdom has fashioned for us guidelines that are not mere legalistic religious mandates but principles that make intimacy with Him possible if sought.

    In the earlier passages, we see how God revealed Himself to the just and the unjust, to the righteous and the unrighteous, to those seeking Him, and to those who need to seek Him. He decides to whom, when, and how according to His sovereign purposes. God desires to be the sole focus of our love because He wants us to know Him. These scriptures reveal how a fear of the Lord always resulted when God was present and recognized as God. In Exodus 33:20, God tells Moses that no one shall see His face and live. God's chosen people are familiar with this principle. Throughout the Old Testament, a fear of death accompanies a fear of the Lord because of this passage. However, those humbly responding in worship to the presence of God usually received God's reassurance, peace, life, joy, and power. His presence did not bring a sense of imminent danger to those who responded to Him in worship.

    Let us reflect more on Israel's fear resulting from God's proclamation to Moses. In Exodus 33:18, Moses asks to see God's glory. He did not ask to see God's face, but when God graciously agreed to Moses's request, God made a point of stating that Moses could not see His face, for no man could see it and live.

God reveals His glory but not His face multiple times in the Old Testament. There are multiple times when the Angel of the Lord, the pre-incarnate Christ, appears in the form of a man. Certainly, these are humbling experiences resulting in great fear due to the majesty, glory, and power of the holy presence. We know from Exodus 34:29–30 that Moses's encounter with God at the burning bush affected his appearance so much that those who saw him were afraid. Perhaps God is protecting humanity because His glory is so overwhelming that our physical bodies could not endure the experience. Perhaps God tells Moses of this protection so Moses will understand why God must shield him from any risk of glimpsing His face. If this is a protective proclamation, not a stern warning, is it legitimate to fear God revealing His face? It does not appear from God's Word that His nature or way of dispensing justice and correction is to reveal His face. Is Satan legalizing this statement in the minds of God's people to so fuel fear of God's wrath that one is discouraged from pursuing intimacy? Has Satan successfully so fueled fear of God's wrath that we fail to pursue His favor? As we focus intently on pursuing God's favor, there is less need to fear God's wrath for the former relies on the indwelling Spirit that overcomes Flesh.

There are two types of a fear of the Lord. First is a reverent fear that honors God's sovereign power. With this type of fear, one is humbled by the reality that God is the Great I Am, the Alpha and Omega who knows, sees, and governs all. This fear fuels a desire for intimacy with God. It empowers us to surrender to God's will and His ways for completing His will. This fear is fueled by the Spirit of God.

Second is a fear of God's wrath or judgment. The consequences of sin fuel this fear along with inadequacies or a failure to please God. A fear of God's wrath may change behavior, but it also is susceptible to legalistic behaviors and mandates. Behavior modification is a step toward change, but without genuine repentance, one is prone to repeat the sin. This fear may be fueled by the Spirit during times of conviction and cleansing, but it can also be fueled by man's Flesh and Satan's schemes to pervert truth and distort God's ways for refining His children.

Notice the difference between these fears of the Lord and the effects of fear we have discussed thus far. A fear of the Lord resulting from an experience with His power does not bring anxiety and stress. A healthy fear of the Lord does not push us away from knowing Him, but fuels our hunger to know Him. Daniel gives insight to the weight of compassion, intercession, and concern that comes from an intense revelation of God's truth and a fear of Him. Daniel 8:27 says, "And I, Daniel, fainted and was sick for days; afterward I arose and went about the king's business. I was astonished by the vision, but no one understood it."

Notice how the burden of God's revelation was intense and confusing to Daniel. He did not have understanding but appeared to seek it. "No one understood it" implies that Daniel sought counsel and advice from others but found no answers. This burden, this lack of understanding did not make Daniel so consumed and distracted with fear and anxiety that he was unable to continue the king's business. This revelation was significant enough to cause physical unrest but not impair his work.

Daniel reveals a healthy fear of the Lord and how revelation can be unsettling to the point of physical distress but not be an unhealthy overreaction emotionally and spiritually. This exemplifies our goal for this study. We want to learn to walk in steadfast faith focused on the plans and purposes of God. We want sensitivity and compassion to God's burdens for His people yet not take the burden on ourselves. We want to give Him the burden and walk in fear of Him, not fear of the burden; while understanding how fear of God invites His revelation and results in the humility to live His purpose for the revelation.

Throughout the Bible, God generally reveals Himself in ways that cannot be overlooked. From a historical viewpoint, it is easy to accept that God would choose to reveal Himself miraculously. In the Old Testament, God's power and Spirit rained down on earth and empowered humanity through outward, visible manifestations. In the New Testament, we see the miraculous preparation for the coming of Christ as well as the Son of God in the flesh. Humanity could actually see Christ in person as well as God's miraculous power at work through Him. Christ modeled and made the way for the miraculous indwelling of God's power and Spirit. However, can we "see" Him today? Hebrews 13:8 says, "Jesus is the same yesterday, today, and forever." He never changes. His love for us never changes. His desire to commune with us never changes. Would it then stand to reason that the God who desired to make Himself known in the Old and the New Testaments would also desire to make Himself known today? If so, how do we "see" Him fully today?

In preparation for the next chapter, write down your understanding of a hardened heart.

As we began this lesson, we meditated on Proverbs 2, which teaches that an enduring resolve to study the Word brings a fear of the Lord that in turn helps us find the knowledge of God. These truths are the key to understanding how we "see" God and are the focus of deeper study in chapters 3–5.

All God's Word reveals His character. When we focus on understanding His ways in scripture, we learn how to see Him. While God's Word is the source for both general and specific promises today, all His promises teach us about the depth of His love for humanity. As we learn to identify His ways for revealing His love and will in scripture, we understand how to better understand His specific will. As we read God's Word, we benefit more by seeking to understand what it teaches us about God more than how it would help us. As we put the focus on God above our own need, we will find the guidance sought. "Seek you first the kingdom of God, and all these things will be added unto you" (Matthew 6:33). "Delight yourself in the Lord, and He shall give you the desires of your heart" (Psalm 37:4).

Before we continue the discussion of seeing or knowing God, we conclude by exploring the effects of fear, doubt, and unbelief to the growth of faith in chapter 2. Meditate on Psalm 112:1–8, which reveals the blessings resulting from a fear of God.

> *Praise the Lord! Blessed is the man who fears the Lord, who delights greatly in His commandments. His descendants be mighty on earth; the generation of the upright will be blessed. Wealth and riches will be in his house, and his righteousness endures forever. Unto the upright there arises light in the darkness; He is gracious, and full of compassion, and righteous. A good man deals graciously and lends; He will guide*

his affairs with discretion, surely he will never be shaken; the righteous will be in everlasting remembrance. He will not be afraid of evil tidings; his heart is steadfast, trusting in the Lord. His heart is established. He will not be afraid, until he sees his desire upon his enemies.
—Psalms 112:1-8

Growing Faith 1
The Unraveling of Fear and the Revival of Faith

Throughout our study, we learn how to see life's circumstances from God's perspective; we learn to see the spiritual realities through physical visibilities. As part of our training, most of the study requires a bird's-eye view of God's Word as much as specific analysis, particularly with Jesus's training of His disciples. We begin and will end the Growing Faith discussions by analyzing Gideon's faith growth. Because of the reverence often given those chosen twelve of Christ, Gideon's situations and deliverances appear more personally applicable and typically human. In addition, this one chapter in Judges gives a complete picture of God's process of raising His child from fear to faith.

Gideon's life reveals an important distinction with fear. When the Angel of the Lord first meets with Gideon, the fear he reveals is a destructive fear that blinds him from the truth about God as well as his circumstances. It is a paralyzing fear preventing Gideon from knowing and completing his life purpose. However, when the Angel of the Lord leaves, Gideon's fear of the Lord is restored. A fear of the Lord is a protective form of fear. Gideon's fear of the Lord postures him to receive further truth and specific instruction from God. It empowers him to depend on God to fulfill his purpose. Gideon's fear of the Lord prepares him for his future role. Notice the opposite extremes in fear and the opposite effects.

I cannot emphasize enough the importance of Gideon's example in bringing understanding of God's faith-growth process. For this reason, I pray we reflect on these discussions of Gideon throughout this study as well as pray for God to bring to our remembrance truths applicable in our lives. This is extremely beneficial for our faith growth for it reminds us of God's faithfulness to prepare His children. It reminds us of God's desire to commune personally with us. It reinforces truths of His character observed in this encounter that repeat in similar ways throughout His Word. All these deepen trust in God.

One of the wonderful aspects of this chapter is its ability to equip Christians at different stages of their relationships with God. As we begin to discuss these, I hope you will find a parallel to your own need and see God's perspective for that need. I pray God meets with you in a personal way.

The three stages of growth we discern from Judges 6 are:

1. the fully surrendered servant (the Angel of the Lord),
2. the deliverer in transformation (Gideon), and
3. the people in need of restoration (the Jewish people).

God's Word reveals the surrendered Servant of God who equips the deliverer of God who restores the people of God who give glory to Him through their repentance.

God uses each one to help the other more fully focus on His presence in their midst. As we begin a discussion of each, we start with the last, those who need restoration.

God Restores His People

God's chosen children need restoration. As mentioned, they feared others above a fear of God. Whom they feared became whom they worshipped. They knew of God's greatness and faithfulness. They lived under His protection and provision, yet they rebelled. The last sentence in the prior chapter (Judges 5:31) states that the land rested for forty years. Israel experienced a season of rebellion, judgment, and restoration. However, during the forty years of rest, they began to fear false gods. The period of rest became a period of failing to maintain intimate fellowship with God.

How the children of Israel responded during this time of rest is still common for Christians. During times of rest and ease, we often lose dependence on God (on His Spirit). We become self-sufficient. Absent difficulty, it is easy to carry on day to day without the power of God (or at least the awareness of it). As fellowship with Him diminishes, so does remembrance of His greatness. When we experience difficulty or see it in the lives of others, we initially may not seek God's help for we have drifted from Him. We may try to fix things in our own way and time often without success. Fear begins to take hold of our hearts. During these times, we may also cry out to God, but like the Israelites, we cry out for deliverance without perceiving our need for repentance. Perhaps one important part of the Christian life most affected by this same pattern is the marriage relationship.

Besides a Christian's relationship with God, the most intimate relationship is marriage. Because of its significance in our lives, to our children, and to the strength of society, it is one Satan sets out to undermine and destroy. Recall his destruction in the garden to undermine what Adam and Eve had together and their fellowship with God. Satan uses fear, self-protection, and doubt to unravel bliss and peace. Once this seed of fear is planted, Satan wields power over thoughts. Refer to Genesis 3 as we revisit how temptation evolved to fuel disobedience.

Satan led Eve to believe there was something missing that she could find apart from God's instruction. This process of deception is easy to conceptualize. God gave them so much, so why would He withhold something else? Did He not make them caretakers of the earth and its fruits? Can she trust Him? Should she care to? If eating the forbidden fruit gives greater knowledge wouldn't this be good for Adam? Once she partook, her desire was for her husband to join her.

Imagine the conflict in Adam as Eve offers him the forbidden fruit. Adam's one flesh partner and wife who shared the bliss of an unbroken world and intimacy disobeyed God, so what would happen to her? What would happen to their relationship? Didn't God say they would die? But Eve has not died, so is it really safe—can he believe God or Eve? Can he live without her if she is to die? Could he return to loneliness in the garden after knowing her? Is the risk of dying with her a better consequence than answering to God?

When Adam succumbed to the forbidden fruit, they both knew shame; they covered themselves from each other and hid from God. Fear, doubt, presumption, and unbelief were integral to the Fall. Sin hindered intimacy with each other and with God. There was a way that seemed right to man, but it was not God's way, and it led to turmoil, guilt, shame, eternal death, and eventual physical death where there once had been everlasting peace.

By eating the forbidden fruit, instead of increasing goodness, Eve's sorrow and conception are multiplied. Eve's desire for Adam to eat the fruit results in a curse upon her relational desire for her husband. Her actions had the opposite effect of those intended. No longer will the desire for her husband result in blissful contentment. Now he will rule over her. Woman will struggle with contentment and oppression.

Prior to the Fall, Adam trusted God and sought God's favor. He experienced peace with God, with Eve, and as caretaker of the garden. Adam's disobedience disrupted this peace. Now he experiences fear of futility and failure in his work and in providing for his family. Through exerted efforts, he will continually deal with great toil, thorns, and thistles just to eat and survive. Because man was influenced by woman and disobeyed God's command, his fear of repeating this failure causes him to rule over her (Genesis 3:13–19).

God's original, distinct but equal roles for man and woman are distorted by the Fall. Wives often look to their husbands to provide the contentment and happiness that before and after the curse comes only from God. Under the effects of the curse men will continually struggle with that proper balance of following God, loving the wife and family, and vocational success. In toil and frustration men seek peace often at the expense of ruling over the wife. The blissful union experienced before the Fall is replaced by a constant tug of war to protect self.

When husbands and wives live trapped by the curse, there is little to no peace, contentment and intimacy. If the marriage continues in this state, spiritual or emotional intimacy is found lacking by one or both spouses and happiness is sought from other sources. Material things, social activities, or roles as parents and providers often captivate more time and devotion than the marriage that's trapped in an unfulfilling state. These roles can become dens of captivity even though they offer protection from further marital tension. If we cannot find happiness through these venues while still in the marriage, we may look for reasons to get out. There seems to be a misconception that God is more concerned with one's happiness than with obedience to the marriage covenant and dependence on Him through even great marital difficulty. There is a crying out to God, but it is often a crying out for freedom from the oppression of a difficult marriage, too often without first perceiving a need for personal repentance and restoration.

Through Christ, God makes a way for the needed restoration, a way to overcome the effects of the curse through eternal life and in marriage. Too often, though, like God's people in Judges 6, we have a fear of circumstances greater than a fear of God. There is a way that seems right to man, but in the end, it leads to destruction. In marriage, the destruction could be emotional turmoil, physical or financial distress, separation, or divorce. But, "a fear of the Lord is the beginning of wisdom" (Proverbs 9:10).

Dear beloved, if you are oppressed by a marriage that falls short of God's design, know that God hears your cry! Even when difficulty is the result of sin, we have hope because God is working to restore intimacy with Him and the marriage. As we continue in this study, let God speak to this need. Hear His words of correction and instruction for they are necessary for the deliverance we seek. He is calling us to be faithful to Him and to our spouses, but He will also empower us to accomplish all He asks.

Some completing this study have already experienced divorce in biblical grounds and others from a path not in accordance with God's Word. Please do not allow the teaching and illustration in this study to be used by Satan as condemnation. Divorce is never an unpardonable sin, but it often occurs because of hardened hearts. God wants to cleanse us from and restore hardened hearts. Satan wants to condemn us for wrong choices; God wants to cleanse us from them. Allow this study to cleanse any guilt or hurt from betrayal that may be lingering in your heart. Both of these are sources of fear that hinder restoration with God. Relinquish either of them if they surface in the course of this study. Ask God to lead you to further resources to bring the restoration you need and He desires.

As mentioned, rooted in fear is the need for self-protection that can distract us from God's truth. However, some may require protection mentally, emotionally, and physically from abusive spouses. If these are your reality, finding specific help for these situations is beyond the scope of this study. If you are in harm's way from an abuser, please do not allow this study to prolong further abuse. If you even suspect this is the direction your relationship is headed, seek protection through wise professional counsel. The marital discussions, illustrations, and guidance in this study do not refer to marital issues where a person's health and welfare are in danger.

The drifting away from one another may lead to what appears irreconcilable. While differences are not abusive in nature, they often result in separation and divorce to avoid prolonged struggles caused by generational sins or bad habits. My marriage is testimony that irreconcilable differences are not beyond redemption. They are not usually reconciled on our timetable or preferred means, but that isn't because God has abandoned the marriage, our spouse, or us. It is because each spouse is in need of restoration, and we typically are not receptive to the depth of restoration needed.

Because of the Fall and Satan's continued temptations, all marriages require work because we all require restoration. There is no perfect person waiting somewhere that will result in a perpetual, conflict-free relationship. Once the newness of relationship fades it takes work from both spouses to deepen intimacy.

We often look to the marriage to ease the effects of everything that ails us, things only Jesus can provide or heal. The intimacy, contentment, and peace desired by man and woman cannot be achieved without God's wisdom and understanding. How we respond to conflict—how we allow God to refine our weaknesses through it—can be a catalyst for eventual marital restoration. Fear of the relationship remaining stagnant in an unfulfilling state fuels self-protection, which is pride. Pride goes before a fall if left unsurrendered. Fear of the marriage not healing in the manner you comprehend can cause you to drift from both God and your spouse. Do not allow Satan to fuel the destruction of your marriage through fear, self-focused protection, or pride. With man, it is impossible; with God, all things are possible. (Our faithful response keeps the door of possibilities open).

Open the eyes of your heart to the Spirit as we continue study of God's ways for growing faith and how they benefit marriage. Allow the Spirit to reveal any pride in your heart that may have contributed to marital issues or even divorce. Allow this study to be a catalyst of cleansing and healing as God strengthens faith and restores a reverent fear of Him.

Allow God to use this study to help navigate you and your children through difficulties of divorce. Anyone experiencing marriage difficulty and especially divorce has certainly battled with fear before, during, and after divorce. God cleanses and heals when we surrender to Him. Go beyond confessing your need for God's power to confess your desire for Him. Allow the expectation of meeting with Him fuel hope through present difficulty.

There can be trials in many areas of our lives besides marriage that cause us to cry out to God. It can come through difficulties with children, parents, financial pressures, grief and hurt, physical hardship and suffering, career pressures, and other major concerns. As we cry out, we should also be sensitive to how God is calling for cleansing and repentance. What He asks of us, He will empower us to accomplish. As with Gideon, God does not expect the power, skill, or ability to come from self. God asks for a partnership of surrender to His power. It will be a partnership that accomplishes more than imaginable on our own.

America is currently facing great difficulty. While some believe that the year 2009 ushered in the worst economy since the Great Depression, I argue we are experiencing one of the most spiritually rebellious times in this nation's history. We have experienced times of great immorality in our past, but even during those times, there still existed an acknowledgment of God as God of our nation. Perhaps for the first time in our history, we have become a nation demanding tolerance of many religions, but Christianity is demonized and ridiculed more than it is tolerated or defended. Even President Obama proclaims to the world his belief that we are no longer just a Christian nation. Our country, like Gideon's, has lost reverence of God. Likewise, many of our households serve other gods be they other religions, materialism, sensuality, self-gratification, or the environment.

As in Judges 6, there is a great and understandable outcry in this nation for the difficulties we face. However, we fail to recognize that many of these difficulties are the result of our rebellion. God has not abandoned us; we have separated from Him. There *is* a crying out for deliverance and security, but not in repentance.

To the extent this is recognized in the public sphere, God is not seen as the source of deliverance. Instead, government is touted as the great arbitrator and deliverer of what is wrong in the nation. We are told by many that our problems will be solved by the government's intervention and regulation of all aspects of our lives. Economic fear is used to fuel class envy and social injustices creating the perceived need for a deliverance from a higher power. However, the higher power is deemed to be the wisdom of men through government intervention and an erosion of individual freedom. God's Word tells us that the wisdom of men is foolishness to Him. Yet even among public leaders who profess to be Christians, fear of political correctness often silences open demonstration of our need of God and a reliance on His truths.

Until we recognize God as the true deliverer, counselor, and source for restoration, our nation will continue to suffer. As Judges 6 reveals, revival happens as God's power is revealed in our lives and then in our own households and extended family. To accomplish national restoration, our families need restoration first.

During these difficult times, Psalm 33 has been a great comfort and reminder of God's sovereignty over our nation. It serves as a model for intercession. This passage acknowledges that we need to recognize God as Creator and to fear and worship Him (more than His creation) to receive protection. It reminds us that we are not to put our trust in kings, rulers, and the military but in our almighty Father. Too many homes do not promote and practice these beliefs in the family.

God wants to restore His children. Perhaps like the children of Israel, the restoration we currently seek is but a shadow of the real restoration we need. Be willing to hear the Word God reveals. He meets with us in our need and makes a way for restoration. Seek Him. Wait on Him. Trust Him, for He is our God worthy of our fear and worship!

God Equips His Deliverer

What we learn of Gideon, his circumstances, and the favor He has with God seems to indicate he did not follow his father's household in worship of Baal. Most likely, the level of oppression and fear is increased in Gideon if he failed to participate in pagan worship with his family. As we begin to look at the depth of Gideon's fear, there are a few important observations to revisit regarding his encounter with the Angel of the Lord. These are the foundational ways God strengthens faith.

- God comes to us—the Lord met with Gideon personally, intimately, face to face in the quietness of his everyday work.
- God meets us as we are—the Lord met with Gideon when he was fearful and helped him rise above his circumstances to become a man of faith.
- God changes us before he changes our circumstances—Gideon sought deliverance, but the Lord's presence empowered surrender (to become the deliverer).

Before Gideon is filled with God's power, he must first be emptied of fear and its effects. As the Angel of the Lord visits with Gideon, He allows him to vent. Gideon voices all that is troubling him while the Angel of the Lord periodically unfolds and restates God's plan. With each interchange, we see Gideon's focus change. He becomes less frustrated and increases his desire to understand God's will.

In Judges 6:11–17, we see the devastating and progressive effects of fear in the heart of Gideon. Let's further look at the many layers and consequences of fear that God begins to cleanse as Gideon confesses his frustrations.

- Judges 6:11: *Fear*—He works in hiding for fear of losing nourishment for his household.
- Judges 6:13: *Depression and Frustration*—He is depressed by the absence of the Lord and frustrated or angry that God allowed this to happen. He is confused as to why God has not intervened to help.
- Judges 6:15: *Insecurity*—Insecurity is a form of pride because it is consumption with the inadequacies of self. It is prideful to presume God would expect him to accomplish such a task in his own strength. Gideon, as we, presumes God is calling him to perform the unthinkable when actually God is calling him to surrender as a vessel for the power of God. It's not about his abilities; it's about the greatness of God!
- Judges 6:17: *Doubt*—Gideon heard the Lord's will but doubts its credibility. He looks for a sign, proof, or evidence to fully relinquish his fear. Even though he has been in the presence of the Lord, he has not fully realized it.

Judges 6 reveals God's perspective of fear's effects. Fear fuels depression, frustration, anger, confusion, doubt, and pride (insecurity). The danger of fear is that absent fellowship with God, we remain isolated and focused on self-protection or self-pity. Just as Gideon progressively reveals how deeply fear affected him, we also must realize the far-reaching effect of fear in our lives.

There are three seeds of fear. I call these the fear trinity as often one fuels the others when left to grow, choking the growth of faith. This fear trinity may spawn other fears. The core categories of the fear trinity are fear of rejection, fear of futility, and fear of failure. Let us examine these more closely.

Fear of Rejection—Genesis 3:16

Fear of rejection fuels a fear of loneliness. It is a fear of separation from those we love, admire, and respect. It also may include a fear of shame, disfavor, mistrust, and alienation of those dear to us resulting in performance-based acceptance in relationships. Performance-based acceptance causes us to perform in ways that please people including self, instead of seeking what pleases God. This form of fear can be very deceptive when the people we seek to please are godly and worthy of respect. Our focus must always be to seek what pleases God. Even other well-meaning Christians may not be able to discern what God wants to reveal. He wants us to know Him and His ways personally, which may not necessarily be His ways for them or what they perceive with human insight.

The fear of rejection can manifest in many different ways. It can lead to codependency or neediness causing us to attach ourselves emotionally to others in unhealthy ways. On the other extreme, it could also cause us to isolate emotionally or socially withdraw in attempt to avoid hurt or rejection. The fear of rejection can also result in proving our loyalty in unhealthy or ungodly ways to gain approval. It may fuel domineering tendencies in us to manipulate, control, and deceive through a lack of openness and honesty to preserve a relationship.

Understanding our identity in Christ empowers us to overcome this fear. As our understanding of who we are in Christ increases, our fear of rejection and our concern with the perception of others become less important to our well-being. We learn to value more what God thinks of us than what others may say or think. We realize that our true worth lies in who God created us to be, not in whom or what others try to create us into. Others, including Gideon himself, thought of him as the weakest leader of the weakest clan. However, God saw him as a mighty man of valor. Gideon might have been the social or family outcast, but God was with him. Gideon had the privilege of intimate communion with the Holy God. This fellowship with God eventually brought fellowship and acceptance of others. Gideon was not as alone as he imagined.

The more we seek God, the more we nurture fellowship with Him, the more we realize we are never alone, never rejected. People are drawn into fellowship with us when our countenances and personalities reflect godliness, not neediness or manipulative insecurity. Fellowship with Him molds us into people who reflect His goodness.

The fear of rejection may lead to some or all of the following:

- materialism
- envy
- gossip/backbiting/criticism
- codependency/neediness
- control/manipulation/bullish intimidation
- insecurity
- paranoia
- sexual immorality—primarily in females as a misguided attempt to find love, intimacy, and affection
- performance-based acceptance

Fear of Futility–Genesis 3:17–19

Fear of futility promotes a fear of uselessness, a lack of purpose or meaning, a fear of harm or even death. This fear causes one to wrestle with the question: does my life really matter in the grand scheme of things? The fear of futility results in despair, discouragement, hopelessness, and depression in varying degrees. It can also manifest itself as idleness and worthlessness causing us not to reach our full potential.

On the other extreme, it results in an obsession with busyness to accomplish, achieve, and prove our value. An unhealthy obsession with overachieving to gain earthly success can destroy marriages and families. Ironically, many who pursue this lifestyle justify their efforts as necessary for the good of their families and sometimes even for the kingdom of God. Nevertheless, these attempts to overcome the fear of futility never truly satisfy the need. They do more to bring failure and disgrace than honor and glory to God.

The fear of futility is not limited to a fear of one's own futility but can also be a fear of losing those close to you such as a parent, child, spouse—the fear of a relational futility.

A fear of futility builds as we focus more on physical visibilities than spiritual realties. This fear works to undermine trust in God's sovereign plan for our purpose or the purpose of our loved ones. When this fear has a stronghold, it shifts focus to temporal things rather than the eternal.

As we gain understanding of our spiritual and vocational purpose, the fear of futility diminishes balancing successfully our calling and responsibilities in ways that honor God. As Gideon reveals, worship brings us into close communion with God and helps us receive specific instructions for our purpose and understanding of God's path. Close communion empowered Christ to survive intense, forty-day temptations as well as prepared Him to endure the cross. Worship focuses attention on our eternal life, not the futilities of our brief life this side of heaven.

The fear of futility may result in a number of negatives:

- control/manipulation/bullish intimidation
- idleness/complacency
- busyness/over-eagerness
- workaholics
- depression/discouragement/suicidal tendencies
- hopelessness/overwhelmed
- sexual promiscuity—primarily for men as reproducing gives a feeling a perpetuating life beyond self

Fear of Failure—Genesis 3:7–13

This is a fear of doing the wrong thing or making wrong decisions. We may fear failing our family, friends, bosses, customers, or even God. The fear of failure can cause us to wear masks of pretense to maintain our reputation or credibility thus concealing who we really are. There is a compelling to protect and project a certain supposedly successful identity. We have difficulty being honest about our weaknesses and shortcomings resulting in dishonesty within and with others. This fear leads to a stronghold of perfectionism, setting standards too high for anyone to meet, thus fulfilling the very thing we fear—failure.

Because failure often results in fear of rejection from those we respect, many of its effects parallel those of the fear of rejection. With a fear of rejection, we seek to combat the fear with relational performance. With a fear of failure, we seek to overcome this fear with vocational performance. Perfectionists cannot tolerate making mistakes—their own or anyone else's, so the desire to control situations and environments is great.

The need for control can result in quenching the move of the Holy Spirit. The fear of failure is so strong that there is little room for trusting the unseen and unknown ways of God; thus, self is exalted to control above surrender. As we become more focused on the accuracy (or potential inaccuracy) of our or others' performance, we become desensitized to our need to surrender and trust the Holy Spirit. Our behavior, our performance, is given a higher value than what is healthy. Our focus shifts to avoiding failure so much that we do not see what God is attempting to do through us. Similar to the fear of rejection, we lose sight of our value or of the value of those we lead in the eyes of God.

Faith gains victory over this fear when we trust God through weakness. We rejoice in weaknesses when we surrender them to God so that His power is displayed through them. But to trust God with our weaknesses, we must first be willing to honestly recognize and accept them. We must learn to trust God all the more when the display of His power is not immediately apparent through our weakness. During the times of waiting for His power to be revealed, we learn that appearing foolish, or even appearing to be a failure can ultimately reveal God's glory when we surrender our reputation to Him. This journey teaches us to surrender as vessels for the glory of God instead of needing others to see us as successes.

These are other sins the fear of failure leads to:

- perfectionism/performance-based acceptance
- narcissism or narcissistic tendencies (self-absorption and self-indulgence)
- pretense/hypocrisy
- pride—either arrogance or insecurity
- control/manipulation/bullish intimidation
- dishonesty with self and others
- envy

- unconfident/indecisive behaviors
- materialism
- immoral sensuality

The Rise of the Deliverer Comes with the Surrender of the Man

Gideon complains to the Angel of the Lord about God's failure to show His power on their behalf and grant deliverance. The Angel of the Lord challenges Gideon to channel this frustration into faith when He charges Gideon, "Go in this might of yours, and you shall defeat the Midianites as one man." In 2 Corinthians 12, Paul also cries out for deliverance from his thorn in the flesh. In this situation, God also refuses to deliver him from the thorn but instead uses the thorn to teach Paul the blessing of a further surrender to and dependence on God. Surrender to God during adverse, unwanted, and hopeless situations is the key to achieving the freedom we long for.

God's removal of the difficulty is not always the marker of His power; it is revealed as He works in us *through* the difficulty. God's power is so vast that He could easily with a word change our circumstances. But if He intervenes this way, how does that teach us more about who He is? While we may have gratitude and mostly relief through this recognized provision of God, what would this miracle do to increase our intimate knowledge of Him or a dependency on Him above His gift of power? As we continue in our study, God's ways for handling difficulty will become clear and more enticing.

The fears of rejection, futility, and failure have at least one common effect—the need to control or manipulate. The need to control is the opposite of surrender. Fear compels us to control; faith calls us to surrender. Remember that fear at its core fuels the need for self-protection. This need to protect self results in the control of people and circumstances to prevent something from happening or not happening. These actions are counterproductive to their intended result for they always hinder intimacy in relationships as well as mutual respect. While in the Flesh we feel the need to control, we should more readily surrender to God in our Spirit allowing His power to overcome the tendencies of the Flesh. We should pray, "Lord my Spirit is willing, but my Flesh is weak."

Another common factor in the fear trinity is the potential for these fears to spiral upon each other compounding the need of self-protection and acceptance. Love conquers fear. 1 John 4:18 says, "There is no fear in love; but perfect love casts out fear, because fear involves torment. But he who fears has not been made perfect in love."

Dear beloved, God is in your midst and is saying through this study, "I am with you." The great I Am is working to restore what fear has destroyed in your life. God has not given you a spirit of fear but of love and a sound mind (2 Timothy 1:7). God is not the author of destructive fear that torments. Fear that destroys is Satan's counterfeit to a reverent, godly fear. God gives His love, His power, and a sound mind to circumvent the schemes of Satan. He wants you to know the depth of His love for He wants you delivered from fear. "He who fears has not been made perfect in love" (1 John 4:18). When fear of rejection, failure, and futility exists, Satan makes us feel diminished in the eyes of God and tries to diminish the perception of ourselves in the eyes of others. *God wants intimate fellowship with each of us where we are as we are so we will more fully experience His love.* He wants us to experience the fullness of His love so fear is diminished as He uses this situation to grow faith. He empowers rising above circumstances to transform us into the persons He intends us to become.

> ... that He would grant you, according to the riches of His glory, to be strengthened with might through His Spirit in the inner man, that Christ may dwell in your hearts through faith; that you, being rooted and grounded in love, may be able to comprehend with all the saints what is the width and length and depth and height, to know the love of Christ which passes knowledge; that you may be filled with all the fullness of God. (Ephesians 3:16–19)

God Uses the Surrendered Servant

The Angel of the Lord graced Gideon with His presence to reveal God's will and to encourage him in this faith-building process. At some time in your life, you will receive opportunities to be this same type of encourager. We at all times are to be reflections of the life, light, and grace of Christ. While we benefit from encouragement at any time, during times of spiritual warfare, during times of testing, and during times of wanted deliverance, it may be our saving grace.

God-focused encouragement granted to a receptive heart gives gentle guidance before sin has an opportunity to bring further harm. The Angel of the Lord gives us an incredible example of how to motivate a person to reach his or her full potential. A surrendered servant is one who has faith in God's redeeming love.

I mentioned earlier about the way husbands and wives should respond to each other in marriage. This is true in many other if not all relationships. If it were practiced more often in the Christian fellowship, there would be more unity as well as more godly leaders persevering for the kingdom of God. "We are to love one another in light of who God intends us to become, without becoming bitter or complacent about who we are."[8] This is an accurate description of unconditional love. It is certainly the depth of love Christ has for us. While we were yet sinners, He died for us trusting the transformation God had in store for all who believe. Christ, our Surrendered Servant, models this calling for us. A surrendered servant is to

1. look beyond who others outwardly appear to be,
2. interact with them as the person God intends them to become, and
3. encourage them with proper balance without engaging in either extreme of bitterness or complacency.

Understanding how to apply this in relationships helps us receive and give love unconditionally dispelling fear. Let us look at each of these elements more closely and meditate on how to model Christlike encouragement and love.

Looking beyond Appearances

It is not surprising that this is the same attitude the Angel of the Lord presented with Gideon. From a purely human perspective, someone could look at Gideon's fear, doubt, pride, depression, frustration, confusion, social ranking, and insecurity and disqualify him as an army commander. God's

---
[8] Ibid.

willingness to choose the less obvious as His leaders is not surprising to students of the Bible; this pattern is consistent throughout God's Word. He chooses the apparently weak, the least, the less obvious because it reveals His power and nature as God.

God's power is more visibly seen and demonstrated by our human senses when His might is revealed through those with no obvious strengths of their own. For this reason, Paul exhorts us to rejoice in our weaknesses for the glory it brings God. Generally speaking, the meek and the weak are also sometimes the humblest; they recognize their need to depend on a greater power. There is little or no reliance on human strengths, talents, and abilities but rather a perceived need for divine indwelling.

In society today, Christians are often perceived as weak, uneducated, easily influenced, and manipulated. It is easy to see how the world draws this conclusion for it measures strengths very different from the way God does. Gideon also illustrates this point. Gideon professes a weak social ranking. Financially, emotionally, and psychologically, he suffers a temporary weakening. However, he is not weak in character. As Gideon's worship results in further revelation of God's ways, these outward weaknesses fade. In Judges 6, the Angel of the Lord did not try to refute Gideon's misunderstandings or focus on his weakness; He restated God's purpose and encouraged Gideon to rise to that calling.

This is an important lesson for the surrendered servant. Looking beyond appearances may also require the surrendered servant not to be too heavily influenced by what others say or think especially when it falls short of God's truth. This requires the surrendered servant to seek understanding of God's plan for others more than relying on human wisdom, intellect, or opinion. Surrendered servants must surrender the wisdom of the Flesh to seek wisdom and revelation of the Holy Spirit. They learn to look beyond appearances and encourage others to rise to their God-ordained callings. For this reason, the surrendered servant must be kingdom focused. Most people have insecurities whether they are apparent or not. Even when we recognize our strengths, learning how to utilize them is a process. During this time, we are susceptible to fear and doubt that undermines growth, and that fuels insecurity. Unbiased surrendered servants—not parents or spouses—who recognize our value and strengths fuels our confidence to trust God's work through us. They can give us hope and perseverance to overcome Satan's undermining tactics that fuel frustration. Sometimes, all we need to overcome is to know that someone else believes we can achieve more than we can comprehend.

Though we may believe in and teach God's redeeming love, do we really live it? Do we gossip about others' sins or failures justifying that as necessary to protect the church, without confronting the sinner directly with the gossip to promote redemption? Or do we provide a restorative atmosphere for believers who stumble? Are we a social club formed by our own rules that alienates those we fear, or a house of healing and encouragement reflecting God's drawing love? Are we as willing to promote faith in others' restoration as we are to spread gossip?

A surrendered servant also willingly encourages even when others' callings may be higher than theirs. Christ models this principle. While we are not higher than Christ, He reveals the great importance of our works. Shortly before His crucifixion, He prepared the disciples for the coming of the Holy Spirit. He said that with the Spirit, the disciples would do even greater works than He had done (John 14:12). Christ, the Word, the Creator, the Son of God came to earth as the Son of Man to empower His followers to do mighty works with the indwelling power of the Trinity; to spread the gospel to all people, not just the Jewish people as was Jesus's earthly ministry. This truth does not diminish the glory of Christ or the greatness of His work as the Son of Man. It further reveals the role Christ played to model and endure everything for us. We have His example of surrender and humility to prepare the way for others to reach their full potential.

Loving Them for Whom God Intends Them to Be

Only God fully knows the purpose He has for His children. However, the more we mature in our faith, the more we are able to discern God's work in the body of Christ. The challenge for us as encouragers is to be sensitive to the work of the Holy Spirit to use someone like Gideon or someone like us. They are in our families. They are in our churches. They are in our workplaces. They are in our neighborhoods. Yet if God is to use us an encourager, we will not have to search to recognize those to encourage. However, we are more likely to encounter the Gideons, those who have difficulty recognizing their potential, than we are to encounter the King Sauls, those who believe they have greater power and authority than what is granted.

Eventually, God brings both into our lives granting us opportunities to encourage them to seek and follow God's path. When we seek God, He brings to our attention those He would have us mentor. He also guides us in what to say. Absent divine revelation, we will not be able to discern specifically how God will use someone the way the Angel of the Lord understood Gideon's purpose. However, God may give us discernment to recognize spiritual giftedness in its early stages. God may reveal to us only one aspect of His purpose for them so that we can encourage them in their faith growth.

We should exhort one another in ways that empower with humility without fueling pride. Even when we do not have understanding of God's purpose for others, we can trust He has one. Until He calls us to eternity, His transformation is in progress. Part of our own transformation into the image of Christ is encouraging others along that path. Paul encourages New Testament Christians in this manner in 2 Thessalonians 3:4: "And we have confidence in the Lord concerning you, both that you do and will do the things we command you."

Who does not want or need to be loved for whom God intends them to become? Imagine the unity and bonds of love fueled in the body of Christ by living His example. Imagine the criticism, gossip, and backbiting that would cease as this call is answered! To love someone as the person God intends him or her to become requires great dependence on the Holy Spirit by the encourager. It requires a continual focus on the will and ways of God to complete His purpose for that individual. It means demonstrating faith in God to use him or her in ways we cannot fully recognize but to genuinely encourage that person with enthusiasm as if we could.

It first requires realizing our need to look beyond their appearances or visible circumstances so our focus can receive God's truth. It leaves no room for the envious, prideful, and skeptical Flesh that functions primarily on intellectual knowledge, apparent realities, or sometimes even experience. God reveals what we need to know as we lay aside our own human wisdom and agendas to genuinely seek His truth.

Encouraging with Proper Balance

We should love others as the persons God intends them to become and do that without becoming bitter or complacent about whom they are. This is a very critical condition on how to encourage. We are not to be bitter during their periods of transformation when they may still be functioning in the Flesh. Their behavior may often be wrong, but we are to help them overcome living in the Flesh to reach the level of faith God intends for them. In our attempts to save them from going over a cliff, we must be careful not to be the hazard causing them to trip and go over it. If we allow fear, pride, anger, or resentment consume our focus, we will not be postured to encourage them perhaps to the degree necessary. This process transforms us into the image of Christ as much, if not more so, as it prepares them. To encourage others in this way requires us to become more Christlike, to surrender more to an understanding of God's ways and purposes, and to demonstrate His love, not His judgment, through us.

But we are not to blindly or complacently ignore their behavior that falls short of God's plan or that is ungodly. Too often, it is easy to look away from any unhealthy behavior rationalizing that this is not who they are or what they want to be, so nothing is said even when it becomes necessary for their repentance. Complacency that leads to an improper silence is just as damaging to someone's growth as lashing out in judgment or anger. Remember James 5:19–20: "Brethren, if anyone among you wanders from the truth, and someone turns him back, let him know that he who turns a sinner from the error of his way will save a soul from death and cover a multitude of sins." To turn someone back requires boldness, but it must be tempered by gentleness, patience, and sometimes long-suffering. But to do so covers a multitude of sins by curtailing the devastating effects of fear.

Through my own failures in this area, I have learned to pray for God to teach me how to respond with bold gentleness. I need not retreat into complacency, but neither do I want my angry demeanor to be an excuse for someone rejecting truth and continuing in sin. As we learn from Gideon's example, confrontation with sin often stirs intense emotion and possibly anger in those confronted; there is no benefit in fueling that anger with an improper countenance. Conduct seasoned with gentleness goes a long way to ease those emotions—"a gentle answer turns away wrath."

When we love others as the persons God intends them to become, we have to maintain an eternal perspective of their purposes. We cannot allow physical appearances to cause us to respond in ways that discourage instead of encourage. As we encourage others to grow in faith, we must be careful to do so in the Spirit, not in the Flesh.

Perhaps one of the most public examples of a surrendered servant is that of Ashley Smith in Atlanta in March 2005. Ashley was taken hostage taken by Brian Nichols, who was fleeing authorities after killing many prior to a court appearance. Humanly speaking, Ashley had every reason to respond in fear, outrage, and in angry disgust toward her captor. Yet her interaction and conduct inspired hope and communicated concern and value toward this ruthless killer. She did not allow anger and bitterness about her husband's murder years earlier to fuel hatred for Nichols. Neither did she complacently disregard the potential for this man to bring further harm to her as well as adversely affect her daughter's life.

Instead, she acknowledged the power he then had over her and gently, lovingly refocused it on the power of God in her heart and miraculously in his. In spite of her extreme difficulty, she responded with compassion; she showed a concern and interest in his life. Ashley did not focus on the outward appearances and circumstances but instead helped him realize the value and purpose God had for him. She gave him hope in an otherwise hopeless situation. Her compassion opened the door for the freedom to read and share with him scriptures and guidance from *The Purpose Driven Life*.

Ashley depended on God to focus her mind on eternal truths rather than her fear of her present circumstances. While she was not fully discerning of God's specific purpose for this man, she helped him look beyond the immediate trauma to understand that there was an eternal purpose and plan for something good to come from someone who had made so many wrong choices. He spared her life and turned himself in to the police. Her willingness to seek God, to find eternal value for her difficulty while still in the midst of it drew this man closer to God. She relied on the power of God to flow through her life to communicate love to a beloved creation of God.

"In this world you will have tribulation, but be of good cheer, I have overcome the world" (John 16:33). In this verse, Jesus exhorts us to "be of good cheer" in the midst of great fear and difficulty. God is with us and is exhorting us to focus faith on Him alone. God desires us to exalt Him as the center of our focus and worship for He longs to fellowship with us. He is working to bring peace, to calm our hearts so we will willingly receive guidance.

The story of Gideon reiterates that God uses all things for His glory. No matter where we are in our walks with Him, no matter how frustrated or inadequate we feel, God has a purpose for where we are right now. Maybe it is restoration to Him.

If the cares, concerns, and desires of this world have distracted you from knowing Him more, turn to Him now. Don't just cry out with your needs; cry out with a passion to know Him, to experience His presence in your circumstances. Watch how subtly but personally He will reveal Himself in response to your cry. God loves you!

Perhaps you are being refined and strengthened to lead others or be the catalyst for restoration of your marriage and family. Fear can be the tool God uses to help you experience the most intimate and personal times with Him. Recognize Him in the midst of your daily routine for He may come to you in your work as with Gideon. He may be near, faithfully revealing His instruction until you focus more on Him than what you fear. Be honest with God and yourself about what troubles you even if it means confessing frustration with His perceived inaction.

Perhaps you are the primary encourager God will use to strengthen the faith of other future leaders. Those who commit themselves to recognize God's perspective above outward appearances position themselves to recognize great spiritual warfare in and around them. Intercede with fervent, consecrated prayer and give verbal encouragement to others as the Spirit leads. Allow God to use your intercession to begin breaking down the strongholds of fear, doubt, and unbelief of others.

God is unraveling fear and finishing faith. Embrace Him today and experience His power that will grow faith from that small seed to the mature tree of life. He will strengthen you. You will shelter others.

⇃ Chapter 2 ⇂

The Power of a Hardened Heart

Today, if you will hear His voice, do not harden your hearts.
—Hebrews 4:7

What Is a Hardened Heart?

Begin with worship, meditation, and prayer.

> Beware, brethren, lest there be in any of you an evil heart of unbelief in departing from the living God; but exhort one another daily, while it is called "Today," lest any of you be hardened through the deceitfulness of sin. (Hebrews 3:12–13)

> "Heavenly Father, let the light of Your love shine through encouraging all those around me. Allow a sensitivity to Your presence and a boldness to let You minister through my thoughts, words, actions, and reactions to the circumstances You allow today."

Early in the study of this subject, I began to poll peers on their understanding of a hardened heart. Generally, the feedback received was the same. I found that most surveyed, including myself, perceive a hardened heart to be a callousness toward God, a refusal to embrace who He is and what He says. I also discovered that this phrase is commonly associated with people who reject God totally or professed Christians who do not attempt to live obediently. Hardness of heart is a phrase most identify as an attribute of those who do not fellowship with God.

In the Old Testament, the words *hardened heart* refer mostly to this type of callousness described above. Five Greek words are used in reference to hardness of, harden, or hardened hearts in the New Testament The most commonly used, *poroo* comes from the root word *poros*, a kind of stone. *Poroo* means to cover with thick skin, make the heart dull, to grow hard, to lose the power of understanding.[9] The second most commonly used root word is *skleros*, meaning hard, or harsh.[10]

During this study, we want to take a bird's-eye view of Jesus's ministry. While taking a broad approach to His interaction with the disciples, we want to compare and contrast this interaction with that of the Jewish leaders opposing Him. We will focus on Jesus's attitude toward and warnings against hardness of heart. We will look at the power of fear, doubt, and unbelief to harden the hearts of believers.

From the gospel of Mark, we want to first gain a deeper perspective of why the disciples struggled to understand Jesus's ministry and message. Many of these men had been followers of John the Baptist, so they anticipated Jesus's coming. At times, though, some questioned if John was the Christ (Luke 3:15). Even with God proclaiming Jesus as His Son during the baptism, this fact was not comprehended by most including the disciples.

Too often, we study the Gospels with a postcrucifixion perspective forgetting this important truth. Their understanding of Jesus as the Messiah is a slow revelation over three years of ministry through His resurrection. Though reasons differ, our perspective is often just as skewed as the disciples' understanding was. They knew so much of Jesus as the Son of Man that they missed the fullness of His power as Christ, the fully surrendered Son of God.

---

[9] Blue Letter Bible, dictionary and word search for *poroo* (Strong's 4456), Blue Letter Bible, 1996–2002, February 7, 2005, http://www.blueletterbible.org/cgi-bin/words.pl?word=44568page-1.

[10] Blue Letter Bible, dictionary and word search for *skleruno* (Strong's 4645), Blue Letter Bible, 1996–2002, February 7 2005, http://www.blueletterbible.org/cgi-bin/words.pl?word+46458page-1.

We know so much of Jesus as the Christ that we miss the fullness of His surrender as the Son of Man. Consequently, we, like the disciples, miss many faith-building lessons from Jesus's ministry even if for different reasons.

Second, as our study of Mark continues, we will focus on the teachings of Christ particularly to His disciples. Mark gives unique insight to the intimate interchange with Jesus's followers behind the scenes of the miracles. While the disciples participated in them, they did not fully grasp what was happening or the role the miracles played in shaping their future or faith. Pay close attention to the nature of the questions Jesus asked the disciples. Reflect on the deeper reasons Jesus was frustrated by their response remembering that He is partly trying to prepare their minds for how His life as the Son of Man would end. Imagine yourself in their place not comprehending the crucifixion coming. How different would you have reacted, or would you have? How would you have responded to Jesus's teachings, miracles, and His questions?

As we look at New Testament scripture, we are reading and observing God's process of grooming faith. We look at the pattern and similarities of equipping believers.

By engaging in this reflective exercise, we will recognize obstacles to understanding God's power at work today and learn how to identify God's faith-building ways for unfolding His plan and purposes.

By examining the disciples' faith growth, our awareness of God's ways to work in our lives increases. By observing their lack of understanding, we are better equipped to see God's eternal purposes at work in the routine and spiritual moments of our lives. We will begin to understand that everything He teaches, every blessing and miracle He grants, is not only a blessing for today but also a preparation to recognize Him and His purpose for the future. What greater encouragement to propel us from fear to faith than to prepare our understanding of God's plan for our lives!

Our understanding of God's purposes will never be complete. As we examine scripture and Jesus's equipping of the disciples, we will see God's ways for gradually unfolding understanding necessary for us to know Him and His will. This knowledge empowers obedience, which nurtures a growth spurt of faith.

In the introduction, I asked you to reflect on your understanding of what God can and will do in your situation. By taking this bird's-eye view, we are also asking you to stretch your understanding of who God is. Future lessons will focus specifically on this subject. However, we cannot fully grasp this chapter's message without perceiving our need to learn more about God.

Write down the following scriptures that all have *poroo* (to make the heart dull, to grow hard, and to lose the power of understanding) as the definition of a hardened heart.

Mark 6:52

Mark 8:17

Mark 16:14

In each of these verses, what group of people did Jesus indicate had hardness of heart?

Read John 12:40 and Mark 3:5. In these verses, what group of people has a hardened heart?

Do you believe your heart is hardened with fear, doubt, and unbelief to a degree? If so, described your understanding of it.

If so, describe your present understanding of how it is hardened against hearing and understanding.

If not, why not?

In the first three verses above, Jesus chastises the disciples for their hardened hearts. As we continue our study, the correlation between a hardened heart and a tendency to lose the power of understanding will become significantly more meaningful especially in reference to Christ's followers.

In Mark 3:5, the Greek word used for hardness of hearts has a stronger meaning than that used with the disciples. It is *porosis*,[11] which means obtrusiveness of mental discernment, a dulled perception; the mind has been blunted and covered with a callous. The account in Mark 3:5 is the only direct confrontation Jesus makes toward the Jewish leaders' hardness of heart. While God repeatedly rebuked this hardness in the Old Testament, only one instance of direct confrontation is made by Christ in the Gospels. In John 12:40 (and the comparable record in Matthew 13:14), Jesus refers to this hardness as prophesied by Isaiah, but it is not a direct rebuke by Him.

To recap, Jesus specifically rebukes the disciples' hardened hearts on three occasions. He repeatedly criticizes their lack of understanding. When Jesus refers to their lack of understanding, He is more gently referring to their hardened hearts. But in reference to Jewish leaders who will crucify Christ, Jesus confronts their hardness only once. He uses many other descriptions as reference such as evil, blind, slanderous, hypocrites, and brood of vipers to name a few. But in Mark 3:5, Jesus was grieved for the leadership because of their hardened hearts.

Because of God's repeated warnings against hardness in the Old Testament and the severity of the opposition of the religious elite in the New Testament, we more commonly associate the term *hardened hearts* with that of the Jewish opposition. Most do not think of it has a hindrance in the disciples' ministry with Jesus given what they eventually accomplish to spread the gospel. Yet we will see that those who fellowshipped closely with Jesus served Him with a faith hindered by hardened hearts in the beginning. Whenever Jesus addresses the disciples' hardness, He speaks with frustration, discipline, correction, and instruction in His early ministry. He makes proclamations regarding the Pharisee's hardness, but He chastises that of the disciples and exhorts them to change.

We will continue to examine why Jesus focused more on the disciples'

---

[11] Blue Letter Bible, lexicon and Strong's Concordance search for 4457, Blue Letter Bible, 1996–2002, February 7 2005, http://www.blueletterbible.org/cgi-bin/words.pl?word+4457&page-1.

hardness and how He revealed the path to freedom from it. With each teaching (His Word), each confrontation (His will), each miracle (His power), Jesus exhorts them to hunger for the provision of faith and understanding God gives to obtain this freedom.

Like the disciples, we can fellowship with, minister alongside, and commune with Christ and yet do so with hearts hardened to His ways and His will, but God wants to bestow His power through us. God wants us to experience the peace that comes when we continually surrender hardened hearts!

Read 1 John 1:8–9. Write in your own words the contrast between these two verses. Pray and ask God to give you spiritual understanding and sensitivity to ways you may be deceived about sin in your life. Be willing to lay your soul bare before the Lord as Christ yielded himself in great humility on the cross so He may cleanse and restore you. As verse 9 admonishes, be willing to confess these sins to God and perhaps to others offended with this sin as God so leads.

Mark's gospel provides a distinct perspective of the disciples' spiritual preparation. From Mark's record, we see how Jesus gives His most earnest followers the tools necessary to empower faith and to obediently sacrifice in their service. Mark uses brevity and bluntness in his detail of the gospel, but he offers more details of Jesus's conversations with the disciples in those teachable moments. The common message of Christ in these interchanges is the focus of our study. Jesus repeatedly asks them (and us) to lay aside fear, doubt, unbelief, and hardened hearts so we may "hear and understand" the will of God. This is the foundation for living in the power of faith. It is both hearing and understanding through faith that empowers us to overcome a fearful, hardened heart.

To facilitate the next study, read Mark 4–6:13. Meditate on the scriptures and begin to frame that bird's-eye view of what is happening. We will continue to look more closely at the correlation of hardness of heart with unbelief and how it hinders growth.

Christ came to grow faith and remove hardness of heart. Allow

God to use the truths of these words to increase your expectations and understanding of His ways.

> *The Spirit of the Lord God is upon Me, because the Lord has anointed Me to preach good tidings to the poor; He has sent Me to heal the brokenhearted, to proclaim liberty to the captives, and the opening of the prison to those who are bound; to proclaim the acceptable year of the Lord, and the day of vengeance of our God; to comfort all who mourn, to console those who mourn to Zion, to give them beauty for ashes, the oil of joy for mourning, the garment of praise for the spirit of heaviness; that they may be called trees of righteousness, the planting of the Lord, that He may be glorified.*
> —Isaiah 61:1–3

Why a Hardened Heart?

Begin with worship, meditation, and prayer.

> Also He said to them, "Is a lamp brought to be put under a basket or under a bed? Is it not to be set on a lampstand? For there is nothing hidden which will not be revealed, nor has anything been kept secret but that it should come to light. If anyone has ears to hear, let him hear." (Mark 4:21–23)

> "Heavenly Father, give me ears to hear! Thank you for letting Your Word be known to me so I may know You. Thank You for growing my faith. Thank You for continually giving opportunities to test my faith so that its growth may be revealed and I may trust You more."

Let the familiar words of this verse resonate freshly in your mind: light is to shine openly; it is not to be hidden. God wants Christ to be known, not parts of the light sparkling through where we try to hide it or cover it up.

God intends full disclosure. He wants the Living Word revealed to those with ears to hear.

We learned that Jesus's disciples, His closest followers, repeatedly struggled with hardened hearts. How could this happen? They were in the presence of the Living God in full witness of His greatness and power. They believed in Him and His power to the extent they were willing to forsake their former lives to follow Him into an unknown future. Yet they still had hardened hearts. If the disciples struggled with this, how can we expect to live in freedom from it? What were their hearts hardened against? What caused their hearts to be hardened? This section will lay the foundation for answering these questions in the lessons to come.

To learn how this could happen to those in the presence of the miraculous Christ, we first need to gain perspective of the disciples as they served beside Him. We need to see them as Jesus sees them. Try to look beyond the elevation we sometimes attribute to them as the chosen elect. Jesus sees their fear, doubt, and weak faith, but He also knows how God designed their faith to grow and how God will use it for His kingdom. Observe how the disciples see Jesus's miracles as earthly visibilities, not spiritual realities. Observe how this limitation affects their trust in Jesus as well as the doubt God could use them as well.

Let us begin to observe Jesus's early faith lessons and notice the parallel ways our hearts harden as well as the ways Christ grows faith. As Christ exhorts them to overcome hardened hearts, He also teaches us more about who He is as God.

Write the definition of faith as recorded in Hebrews 11:1.

Write down Romans 10:17.

Refer to Mark 4–6:13 as we sharpen our focus on Jesus's preparation of the disciples to know Him.

After the twelve disciples were chosen, multitudes surrounded Jesus. Mark 4 includes parables Jesus gave the crowd. Allow the response to these parables frame our focus. The crowds, the disciples, and Jewish leadership all responded differently to the same eyewitness accounts. All were God's people, but each group had different perspectives of God. There is a recurring message or theme in these parables, a message that lays the foundation for faith. With each parable and the recorded miracle that follows, Jesus repeatedly emphasizes the need to hear and receive the Word of God, the source of faith as we verified from the above verses.

In Mark 4:30–34, Jesus shares the parable of the mustard seed as the last parable in this series. Recall that this gives us the picture of an herb becoming great when it grows into a tree; meditate for a moment on that. Jesus is teaching how to cultivate and grow faith. He reveals the benefit of that growth. He lays the foundation for understanding what God can do, of who God is, and of what God will do.

In Mark 4:35, who is in the boat with Jesus?

In Mark 4:30–34, what does God teach us about who He is and what He is capable of doing?

In the parable of the mustard seed, God revealed what His power can do. He reveals who He is as Creator of all things. After this teaching, there is a test, an opportunity to apply or demonstrate belief in His teachings, a pattern consistent throughout His Word. God now gives the disciples opportunity to have faith in what He is willing to do to help them know Jesus as the Son of God. He asks them to trust God. This test is not for the crowds or the oppositional Jews; it is for the chosen twelve alone. From Judges 6, we learned that before God would deliver and restore His people or gain victory over the enemy, He first strengthened the faith of His chosen leader. Christ now repeats this process with the disciples.

In Mark 4:35–41, Jesus demonstrates His power over nature by calming the sea. In verse 40–41, Christ says, "Why are you so fearful? How is it that you have no faith? And they feared exceedingly, and said to one another, 'Who can this be, that even the wind and the sea obey Him!'" The disciples failed to exercise faith. They heard the Word but failed to understand it.

They heard teaching about God's power over creation but failed to trust His power in the fearful situation. They missed an opportunity for faith to grow. Their knowledge of Him was expanded by His teaching, but not their trust in Him as Lord. They were His followers, but there was still much about God's power in Jesus they did not understand.

The first miracle recorded following the parables is one that Jesus performed alone with His disciples. Their lack of faith did not prevent God's power from working, but it did affect their celebration of it and a peaceful restoration. While the disciples awoke Jesus, they did so to inform Him of the pending danger, but they were not asking for or expecting His intervention. They seemed perturbed with Jesus's nonchalant concern for their plight. Once God revealed His power, they asked, "Who can this be?" Through this miracle, God was teaching more of who He was as God in Jesus. Through God's power, Jesus could control nature. They could not mentally process what they had witnessed. Their hearts were hardened with unbelief. They failed to spiritually comprehend the physical visibilities, and as a consequence, their fear intensified.

Why couldn't the disciples correlate the truth of Jesus's teachings with the demonstration of truth in the miracle? Perhaps it was because there were no concrete similarities between the teaching and the miracle. Parabolic teaching confounded human understanding. Jesus did not include in His parables a specific proclamation that God had given Him power to calm the sea. If that had happened, the disciples would need only to see with their physical eyes to accept God's Word as truth.

Through parables, God exercises spiritual senses. The disciples need to see with spiritual eyes. Jesus tells the disciples later in ministry that He will not always be with them. He also later teaches of the sending of the Spirit. This will be a form of the Spirit new to them for it will indwell them. It will not be visible with physical eyes. It will take faith—spiritual senses—to believe God's Spirit is in them. It will take spiritual senses to learn to hear its leading over the will of Flesh.

Can you recall a time when you failed to comprehend the vastness of God's power at work in your midst? Has time, maturity, and understanding allowed you to recognize what you could not at that moment? Have you talked about your problems to God informing Him of the grave difficulty but failed to expect a remedy in the way it came?

In an earlier discussion, we noted a pattern of God's ways from Judges 6 used to begin Gideon's revival of faith. To accomplish our faith growth, God reveals Himself, the Word; His will, and His power.

Before you answer the questions below, reflect on the passages in Mark 4–6 and observe this pattern also used by Jesus with the disciples.

Himself: What principles from His Word has God recently taught or reinforced in your life? This could be a passage, a verse, or a theme.

His will: Meditate on pending decisions or difficulties in your life right now. Journal any understanding of His will God may reveal through His Word documented above.

His power: Reflect on how He may be demonstrating the truth of these teachings in your life (i.e., How is He demonstrating the power of His Word). Meditate on how this reveals who God is.

Had the disciples understood, they would not have feared the storm and His authority over nature would not have surprised them. Their expectations of what God could do would had fueled their faith in what He would do. But their hearts were hardened. Jesus, however, continued to give them opportunities to exercise faith.

In Mark 5:1–20, what miracle does Jesus perform?

Whose power does Jesus now exert authority over?

Jesus progressively reveals His power. After demonstrating power over nature, He now expands the knowledge of that power to control the demonic, spiritual realm. Remember how the disciples questioned, "Who can this be?" as Jesus calmed the sea. Maybe the disciples asked that rhetorically, but God intended for them to have an answer. The answer would come miraculously. The disciples witnessed the demons "begging earnestly" for Jesus to leave them alone. God used demons to reveal to Jesus's followers the vast reach of His power. The demons testified that they were solely at the mercy of Jesus's command—to leave them be or to cast them back into eternal misery. These spiritual beings were exposed to the crowd long enough to reveal the far-reaching power of this Man.

Continuing, Mark 5:25–34 reveals a woman with an "issue of blood" who is healed when she makes her way through the crowd and touches the hem of Jesus's garment. Thus far, Jesus actively exercised power, but verse 30 tells us that His power "went out of Him." He did not actively administer the power, but He was aware of its release. Jesus, "knowing power had gone out" of Him, asked, "Who touched my clothes?" The disciples disputed the relevance of Jesus's question in Mark 5:31. But Jesus had a perspective the disciples did not. Even among the crowds bombarding Jesus, He discerned the one who was reaching out in faith, trust, and recognition of His power. There seems to be a difference between what she and the crowd comprehended. As the woman shared what had happened, He told her that her faith had made her well. Her act of faith testified that "Jesus is power." This woman could see what the disciples could not. She believed who Jesus was and acted on that faith.

In these passages, it seems the disciples were just as confused as and sometimes more so than were the crowds. Nevertheless, Jesus highlighted people who demonstrated faith. Those with faith were healed, and Jesus publicly honored their faith. Jesus drew attention to the correlation of faith with the release of His power.

Jesus's first miracle demonstrated what He could do. It did not require a partnership of faith with the disciples. It spared their lives but left them in fear without any obvious growth in faith. The second demonstrated who He was as Lord. Not only was there no partnership of faith, Jesus's power was victorious over the demonic realm, which opposes God on all levels. The third demonstrated what He would do with a partnership of faith with His will.

Three miracles. Three demonstrations of God's power. One partnership of faith. God can and will fulfill His will without us, but as we continue to learn, He longs for the partnership of faith to participate in His work. His love for us desires our fellowship. He invites us to partner in the completion of His will on earth. The partnership does not change His plan; it changes us in its execution. It brings a blessing in the moment and preparation for His plan for the future.

To live a life of faith is to learn to "hear and understand" His will so we may echo it in prayer and respond in faithful obedience. God is sovereign and omnipotent; He can release or withhold His power. However, Christ repeatedly exhorts us to hear and understand, to believe and not fear during demonstration of His power. He wants us to experience the fullness of the blessing in the moment. But as we continue to learn, chasing the blessing for the moment only or primarily circumvents our understanding of God's purpose for it. Experiencing a demonstration of God's power is not the goal; it is not the pinnacle of experiencing God. It is just the door to further understand the depth of God's love. It is fertilizer to fuel faith's growth. It is a step to further discover the fullness of God.

Jesus continues to reveal the power of God over all situations. In Mark 5:35, what was the attitude of Jairus's household?

How would you characterize their depth of faith and its effect, or lack of, on the eventual healing?

Did all the disciples enter Jairus's household with Jesus? (v. 37).

Describe your understanding of this leading.

When the woman is healed, Jesus is on His way to Jairus's house to see his daughter, who was dying. As Jesus speaks with the healed woman, they learn of the daughter's death. Jesus tells him, "Do not be afraid; only believe." Once again, Jesus gives an exhortation to lay aside fear and choose faith.

As they approach the house, Jesus permits only Peter, James, and John to enter with Him. This trio of disciples is the inner circle of followers often drawn away into the secluded presence of Jesus. In this progressive demonstration of His miraculous power—when it came to conquering death—Jesus once again restricts His audience. He allows only those who have demonstrated a deeper understanding of Him to witness this miracle to further that understanding. Later, He commands them to keep this miracle secret. Jesus needs the disciples' faith to grow. His ministry also needs to expand. For both to happen, there needs to be an environment free of controversy, doubt, ridicule, and persecution in the circle of disciples as well as publicly.

Jesus and the disciples return to Nazareth, where He teaches with great wisdom in the synagogues and performs some miracles. In Mark 6:2–4, what was the response to Jesus and His wisdom in Nazareth?

In verses 5–6, what reason does Jesus give for the lack of miracles?

Jesus taught the Word, the foundation for faith. He demonstrated truth of this teaching through miracles gradually unfolding the extent of His power with each. God's glory through His Son testified to His power over nature, over the demonic, over illness, and finally death. At each progressive revelation, He exhorted all to hear and believe. He encouraged them not to fear but to be strengthened in faith.

This process reveals the importance of hearing God's Word. However, the disciples' weak faith reveals that hearing alone limits peace. Christ further exhorts us to understand the Word. We must be willing to learn who God is so our understanding of what He can do and will do is increased. As our knowledge of God expands, so do our expectations of His ability to reveal His power and goodness. As we understand more of His fullness, trust deepens.

The disciples reveal what happens with limited expectations of God. They limited Jesus's ability to great knowledge of God, His will, and His plan to wisely execute a plan for ending Roman rule of the Jews and establishing an earthly kingdom. Though the parables told of God's power, they were not expecting it to overrule the laws of nature and physical constraints such as lifelong illnesses and death.

Read the parable of the householder in Matthew 13:51–52. This parable is given within the teachings of those shared in Mark though Mark does not record this one. Matthew gives additional insight into Jesus's preparation of the disciples in this final parable. Recognizing the response to Jesus is important.

Understanding His Word will strengthen the faith of His disciples to trust Him in future difficulty. He poses a question that gives them the opportunity to search the level of their understanding. Jesus teaches that every scribe who understands the kingdom of heaven is like the householder who brings out treasures new and old. A scribe is a disciple, a student of God's Word, a seed of faith. Faith causes one to trust in what they have learned (the old), as well as trust in things yet unseen (the new). At the time this parable is given, treasures old would refer to the Law, the old covenant promise through Abraham and Moses. New treasure refers to the covenant God is making through His Son. Even today, we rely on treasures in God's Word, but God's Spirit reveals the Living Word of God, or treasures new revealed according to God's will through revelation of the Spirit.

Write Matthew 13:51–52.

Reflect on recent demonstrations of God's power or His miraculous intervention (either pleasant or difficult) in your life and circumstances. Can you see a progressive demonstration of God's power? Recap them.

Ask God to reveal some aspect of Him (not you, not your circumstance) He wants you to discover. Write His response to serve as a reminder of His goodness to you.

Hardened to Understanding

Begin with worship, meditation, and prayer.

> Therefore the Holy Spirit says: "Today, if you will hear His voice, do not harden your hearts as in the rebellion, in the day of trial in the wilderness; where your fathers tested Me, tried Me, and saw My works forty years. Therefore I was angry with that generation, and said, They always go astray in their heart, and they have not known My ways. So I swore in My wrath, they shall not enter My rest." Beware, brethren, lest there be in any of you an evil heart of unbelief in departing from the living God. (Hebrews 3:7–12)

> "Heavenly Father, grant me the focus on Your will and ways so I may have understanding of Your Word. Help me follow You, walk with You, and abide in You. Father, I desire to enter Your rest. Show me how, I pray."

Some commentators subtitle this passage in Hebrews as "Warning against disbelieving the 'voice' of God." Hearing God's voice and understanding God are critical in preventing hardened hearts. In this passage, failing to understand God led to ignorance of His ways and physical and spiritual strife. In chapter 4, we will discuss more about hearing God. For the remainder of this chapter, we will explore how hardened hearts are obstacles to hearing God and understanding His ways. Earlier, I mentioned God's leading me to be still, but like the disciples on the stormy sea, sometimes, it seems an impossible request.

I Thought We Were Being Still

It is difficult to embrace stillness when family members are gravely ill and facing mortality. Stillness isn't easy to live when series of hurricanes require evacuation, property destruction, financial setbacks, and reordering of plans. Stillness is hard to find when market forces dictate career modifications.

Stillness is feared greatly when these stresses burden a marriage that needs strengthening. Time stops for no one and no thing.

Life has a way of leading us through turbulent times often out of our control. The circumstances above were experienced by my family during God's instruction for me to be still. Emotional, financial, physical, spiritual, and professional unrest fuels fear.

Human nature tends to compartmentalize aspects of life, but the spiritual reality is that all things work together for God's purpose to those who love Him. Satan preys on the tendency to compartmentalize our walk with God from work life, social life, and family life. Compartmentalizing puts self, not God, in control. With self or Flesh in control, God is far away "somewhere" and called upon only when we think we need Him.

Like the disciples, we often fail *to recognize His power or presence* in the midst of difficulty even if we know He is there. Focusing on difficulties in these areas makes us consumed with the problem, not the problem solver. It fuels fear over faith. My difficulty described above is not a surprise in comparison to scripture. Let's look at the context of God's command to "be still and know that I am God" in Psalm 46:1-11.

> ...God is our refuge and strength, a very present help in trouble. Therefore we will not fear, even though the earth be removed, and though the mountains be carried into the midst of the sea; though its waters roar and be troubled, though the mountains shake with its swelling. There is a river whose streams shall make glad the city of God, the holy place of the tabernacle of the Most High. God is in the midst of her, she shall not be moved; God shall help her, just at the break of dawn. The nations raged, the kingdoms were moved; He uttered His voice, the earth melted. The Lord of hosts is with us; the God of Jacob is our refuge. Come, behold the works of the Lord, who has made desolations in the earth. He makes wars cease to the end of the earth; He breaks the bow and cuts the spear in two; He burns the chariot in the fire. Be still, and know that I am God; I will be exalted among the nations, I will

be exalted in the earth! The Lord of hosts is with us; the God of Jacob is our refuge. Selah

When disaster strikes, the need of the moment usually requires anything but physical stillness. Recall the devastation Americans and perhaps you personally have experienced—terrorist attacks, hurricanes, fires, floods, earthquakes, tornadoes, and volcanoes tearing apart in minutes a lifetime of work, affecting our dearest loved ones and requiring sacrifice and devotion. During these times, our survival instincts spring into action in escape to safety, to prepare, rescue, or rebuild. In this passage, God demonstrates His understanding and communicates His empathy; but most important, He reveals His way to survive emotionally, mentally, and spiritually. "Be still and know that I am God." Bad situations disrupt our physical surroundings and work to destroy us on every level. Psalm 46 is also consistent with our observation of Jesus's demonstrated power over nature, the demonic, illness, and death. God continually reminds us of His sovereign control over difficulty and His great love for us. "Be still and *know* that I am God."

In New Testament scripture, Jesus, the Word, appears in the flesh. The essence of God's truth proclaimed in Psalm 46 is revealed by Jesus in the early miracles in Mark. Though we do not have the benefit of Jesus among us in physical form, we have His Spirit in us and at work around us—His power is at work. Just as the disciples were hardened to comprehend the significance of Jesus's power and how it revealed God's will, we can be hardened to comprehend the Spirit's power at work or its significance to reveal God's will. This is especially difficult when circumstances seem to contradict His instruction as in my described situation above.

This passage speaks of past, present—and future—natural disasters as a reality beyond our control, and it speaks of God's eternal power: "There is a river whose streams shall make glad the city of God, the holy place of the tabernacle of the Most High. God is in the midst of her, *she shall not be moved*" (emphasis added). In the midst of unrest and earthly disturbances, God's heavenly, spiritual realm is not moved. God's love is constant. His power is certain. I Am is I Am, always. When surrounded by physical unrest and chaos, there is an eternal constant—His power. Let's compare this excerpt to John's description of heaven in Revelation 22:1–3.

> And he showed me a pure river of water of life, clear as crystal, proceeding from the throne of God and of the Lamb. In the middle of its street, and on either side of the river, was the tree of life, which bore twelve fruits, each tree yielding its fruit every month. The leaves of the tree were for the healing of the nations. And there shall be no more curse, but the throne of God and of the Lamb shall be in it, and His servants shall serve Him.

While describing a cursed earth, the psalmist also reveals God's deliverance from the curse. As we continue this study, we must recognize what these passages reveal: there are *always* spiritual realities superseding the physical visibilities, and they offer hope. Hope strengthens our resolve to persevere and leads to peace that postures us to overcome hardened hearts. When God tells us to "Be still," it is more often than not in times that require physical busyness. His command may in fact want the physical busyness to slow down or halt, but usually, the command is to calm the busyness of our minds consumed with fear, doubt, and unbelief more than faith. He commands us to be still so we can discern the spiritual reality amid the physical visibility.

While it is common for us to recognize signs of God's hope in a disaster, what is less commonly understood or sought is God's purpose for us through the difficulty. We may seek to understand why it happened physically without seeking why it happened spiritually, or what God intends spiritually in us. Often, as with the disciples, it is to reveal God's way for removing hardened hearts. It is to reveal more of Himself.

In viewing the church through my window of experience, I think there has been an unintended message to believers—a message Satan wields from a perversion of truth. This perverted message says that since Christians know there are ways of God beyond our comprehension and understanding, there is very little understanding that we should seek or that we are incapable of understanding God's ways. Since we know we are not God and cannot be all knowing, we often fail to seek what understanding He does offer. In difficulty or great sorrow, the emotional strain is often so intense that we suppress spiritual understanding to avoid dwelling on anger or mistrust of

God's ways. This paralyzes us from seeking the survival tools God provides through Christ. Hearts hardened to understand truth.

Since we may not perceive our need to seek understanding as a church, we have neglected to train how to receive it. This study exposes this misperception through scripture, and teaches what a healthy pursuit of understanding is based on in scripture and what it does to grow faith. We learn how to surrender our emotional unrest to receive God's peace even in difficulty; that positions us to receive the provision of understanding God graciously gives.

Luke 4:1–14 reveals an important time of preparation for Jesus's ministry on earth. After His baptism, it says that "being filled with the Spirit,"[12] *the Spirit led Him* into the wilderness. At the end of this forty-day wilderness experience, it says that He "returned in the *power*[13] *of the Spirit*." Something unique and transformative happened to Jesus in the wilderness. Something happened that intensified His empowerment. While the Spirit is present and leading Jesus in all things, though He is complete in the Spirit, there was a time of stillness during which God filled Jesus with the power needed to fulfill His miraculous purpose. But the process was not without difficulty. He was tempted on three levels—body, mind, and soul—yet He overcame with prayer, fasting and utilizing the weapon of God's Word. Jesus's victory over temptation resulted in an empowerment to fulfill His purpose God's way.

Life is certain to lead us in directions we don't want to go. Sometimes, that may be the result of our failures, weaknesses, or sin. Sometimes, it is the Spirit leading us into times of testing. All these can produce fear, but they can also strengthen faith because God is constant. The Spirit guides us in all truth. Spiritual realities supersede physical visibilities. Following Jesus's example, we can learn to overcome and receive God's power to fulfill

---

[12] Being filled with the Spirit in the Greek translation means to be full and complete in the Spirit, G4134—plērēs—Strong's Greek Lexicon (KJV), Blue Letter Bible, accessed 29 August 29, 2016, https://www.blueletterbible.org//lang/lexicon/lexicon.cfm?Strongs=G4134&t=KJV

[13] The Greek translation for power means a strength and ability, a power for performing miracles, a moral excellence of soul, G1411—dynamis—Strong's Greek Lexicon (KJV), Blue Letter Bible, accessed August 29, 2016, https://www.blueletterbible.org//lang/lexicon/lexicon.cfm?Strongs=G1411&t=KJV.

our purpose. Just as Jesus was led by the Spirit into the wilderness for forty days of fasting, prayer, and testing, so God leads us to be still before Him in a time and manner suited for His purposes and according to His specific calling for us.

God also led Israel into the wilderness. Unbelief caused them to test and try God though God remained faithful to provide and protect. God says, "They saw my works forty years." Forty years of living in the faithfulness of God, yet they rebelled because "they have not known My ways." They knew His will, His promises, His many miracles, yet through all this, they failed to learn His ways. That failure limited their faith's growth and knowledge of God. It hindered intimacy with and obedience to God.

A lack of understanding caused strife with God. It prevented the rest they desperately wanted. Learning God's ways would have expanded knowledge of who God is. It would have enhanced ability to partner with His purposes through prayer and worship. To seek understanding is to stretch faith to the next level. Availing ourselves to hear God and to learn His ways protects us from hardened hearts.

The earlier passage in Hebrews refers to unbelief as "evil." Unbelief blinds us from seeing God at work or from believing that He can or will provide. Jesus repeatedly rebuked the disciples' unbelief. Unbelief consumed the most ardent followers of Christ. Unbelief is evil because it causes one to reject God's power. Satan seizes the moment and offers fear and doubt as a "protective" substitute.

Let's return to Jesus's teaching on the dangers of hardened hearts and the power of understanding. Matthew 13 contains the parable of the soils, a prelude to the parable of the sower. Both parables reveal the power of understanding.

Pause to read Matthew 13:1–23.

While the Pharisees are hardened from accepting Jesus as God's Son, the disciples have the ability to hear and understand Jesus and learn of His nature and purpose as the Son of God. Thus, when Jesus admonishes the disciples to hear and understand, He is not asking them to do the impossible. He asks them to seek and receive the available provision!

Through God's gift of understanding, He has made a way for His parables, His Word, to be known. Yet those who would abuse this truth for their own purposes or to silence Jesus are prohibited from understanding parables.

As Christ's followers, this is also our hope for overcoming hardened hearts. God gives us the ability to understand. Remember that *poroo* is the most commonly used Greek word for hardened hearts, and among its definitions is "to lose the power of understanding." We cannot lose something we did not already have. As followers of Christ, we have the ability to understand. When we fail to receive and respond to it, we lose the power of understanding. We also lose it to fear, doubt, unbelief, complacency, disobedience, or rebellion. Understanding is still an available provision, but its power is quenched, hardening hearts and desensitizing us to the power of God in our midst.

The Pharisees knew the Word of God, but their hearts were hardened to recognizing the Living Word, Jesus Christ, in their midst. A callousness prevented a desire to remain open to Him.

Can you recall a situation in your life where unbelief blinded you from seeing or experiencing God's power even though you may have been praying for it?

Ask God to reveal the attitudes, presumptions, doubt, or fears that may have fueled your unbelief.

How did God demonstrate His faithfulness regardless of your unbelief?

In verse 15, what does God state would have happened if they had seen with their eyes, heard with their ears, and understood with their hearts?

When we see, hear, and understand God, we are moved to repentance releasing His healing. The power of God is released to restore us to Him when there is understanding. Just as the woman's faithful touch released the power of God to heal, so God's Word teaches about the faith that understands.

Some years ago, I noticed a remarkable principle of nature that illustrates the power of understanding. We had a coral vine on a trellis behind our frequently used gas grill. Glancing out the window one Sunday afternoon, I noticed a four-foot long branch of the narrow vine suspended horizontally in the air. Because branches are delicate, I was surprised that it was so straightly supported. As I approached to observe, I noticed a small, thread-like tendril extending straight up from its middle to a hook anchored in the porch ceiling above. The tendril did not grow at a slanted angle from the branch to the hook. Instead, the tendril and the branch made a perfect ninety-degree angle, one extending vertically and the other horizontally. This process in plants is phototropism. The plant responded to the provision of the hook anchored above. As it grew upward and wrapped itself many times around the hook, the branch was supported for its continued growth. This seemed to have happened overnight. We were in that area the day before and did not see this process beginning even though we used the grill. Even on this day, the very thin tendril wrapped around the hook was visible only with close observation, not from a distance.

Just as the plant miraculously grew a tendril in the exact place necessary to attach to the above hook, so God empowers the Christian to respond to His provision of understanding. He put the Spirit in us causing us to respond to Him. When we respond, our faith is securely bolstered in the anchor of His Word, positioning us to grow supported by His strength. This miracle of nature is amazing because a plant does not have eyes to see the hook above but instinctively knows it's there. Likewise, faith causes us to respond to our God we cannot physically see.

Let us look at the verses that define faith and its source (Hebrews 11:1; Romans 10:17): "Faith is the substance of things hoped for, evidence unseen; that comes by hearing, and hearing by the Word of God." To live by faith, we may not always see God's plan, but we have been given the ability to hear and understand the portion He reveals. Throughout the New Testament, we are admonished to put away Flesh and take on the Spirit. Like the disciples, we often adopt the "seeing is believing" motto. But Jesus repeatedly teaches that hearing with spiritual ears and understanding with spiritual eyes is the basis for knowing God and His will. In Matthew 13:16,

Jesus says, "Blessed are your ears for they hear and your eyes for they see." Believers in Christ have received the ability to gain spiritual understanding, and we continue to explore this truth in chapter 5. For now, begin to let the Spirit transform our traditions, presumptions, and preconceived ideas about receiving understanding. Draw near to Him and know Him as He draws near to you! God responds to those who respond to Him.

Ezekiel 36:26–27 says, "I will give you a new heart, and put a new spirit within you; I will take the heart of stone out of your flesh and give you a new heart of flesh. I will put My Spirit within you and cause you to walk in My statutes, and you will keep My judgments and do them." When our hearts are sensitive to God, He pours Himself in us. Don't fear; ask Him for understanding. Ask Him for more. Rest in a deeper understanding of Him as the God who responds to those who understand Him. You can trust Him. "Blessed are your eyes for they see, and your ears for they hear." God grants restoration through understanding.

Hardened By Unbelief

Begin with worship, meditation, and prayer.

> Happy is the man who finds wisdom, and the man who gains understanding; for her proceeds are better than the profits of silver, and her gain than fine gold. She is more precious than rubies, and all the things you may desire cannot compare to her. Length of days is in her right hand, in her left hand riches and honor. Her ways are ways of pleasantness, and all her paths are peace. She is a tree of life to those who take hold of her, and happy are all who retain her. (Proverbs 3:13–18)

> "Lord, I seek understanding of Your ways and will. Thank You for teaching me how to experience the truth of Your Word in my life. Thank You for the blessing understanding brings to my body, mind, and soul."

Understanding is a tree of life to those who take hold of it. Understanding comes from seeking God's heart and learning His ways. We hear Him and then are given the opportunity to experience the truth of that Word in life's circumstances. As we look at unbelief as a hindrance to understanding, we will continue to look at Jesus's admonishments to seek understanding.

Doubt is skepticism that if unaddressed can become so great that we will not receive spiritual truth without physical evidence, and sometimes even with it. Absent spiritual truth, fear builds to further fuel doubt. This anxiety and uncertainty undermines hope, which eventually gives way to unbelief. As unbelief fills the heart and mind, we fail to trust. This process is summarized as follows.

- Doubt fuels a seed of fear.
- Fear distorts focus on God.
- Misdirected focus quenches faith.
- Weak faith prevents understanding.
- No understanding fuels further unbelief.
- Unbelief fuels hardened hearts.
- Hardened hearts diminish trust.

Earlier in this chapter, we contrasted hardened hearts in believers—*poros*—to hardened hearts of unbelievers—*porosis*. *Poros* means to become calloused, to lose the power of understanding. The process outlined above reveals how this callous develops. Jesus uses another form of hardness in Matthew 19:8 and Mark 10:5 to describe disobedience or rebelliousness. Those who pursue God but lack understanding or spiritual discernment have hardened hearts. In the Old Testament, hardened heart was used in reference to Jewish people who had turned against pursuit of and trust in God's commands and guidance. In the New Testament, hardness refers to those who have the capacity to understand. Fear and doubt overshadow faith and trust, clouding spiritual discernment to fuel unbelief.

Unbelief, a lack of faith, is the result of failing to understand; it also hinders further understanding. It is truly a vicious cycle. To understand God's will for our situation, we have to believe God is able and willing to act outside our limited comprehension. Unbelief hinders our willingness to accept what He is accomplishing or our acceptance of what He appears to withhold.

This study reveals ways we can recognize and minimize fear, doubt, and unbelief from clouding spiritual discernment. This hardening process undermines faith's growth. These are the weeds, thorns, and thistles we must contend with daily so that the seed of faith grows in a healthy environment. Initially, this is a disheartening truth—the prospect of perpetual hard work just to keep our heart and mind free of such invasive intruders. What I pray you will glean from this study is how to draw on the strength and power of Christ to assist in this process. Christ is light; in Him is no darkness, and where He is, there can be no darkness. Christ's presence acts as a laser that eradicates fear, doubt, and unbelief. We will continue to see how and why the chosen disciples, the founders of our church, were hardened by unbelief—failing to embrace this provision of power. We can learn from their hardness. We have the indwelling Spirit to assist us in ways they initially did not when we choose to surrender to it.

"Faith is the substance of things hoped for, evidence unseen." Evidence unseen is critical to understanding. Faith empowers spiritual sight beyond earthly perspectives to trust in God's eternal perspective. Unbelief diminishes the ability to discern these truths. Unbelief diminishes who God is or what He is willing and able to do. Unbelief puts constraints on how God fulfills His plans and purposes. Unbelief blinds us to perceiving God's ways. Isaiah 55:8–11 says,

> "For My thoughts are not your thoughts, Nor are your ways My ways," says the Lord. "For as the heavens are higher than the earth, So are My ways higher than your ways, And My thoughts than your thoughts. For as the rain comes down, and the snow from heaven, and do not return there, but water the earth, and make it bring forth and bud, that it may give seed to the sower and bread to the eater, so shall My word be that goes forth from My mouth. It shall not return to Me void, but it shall accomplish what I please, and it shall prosper in the thing for which I sent it."

God's plans are higher than ours. They surpass affecting our physical well-being and include an eternal plan. He reveals the Word for accomplishing that plan. It *will* be accomplished. When circumstances are difficult, Satan wants us focused on the misery and difficulty of the moment. He works to consume us with fear, doubt, and unbelief. He wants us blind to God's plan and deaf to His Word so we will be isolated from God. Satan destroys hope that undermines perseverance. Faith fuels hope to trust and positions us to receive understanding of God's plan.

Returning to Jesus's preparation of the disciples, we gain insight on the power of unbelief to fuel hardness of hearts. The disciples struggled with unbelief. By framing their experiences of Jesus using natural versus spiritual understanding, they were not grasping all Jesus could accomplish. We can fall into the same trap by failing to seek revelation of the Spirit. The disciples had the presence of Christ without the indwelling Spirit. We have the indwelling Spirit without the physical presence of the Son of Man. We can make the same mistakes as the disciples, but we can also learn from God's Word how to overcome them.

In Matthew 17:14–21, why couldn't the disciples heal the epileptic child? (Note this conversation happens right after Jesus's transfiguration but the failure of the disciples occurred during the transfiguration.)

What does Christ say is necessary to bring healing in this situation?

In Matthew 15:10, how does Jesus begin His teaching of the multitude?

Notice the response by Jesus in Matthew 15:16–17 (emphasis added): "So Jesus said, 'Are you *still without understanding*? Do you *not yet understand* that whatever enters the mouth goes into the stomach and is eliminated? But these things which proceed out of the mouth come from the heart, and they defile a man.'"

Reread Mark 6:1–6. What limited Jesus's ministry in His hometown?

In the last chapter, we focused on the effects of presumption, doubt, and fear on faith. While we have few details of Jesus's youth and adolescence, what we know of His nature as the Son of God tells us He was without sin (Hebrews 4:15). It seems that the people of Nazareth failed to recognize this trait of Jesus; they were preoccupied with too many other facts. Human nature causes me to conclude what these facts may have been: He was the carpenter's son, "you know that poor man, the one who can't afford to send his children to all the right schools." "He was homeschooled by Mary. Yeah, that's Mary's son, you know the girl who 'got herself in trouble' too young and unwed. What of God's truth could she teach him?" "Who are his brothers and sisters but those who live among us—they are certainly no better than we are? Where are his credentials for these mighty works? How could someone like Him possibly be so wise? What makes Him think He could possibly know more than me about God?" You know full well how the gossip goes. We have all witnessed it or been the recipient of it if not participated in it.

Notice they do not deny that Jesus's wisdom and mighty works are real. Their presumptuous notions about Him and His family prevent them from embracing His truth. Matthew's version says that Jesus *would* not do many miracles there. They are consumed with prejudicial unbelief that keeps them from experiencing the miraculous power of God that would change their lives. Unbelief hardened their hearts and restricted the work Christ offered in their midst.

Read John 20:19–29. What evidence does Thomas need to see in order to believe?

What evidence does Christ offer?

What does Christ say about seeing and believing in verse 29? Thomas needed to physically see in order to believe. Jesus graciously supplied the evidence, but He also stated that *blessed* is the one who believes *without* seeing.

Read John 16:1–3, 12–15, 25–33.

Christ realizes that one of the greatest tests of their faith is coming. It is later in Jesus's ministry, and Christ's time for strengthening the disciples' faith prior to this difficulty is waning. But the disciples are now certain they have understanding. They express their belief to Jesus. They now realize He is the Messiah, but they still believe He is on earth to establish an earthly throne. They understand God's will, but they still lack understanding of His ways and timing. When the soldiers come to arrest Jesus in the garden, Peter was ready to fight. His limited understanding fueled the perceived need to defend Jesus, to protect His life. Peter heard Jesus's truth but failed to wait on understanding God's ways. Peter was operating in the Flesh. God's purposes are higher and farther reaching than Peter's comprehension.

Peter and the disciples were devoted followers of Christ, but they failed to measure Jesus's warnings and preparation with the entirety of God's Word. Since creation, God has had an eternal plan. His Word tells us some of His plan. As we will continue to study, we have His Spirit that continues to reveal His ways for completing His plan. What God has revealed in His Word will not contradict revelations of His Spirit. Conversely, revelations of His Spirit will be a fulfillment of His Word and not contradict it. But if we focus solely on the written word or solely on revelations of the Spirit, understanding will be limited or perhaps even distorted.

The disciples were overwhelmed. For reasons I can only imagine given the circumstances, they did not fully correlate God's prophesy from scriptures with Jesus's teachings to capture the full story. As a consequence, when God's plan began to unfold, doubt, fear, and unbelief reigned in their hearts. Failure to understand God's ways left them ill equipped to withstand what was to unfold in the near future. Without understanding, they were dumbfounded with unbelief. "How could this be happening to Jesus? What will happen to us now?"

It would take a while to gain understanding. In Luke 24:1–12, we are given announcement of Jesus's resurrection. The women in the tomb initially are disturbed by the absence of Jesus's body. However, the encounter with the Angel causes them to remember the words of Christ, and they believe. When this news is shared with the disciples, they refused to believe. Without the indwelling Spirit, there was no spiritual prompting to cause them to remember the words Jesus had spoken. The women believed only as the angel caused them to remember. It takes spiritual revelation.

Without understanding, fear and unbelief continued to trouble them. As we continue to read John 16, we see how Jesus comprehends their lack of understanding. He tells of the Holy Spirit's soon coming that will "bring to their remembrance" all that Jesus says.

Like the disciples, we often are so consumed with the present difficulty that we fail to fully comprehend God's ways, which limits understanding. Fear, doubt, and unbelief can overshadow remembrances of God's past faithfulness and His revealed promises for the future. As we confess our lack of understanding, God's Spirit in us brings to remembrance truths from His Word to empower faith.

While we may believe in what God can do, we may fail to seek what God will do. We may underestimate the extent to which God intends to reveal His power just as we learned from Jesus's early faith training of the disciples. Furthermore, even when we do acknowledge His power, we still may limit His purpose for it.

Ask God to reveal any provision you may be hardening your heart to understand or receive. What are you fearing? Are you doubting God's ability or willingness to bring victory over your burden? How are you presuming God will or will not respond? Are you limiting your expectations of God? Are you informing Him of your need, or are you crying out to Him amid it? Journal what God reveals.

Meditate about the significance of Christ's resurrection on the disciples' understanding of Jesus's teachings. Reflect how understanding could have better prepared them to endure this difficulty. Reflect on how their lack of understanding also figured into God's plan, for Christ had to bear the burden of our sins alone in shame and disgrace. Reflect on how you may have been asked to endure difficulty without the understanding from those who should have offered it the most. What does God want you to learn from those moments of isolated suffering?

Ask God to open the eyes of your heart to understand His ways so you will know Him and His faithfulness more fully. Surrender to receive understanding for the situations causing you the most fear and anxiety. What greater good is He preparing you to receive? Ask Him to unfold His provision to prepare understanding. We will reflect more on this process.

God wants to reveal His goodness so that faith grows. He has a plan, a provision, and a path that is higher than what you perceive. It will be accomplished. It will not return void. What a promise! He is your heavenly Father calling you near to reveal His gentle, pure love. Even when the path becomes difficult, we can trust His nature as God is to respond with good to those seeking to know Him. Let these truths encourage you to embark or persevere through the journey's end. Understanding is the key to deliverance from a heart hardened to the purposes of God. Seek it!

> *For the Lord gives wisdom; from His mouth come knowledge*
> *and understanding; He stores up sound wisdom for the upright;*
> *He is a shield to those who walk uprightly ... When wisdom*
> *enters your heart, and knowledge is pleasant to your soul,*
> *discretion will preserve you; understanding will keep you.*
> —Proverbs 2:6–7, 9–11

"I Believe, Help My Unbelief"

Begin with worship, meditation, and prayer:

> Wherever He entered, into villages, cities, or the country, they laid the sick in the marketplaces, and begged Him that they might just touch the border of His garment. And as many as touched Him were made well (Mark 6:56).

> "Jesus, enter my heart with the fullness of Your Spirit and remain with me wherever I go today. Strengthen my faith to touch You today. Thank you for making me 'well.'"

An act of faith in God's will releases His power. "As many as touched Him were made well." What great faith! Wherever He entered, they begged

Him. What trusting persistence! This level of faith was not always as strong. Remember how Jesus was received in Nazareth at the beginning of this chapter in Mark. What a stark contrast.

Let's return to Jesus's preparation of the disciples' faith. Previously, we looked at the first signs of ministry opposition shown Jesus in Nazareth. While His ministry was rejected, more than the locals opposed it.

Opposition is building from Jewish leadership. Following this experience, Jesus sends the disciples out in pairs to experience ministry on their own. This is their first trial-run opportunity to replicate the ministry they have assisted Jesus in bringing to the crowds. Given this level of empowerment is new to them, let's more closely examine Jesus's exhortations prior to their departure.

Read Matthew 10:5–11:1 and summarize Jesus's instructions in the parallel account from Mark 6:8–11.

1.

2.

3.

Jesus exhorts the disciples to depend on God for their physical needs. He gives guidance for discerning where to minister. Matthew's account reveals Jesus's instruction to share only with those who are "worthy." As the disciples' faith is still developing, Christ establishes parameters for them to minister in a safe, encouraging environment. God knows the lack of understanding still in the disciples as well as the severity of opposition that is building with the Jewish leadership. Remember that God intends for faith to grow. But what He calls them to do shortly will offend and disturb those not willing to understand God's power in them.

For now, God incubates their faith. He provides the opportunity and protection for the disciples to grow into that challenge. God further protects the disciples by giving them a worthwhile task that will separate them from Jesus momentarily. As the disciples are expanding their ministry experience, Jesus speaks out against sin, and some of this brewing opposition.

What are Jesus's exhortations in Matthew 10:26–28, 31?

What do the disciples accomplish in Mark 6:12–13?

The disciples' faith is being stretched to believe in what God can do for them and through them. Jesus has faith in their obedience, but He knows the price they will pay for it. They will be misunderstood and persecuted by those closest to them including friends, family, and fellow religious servants (Matthew 10:32–42).

Jesus exhorts a fear of God above fear of persecution. Remember how fear of God, worship of God, postures us to keep our focus on spiritual realities not earthly visibilities. Jesus reminds them that the persecution comes from a rejection of God in them, not them personally. Jesus's teachings on persecution are accentuated by the news that John the Baptist has been beheaded. (Mark 6:14–29).

In Mark 6:30–31, the disciples reunite with Christ. They report on their ministry efforts, and Jesus tells them to rest. The crowds, however, prevent rest. Describe the spiritual hunger of the crowd in Mark 6:33.

As Jesus teaches, time passes. The spiritual hunger is overshadowed by a physical hunger. Let's look at the interchange between Jesus and the disciples. In verses 35–36, how would you characterize what the disciples say to Jesus?

Once again, we see the disciples informing Jesus of the gravity of the situation without seeking how He recommends handling it. They are dutiful advisors. They make reasonable recommendations. They have assessed the need and brought it to the attention of their leader. Even at this point in their faith growth, they still do not anticipate a solution that exceeds physical visibilities perhaps, because like us, they surmise *this* situation is different; it is overwhelming. "We are too few, and the magnitude of the need is too great. After all, these are the facts: The area is deserted from any food sources. The hour is late. The crowd is vast and will take time to dissipate. Virtually no one came prepared to take care of their need, and their need is too great for our ability to provide."

Jesus responds with apparent disregard for these facts. "You give them something to eat," He states. Jesus responds to their lack of faith, with an exhortation of faith. Jesus wants them to exercise spiritual power, to look beyond themselves for the solution. But the disciples still define His response in earthly limitations, "Shall we go and buy two hundred denarii worth of bread?" They have estimated the costs and know they are lacking. Furthermore, they know Jesus is aware of their limited finances. He had just sent them out to minister in the countryside without money. "What is He thinking, telling us to feed this crowd?"

But Jesus also told them God would provide for them without money as they ministered in pairs. And He did. The rationalizations are imaginable. "But that was then, this is now." They have just returned from God's power working through their ministry. They know the power was God's, not their own. Or do they? Now, when presented with another opportunity to believe God will use them, they doubt. Their expectations of God are small. They still resort to physical solutions for a supernatural dilemma. Doubt and unbelief overrule faith.

Jesus's statement reiterates what they know to be true. "There is no possible way we can feed this crowd." The disciples miss the opportunity to express trust in God to do a mighty work. But this exercise has still been productive for their faith growth. The disciples have established that their talent and ability is inadequate. "With man it is impossible" is clearly evident. Now the faith lesson continues. Jesus is about to reveal how "With God all things are possible."

> And when He had taken the five loaves and the two fish, He looked up to heaven, blessed and broke the loaves, and gave them to His disciples to set before them; and the two fish He divided among them all. So they all ate and were filled. And they took up twelve baskets full of fragments and of the fish. Now those who had eaten the loaves were about five thousand men. (Mark 6:41–44).

God revealed His ability to provide for a most basic need in a most supernatural way. But the miracle provides more than satisfaction of physical hunger. The miracle also provided for God's dutiful servants though they still lack faith and understanding. Let's review Jesus's instructions for the disciples' recent ministry.

Reread and write Matthew 10:9–10.

"Provide neither gold nor silver nor copper in your money belts, nor bag for your journey, nor two tunics, nor sandals, nor staffs, for a worker is worthy of his food."

"A worker is worthy of his food." God's miraculous leftovers—one basket per disciple—demonstrates His abundant provision for the worthy workers. A basket of bread was an acceptable, valuable form of exchange at that time and society. Serving others did not cost the disciples anything financially, but much was received through their obedience and availability even amid doubt and unbelief. God provided for their physical need for food and shelter, and He provided rewards for their service.

Read Psalm 34:4–10. Ask God to reveal any overwhelming situations that you may be "instructing" Him how to remedy.

Is He responding with an instruction that you believe is impossible to fulfill? What is that instruction?

Do you think God could be giving you an opportunity to exercise faith in His supernatural power? Write what He reveals.

The disciples ministered in pairs through faith and away from Christ's immediate assistance. Through this faith, God demonstrated His power by healing the sick and casting out demons. Yet when faced with another opportunity to expand their knowledge of God, they responded with doubt and unbelief. The following verse models for us a more appropriate response when faced with circumstances that seem beyond our ability to overcome. God wants to grow faith. Doubt and unbelief hinder that growth. Be willing to confess unbelief or even the possibility of it. Be encouraged that God does not always punish unbelief but instead continues to grant opportunity for faith to grow. To him who is willing to believe, all things are possible: "Jesus said to him, 'If you can believe, all things are possible to him who believes.' Immediately the father of the child cried out and said with tears, 'Lord, I believe, help my unbelief'" (Mark 9:23–24).

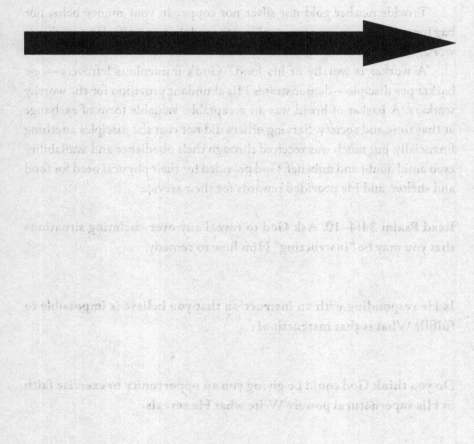

Growing Faith 2

An Immediate Test of Faith

Through feeding the five thousand, the disciples had opportunity to demonstrate deeper faith in the power of God. When they previously went out two by two, God used them as vessels for His miraculous power away from Jesus, their teacher. Now back in His presence, they doubted God's ability to continue using them miraculously. Their return to Jesus's presence seemed to result in complacency. Later, we look at the second opportunity God gives them to feed the multitudes by faith in His power.

Following this miracle, Jesus gives another chance to demonstrate faith. This is a second chance in light of the miracle and test they just encountered with the crowd; it is also a second chance in another familiar situation. Once again, they are away from the crowds on a storm-tossed sea. Recall that the prior stormy sea miracle in Mark 4:35–41 was the first recorded demonstration of Jesus's power after extensive teaching on faith. Many miraculous things have occurred since coupled with further teaching and ministerial instruction. They have had many opportunities for their understanding and faith to grow.

Unlike the previous miracle on the stormy sea, this time, Jesus is not with them in the boat. Observe how Jesus again sends the disciples away from Him. He begins to prepare them for His permanent physical separation. We will see, though, that Jesus is nearer than the disciples imagine. Let's read the current passage and look at how this difference adds another dimension to strengthen the disciples' faith.

> Immediately He made is disciples get into the boat and go before Him to the other side to Bethsaida, while He sent the multitudes away. And when He had sent them away, He departed to the mountain to pray. Now when evening came, the boat was in the middle of the sea; and He was alone in the land. Then He saw them straining at rowing, for the wind was against them. And about the fourth watch of the night He came to them, walking on the sea, and would have passed them by. But when they

saw Him, walking on the sea, they supposed it was a ghost, and cried out; for they all saw Him and were troubled. And immediately He talked with them and said to them, "Be of good cheer! It is I; do not be afraid." Then He went up into the boat to them and the wind ceased. And they were greatly amazed in themselves beyond measure, and marveled. For they had not understood about the loaves, because their heart was hardened. (Mark 6:45–52)

The first line in verse 45 subtly reveals important aspects for the setting of this miracle. The Word says that Jesus "immediately made" the disciples get in the boat. As previously mentioned, they just failed to demonstrate faith but instead doubted with the feeding of the five thousand. Immediately following the miracle—with the power of God still fresh in their minds, spirits, and emotions—they have another opportunity to trust in the power of God. It is reasonable to describe the disciples as still relishing in a mountaintop experience. Their physical senses have just witnessed miraculous supernatural power. However, their previous doubt overshadows any lasting awe and understanding. The strong power of doubt to fuel fear and unbelief is revealed through the disciples' response on the stormy sea.

With the expectations of what God can and will do just stretched, Jesus gives them another faith-building lesson. Verse 52 states that their present unbelief (and fear) existed because they "did not understand about the loaves for their hearts were hardened." The doubt present after witnessing the miracle of the loaves combined with their present fear of the storm fuel unbelief, spiritually disabling them from trusting and responding in faith. (This same account in Matthew 14 also describes the disciples as given over to both doubt and fear.) Remember we discussed that doubt and fear are like two sides of a coin; when there is one, the other is a near temptation. In the miracle of the five thousand, doubt blinded them to God's available power. This doubt fuels fear in this following circumstance on the sea.

This should serve as both a caution as well as an encouragement with our own faith-building lessons. We should be cautioned and sensitive to the possibility of back-to-back situations that would fuel doubt and fear. We can learn from the disciples the need for maintaining spiritual sensitivities in the presence of overwhelming and difficult physical visibilities. However, we can also be encouraged by the repeated opportunities Jesus gives the disciples to build their faith even when they appear to repeatedly fail the tests.

Verse 45 also says Jesus made the disciples get in the boat. Why would Jesus make them get into the boat? Perhaps they wanted to cling to a mountaintop experience with Jesus. After witnessing such a miraculous provision, perhaps they desired to remain with Jesus on the mountain in prayer. The growing multitudes curtailed their rest. Thus, the desire for physical rest and spiritual solitude with Jesus has probably increased given the recent events.

Their desire to remain in Jesus's presence could be true in light of another theory. Many of the disciples were trained professional fishermen. This vast sea experience fueled sensitivity to weather patterns. It is highly possible that they discerned the rough winds approaching. While they had previously witnessed Jesus calm the storm, they did not fully understand the power displayed. Furthermore, Jesus performed this miracle while still on the boat. This time, He sent the disciples ahead of Him while He dismissed the multitudes and went up the mountain to pray. They possibly doubted Jesus's ability to provide protection from afar. Perhaps they doubted the power of God to work through them. "Who wants to willingly head across a stormy sea in the middle of darkness when you could finally be resting in the presence of Jesus on the mountain?"

Jesus *made* the disciples get in the boat. The Spirit led Jesus into the wilderness to be tested in a way that would empower Him miraculously. Likewise, we learn from what follows that God had a plan to display His power for the disciples' faith to grow (notice the pattern of God's ways). This opportunity to grow did not come from comfortably and safely residing in Jesus's presence; it came as He sent them ahead of Him to face the storm. Unknown to them, Jesus was always aware of their situation and remained nearby in intercession for them.

Reflect on the progressive surrender to God's power. He sends them out in pairs to perform healing miracles. Jesus faces opposition with the Pharisees, and John the Baptist is beheaded. Jesus gathers them to give them the opportunity to perform a miraculous provision for multitudes in His presence. Now He sends them alone on a turbulent sea. But this is an experience in which they have already witnessed His power. Not only has Jesus demonstrated God's power in their presence, He has also already overcome a similar situation. He grants them an opportunity to exercise faith and increase His power in them. Therefore, there is a benefit, not harm, from this experience.

Jesus made them face the storm so their faith, dependence, and knowledge of the power of God would grow. When we read Matthew's account in 14:22–32, we are told of Peter's willingness to get out of the boat and walk on the water to Jesus. Peter's willingness to trust, his willingness to lay aside fear empowered him to walk on the stormy sea. But when he became consumed with doubt and fear, the power to walk on water was not available to sustain him.

We have studied the events leading to this time and discussed the hardness of the disciples' hearts existing at each opportunity to demonstrate faith. While in the presence of Jesus witnessing the miraculous power of God again and again even to the extent of being a vessel for that power; their hearts are still full of unbelief. This causes them to settle for less than what God desires to give. Only Peter seems to have stretched his expectation of what God will do as demonstrated by leaving the boat.

Notice the relentless determination Peter had to be near Jesus in the demonstration of power. When the others realize Jesus walked across the turbulent waters and boarded their boat, they were amazed.

Jesus was near the disciples on the stormy sea. He would have passed them by except that they cried out. However, like the children of Israel in Judges 6, their cries were not in repentance but in a response to the crisis. They were not inviting Jesus in the boat to celebrate trust in God to protect them; they were crying for help.

Like the disciples, do we doubt God's ability to provide for us through the Holy Spirit? God is not far but near through the Holy Spirit—a call away. While we should learn from the disciples' response to fear, we are reassured that God also responds even to our fearful cries and unbelief. In both situations, God is willing to make Himself known regardless of fear. We have the blessing and opportunity to learn from these examples and perhaps our failures.

The disciples teach us to be more sensitive to the desire of God to make Himself known and to reveal His power. Even though we may have great testimonies and firsthand knowledge of God's power, we may yet find ourselves in new situations doubting and fearful just like the disciples. In these times, we should call out to the Spirit in faith, not in fear, and surrender as a vessel for the power of God. We can be a vessel of peace in the midst of confusion and chaos.

The winds ceased after Jesus came close. They saw Him from afar, yet the seas still raged. They witnessed His power from afar as He and Peter walked on the water while the seas still raged. And the seas continued to rage until Christ was in the boat next to them. Notice how scripture tells us that He went in the boat to them. They are in the boat stunned, marveling, amazed beyond measure, seemingly paralyzed by their confusion. Except for Peter, they are not going to Him. It does not appear they help Jesus in the boat. He is going to them. Once there, the wind ceases. His mere presence brings peace to the sea only in His closeness to them! What a lesson and comfort this should be for us! What an admonishment to rush out to meet Him.

Jesus brought peace to still the sea. But the disciples were initially unable to receive the fullness of the peace He offered because of the hardness of their hearts. It is interesting that it is at the end of the stormy sea miracle that scripture says, "They did not understand about the loaves, because their hearts were hardened." Mark is making a distinct observation about the hardness of heart to diminish embracing the fullness of God from one miracle to the next. Unbelief about the loaves fueled fear further when on the stormy sea.

Yes, they were in the presence of Christ. Yes, they witnessed the miraculous power of God with the feeding of the crowds. But how did that change their hearts? Their hearts remained hardened. Yes, they are still God's chosen leaders. Yes, He continues to use them as vessels of His power and glory, for with this immediate test, they are given another opportunity to grow faith on a stormy sea. Matthew 14:33 gives a better description of how this additional miracle affected the disciples, "Then those who were in the boat came and worshipped Him saying, 'Truly You are the Son of God.'"

Remember what they said after the sea was calmed the first time: "Who can this be that even the sea and the wind obey Him?" Jesus now answers this question, perhaps a rhetorical question from the disciples' perspective. God always wanted them to have understanding. The capacity to understand was always there but covered by fear, doubt, and unbelief. God answered their question by placing them in a similar situation giving them another opportunity to trust. The disciples' understanding finally expands to comprehend who Jesus is: The Son of God.

Are you seeing the process of God's ways to strengthen faith? One may ask, "What is so wrong with the disciples' unbelief given that God uses them in miraculous ways to further His kingdom?" As mentioned above, they missed the opportunity to embrace the power of God and learn more about God's character. But perhaps the greatest danger with the presence of unbelief, fear, and doubt is that there is coming a crucial time when Jesus's presence will not be so near. The disciples will then experience situations and be prone to greater fear and doubt requiring strong faith instead of incubating it. Currently, Jesus gives opportunities to grow faith to prepare them for the future. If they struggle to find peace in Jesus's physical presence and in the presence of God's power, how will they find peace in His absence and in the presence of spiritual persecution? If they can't trust in the Son of Man they physically see, how will they surrender and trust in the Spirit they cannot see?

Fear, doubt, and unbelief also restrict our ability to embrace and know God. We too need intimate experiences with God to sustain faith when later the presence and power of God is not as obvious. God may allow Satan to stir a crisis just as the disciples eventually experienced. God may also orchestrate circumstances to reveal the devotion, obedience, and understanding (or lack of them) in our hearts. The Bible says that the heart is deceitful above all things. God allows tests not for His need but for ours. Through tests, we truly "see" our heart with "faith markers" revealing strong and weak faith. These tests can come in the form of physical, financial, emotional, mental, or spiritual (or ministerial) difficulty. They may come in the form of temporary tests or lasting thorns in the flesh.

God's ways teach that before these tests, He gives opportunity to experience His mighty power. The tests reveal our inadequacies and need for this power that reaches us from afar and calms us. He wants to give greater understanding of who He is while He is near. God allowed similar tests for the disciples to answer their questions and build faith. He may repeatedly allow similar difficulties to afflict us until we receive the understanding He longs to reveal about Himself and about our need for Him.

While we have the continual presence of the Holy Spirit, we have already discussed how we can grieve and quench the nearness and power of His presence. A question worth echoing, the Holy Spirit has us, but do we always have the Holy Spirit? We are sealed by the Holy Spirit, but are we walking in the Holy Spirit rather than in the Flesh? When unbelief, fear, and doubt consume our focus more than the presence and power of God, we are extremely vulnerable to the schemes of Satan. Because we have grieved or quenched the Holy Spirit, we are momentarily out of His fellowship and may not be aware of His nearness (just as the disciples were unaware of Jesus's nearness on the stormy sea). God's ways and the disciples' experiences teach us to seek opportunities to safely grow in faith through these difficult seasons. The strengthening of faith during these periods of growth will help sustain us when Satan attacks to undermine faith.

Most of us would never consider crossing a stormy sea a safe thing to do or God's perfect will. We sometimes presume that when we cooperate with God's will in obedience, it results only in pleasant, smooth journeys. We may also presume that a rocky journey is one outside of God's will. We can trust the Spirit to lead us to the center of God's will, but we are not assured it will always be easy. God may lead us willingly or unwillingly into a wilderness because He wants to reveal to us and fill us with His power that can be received only in solitude. He may keep us in the wilderness until we learn what He attempts to teach us or until the circumstances are prepared for further growth and purpose

He wants us to know Him more just as He wanted the disciples to realize Jesus as His Son. Are we amazed, frustrated, confused, and stunned by the experience, or do we recognize His presence and power?

God is faithful to work difficulty for our good when Satan tempts us. In spite of the difficulty, we should expect a display of God's power. Through faith, we trust His power and like Peter get out of the boat and move closer to Him. Faith is our sustaining grace. He wants us to see the strength of it, and He wants to strengthen it more. When you perceive to be drowning in difficulty, Christ is near encouraging you to lay aside unbelief, *face everything and rise* by faith.

As I shared previously, some years ago, God had me rest from ministry. I knew He was leading me into a time of equipping, but I was unsure about the specifics. He reiterated, "Be still and know that I am God." He began to teach me more about the process of prayer and greatly intensified my personal and intercessory prayer. It was also during this time that God prompted meditation on the purpose of Jesus's wilderness equipping in Luke 4. I more fully understand now how God equipped me through solitude with Him as well as through great temptations.

About a year and half later, I had a very intense, two-day period of revelation that included a call to teach others about prayer. But it was also a warning of pending attacks by Satan and an exhortation to willingly embrace the cross. Though I was reassured of God's nearness, I was also very concerned, confused, and fearful.

Given the events of the next six months, most of these warnings were fulfilled. Without the warning, the circumstances would have undermined God's work. God provided revelation to protect His work in me and His purpose for me. The teaching on prayer came under great attack by Christian leaders who had a focus more on outward appearances and human reasoning than spiritual understanding. Without such clear direction, I would have greatly doubted my purpose because the teaching experience was anything but smooth.

In retrospect, I understand God's preparations and leading that made me walk that path. I wish I could say His warnings caused me to understand fully the situation and to know how to respond flawlessly, but like the disciples, it did not. However, the preparation kept me grounded in His will so that fear and doubt of His plan, purpose, and promises for ministry did not overtake me. I was shaken, but my faith in the promises of God and His purposes did not fail. God assured me of the study's benefit to those who persevered and used this experience to test understanding and commitment for further ministry. Despite great spiritual warfare and emotional strain, that test strengthened God's call on my life. The experience caused me to depend more on God, which prepared my understanding of many things to come.

When we are still and focused on God, He prepares us for revelation of His will and purpose. We have seen this in the life of Gideon, and Jesus progressively revealed the power of God to the disciples to prepare understanding and grow faith. But often, the crowds seem to more easily accept the power of God than do some of God's apostles. Mark 6:54 tells us the people recognized Jesus when He came out of the boat. Remember that

Jesus made the disciples get into a boat on the shore of the Sea of Galilee while the multitudes were present. They knew Jesus could not have quickly joined the disciples because He returned to send the crowds away, which probably did not happen quickly.

News of the feeding of the five thousand probably spread throughout the land. No doubt there were witnesses in and near Bethsaida who knew Jesus did not get in the boat with the disciples. Therefore, to see Jesus get off with them would testify even further to that power they sought and believed in.

Verses 55–56 speak of the peoples' expectations of God's power and their great faith.

> They ran through the whole surrounding region, and began to carry about on beds those who were sick to wherever they heard He was. Wherever He entered, into villages, cities, or the country, they laid the sick in the marketplaces, and begged Him that they might just touch the border of His garment. And as many as touched Him were made well.

This is a sobering lesson revealing how God's chosen, very available, and effective leaders can have hearts hardened with unbelief even in the midst of great service for God. Leaders sometimes struggle to recognize God more than do the multitudes. This was true for Jewish leadership as well as the disciples. Unbelief prevents faith from maturing. As long as we ignore unbelief or refuse deliverance from it, we find ourselves intensely battling fear and doubt. We fail to understand God's power and purposes at work.

God wants us to experience victorious, abundant living. God has an available provision of understanding that dispels unbelief, but it is not automatic. In the next chapter, we will realize more fully the provision He gives. He wants us to know Him. He wants us to hear Him. He wants us to understand His revealed will. Most important, He wants us to realize how knowing, hearing, and understanding Him grows faith in remarkable ways.

Is He calling you now? Only you can choose to get out of the boat to walk on the stormy sea and meet Him amid your fear. He is nearer than you realize.

Chapter 3

The Power of Knowing God

And this is eternal life, that they may know You, the only true God, and Jesus Christ whom You have sent.
—John 17:3

To Know Christ as the Way

Begin with worship, meditation, and prayer.

> I will give you a new heart, and put a new spirit within you; I will take the heart of stone out of your flesh and give you a new heart of flesh. I will put My Spirit within you and cause you to walk in My statutes, and you will keep My judgments and do them. (Ezekiel 36:26–27)

> No more shall every man teach his neighbor, and every man his brother, saying, "Know the Lord," for they shall know Me, from the least of them to the greatest of them, says the Lord. I will forgive their iniquity and their sin I will remember no more. (Jeremiah 31:34)

"Lord, thank You for making a way for me to know You. I praise You for being my way, my truth, and my life. I worship You as my almighty Lord who desires for me to know Him and empowers me to walk with Him."

During Old Testament times, the only written Word of God was the Torah. For families privileged to afford one, it is a most prized possession. In addition to the Torah, the Jews also had the oral law taught from priest to priest. Most of God's Word was taught orally from brother to brother or neighbor to neighbor. In the passages above, God is prophesying the day when the need for this type of teaching will not be great because of the teaching He puts in us. This is the prophecy of Christ's coming to redeem the world and to send His Holy Spirit. His Word lives in believers teaching from within. He removes the hardness of hearts, pours His Spirit in us, and strengthens the focus on His Word in our thoughts affecting our response and obedience to Him.

Christ exhorts us to receive the understanding God provides those who believe in Him. Sin separates us from God. Jesus's sacrifice on the cross and His resurrection give us the right, the power or ability, to know God. Jesus is the only way to have a relationship with God. When we accept Christ as Savior and Lord of our lives, the door to knowing God opens, but this is just the beginning.

Just as the disciples gradually understood who Jesus was and God's will for Him, so is our progressive understanding of God's fullness. Initially, the disciples lacked understanding that Jesus was a vessel for God's power. As God's servants, we also often strive to work for God or alongside kingdom work instead of allowing God to work through us.

Our understanding and experience of God should surpass knowing *about* Him; God wants us to know Him. He teaches us about His character. We learn about His majesty. We experience or witness His power. We study things He has done. We go to Him in prayer with our needs because we know He is our sovereign provider. But each one of these is merely an avenue to know Him more fully than we do. Each of these reveal more of Him when spiritual senses are open to understanding. The goal of all that He gives and does is for us to know Him and for the intimate communion to intensify worship of Him. God wants us to know the depth of His personal love.

As a bivocational pastor for over sixty years, my father pastored small retirement community churches and served in many positions in public education. In our home, we always went to church, and a love for learning was stressed. As a young child, I knew that God loved me, that He loved the whole world. I knew Christ was His Son who died on the cross to save the world. But that was just knowledge about God. One Sunday morning when I was five, I was singing with the choir, praising God, and expressing my gratitude for God letting me know Him, but I yearned to know Him more. While I had learned about the love of God, I had not yet begun to understand its depth or how sin separated me from Him. I did not feel separated from Him; I loved Him and knew He loved me. I certainly knew He felt the same way for everyone in the world for "He has the whole world in His hands." Not only did I not really know God, I did not realize there was more to know.

A year or more later, I came to realize that I was a sinner and that my sin kept me from God. I had not felt kept from God but I was. I confessed my sin to Him and accepted Him in my heart. Even though I was young, I remember the elation of discovering that there was more of God He wanted me to embrace and the sorrow of what had kept me from that deeper relationship.

Even after accepting Christ as my Savior and Lord, my desire to know Him intensified. I trusted that God had a purpose for me though I did not know what it was. I also knew He would make it known to me though I did not know how. Many years later and despite many detours, that yearning has never left. While God has been faithful to allow me to know Him, the more I come to know Him, the greater He intensifies my hunger to know Him more.

Though you may be a Christian, I pray this study fuels a deeper hunger in you to know God more.[14] God often accomplishes so many miraculous

---

[14] You may know many things about God, but if you have never confessed, you are a sinner and need Him to be Lord of your life. Stop now and pray a prayer to invite Him into your heart. This is the first step to knowing God on an intimate level. Romans 3:23 tells us, "For all have sinned and fall short of the glory of God." However, Romans 10:9 says, "If you confess with your mouth the Lord Jesus and believe in your heart that God has raised Him from the dead, you will be saved." If you have just prayed to God inviting Him to live in your heart, tell a Christian friend or pastor. Invite them to celebrate your new journey of knowing and living for God.

things in our lives when we come to salvation that we cannot conceive there is more He desires to give. Sometimes, we think God too almighty and us too undeserving to receive such moment-by-moment intimacy and presence of God. Perhaps unconsciously, we resign to muddle through life the best we can, often in our own strength hoping we do not do too many things contrary to His purpose.

This chapter marks the middle of our study. I hope God is breaking down misunderstandings about His desire to make Himself known to you. This chapter furthers our understanding of Jesus's role as the Son of Man and how there is much to learn from this ministry and His teachings to the disciples. While we reiterate God's will for us to model Jesus's and the disciples' ministry, we continue to look at how misperceptions and edification of these ministries sometimes keep us from reaching our full faith potential. As we begin to study what it means to know God, let us look at what Jesus reveals about that indwelling relationship we have through Him with God.

Read John 14:1–7. What does Jesus reveal as the key to knowing the Father? (vv. 6–7).

In John 14:8, how does the disciple Philip respond to these words of Christ?

Read John 14:9–12. What does Jesus indicate as the source for "seeing" the Father?

The disciples now realize Jesus is the promised Son of God. They have served with Him under His teaching and fellowship for almost three years. However, they seize the opportunity to see God the Father also as further testimony of Jesus's teachings. This revelation is very important. During these three years, Jesus helped them understand the fullness of who He is. Now that they finally get it, they are not content—they want more. Understanding fuels an intense desire for all that God represents.

Jesus teaches that to see the Father requires only believing in who Christ is for His life is a reflection of God's. He further tells them that even if that is difficult for them, they should "see" (i.e., understand) based on the works of God Jesus completes in their presence.

The disciples want to see in a physical sense. Jesus instead tells them to see spiritually with faith, with a belief in the unseen but evidenced partly by what they can physically see and know. The sight Jesus offers is far greater than physical sight. The physical realm is able to testify to the spiritual, but faith is the root of that understanding and sight. Jesus seems slightly frustrated with His closest followers because they have seen with their eyes yet still struggle to believe or see through the spirit.

At the tomb of Lazarus, Martha questions Jesus's command to remove the stone because of the stench of death. In John 11: 40, Jesus responds, "Did I not say to you that if you *would believe you would see the glory of God?*" (emphasis added; see also John 11:4). In verses 41–42, Jesus verbalizes what He has been silently praying as a witness of who He is: "Father, I thank You *that You have heard Me.* And I know that You always hear Me, but because of the people who are standing by I said this, *that they may believe that You sent Me*" (emphasis added). By vocalizing His prayer before those assembled, He asks God to testify that He and the Father are one. In this passage, we again see Jesus's admonishment to have faith and to receive the fullness and glory revealed by God in response to faith. We also see God use this experience to teach more about Jesus—the One who has power over the stench of death.

As followers of Christ, we too must realize our weakness of failing to experience the Father in situations and circumstances. We can be in the presence of God's miraculous power and miss the fullness of His provision if our eyes of faith do not remain opened. Unlike the disciples, we cannot physically see Jesus, but He has given the Holy Spirit to reveal His power. Jesus makes Himself and God known through the revelation of the Spirit. As we continue to explore what it means to know God, to hear God, and to understand God, we learn how to face all aspects of our lives with opened eyes of faith. The foundation needed is a continual focus on God's presence.

Now we exhort you, brethren, warn those who are unruly, comfort the fainthearted, uphold the weak, be patient with all. See that no one renders evil

> *for evil to anyone, but always pursue what is good both for yourselves and for all. Rejoice always, pray without ceasing, in everything give thanks; for this is the will of God in Christ Jesus for you. Do not quench the Spirit. Do not despise prophecies. Test all things; hold fast what is good; abstain from every form of evil. Now may the God of peace Himself sanctify you completely; and may your whole spirit, soul, and body be preserved blameless at the coming of our Lord Jesus Christ. He who calls you is faithful, who also will do it.*
> —1 Thessalonians 5:14–24

To Seek His Face

Begin with worship, meditation, and prayer.

> I am the good shepherd; and I know My sheep, and am known by My own. As the Father knows Me, even so I know the Father, and I lay down my life for the sheep … My sheep hear My voice, and I know them, and they follow Me. And I give them eternal life, and they shall never perish; neither shall anyone snatch them out of My hand. (John 10:14–15, 27–28)

> "Lord, help me realize the ways I prioritize Christian service above fellowship with You. Teach me how You desire me to personally seek Your face. Open my heart to receive Your fullness. Thank you for the vastness of Your love."

Jesus is our Shepherd. We respond only to our Shepherd, the one we have come to know, whose faithful voice we recognize and whose proven care we trust. As our Shepherd, He knows us and we know Him. But how do we know Him? Is there a difference between knowledge of God and knowing God? Is it prideful to suppose we should seek the fullness of God as we come to know Him?

As we study the power of knowing God, the answers to these questions will become obvious. God knows us. He wants us to understand just how deeply He loves us. He gives us the desire and understanding to receive this provision. We find it when we realize the need to seek His face more than we seek a provision from His hand. The interchange with Martha and Mary when serving Christ in their home gives us an example of the difference between seeking God's hand and seeking God's face.

Read Luke 10:38–42. In Luke 10:40, what was Martha asking Jesus to do for her?

From Luke 10:42, what does Jesus say about Mary choosing to seek Him?

From this passage and other interchanges with Jesus, we know Martha and Mary were followers and students of Christ. In a time when women were not permitted to be taught in the temple, we see Christ desiring Martha and Mary to be with Him, students "at his feet," an honored position for hearing His teachings and enjoying conversation. He loved them as well as their brother, Lazarus. In this passage, we see Martha desiring to serve Christ. The provision from Him she sought was assistance for that service. Martha came to Christ, but she was seeking His hand of authority and influence. She was not coming to Him for the sole pleasure of being in His presence. Christ's response was not to encourage Mary to serve but allow her to remain at His feet in intimate communion and fellowship. He subtly pointed out that the greatest service Martha could offer was the fellowship of undivided devotion.

Martha loved Christ; that motivated her to serve and please Him, to provide for His physical need. However, in this passage, Christ stressed His desire not just to have our service, but also to have our undivided attention in fellowship. He implied that His greatest need, that "one thing" needed, was fellowship. His desire, or "need," surpassed the physical. Jesus cares more for communion than service for Him. He does not diminish the physical need but rather reveals His greater need—spiritual fellowship. He wanted Martha to seek His face, not just His hand. He wanted Martha's priority to fuel offering herself, not just her hand.

While I do not believe this passage indicates we should always sacrifice service to God for communion and fellowship, I believe it reiterates the importance for us to "be still and know that I am God" (Psalm 46:10). Church activities and service can enslave us to the neglect of deepening surrender to God. This interchange teaches the importance of intimate communion and His will for the place and time for service.

I can say this forcefully because I am a Martha. As previously mentioned, God brought me through a refining season lasting many years of being still before Him in service. While it is very difficult for a Martha to be still, and I am no exception, this has been one of the most intimate seasons of my relationship with God to date. During this time of resting and testing, I have gained greater understanding of His scriptures and received clear instructions in powerful ways. It has been a necessary season of empowerment to surrender to His will and ways for my life.

David also echoes seeking this "one thing" and reveals the importance of seeking God's face.

Read Psalm 27:4: What is the "one thing" David is seeking, and what does he hope to receive from this seeking?

In Psalm 27:8, what does David say that God commanded him to seek?

In Psalm 27:9, what does David request God not to withhold from him?

To know God more, we must desire to seek Him. In the above passage, we see David as one who wants to abide in the presence of God continually so he may behold His beauty and gain His counsel. Seeking the face of God, beholding His beauty, brings wisdom and understanding.

To seek His face is to seek a more intimate level of relating to or knowing God. When we seek the face of God, we move beyond learning about God, beyond serving God, to interacting intimately with Him through worship, prayer, and fasting. When we seek His face, we realize more than what He can do for us or what we can do for Him. It goes beyond to focus on who

He is as the I Am. Those with a hunger to seek His face understand the empowerment that comes from resting in His presence. Let us examine a few more of these scriptures.

Read 2 Chronicles 7:14–15. What happens when we seek God's face?

Before He tells us to seek His face, what does God mention we must do?

How will God respond to someone seeking His face? (v. 15).

In Psalm 24:1–6, what characteristics describe the generation that seeks God's face?

In 1 Peter 3:12, what is God's response to those who do evil?

Read Revelation 22:1–5. In John's vision of heaven, what is the blessing described in verse 4?

From reading these passages and verses, do you believe seeking the face of God is the goal or the means to a goal?

Seeking the face of God should be a desired pursuit, but in Exodus 33:20, God tells Moses no man shall see His face and live. How can these two be reconciled when repeatedly throughout God's Word He exhorts us to seek His face? As we learned, Jesus is our way to know God and see His face. Until we reach our eternal glory, we can see His face only in a spiritual sense, but then we shall see Him through sight.

For us to seek the face of God this side of glory requires more than a casual attempt to approach Him. This is more than giving Him our needs in prayer, going to church on Sunday, and routinely serving Him. A desire to seek the face of God is a relentless pursuit to find His favor. It is seeking to rest in His glory. It is to abandon self to receive whatever He in His sovereignty will bestow on us. To seek His face is to express our desire to know Him.

The reward of seeking His face is to receive His favor. It is to glimpse His glory as we in our earthly state are able to experience. A failure to seek His face results in God turning His face away and removing His favor.

In the next two lessons, we will look at different ways God reveals His face and glory. His glory manifests through earthly powers that often fuel fear. For example, He reveals His presence in fire (Deuteronomy 5:24), lightning, thunder, clouds (Exodus 19:9), and earthquakes (Revelation 11:13). From an earthly perspective, these forces of nature cause us to fear because of the harm and danger they bring. However, when these forces are the effect of God's glory, they bring a godly fear that empowers trust and obedience. While giving the Ten Commandments to Moses, His presence resulted in great thundering, lightning, and a dark cloud on the mountain (Exodus 19:16). Because the children of Israel were unaware that this represented the glory of God's presence, they feared greatly for their lives (Exodus 20:18–20). They presumptuously framed their knowledge of God on their experience of thunder and lightning. This presence of God's glory caused the face of Moses to radiate so brightly that he had to veil his face before the fearful Israelites.

Revelation 22:5 says that God's face is the light of all heaven. The glory of His face is so bright that there is no night there. His face is representative of His purity, holiness, goodness, and power. The fire of His glory in the burning bush is a holy fire that did not consume the bush. Daniel's three friends while in a fiery furnace receive protection by a fourth person, the Angel of the Lord. This fire also becomes a holy fire in the presence of the Lord. The fire did not even singe the hair of Daniel's friends.

These passages teach that God's face, God's presence, is power! It is a power that humbles, provides, protects, and heals. It reveals His will. It guides and corrects. To seek the face of God is to seek His power and be changed by it. To seek the face of God is to be kept by the power of God in obedience to His will (1 Peter 1:5).

In 1 Corinthians 8:1a–3, we read, "We know that we all have knowledge. Knowledge puffs up, but love edifies. *And if anyone thinks that he knows anything, he knows nothing yet as he ought to know.* But if anyone loves God, this one is known by Him" (emphasis added).

Let us also look at Ephesians 3:17–19: *"that Christ may dwell in your hearts through faith;* that you, being rooted and grounded in love, may be able to comprehend with all the saints what is the width and length and depth and height—to *know* the *love* of Christ *which passes knowledge;* that you may be filled with all the fullness of God"* (emphasis added).

No matter where we are in our knowledge of God, we have so much more to learn. When we accept Christ as Savior, we merely open the avenue to know Him; what we have to learn is far greater than knowledge—it is to experience the fullness of God Himself. This is not a calling to exalt one's self to become like God; this is a continual process of humbling self, a sacrifice of our Flesh, so God will reveal His fullness through us.

As modeled by Gideon and Jesus's teachings of the disciples, we embrace God's fullness when we embrace His Word, will, and power. As mentioned, we generally understand and embrace God's truth in His Word and seek His will, but too often like the disciples, we miss completely or misunderstand His power. Even when His power is evident, we may fear it. We may not initially discern its fulfillment as a testimony to God's Word and will. Even if we recognize it, we may miss the fullness of its blessing and peace.

We often fail to seek His power with the same devotion with which we seek His Word and will. Ephesians 3 reveals the eternal prayer covering that fills us with the fullness of God, His power. This comes through faith, through knowing the love of God.

Part of knowing God is realizing how much He knows us and everything that happens to us. He cares for us because He is our Father who desires to reveal the depth of His love. His Son, our Shepherd, leads us near Him. Moses gives us an example of seeking God's fullness.

Read Exodus 33:12–23. In verse 13, why does Moses tell God he needs to know His way?

After God assures Moses His presence will go before him, what does Moses ask God to do in verse 18?

From the first half of verse 19, what glory does God promise to reveal to Moses?

In Exodus 33:11, how does it say Moses speaks with God?

Moses had an intimate relationship with God. Moses sought the face of God. Yes, he wanted the hand of God's provision, but from this passage, we see Moses as a man desiring intimate communion with his Father. Moses wanted to know Him. While he received the Ten Commandments, the Israelites rebelled wildly in the camp. God was angered and Moses was frustrated, but God's purposes prevailed.

After Moses intercedes for them, he intimately communes with God. Given all the previous miraculous, overwhelming, intimate, and unbelievable encounters with God, Moses still wants more! I respect Moses' tenacity in what he asked, relentlessly pursuing the fullness of God.

Think about all God's power Moses experienced thus far. Moses' miraculous survival as an infant, his encounters with God on the mountain, the miracles and plagues before Pharaoh, Israel's deliverance from the Egyptian army, the provisions of water, and writing the commandments in stone by the finger of God. Moses experienced more than any of God's servants. God responded to his request by giving him all of God he could bear by allowing all His goodness to pass before him. The Hebrew word used for "goodness" in this verse is *tumb*;[15] it comes from the root *towb*,[16]

---

[15] Blue Letter Bible, lexicon and Strong's Concordance search for 02898, Blue Letter Bible, 1996–2002, February 8, 2005, http://www.blueletterbible.org/cgi-bin/strongs.pl?strongs=02898&page=1.

[16] Blue Letter Bible, dictionary and word search for towb (Strong's 02895), Blue Letter Bible, 1996–2002, February 8, 2005. <http://www.blueletterbible.org/cgi-bin/words.pl?word=02895&page=1>.

a verb meaning to be pleasant, delightful, glad, and pleasing. God allowed Moses to "behold the beauty of the Lord."

From previous scriptures, we learned of the radiant effect of God's face. It is therefore understandable why Moses in this earthly state could not withstand viewing the full glory of God's face. While God does not grant the pleasure of seeing His face, He instead allows Moses to experience God's goodness. He says He will proclaim the name of the Lord before him, meaning God will establish, direct, and ordain the glory and reputation of the Lord before Moses.[17] Though Moses cannot see God's face, He allows him to see His back after all of His goodness passes by.

While I cannot even begin to comprehend what God's presence must have been like, I certainly can imagine Moses' other surroundings. Gain a mental picture: God has Moses stand near Him. He places Moses in the cleft of the rock; his face and body are pressing against the hard, musty, earthen mountain. This rock is Horeb, from which God provided water, a symbol of the spiritual Rock that provides Living Water (1 Corinthians 10:4).[18] The hand of God covers him in the cleft. What peace must have flooded his body! I can imagine the discomfort of the rock becoming unnoticeable as rest calms his nerves and muscles as the hand of God covers him. This is the presence of the almighty God with man, who experiences His presence and glimpses the form of God![19] Recall Jesus's invitation from Matthew 11:28: "Come to Me all you who are weary, and I will give you rest." Imagine the rest that must have swept over a weary, frustrated, Moses.

What in this world has you hard-pressed against the ruddy rock? Do you fully realize what it means to be in the cleft of the Rock? Do you realize God is nearer than you can imagine? How are you seeking God? How great is your hunger to seek His face, His power? How may God be using this rock, this difficulty, to reveal the Rock and release His Living Water, goodness, power and peace?

God may use circumstances to push us closer to Christ, the Rock. His

---

[17] Hebrew word shem, http://www.blueletterbible.org/lang/lexicon/lexicon.cfm?Strongs=H8034&t=NKJV.

[18] 1 Corinthians 10:4.

[19] Moses in his mortal form could not bear to see the full glory of God's countenance, yet Moses as a glorified saint was present on the Mount of Transfiguration when the glory of God radiated the body of Christ (Mark 9:2–4).

purpose may be to envelope us in His embrace. Do you hunger for God's goodness? Are you seeking Him on the mountain or rebelling in fear, doubt, and self-indulgence down in the camp? Through faith, Christ wants to dwell in our heart so we may know the vastness of God's great love. God wants us to surpass knowledge about His love. He wants us to experience its width, length, depth, and height. He wants us to go beyond knowing about it to experiencing it. He wants us to know His goodness! Are we willing to seek His face?

> *The Lord is in His holy temple, the Lord is on His heavenly throne. He observes the sons of men; His eyes examine them ... For the Lord is righteous, He loves justice, upright men will see His face.*
> —Psalm 11:4–7

To Know His Glory

Begin with worship, meditation, and prayer.

> For it is the God who commanded light to shine out of darkness who has shone in our hearts to give the light of the knowledge of the glory of God in the face of Jesus Christ. But we have this treasure in earthen vessels, that the excellence of the power may be of God and not of us. (2 Corinthians 4:6–7)

> "Lord, thank You for choosing me to be a vessel of Your honor and glory. Teach me to be sensitive to ways I try to hide Your glory and help me to reveal more of You this day."

To seek God's face is to glimpse the fullness of His power and glory. From Genesis, to the power of Christ over sin, to the eternal reign of the glory of God, God is perpetually causing light to shine out of darkness. If this is an aspect of His general purpose, can we not believe this is also central to His specific purpose for our fears? If we respond to fear by drawing near to God, we will come to know, trust, obey, and glorify Him even through fear.

God wants us to know Him. When we know Him, we will trust Him. Trust in God empowers obedience. He is glorified through obedience. When we know God, we know His glory and will reveal it. Sound impossible? It is if we fail to understand fully what Christ came on earth to demonstrate. Jesus came to earth as a vessel so the "excellence of the power may be of God and not of Him" as an example of this truth for us.

Jesus came to earth with the nature of deity as the Son of God, who humbled himself on earth as the Son of Man in human form. The fullness of Jesus's humanity does not diminish the fullness of His deity. To understand the power of the One living in us, we need to explore fully what it meant for Jesus to humble Himself in the form of man. We realize we are not and cannot be deity, but we are human, and Jesus's life models for us how to live the human life surrendered as a vessel for the power of God. In this session, we carefully observe His example to allow the power of God minister through Him as Son of Man.

This lesson stretches our understanding of Christ's ministry in the Gospels. Our postcrucifixion knowledge of His deity may obscure all there is to learn about His humanity. We hope to spiritually see the difference between two truthful perspectives: Christ as deity coming to earth committed to fulfill God's plan versus Christ as Jesus, the Son of Man coming to earth surrendered to the power of God. While both are true, focusing on the first to the neglect of understanding the second impairs fulfillment of our purpose as well as faith's growth.

Commitment to a Plan versus Surrender to a Power

John chapters 14, 15, 16, and 17 record some of the most intimate teachings of Christ not recorded in the other Gospels. To appreciate the heart of these messages, consider the time and context of His preparation. It represents Jesus's teachings the final moments prior to His crucifixion. Because of the urgency of the hour, it is reasonable to assume that what Jesus has to share is a vital part of what we need to learn. These are very important last words as the Son of Man ends His ministry in the flesh to resurrect to His eternal reign.

In these passages, Jesus reveals how He is a reflection of God. His life reveals the fullness of God (Colossians 2:9-12). Yet in these chapters, He also teaches it is through Him that we also reveal the fullness of God.

Read John 1:18, 14:1–7. What does Jesus say is the key to knowing the Father?

From John 14: 5 and 8, describe the disciples' level of understanding of Jesus's words.

In John 14:10–11, Jesus continues instructing the disciples about the source of His power to accomplish the miraculous. Twice in these two verses, Jesus makes a point about how God indwells Him and how He is protected by God: "The Father is in Me, and I am in Him." There is unity. They are one. But how are they one, and are we one with them also? Let us see.

The disciples now realize Jesus is the Son of God, but this knowledge skews their (as well as our) understanding of what God is doing through Him. It is easy for us to accept that Jesus performs the miraculous when we consider His deity. However, at this specific time, Jesus is also the Son of Man, meaning He has laid aside His rights and power (but not His nature) as God's Son to take on the form of man.

Consider the role the President of the United States has in and outside our country. In our land, he has power and authority established by the Constitution. However, when he leaves the United States, he may have influence, respect, and deference for his position, but he has no authority to exert his presidential power abroad. Yet he is still the President of the United States. His personhood has not changed, but his power has. Only through his cooperative work with the governing body of a foreign country can he effect changes outside the United States.

We know from John 1 that God gave Christ the authority and power to create, hold in place, and rule heaven and earth. But God also had a plan for Christ to leave the presence of God for a season to complete a purpose on earth in the form of man. While on earth as the Son of Man, His nature as the Christ, the deity, is still the same, but His power and authority are different from what He held in heaven. His power to effect change on earth comes only by His surrender to and joining with the authority and power God grants while on earth in the form of man. God, as supreme Governor of earth, gave Jesus power to heal physically and spiritually on earth, yet Jesus did not automatically heal all people. There was a specific plan, purpose, and power of God that Jesus surrendered to follow. To understand further, let us look at more scriptures.

Read John 6:38. Whose will has Christ come to complete?

Read John 1:1–5, 14. Describe the power *given* to Jesus, the Word.

What did Jesus, the Word, have to do so that we could know Him and thus God?

Read Philippians 2:6–11.

The NLT translation states in verses 6–8,

> Though he was God, he did not think of equality with God as something to cling to. Instead, he gave up his divine privileges; he took the humble position of a slave and was born as a human being. When he appeared in human form, he humbled himself in obedience to God and died a criminal's death on a cross.

Verse 7 (NKJV) says, "He made Himself of no reputation ... coming in the likeness of men." "He gave up His divine privileges." Christ willingly laid down His rights, not His nature as God. He emptied Himself to become a servant of God, a vessel for God's power and authority. He came to earth as a human to fulfill the will of God. Setting aside His right to assert Himself as deity, in His humanity He became a servant of God; He came to fulfill God's purpose through His humanity. He is perfect deity fulfilling humanity perfectly. Coming in human flesh, He had no spiritual power except what God granted in accordance with His will—according to the measure given Him, His spiritual giftedness. John 3:34 says that God has also *given Him, as the Son of Man*, the Spirit without measure. What He accomplished on earth as the Son of Man was accomplished through obedience to the Father's will, not because He was exercising His godly power as the Christ but because of His surrender to His Father's power as Jesus, the Son of Man.

Our knowledge of Jesus as deity often overshadows comprehending Him also as the Son of Man who exemplifies the glove analogy. As the Son of Man, Jesus modeled how to be a glove that the hand of God works through. God is in Jesus, and Jesus is filled with God's power so Jesus fulfills the will of His Father (John 14). Upon fulfillment of Jesus's purpose, God sent the Holy Spirit, making a way for Christians to follow Jesus's example.

Think about the times you have felt inadequate as a Christian, unable to exemplify the godliness you know God desires and you want to reveal. When you consider a calling to be Christlike, you may be discouraged because you know you are not Christ. That level of perfection and obedience seems far too great to achieve. It seems to be an unrealistic expectation. "Sure Jesus could do it, He is Christ," we rationalize. With this focus, our understanding of what God asked Jesus to do on earth as well as what He asks of us is misguided and will render us powerless to fulfill our purpose.

Because of a postcrucifixion understanding of Jesus's deity and His position in the Trinity, our understanding of His humanity may be distorted. God asked Him to become *like man*, like you, like me. Jesus had to live, experience, and model everything you and I would experience. For around thirty-three years, He gave up his divine privileges as the Christ to become like us. To expand on the presidential analogy, unlike our presidents who go into foreign lands with great fanfare, media attention, and recognition, Jesus set aside the right even to that glory. He came incognito, as an average citizen. The distinction that He bears in function is that God gave Him a supernatural measure of the Spirit because His purpose supernaturally surpasses what God asks of us. His purpose as the Son of Man was uniquely distinctive, but the power God gave according to His calling is also the power God gives according to our calling. God reveals His calling for us through His Word and His will, and He will fill us with His power to complete that will. Jesus models how we surrender to this empowerment and overcome the temptation that attempts to undermine empowerment.

Jesus's power was God given. Just as God gave Jesus the fullness of the Spirit to fulfill the purpose for His humanity, God also gives us power to fulfill our eternal purpose. Jesus overcame fear and temptation to allow the fullness of this empowerment to accomplish His purpose. Jesus teaches the disciples, and models for us, how we too grow in faith to overcome fear so the fullness of God empowers the fulfillment of our eternal purpose.

There is nothing God asks of us that Jesus did not experience or model as an example of surrender. Hebrews 4:15 says, "For we do not have a High Priest who cannot sympathize with our weaknesses, but was in all points tempted as we are, yet without sin." Because of who God is through Jesus's humanity, Jesus was empowered to surrender and obey. Thus, when the disciples see and know Jesus, they see and know God. They are not witnessing the authority of Christ; they are witnessing the power of God through Jesus (John 14:10-11). Jesus's earthly ministry as the Christ is complete only when He resurrects from the grave and ascends to the Father. Until then, His work was empowered by power given to Him by God and His perfect surrender to be in unity with it. This is a very subtle yet profoundly important distinction. Let us continue to explore its significance.

Read John 8:38, 49–50, 14:13, 17:1–5. Who did Jesus come to glorify—Himself, God, or man?

Read John 12:44–50. In verse 49–50, whose authority is Jesus exercising?

What command did God give Jesus?

What command in John 12:50 does Jesus say God gave?

Jesus possessed and exhibited power and authority on earth, but it was power and authority given to Him by God to complete God's will. He came as an empty vessel to reveal and glorify God. He came to say, speak, and minister the commands of God. Remember what Jesus said to Peter in the garden, "Or do you think that I cannot now *pray to My Father,* and *He will provide Me* with more than twelve legions of angels?" (Matthew 26:53; emphasis added). Jesus could ask His Father for supernatural protection, but the power is of God, not of Jesus. Jesus did not act independently from God. To the extent Jesus received glory, it was because of His obedience in glorifying God. Through acts of obedience and verbal exaltations, Jesus continually gave all glory and praise to God. In Mark 10:18, Jesus says to the rich young ruler, "Why do you call Me good? No one is good but One, that is, God."

Jesus's power and glory as the Son of God would be restored and revealed only after He is resurrected and restored to the right hand of the Father.

Philippians 2:8–11 and Ephesians 1:20–23 teach us about Jesus's power and authority as Lord being restored. What does this Ephesians passage say Jesus must do before that could happen?

Describe the power and position of Christ *after* His resurrection recorded in these verses.

Jesus became obedient—even to the point of death—humbling Himself, laying down His rights as the Son of God, and surrendering His fleshly desires as man so the will and power of God is accomplished through His surrender. Jesus's power is restored when He is seated at the right hand of the Father in heaven. All things are "put under His feet," and He has been made head of the church, which is His body, "the fullness of Him who fills all in all."

To live a life pleasing to God, we should follow Christ's example: God does not call us to do things *for* Him; He calls us to surrender so He can do His will *through* us. God does not expect us to do great things with our personalities and natural gifts alone. Jesus models how we are to set aside those God given natural traits and surrender them to the Spirit at work in us.

Let us again look at what Christ teaches in John 14:10–14 (emphasis added).

> Do you not believe *that I am in the Father, and the Father in Me?* The words that I speak to you *I do not speak on My own authority; but the Father who dwells in Me does the works.* Believe Me that I am in the Father and the Father in Me, or else believe Me for the sake of the works themselves. Most assuredly, I say to you, he who believes in Me, the works that I do he will do also; and greater works than these he will do, because I go to My Father. And whatever you ask in My name, that I will do, that the Father may be glorified in the Son. If you ask anything in My name, I will do it.

John 14:10–11 reveals God is in Jesus. Jesus is in God. Read also John 14:12–20. Christ, through the sending of the Spirit, makes a way for us to be one with God also. "I am in My Father, and you are in Me, and I in you" (v. 20). Nothing that happens to the surrendered Christian happens without going through God first, then the Son, before it reaches us. Once it reaches us, Christ (who is One with God) lives in us through the Spirit. God wraps us in His power. The Trinity is in us to empower us to persevere and overcome. In John 14:18, Jesus says, "I will not leave you orphans." We are not without guidance and protection. As the remaining verses in John 14 reveal, Jesus encourages us not to rebel against God's instructions but to keep them to ensure we remain in His protection and empowerment.

When Jesus through prayer surrendered to God's will, He received power and authority to accomplish it. Jesus in this passage exhorts us to follow His example and gives us the authority to approach God through Him. "Whatever you ask in My name, that I will do so that the Father may be glorified through the Son." By ascending to the Father, Jesus gives the provision of the Holy Spirit. Through this provision, we are joined with God. Through Christ, we have the indwelling power of God to accomplish His will.

Christ models the necessity of laying down our lives, our rights, our desires, our talents, our glory or ego so we do only the desires of our Father. The privileges Christ laid aside are a far greater sacrifice than the human, fleshly desires God asks us to surrender. Not only has Christ demonstrated the need for this surrender, He also sent the Holy Spirit to accomplish it. He teaches us not to respond or react from our nature but to respond and react from the power of God through Christ in the Spirit living in us. Our focus as Christians should not be on living a perfect life like Christ but to allow the power of the perfect life to live through us. It is not about commitment; it is about surrender. We can have commitment by the power of self-determination without complete surrender of the Flesh. But when one surrenders Flesh, the Spirit is revealed in us.

Just as Jesus's nature as deity influenced His purpose and the power God gave, our natural personality and gifts are foundational for our spiritual purpose. We are born with God-designed natural gifts and personalities, our unique nature. However, when we are spiritually born through salvation, we also receive spiritual gifts to fulfill God's purpose. Just as Jesus was given the measure of spiritual power necessary to complete God's will, God also endows us with spiritual gifts and power. Likewise, the measure we are given is unique for our purpose in accordance with His plan. Yet too often in practical living, we fail to recognize this principle and often reverse the order of our natural and spiritual attributes. We fail to model Christ's example of surrender. We fail to recognize our need for God's power more than our own strengths. Since we usually spend more time and energy developing and using our natural gifts, we usually make our spiritual gifts the second priority if we make them a priority at all.

The point made is very subtle, yet it makes a tremendous difference on the successful completion of our purpose and the peace with which we live life. It is the reason we have repeatedly reviewed the differences between Christ's nature and His purpose as the Son of Man.

In the next lesson, we will look at the dangers of our strengths and weaknesses to fuel pride (both arrogance and insecurity). Let us illustrate what the incorrect reversal of our gifts looks like in practice. Suppose certain people are naturally incredible communicators. They are good at networking with people, inquiring and learning more about others. Engaged conversation intensifies their passion for life. When these natural gifts are surrendered to the Spirit, they exemplify the surrendered servant by encouraging others in their faith growth. If, however, they fail to surrender these natural gifts, they easily become divisive skills. The need to know or to gain importance through fact-finding can also fuel gossip, envy, or betrayal of confidences. The hunger for information distorts a sincere and accurate attempt to relate to others, which leads to mistrust. Information gained can fuel prideful and misplaced importance in a body of people.

Suppose these people also have the spiritual gift of prophecy. If the natural gifts described above are not fully surrendered to the Spirit, the revelations or discernments God grants to them are used in ill ways or in a divisive manner. The gifts God gives to guide instead results in condemnation and usually erroneous, not righteous, judgment.

When we seek to understand spiritual gifts and God's purposes for them, we are equipped to understand how to bring our natural gifts into submission to the spiritual. When through the Spirit we communicate revelations with the natural gifts surrendered to God's purpose and not fleshly desires, there is conviction, grace, restoration, and healing.

Reflect on your natural talents and giftedness. How can these God-given gifts become a hindrance to God's power revealed through you? Are they a hindrance? (Take time in prayer for God to reveal understanding of His perspective.)

How is God asking you to surrender these to the Spirit so your spiritual gifts demonstrate the glory of God?

Are you striving to do things *for* God, or are you surrendering to allow His power to do His work *through* you?

Reflect on this final prayer of intercession Christ prayed for you as the Son of Man echoing the will of His Father. It serves as another reminder of the vast love of God that has made a way for you to know Him. It is a reminder that we are to seek Him and His power and not rely on our abilities. It is a powerful exhortation to reflect His glory.

I do not pray for these alone, but also for those who will believe in Me through their word; that they all may be one, as You, Father, are in Me, and I in You; that they also may be one in Us, that the world may believe that You sent Me. And the glory which You gave Me I have given them, that they may be one just as We are one: I in them, and You in Me, that they may be made perfect in one, and that the world may know that You have sent Me, and have loved them as You have loved Me. Father, I desire that they also whom You gave Me may be with Me where I am, that they may behold My glory which You have given Me; for You loved Me before the foundation of the world. O righteous Father! The world has not known You, but I have known You; and these have known that You sent Me. And I have declared to them Your name, and will declare it, that the love with which You loved Me may be in them, and I in them.
—John 17:20–26

To Know God's Fullness

Begin with worship, meditation, and prayer.

> But he denied it, saying, "I neither know nor understand what you are saying." And he went out on the porch, and a rooster crowed. (Mark 14:68)

> "Father, grant me strength to boldly face my fear so I am not blind to denying truth of my circumstances and Your will. Help me honestly accept Your correction and guidance so I may walk in the freedom of knowing and understanding Your will to transform me more into the image of Christ."

Fear hinders embracing God's fullness. Peter's life reveals how it played a key role in hindering his understanding of Christ's revelations (we will also return to this passage later). As we discover, a fear of rejecting Christ and a fear of failing to honor God were obstacles to his willingness to see his true need. His need, as well as ours, is to realize the weaknesses that promote self and hinder godly dependence. Our study reiterates the need to lay aside fear so we can honestly acknowledge the weakness God desires to use for His glory.

Read Jesus's prophesy of Peter's denial in Mark 14:27–31. What is Peter's response?

In pride, Peter boasted to Jesus that he would not stumble, even when all others did. Initially, Peter did not forsake Christ. He attempted to prove this earnest devotion. Humanly speaking, he in fact took a courageous stand in Christ's defense by drawing a sword on soldiers in the garden and cutting off one's ear. Peter did have commitment, but he lacked surrender to understand God's plan, and he lacked surrender to God's power to fulfill God's plan. Listen to Christ's response to Peter in Matthew 26:52–53: "Put your sword in its place, for all who take the sword will perish by the sword. Or do you think that I cannot now pray to My Father, and He will provide Me with more than twelve legions of angels?"

Jesus tells Peter that to take the sword up is certain death because this is not God's plan. There would be no protection acting outside of God's plan. "There is a way that seems right to a man, but it leads to death." Jesus could pray and receive provision, but He will not ask that of God for He knows that is not God's will. Jesus and the Father are One. He is to fulfill the will of the Father. Because of consecrated prayer in Gethsemane, Jesus surrenders to God's plan, not His own protection or comfort. In this interchange, we have an example of surrender and get a glimpse at how our Intercessor takes our actions—or our prayers—and refocuses them on the will of the Father even when we fail to comprehend!

Following, we learn in Matthew 26:56 that "all disciples forsook Him and fled." From our perspective, we realize Peter would in fact follow Christ to a crucifixion death. Therefore, Peter's response to Jesus's prophecy included truth—he would eventually defend Jesus until his own death, but not today. Peter had desire, determination, and resolve to follow Christ, but he lacked understanding that would deepen faith, and he lacked a spiritual empowerment to surrender.

Read Peter's denial in Mark 14:66–72. From verse 71, describe Peter's emotional state and reaction.

Peter boldly proclaimed his devotion to Christ and acted on His behalf only to have his actions rebuked and corrected. Peter seems determined to prove Jesus mistaken about his level of devotion. Imagine his confusion when Jesus corrected him in the garden. He in fact was not at that time fulfilling Jesus's prophesy of denial. Imagine how this confusion and correction probably played a role in fueling the eventual denial. Jesus rebukes what Peter perceives to be faithful, obedient devotion. He witnesses an unjust trial of Jesus by the Jewish Sanhedrin. Jesus is labeled a blasphemer for speaking the truth. Animosity against Him is escalating to an unbelievable level. Imagine the intense fear that must have consumed Peter as he witnessed the Jews' destruction of his Messiah, his future King of the Jews, which he himself now denies just as Jesus prophesied.

When Peter proclaimed his unwavering support, he rejected and denied his own need of Jesus—to Jesus Himself, even before his three public denials. Peter believed he already had everything he needed to remain committed to Jesus. In pride, Peter believed the power to obey was his own strength, gifts, and goodness. Peter reveals how we try to do things *for* God, instead of allowing God to do His will *through* us. This is an incredible lesson to comprehend for our faith growth, for this mind-set is perhaps the greatest obstacle to knowing God more and for living in His presence and power. Self-sufficient pride hindered faith.

Could Peter not accept in his heart that he, as this great defender of Christ, would so easily reject Him publicly? Could he not admit that he needed strength and courage beyond his own ability? Can we? Do we? Jesus previously stated that Peter was the rock that His church would be built upon. Shortly after this spiritual insight, Jesus rebukes Peter as an instrument of Satan. Jesus saw the root of sin in Peter's heart that still needed cleansing to prepare Him for that work. Jesus knew Peter would stumble, but He also interceded for Him so that his faith would not fail during this time of crisis.

Peter and Gideon reveal how the fullness of God is progressively revealed. Peter first committed to follow Jesus as His disciple. Then he surrendered to be a vessel of God's power in ministry. Then he understood the fullness of who the Son of Man truly was as the Christ. Even with these progressive understandings, there was more for Peter to learn. He failed to comprehend how the current crisis (and personal failure) was a catalyst in God's eternal plan. He failed to comprehend the fullness of God's redeeming power to work through him. He failed to comprehend the fullness of the promised coming of the Holy Spirit.

Even when we receive revelations and understanding, fear leads us down a path of denial of God's truth, dishonesty with others and ourselves, and a mistrust of God's purpose. As devoted followers of Christ, we encounter circumstances designed to further reveal the fullness of God. When Flesh is surrendered, we further testify to God's power at work and receive the blessing of more of His presence. For this reason, we cannot know the fullness of God until we are willing to understand, not just recognize, our weaknesses. God desires to transform us into the image of His Son. He wants to prepare us for His purpose. As we honestly acknowledge our weaknesses, we are humbled to surrender them and allow His strength to work through our inadequacies. This humble surrender prepares us to receive the revelation Christ offers to embrace God's fullness. We will comprehend how God's power substantiates and fuels obedience to His Word and His will. Our growth will guide and protect others in our sphere of influence. God will be exalted in even those small moments of life.

Jesus's response to Peter's weakness should be an encouragement. Jesus did not rebuke him during this prophecy; He honestly spoke of things to come and interceded for Peter's faith to remain. (Sound familiar? Remember this same process with Gideon?) Even in the presence of a prideful Peter, Jesus saw him as the rock for His future church. Jesus focused on helping Peter become the person God destined him to become. As already stated, Peter intently focused on following God. However strong his faith had been, God was revealing the need for it to mature. He who began a good work in us is faithful to complete it even when the physical visibilities seem to contradict this truth (Philippians 1:6; Hebrews 13:21).

This was God's intent with Gideon and Peter and it is with you and me. God allows tests of faith and trust to reveal the weaknesses and barriers to surrender.

Peter failed to recognize fully His need to depend on God. From

Peter's perspective, he did not need strength or courage to follow Jesus. He thought he had all he needed to prevent stumbling (he "proved" it in the garden). Peter had a desire for obedience in his heart but failed to recognize the supernatural power needed to fulfill that obedience. These tests were necessary for Peter to recognize this need. When Peter finally realized his pride and weakness, he went out and wept. His faith did not fail. He repented.

What strengths mask your needed dependence on God?

What tests or trials is God allowing in your life to help you realize a greater need of Him, a greater need of surrender to His power, not your own strengths? How are you denying this in your life or trying to disprove it?

In Philippians 3, Paul also exhorts us not to put confidence in our Flesh, our abilities or strengths, our "righteousness." Paul reflects on his own religious qualifications that led to self-reliance, confessing that the only qualifications he needs is the knowledge of Christ and His righteousness coming from faith.

Read Philippians 3:4–15. In verse 6, how does Paul describe his obedience to the law?

In Paul's righteousness of the law as "Saul," what were his actions toward Christians?

From verses 8–11, how would you describe Paul's desire to pursue Christ?

How are Paul's exhortations similar to the lesson learned by Peter discussed above?

Fill in the blanks from verse 10.

"that I may _____ Him and the _____ of His resurrection, and the _____ of His sufferings, being _____ to His death, if, _____, I may attain to the _____ of the dead."

In 2 Corinthians 12:8–10, what does Paul say is the benefit of accepting your weakness?

Too often, like Gideon, like Paul, in fear and uncertainty, we pray for deliverance from our situation or help for a quick remedy that seems never to come. God allows tests, trials, and difficulties to strengthen our dependence on Him. Trials reveal weaknesses, but they are also vehicles for knowing Him on a level we may have been unwilling to realize apart from the difficulty. Trials and tests cause us to see God more fully, which also causes us to see our fellow man differently—through God's eyes. Paul certainly bears witness to this truth as the prior persecutor of Christians. Paul learned to pray that he would have the "fellowship of His sufferings," realizing in his spiritual maturity that suffering provides opportunity to know God more. This understanding empowered Paul to embrace the thorn in his flesh that God allowed to remain.

In the situations you have identified as a source of fear, ask God to identify any weakness He wants you to surrender. Open your heart to embrace what the Spirit reveals.

How has this weakness brought suffering into your life?

How can this weakness cause you to depend more on Christ?

How is this life experience helping you know God more?

John 17 is probably my favorite chapter in that book because it reveals Jesus's prayer prior to His crucifixion. By the time Jesus prays this prayer, the struggle to surrender to His horrible suffering is complete. Nothing about this prayer is self-focused as it is not asking for deliverance from the suffering but instead prayers of intercession!

Let me restate this significance: Jesus's last detailed prayer, prior to the inevitable brutality was a prayer for others! Verses 1–5 express His desire to be restored to His former glory, an expression of hope that empowers surrender to the pending difficulty. In verses 6–19, He tells His Father how He has obediently completed His purpose to equip the disciples. In verses 20–26, He intercedes on behalf of all future believers (you and me) who come to know God, expressing His desire for us to grasp the depth of His love.

Read John 17. In verse 3, how does Jesus describe eternal life?

Jesus's prayer in John 17 reveals the depth of God's love and more important, Jesus's willingness to make it available. When I read this prayer knowing what Jesus is about to endure so we may know Him, I am immersed in the depth of His love and humbled. Jesus wants us to know Him so we may know God!

As preparation for the next lesson, read and meditate on the prayer in John 17 along with the following assurance by Christ to provide a way for knowing Him. We will examine this empowerment more closely in the next section.

> *If you love Me, keep My commandments. And I will pray the Father, and He will give you another Helper, that He may abide with you forever, even the Spirit of truth, whom the world cannot receive, because it neither sees Him nor knows Him; but you know Him, for He dwells with you and will be in you. I will not leave you orphans; I will come to you. A little while longer and the world will see me no more, but you will see Me. Because I live, you will live also.*
> —John 14:15–19

Empowered to Know Him

Begin with worship, meditation, and prayer.

> "Eye has not seen, nor ear heard, nor have entered into the heart of man the things which God has prepared for those who love Him." But God has revealed them to us through His Spirit. For the Spirit searches all things, yes, the deep things of God. (1 Corinthians 2:9–10)

> "Father, help me comprehend the depth of Your desire for me to know You. Grant me the desire to hear what You give the Holy Spirit to reveal about Your specific will for my situation. Help me embrace Your truth, to live it obediently, and to glorify Your name."

Central to knowing God is knowing His will and surrendering to it. Peter and Paul's shortcomings reveal how we can be caught up in service or righteousness "doing things for God" and still fail to comprehend God's will with devastating results to ourselves or others. Continual prayer empowered Jesus to surrender to God's will. For us to know God and His will, we must learn the "deep things of God"; we must learn how fully God empowers us to know Him through Christ and the Spirit. From Gideon and from Jesus's teachings, we identified the Word—will—power—ways of God to make Himself known. Recognizing and receiving His power is the key element to fulfill our purpose. Without His power, we attempt to complete His will in our own strength, which is often inadequate for the calling. As seen with the disciples, without recognizing it as an available provision, we do not look beyond ourselves for the wisdom to fulfill His will. This leaves us full of doubt, fear, and discouragement and lacking the desire to obey.

First Corinthians 2 correlates the gift of the Holy Spirit and wisdom. The Spirit empowers us to know the things of God. As we look at Paul's teachings, reflect on how the societal influences of Paul's day parallel similar influences of our time. This passage is part of a letter written by Paul to the church of Corinth in response to reports of divisions and disputes in the church. This missionary church started by Paul was amid a very pagan, evil society. Corinth was a coastal city in Greece somewhat analogous to a resort city today. However, the level of sin and immorality were great. Reportedly, "Corinth became so notorious for its evil that the term *Korinthiazomai* ('to act like a Corinthian') became a synonym for debauchery and prostitution." Corinthian society had no modern philosophical influences yet remained very much shaped by ancient Greek philosophies and religions. This influence fueled a prideful reliance on the wisdom and intellect of men.[20]

Keeping in mind the influences mentioned above that also infiltrated the church, read 1 Corinthians 2:1–5 and briefly describe the contrast Paul makes between what has empowered him and what has not.

Why does Paul indicate this distinction was important? (v. 5).

Read 1 Corinthians 2:11–12. From verse 11, who is the giver of wisdom and all things spiritually discerned?

Looking back at verse 10, how has the Spirit come to know the deep things of God?

In verse 12, what does Paul give as the reason for the gift of the Spirit?

God gives the Holy Spirit authority to search the knowledge and wisdom of God and make it known in accordance with His will. Verse 12 reiterates that we have a gift greater than human or worldly wisdom because we have knowledge of our almighty God from the Spirit. The Spirit's empowerment enables us to discern the worldly from the spiritual. We learn the deep things of God through the Spirit.

---

[20] Thomas Nelson NKJV Open Bible commentary, 1342.

As we read 1 Corinthians 2:9-13, recall our recent look at John 14 and Jesus's instruction about God being in Jesus and Jesus being in us.

> But as it is written: "Eye has not seen, nor ear heard, nor have entered into the heart of man the things which God has prepared for those who love Him." But God has revealed them to us through His Spirit. For the Spirit searches all things, yes, the deep things of God. For what man knows the things of a man except the spirit of the man which is in him? Even so no one knows the things of God except the Spirit of God. Now we have received, not the spirit of the world, but the Spirit who is from God, that we might know the things that have been freely given to us by God. These things we also speak, not in words which man's wisdom teaches but which the Holy Spirit teaches, comparing spiritual things with spiritual.

We understand God only through revelations of the Spirit that empower us to discern what the natural man cannot—the spiritual realities amid earthly visibilities. The Christian who relies on the same senses of understanding as the natural man will not be able to discern spiritual truths. When we try to discern the spiritual using the strengths of the physical, we gain only man's wisdom. Man's wisdom falls vastly short of God; it is foolishness to Him. The child of God who wants to know His will and how to surrender to it must surrender to the power of the Holy Spirit. This surrender begins with consecrated study of His Word, prayer, worship, fasting when He leads, and obedience where He leads.

In chapter 4, we continue to explore what it means to hear God. This passage above lays the foundation for understanding God's desire to speak, to reveal Himself, and to make a way to commune with Him. At the end of this chapter, we see how the Jewish religious leaders believed they knew God and had insight into His Word and commands. Yet their true knowledge of God and His power resulted in total rejection of the One He sent.

We possibly find ourselves behaving no different from the Jewish leadership when we refuse to allow the Holy Spirit to empower Christian living. If we treat Christ's ministry in the gospels as little more than a history lesson to be revered or as teaching primarily for the New Testament disciples, we limit understanding of God and His ways. This often prevents embracing God's presence and power at work though we bear witness with our physical senses. Though our rejection is not as severe as the Jewish leadership's, we are victims of the same pitfalls as were the disciples, who refused to receive the insight and peace Jesus offers.

When we first became a Christian, the Holy Spirit moved in our lives to reveal the truth of Christ. However, until we responded in faith and received His gift of salvation, that knowledge of Christ as Savior and Lord was not fully ours. This same principle and process is true for our daily relationship with Christ; it is the key to receive the deep things of God. Continual surrender to the Holy Spirit is a must. We can be Christians yet still respond to people, circumstances, and even interpretation of the Word with human wisdom and intellect. We may be aware of God's truth, but for it to shape our circumstances, we must respond in faith to the provision available through the Spirit.

Let me illustrate by returning to the marriage relationship. I have a deep need for my husband to share emotional and spiritual intimacy. I want him to be my best friend as well as my soul mate. I desire romance and spiritual leadership. My husband has a need for me to be his intimate companion sexually and recreationally. Each of these needs very much express some of the basic roles God intended when he created husband and wife.

However, we are also aware of what God's Word says about the curse of man and woman from Genesis 3 and how that affects marriage. When sin entered the world through Adam and Eve's sin, fulfilling our God-designed roles in marriage became impossible on our own. "The woman's desire shall be for her husband but he will rule over her," and the man shall struggle with fear of failure and futility (Genesis 3:16–19). When I express my need or respond to my husband as a natural woman or "carnal" Christian, my needs can become self-centered. I can be consumed with a need for emotional closeness to a degree that actually pushes my husband away. My reactions may fuel his fear of failure, which in turn may increase his desire to pull away from home life and throw himself more into recreational or vocational interests.

Increased efforts at work may give him some sense of accomplishment, which serves to minimize his fear of futility. But his need for an atmosphere of peace and rest at home then becomes another environment of futility and failure because of my dissatisfaction. If he "demands" me to meet his needs, he is ruling over me with his fears. If I respond to him with a lack of respect, my response further fuels his failure and fear of futility. When one or both tries to relate to the other in the Flesh, the intimacy, joy, and peace we desire is short-circuited. Fear and self-protection cause us to remain at the mercy of the curse without the intervening strength of the Spirit.

Ephesians 5:22–33 gives the married couple instructions about how to fulfill our roles as husband and wife to overcome the curse. Generally speaking, husbands are to love, honor, and cherish their wives just as Christ sacrificially loved the church. They are to love their wives more than their own bodies, taking great concern for their welfare. Husbands are to prioritize sacrificial love above their own fears. The love husbands have for their wives is to be a love that perfects her the way Christ perfects the church. This is a wooing love, a persevering love. It is a love that is faithful, trustworthy, and dependable even in the moments when wives are not the most lovable. A husband's provision and care for their wives should supersede efforts to calm his fears in unhealthy ways. Do you see how this instruction minimizes a wife's fear of rejection or defuses an unhealthy desire for her husband?

Wives are to respect their husbands; showing respect is not optional based on their husbands' performance. Wives are to honor and respect their husbands for they are in the process of growth that will perfect the wives as Christ perfects the church. Given the challenge of his calling and given that husbands are themselves maturing, a wife's respect fuels the husband's confidence to rise to this calling. Wives are to honor their husbands as the church honors Christ. Wives are to trust the leadership of their husbands just as the church patiently trusts and follows Christ. This trust of the husband's leadership is the redemptive anecdote for Eve's original tempting of Adam. Do you see how this instruction minimizes a man's fear of futility and failure and provides a place of rest from an otherwise tumultuous struggle to provide for his family? Do you see how this respect defuses a husband's unhealthy ruling over the wife?

This is my summary knowledge of God's truth about marriage but this knowledge alone is insufficient to help me love and respect my husband. I must not turn my back on God, who fills me with His love that dispels fear and calms my emotions. I have to allow faith in God teach me how to love and respond to my husband in tangible ways. I have to seek God's knowledge, wisdom and understanding that empowers my role as an Ephesians 5 wife. I must trust the Spirit to give guidance and creativity in meeting my husband's needs and affirming him. I must allow faith in God to help communicate needs in a way that encourages without intensifying fear. I must allow the Spirit to teach me how to respond to unmet needs or insensitive communications in a Christlike way. I must be sensitive to how the Spirit fuels intercession, surrendering to God's purpose for my husband above my own ideals. With long-suffering and patience, I must realize my husband is learning the same.

Commitment in marriage is vital. A commitment to remain married even through great difficulty keeps the door to intimacy open. Too many marriages today lack commitment. However, for there to be intimacy, contentment, and satisfaction in marriage, there must be more than commitment—there must be surrender to the Spirit.

God may reveal a specific word and will to help your marriage. But where there is disunity, hurt, and unresolved issues, to overcome requires the power of His Spirit to calm emotions and grant peace even before there is restoration. His power will "calm the child before He calms the storm." How He displays His power is specific to you and your situation.

Learn this from the disciples and Gideon: worship and prayer when doubt, fear, frustration, and disappointment are high will sustain and guide us. God is the finisher of faith. His is stretching, growing the faith of each spouse through marital difficulty and transforming each into His image. This process will reveal more of God's fullness and His personal love for your family. He is trustworthy.

Do not allow Satan to use conflict to destroy intimacy. Strength results when conflict resolution takes each spouse to deeper intimacy. This possibility should motivate desire to successfully navigate the relationship through conflict. One cannot navigate conflict in healthy ways before finding personal, emotional restoration and peace through God's love and strength.

We fail because knowledge and intellect alone do not empower us to love. While this is important, a continual response to the Spirit teaches how to love one another, how to be patient, how to forgive, and how to communicate repentance that rebuilds trust. These principles are not often sought by, or taught to, couples. Even when this instruction is available, young love is so great it often blinds the need for it (remember that Peter also thought he had all he needed). Even when the principles are received, it takes a lifetime to get to know your spouse's uniqueness and how to apply the principles through good and bad times. Without this understanding, true love drifts apart often leading to irreconcilable differences.

No one marries with the goal to end the love in divorce. When marrying young, there is much maturing and transforming that takes place in each person. People learn and grow differently and at unique stages. If we are so focused on our own personal growth, we can inadvertently not use that positive change to also grow the relationship. When we follow the teachings of Ephesians 5, God will grow us together as He grows us individually. When we don't follow Ephesians 5, we will suffer in the effects of the curse and feel trapped by an unfulfilling marriage.

Christ, as the Son of Man, lived this example for us on earth. He, victorious in His sacrificial role as the Groom of the church, lives in the Christian husband. He, victorious in loving humanity, in honoring God's purpose for His surrender, in nurturing relationships with respect, lives in each Christian wife. Learning from Christ the unique how-tos is what makes your relationship with Christ—your revelations from His Spirit—immensely personal and intimate. Deepened communion in prayer with Christ improves communication with your spouse and ultimately minimizes conflict. Lean on Him. Depend on Him. Trust Him. Find joy and peace in the wisdom only the Spirit can reveal for your unique situation.

This need of Christ is so great to sustain a marriage that I believe it is the reason marriage is the primary relationship where we should avoid being "unequally yoked" (2 Corinthians 6:14). If a husband and wife each do not have a hunger to grow with God, the success of marriage is handicapped from the beginning. God is a redeeming, intervening God, but the path is made more difficult and less peaceful.

As a husband, how are your strengths or weaknesses perfecting your wife into the person God destined her to become? Which is the greatest catalyst—the strength or the weakness? Are these ruling over her to ease your own fears or, like the surrendered servant, drawing her to seek and embrace *God's* purpose? What fears do you need to surrender to be a vessel of God's love, provision, and security to her?

As a wife, how are you trusting God to work through your husband's strengths and weaknesses to lead your family? How are you—or will you—communicating respect for him? How do you nurture the marital relationship through both good and bad times? Is it a manner that creates an atmosphere of peace, or failure, futility, and discord? What needs, strengths, or weaknesses do you need to surrender to be a vessel of God's love and respect to your husband?

Trusting God's refinement in each other's life empowers us to remain committed to one another and the marriage. But we must also surrender to God as an instrument for the other's refinement. Seek God's power to fuel intimacy so the marriage is not "faithfully trapped" by your commitment. God grants understanding of the wife to her husband. God grants understanding of the husband to his wife. Relationships thrive when each spouse receives God's understanding of how to express love to one another.

Read 1 Corinthians 2: 6–8. To whom does Paul speak the wisdom of God?

In 1 Corinthians 2:14–15, describe how the natural man responds to things of God.

In 1 Corinthians 3:1–3, how does Paul describe the level of spiritual maturity of the Church of Corinth?

These passages reveal the need to guard against living and responding to life's situations as carnal Christians unable to comprehend the deeper ways of God. In 1 Corinthians 3:2 as well as 2:14, Paul indicates that a lack of maturity, wisdom, or spiritual discernment occurs when one does not receive the provision made available. The natural man does not receive because God's wisdom appears to him as foolishness. Babes in Christ cannot fully receive spiritual discernment because of a lack of holiness. Babes in Christ live with envy (ungodly jealousies), strife, and divisions rooted in pride, doubt, and fear.

Read 1 Corinthians 2:16, then fill in the blank.
"...But _____ have the _____ of _____."

Paul reminds the carnal Christians of Corinth and us that Jesus is the way for the things of God, the mind of God, to be revealed. We have a far greater source of wisdom and understanding indwelling us for we have the mind of Christ. We do not become all knowing as Christ, but we receive all we need to know to live obediently as we respond to the Spirit's revelations. Remember, Christ said He would not leave us orphans but would provide the Holy Spirit to reveal the truths of God. In the next two chapters, we will more closely study what Christ reveals.

So many times in the Christian life, we generally know *what* to do but do not always know God's best way for *how* to do His will. The Holy Spirit continually searches the deep things of God to reveal them to us. God does not reveal His will and then leave us helplessly to figure out the details. As revealed throughout the Old Testament, He is a God of details. God helped Gideon understand the what before he could receive the how. Satan attempted to use doubt and fear to circumvent Gideon's understanding and obedience. At the end of this study, we more closely study the how. Both of these revelations came when Gideon surrendered fear and worshipped God. God did not leave Gideon alone with generalities but revealed a detailed plan. God wants us to know His will and His ways because He wants us to know Him! The more we know Him, the easier it is to discern His ways for completing His will. The deeper we search to understand the details of His specific will for us, the more intimately we know Him.

In Romans 12:1–2, Paul gives an exhortation to mature in Christ and live sacrificial and holy lives. He admonishes us to put aside the things of the world to live in the will of God. Paul says we may "prove" what is that "good and acceptable and perfect will of God." We go beyond knowledge of it; we are empowered to prove it through our obedience to Him.

> I beseech you therefore, brethren, by the mercies of God, that you present your bodies a living sacrifice, holy, acceptable to God, which is your reasonable service, And do not be conformed to this world, but be transformed by

the renewing of your mind, that you may prove what is that good an acceptable and perfect will of God.

What things of the world (an attitude, comfort zone, fear, person, habits, religious tradition, material things, envy, gossip, and strife) may be distracting you from receiving the wisdom of God for your circumstance? If you have received the what of God's will but not the how, follow Gideon and Jesus's example of prayer and worship until God reveals the how.

Pray God increases sensitivity to His specific will through the power of the Holy Spirit. Surrender to understand the deeper truths God wants to reveal. Allow the Spirit to reveal what perhaps is keeping you a babe in Christ or a carnal Christian. Allow Him to begin renewing your mind or replacing your fearful, self-focused thoughts—any worldly thoughts limited by physical visibilities—with His truth. Rejoice that God has a divine plan and purpose for the circumstances causing fear. His ways may seem foolish to the world and sometimes to other Christians, but receive His path in faith and trust He has prepared a provision of understanding for those who love Him!

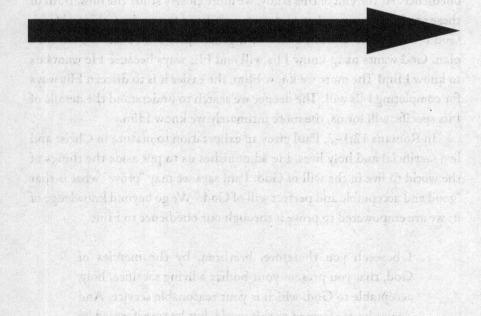

Growing Faith 3

Knowing God versus Knowing Religion

In this section, we return to Mark for a bird's-eye view of Jesus's preparation of the disciples. We left off at the end of Mark 6, where Jesus was healing multitudes. As we focus on Mark 7, we learn of Jesus's ministry at the end of the chapter.

> Then He commanded them that they should tell no one; but the more He commanded them, the more widely they proclaimed it. And they were astonished beyond measure, saying, "He has done all things well. He makes both the deaf to hear and the mute to speak." (Mark 7:36–37)

The witness of Jesus that spread despite his command of secrecy is that "He has done all things well; He makes both the deaf to hear and the mute to speak." However, as Mark 7 begins, we find this is not everyone's opinion. Once again, Jesus is in the middle of debate and controversy with the Jewish leadership. As we study the core of this controversy, the miracles Jesus performs take on a more significant meaning in our faith growth.

Beginning in Mark 7, the Pharisees question the disciples' violation of Jewish tradition.

> Then the Pharisees and some of the scribes came together to Him, having come from Jerusalem. Now when they saw some of His disciples eat bread with defiled, that is, with unwashed hands, they found fault. For the Pharisees and all the Jews do not eat unless they wash their hands in a special way, holding the traditions of the elders. When they come from the market place, they do not eat unless they wash. And there are many other things which they have received and hold like the washings of cups, pitchers, copper vessels, and couches. Then the Pharisees and scribes asked Him, "why do Your disciples not walk according to

the tradition of the elders, but eat bread with unwashed hands?" (Mark 7:1–5)

Notice from verses 1–2 that *they* came to Jesus (from Jerusalem) and immediately found fault with Him and the disciples. The religious ones were not seeking to gain further understanding or knowledge of God's power but to take issue with God's servants. I once read, "A religious spirit is one that glorifies what God has done in the past but fails to acknowledge what He is doing in the present." The Jews adamantly refuse to acknowledge (and aggressively attack) what Jesus is doing. However, the disciples also failed to recognize the power of God initially. In verses 6–9, Jesus responds to the criticism by exposing the Pharisees' hypocrisy of placing more emphasis on the traditions of men than obedience to God's commandments.

> This people honors Me with their lips, but their heart is far from Me. And in vain they worship Me, teaching as doctrines the commandments of men. For laying aside the commandments of God, you hold the tradition of men-the washing of pitchers and cups, and many other such things you do. And He said to them, All too well you reject the commandment of God, that you may keep your tradition.

Jesus reveals to the leadership and the crowds how little they know God. They have placed greater importance on religious tradition and practices than on obedience to God's command. Satan slowly and very subtly caused the Jewish leadership to substitute commitment to religious tradition for absolute surrender to the love of God. Jesus gives one example of this substitution in verses 10–13 and concludes by saying, "and many such things you do."

Jesus continues in Mark 7:14–16 speaking now to the multitudes: "Hear Me, everyone, and understand: There is nothing that enters a man from outside which can defile him; but the things which come out of him, those are the things that defile a man. If anyone has ears to hear, let him hear!"

Away from the crowds, the disciples ask Jesus the meaning of this parable. Jesus is disturbed by the hypocrisy of the Jews and appears frustrated by the disciples' persistent unbelief that prohibits understanding.

The purpose of this interchange with the Jews and the disciples is to focus on the conduct of the heart. Jesus reveals their need to be cleansed of sin. In accordance with God's Law, the priests atone for their sin. Therefore, they do not perceive a need for any other cleansing. Their tradition of sacrifice may restore them in a right relationship with God, but it does not empower holy living. Sin corrupted the religious elite. They seek to enforce the law and religious tradition but are themselves powerless to accomplish inner change and obedient living. Through this discussion, Jesus calls attention to the need for this level of cleansing. While the Jews recognize a need of atonement for sin, they do not express a need for power to overcome the temptation to sin. They are so locked into religious tradition that they miss God's desire for relationship and the resulting empowerment over sin.

We may recognize our need for Christ in regards to salvation, but too often, we try to live the Christian life in our own strength apart from Christ. We can be disciplined Christians living good, moral lives but miss Christ's presence and power. Or perhaps we are carnal Christians casually confessing sin but failing to seek how to resist the temptations to sin. The purpose of spiritual routines or disciplines is to provide the opportunity for intimacy. When we focus more on the traditions of church attendance, service, good behavior, prayer, and study because we are supposed to, we are missing the blessing and power of comprehending the fullness of Christ in our midst.

Intimacy with God empowers us to surrender to His Spirit, but fear restricts surrender. Our culture and accomplishments as a nation fuel self-empowerment that sends the message that control is strength and surrender is weakness. Fear fuels insecurity. The human response to insecurity is to control people or situations to gain the security we crave. True strength, security, and confidence come in surrender to God. Surrender is a state of mind; it is a constant communication with God, seeking through silent prayer His understanding, guidance, purpose, and direction. It is a continual openness of one's mind and heart to glean the spiritual realities through the earthly visibilities.

Fear fuels mistrust of God. What if God asks me to surrender something I don't want to? This fear fuels self-protection, which in the long term will not result in peace. Even if you find happiness in the short term, is it at the expense of others? Is that godly love? Satan is highly successful at using fear to thwart surrender. We have the tendency to equate surrender with perpetual suffering or depravation, to think one ensures the other. This is often his message to us: "If you surrender to God, you will have to go live in the wilderness like John the Baptist ... If you surrender to God, you will live a life of suffering ... If you surrender to God, your dreams will never come true ... If you surrender to God, you will have to give up what brings you happiness." We too often surrender to this fear, not faith, leaving us to muddle through life relying on our own strength. Like God's people in Judges 6, we are oppressed by a vast enemy of fear retreating into caves to exist and missing the very abundant life we dream about. Because we fear presumed suffering, we suffer needlessly. The only thing we have to fear is fear.

"Delight yourselves in the Lord and He shall give you the desire of your heart" (Psalm 37:4). The Jews partially committed themselves to God. They surrendered their hearts to religious traditions. At that point in their ministry, the disciples committed themselves to God but surrendered only to service. Their dedication to service is no small sacrifice, but complete heart surrender is lacking because of fear, pride, and unbelief. We saw this through Peter's denial of Christ. They and we often unintentionally withhold total surrender because of fear, unbelief, and hidden pride.

Christ teaches what is required for absolute surrender in Luke 9:23: "If anyone desires to come after Me, let him deny himself, and take up his cross daily, and follow Me." This does not speak merely of commitment to service or Christian discipline but of absolute surrender to follow the path of Christ daily. This is not a one-time act of commitment or periodic atonement but of continually setting aside Flesh ... daily. God understands how we allow fear to resist taking up this cross. For this reason, Christ reminds us that man must first "deny himself." Christ, the One who had every right as deity to cling to His power, set aside the glory and rights to come to earth as the Son of Man in obedience to God's power. The strength of this surrender, the power of this surrender, is the resurrected Life living in the heart of each Christian. He did not leave us orphans but sent His Spirit. We will not and cannot surrender selflessly without embracing His Spirit. Self-protection is the opposite of surrender. It is an obstacle to spiritual discernment.

Earlier, I spoke of a time in ministry when a prayer study came under attack by Christian leadership. The revelation given to prepare me was in part the song "Embrace the Cross." Over a three-day period, in many ways God reinforced the message of the song, which says this in part, "Embrace the life that comes from dying. Come trace the steps the Savior walked for you. An empty tomb concludes Golgotha's sorrow. Endure it 'til tomorrow, your cross of suffering."

The death I was to experience was not a physical death. At the time, it seemed like the death of many things desired—ministry, reputation, leadership, friendships. Those have not died; they have just refocused. A more abundant life has come from it. This study has come from it. Another part of the song says, "receive from Jesus fountains of compassion, only He can fashion, our hearts to move as His." My longing since childhood was to know God. How can I know God fully without also knowing the fellowship of His sufferings, the pain of rejection from fellow believers? True, these are paths we do not desire or dream about. These are paths we fear. These are paths we do not willingly choose. Just as the Spirit led Jesus into the wilderness for prayer and great temptations and tests to prepare Him for ministry (Luke 4), He will sometimes lead us there as well. We have hope since this is a path Jesus walked victoriously.

At the end of Luke 4, it says that Jesus returned in the power of the Spirit to begin His ministry. What did prayer, fasting, and resisting temptation glean? Empowerment! Preparation and equipping for ministry! The resurrection coming from difficulty results in cleansing more of our Flesh life. It lessens fear of embracing the cross daily denying ourselves, our perceptions of our purpose, and our limited dreams. His ways are higher than our ways. Spiritual realities supersede physical visibilities.

Surrender is a willingness to embrace the cross with a faith focused on eternal purposes. Jesus's surrender was the result of continual prayer. Prayer empowered surrender. Surrender empowered trust and obedience. Jesus had faith in the promises of God through His resurrection. Jesus understood God's plan. Jesus heard God. In all points, He was tempted as we are. The temptation was intense. The battle to resist resulted in sweating great drops of blood. Yet the Spirit working in Him was victorious. This power lives in us.

Service for the kingdom of God is a by-product of obedient surrender to fulfill God's purpose. We often try to serve without surrender, and that results in frustration, disappointment, or exhaustion. Without surrender, we are serving in the Flesh and thus may not be fully serving God's way. "There is a way that seems right to a man, but it is the way of death." We may fear the path of surrender, but it leads to the life of God's goodness and peace.

God has not put us on earth for the establishment of religiosity but for the deepening of relationship with Him. The disciples believed Jesus would establish an earthly throne. This belief fueled great diligence in their service to Him. Unbelief, doubt, and fear have been just as evident. We know God matures faith to surrender to the point of death eventually. This seed is in them. However, that faith is young. They are in the early stages of its growth, when it is the most vulnerable.

This is how Christ responds to the disciples' request for understanding.

> "Are you thus without understanding also? Do you not perceive that whatever enters a man from outside cannot defile him, because it does not enter his heart but his stomach, and is eliminated, thus purifying all foods?" And He said, "What comes out of a man, that defiles a man. For from within, out of the heart of men, proceed evil thoughts, adulteries, fornications, murders, thefts, covetousness, wickedness, deceit, licentiousness, an evil eye, blasphemy, pride, foolishness. All these evil things come from within and defile a man." (Mark 7:18–23).

Notice how Jesus states the unclean taken into the body is used for good: it is waste that purifies all foods. This reiterates the truth in Romans 8:28: "For we know that all things work together for good to those who love God and are called according to His purpose." For the Christian, God uses what is unclean, the unrighteousness we allow in and out of our life, to bring His good when we surrender to His way. However, a failure to surrender the iniquity in our hearts, our self-promoting desires and self-will, leads to self-destruction contrary to the best intentions. It is not so much about commitment to God … it is about surrender of self.

Later in His ministry, Christ chastises the Jews for prioritizing religious tradition above intimacy with God.

Then Jesus spoke to the multitudes and to His disciples, saying: "The scribes and the Pharisees sit in Moses' seat. Therefore whatever they tell you to observe, that observe and do, but do not do according to their works; for they say, and do not do. For they bind heavy burdens, hard to bear, and lay them on men's shoulders; but they themselves will not move them with one of their fingers. But all their works they do to be seen by men …

"Woe to you, scribes and Pharisees, hypocrites! For you cleanse the outside of the cup and dish, but inside they are full of extortion and self-indulgence. Blind Pharisee, first cleanse the inside of the cup and dish, that the outside of them may be clean also. "Woe to you, scribes and Pharisees, hypocrites! For you are like whitewashed tombs which indeed appear beautiful outwardly, but inside are full of dead men's bones and all uncleanness. Even so you also outwardly appear righteous to men, but inside you are full of hypocrisy and lawlessness. "Woe to you, scribes and Pharisees, hypocrites! Because you build the tombs of the prophets and adorn the monuments of the righteous, and say, 'If we had lived in the days of our fathers, we would not have been partakers with them in the blood of the prophets.' "Therefore you are witnesses against yourselves that you are sons of those who murdered the prophets. Fill up, then, the measure of your fathers' guilt. Serpents, brood of vipers! How can you escape the condemnation of hell? Therefore, indeed, I send you prophets, wise men, and scribes: some of them you will kill and crucify, and some of them you will scourge in your synagogues and persecute from city to city, that on you may come all the righteous blood shed on the earth, from the blood of righteous Abel to the blood of Zechariah, son of Berechiah, whom you murdered between the temple and the altar. Assuredly, I say to you, all these things will come upon this generation. "O Jerusalem, Jerusalem, the one who kills the prophets and stones those who are sent to her! How often I wanted to gather your children together, as a hen gathers her chicks under her wings, but you were not willing! See! Your house is left to you desolate; for I say to you, you shall see Me no more till you say, 'Blessed is He who comes in the name of the LORD!'" (Matthew 23:1–5, 25–39 NKJV)

Jesus is not content with outward righteous appearances. He is concerned with inner cleansing and glory. Failing to acknowledge unbelief, doubt, and fear leaves Christians vulnerable to live lives with the outward appearance of goodness. When we choose to live in the Flesh, we remain babes in Christ unable to discern deep truths of God. We may embrace the truth of God's Word but be ill equipped to recognize how He moves in our midst—a failure to understand and receive His power. Like the disciples, the seed of faith is in us, but we must recognize the need for it to grow and how even religious devotion may obscure partnership with its growth.

Growth does not happen through commitment to religion or religious practices as the Pharisees reveal. Growth happens through surrender to the Holy Spirit. Ministries, churches, and Christian leaders today fall into the same pit as the Jews did. We must guard against Satan, the roaring lion who seeks to undermine holy preaching and teaching not paralleled with holy living. We must guard against kingdom growth when it is burdensome and results in divisiveness in the church and when its efforts do more to undermine than strengthen marriages and families. We must further beware of ministries and churches promoting an image or reputation above humbly glorifying God.

Guard against those who seek to build reputations and expansive or impressive ministries to advance a vocation. It is common to see expansive church ministries where its members are doing great works for God. Yet in those same churches, divorce, sexual immorality, burnout, gossip, envy, and strife are very prevalent among leaders. It is not about commitment to perform; it is about surrender to relate to the God living within who then ministers through that relationship.

While obedient living is successful only by the Holy Spirit's power, chasing manifestations of the Spirit can become a form of religious practice that minimizes the priority of intimacy with God. This is another subtle but potentially harmful distraction from knowing God. To focus on an experience, we may come to rely so heavily on a constant closeness to God that we paralyze or limit our trust of Him without this spiritual experience. When the need for the experience interferes with other relationships or service to God, our priorities may be misplaced. God anoints and reveals His power as He chooses. We should not allow an absence of His special anointing hinder other aspects of our lives. A constant spiritual experience can fuel pride and self-righteousness among fellow believers. It can subtly put an unhealthy importance on self to the neglect of the needs of the church body.

Sometimes, Christ may send us ahead of Him seemingly alone on a turbulent sea to strengthen faith. It does not mean He is not close or unaware of the situation. He may be teaching a deeper reliance on God's fullness than the routine or experience we have grown to depend on in perhaps unhealthy ways.

Remember how Christ in Matthew 7:21–23 warns those who do work in His name yet know not the will of His Father or Him.

> Not everyone who says to Me, "Lord, Lord," shall enter the kingdom of heaven, but he who does the will of My Father in heaven. Many will say to Me in that day, "Lord, Lord, have we not prophesied in Your name, cast out demons in Your name, and done many wonders in Your name?" And then I will declare to them, "I never knew you; depart from Me, you who practice lawlessness!"

Those who do the will of the Father proclaim Jesus as Lord and know Christ in an intimate, daily fellowship. The religiosity of the Jews warns us not to live with commitment to religion, not to build the kingdom of God for selfish gain or exaltation. Notice that Christ does not say that those he does not know will not build the kingdom. Demons are cast out. Wonders are done. God uses all things for His glory, which includes the evil, the ungodly, and even religious piety and practice. We can be drawn away and enticed by pride, arrogance, and self-fulfillment just as easily as the Jewish elites were. It was also a near temptation of the disciples as they fought over who was nearest and dearest to Christ. However, with pride, arrogance, and self-promotion, there can be no lasting peace.

To know the will of the Father, we must live in daily surrender to His Spirit, who reveals and teaches all things. Given this focus on the cleansed heart as the key to knowing God, the healings that follow are a further demonstration of these truths. Watch how Jesus's power illuminates this word and God's will for inner cleansing.

> From there He arose and went to the region of Tyre and Sidon. And He entered a house and wanted no one to know it, but He could not be hidden. For a woman whose young daughter had an unclean spirit heard about Him, and she came and fell at His feet. The woman was a Greek, a Syro-Phoenician by birth, and she kept asking Him to cast the demon out of her daughter. But Jesus said to her, "Let the children be filled first, for it is not good to take the children's bread and throw it to the little dogs." And she answered and said to Him, "Yes, Lord, yet even the little dogs under the table eat from the children's crumbs." Then He said to her, "For this saying go your way; the demon has gone out of your daughter." And when she had come to her house, she found the demon gone out, and her daughter lying on the bed. (Mark 7:24–30 NKJV)

Jesus's primary purpose at this point in His ministry was to minister to the Jews. Conversion of the Gentiles would be the ministry of His followers after His resurrection. Jewish tradition precluded association and interaction with Gentiles. The Pharisees did not deem them worthy of God's favor as they were not born into God's chosen nation. Jesus refers to this in His response. In verse 27, the "children" refer to Israel, "bread" refers to the Word of God, and "little dogs" references Gentiles. Jesus states to the mother and those present that His first obligation and ministry of healing is for God's chosen nation, the children of Israel.

The woman's response indicated a heart that understood the far-reaching favor and blessings of God; she fervently sought even the slightest touch of Christ's power. She approached Jesus openly and humbly and sought His favor confidently. By her faithful response, she (the Gentile) revealed greater understanding than did the Pharisees, the spiritual leaders of God's chosen nation. She did not allow religious tradition and societal protocol to hinder provision from Jesus. She demonstrated a heart that desired to know God. She recognized the power that could cleanse from within. This Gentile, "ungodly" woman discerned more than the religious leaders did. Commitment to religious tradition could not (and did not) help her child, but a humble surrender to the power of God was more than sufficient to cleanse and restore.

Meditate on the healing requested. What was the specific need? Notice how Christ cleansed the demon-possessed soul (inner man) of this Gentile. The Jews were concerned with outward cleansing of their own religious people. They tested Jesus's understanding of their traditions for outward cleansing of the Jews by hand washing. Yet Jesus demonstrated His power to cleanse on a greater level once again. He cleansed the "filth" from within the heart of a Gentile. He spiritually cleansed the "inside of the cup," which truly defiles a man. In this entire interchange, He reminded them of their need to be cleansed of sin within their hearts, and He laid the foundation for understanding His power to accomplish that cleansing. Through this miracle, He proclaimed, "I am your salvation. I have the power to cleanse the unclean inside of you, that which defiles from within."

The healing that follows in Mark 7 also bears some relation to Jesus's previous discourse with the Pharisees and the disciples. He heals the deaf and mute man, "opening his ears, and loosing his tongue." Jesus restores physical senses and increases spiritual sensitivity. He miraculously illustrates His teachings to save the unbelievers (the Jews) as well as equip the believers (the disciples).

The disciples are still learning how to use their spiritual senses to gain understanding. They are still learning how to see and hear on a spiritual level through the revelation of the physical. A deaf and mute man begs Jesus to put His hand on him. As we see how Jesus heals, keep in mind these recent discussions regarding the importance of outward cleansing emphasized by the Jews. Notice how Jesus physically touches the man to heal. Consider how this method might have further outraged the Pharisees. Meditate on the significance of this miracle performed in the presence of the disciples with a command of silence. Consider how Jesus equips His disciples with this further mocking of Jewish tradition.

> And He [Jesus] took him aside from the multitude, and put His fingers in his ears, and He spat and touched his tongue. Then, looking up to heaven, He sighed and said to him, "Ephphatha," that is, "Be opened." Immediately his ears were opened, and the impediment of his tongue was loosed, and he spoke plainly. Then He commanded them that they should tell no one; but the more He commanded them, the more widely they proclaimed it. (Mark 7:33–36)

With the aid of what appears to most as outwardly unclean, Jesus brings miraculous healing power. Everything in Jesus is power. What some would label unclean, Jesus uses to heal supernaturally. Jesus has the power to physically open the ears and release the tongues of the deaf and mute just as He has the power to spiritually open the ears to understanding and loose the tongue to widely proclaim His power.

Do you grasp Jesus's progressive equipping? Do you see how again He verbally instructs and then demonstrates His power in a way that validates and illuminates His teachings? Do you see how important it is to seek the spiritual realities present in the midst of physical visibilities? Certainly, God's power is evident through the miracle, but His character, nature, and purpose are revealed to those with ears to hear and eyes to see spiritually. His power validates His Word and will. Do you see how God's Word again reveals His ways for growing faith? Do you see how Jesus further expounds His nature as God's Son and His power? Jesus continues to lay the foundation to know Him as the One who heals and cleanses the heart. Do you see how Jesus continues to make a way for all to understand who He is? While we know Jesus as our salvation, there is more He longs to reveal about His will and ways for fulfilling our purpose in God's kingdom.

These patterns revealed in God's Word can be revealed in our lives. He wants us to hear Him. He wants us to know Him as the One with the power to cleanse the filth within. Unlike the Pharisees, Jesus has come not to draw attention to Himself but to reveal the kingdom of God. Therefore, if anyone has an ear, let him hear!

Then He said to them, "These are the words which I spoke to you while I was still with you, that all things must be fulfilled which were written in the Law of Moses and the Prophets and the Psalms concerning Me." And He opened their understanding, that they might comprehend the Scriptures.
—Luke 24:44–45

Chapter 4

The Power of Hearing God

He who has an ear, let him hear what the Spirit says to the churches.
—Revelation 3:6

"Can You Hear Me Now?"

Begin with worship, meditation, and prayer.

> I still have many things to say to you, but you cannot bear them now. However, when He, the Spirit of truth, has come, He will guide you into all truth; for whatever He hears He will speak; and He will tell you of things to come. He will glorify Me, for He will take of what is Mine and declare it to you. All things that the Father has are Mine. Therefore, I said that He will take of Mine and declare it to you. (John 16:12–15)

> "Lord, open my ears to hear You. Heavenly Father, I also pray You will develop all my spiritual senses so I may be fully aware of Your presence at work in my life."

"Can you hear me now" is the advertising slogan made famous by a cell phone service. It is also applicable to Jesus's interactions with the disciples.

Their fear, misunderstanding of God's ways, and unbelief interfered with their ability to hear and understand Jesus. Spiritual signals need strengthening for Jesus to be heard and understood. Jesus states that He has many things to say but they cannot yet bear to hear them. We can imagine how difficult it would be to accept horrific details of His coming physical abuse and crucifixion as well as their own persecution. They are not yet prepared to comprehend the entirety of God's plan. But Jesus lays a foundation for future understanding.

Jesus reveals God's perfect will, yet His ways seem too contradictory. Beyond accepting Jesus's physical brutalities, the disciples had to face realities far different from their expectations. He will be King, and these are His closest, most-devoted servants. However, they expect Jesus's kingship to be established on earth. James and John selfishly ask Jesus to grant them seats beside His throne (see Mark 10:35–45). Jesus responds, "You do not know what you ask." They did not fully understand how far reaching His kingdom would be let alone the sacrifices required for establishing it. Notice how they imply through this request that as King glory would be for Jesus, not God directly, contrary to our prior discussion of Jesus's purpose. And they want to share in that glory.

Jesus grooms them for expanding His *spiritual* kingdom. Their purpose exceeds what they presently comprehend and see physically. Jesus will leave their presence, but He will send the Holy Spirit to "guide them into all truth." He does not leave them without a way to gain understanding necessary to fulfill His purpose (John 14:18). This passage reveals that God progressively grants understanding. Jesus reveals only the portion of God's will they are able to comprehend, but even this level of revelation is often misunderstood by most of the disciples. However, He also gives assurance that a deeper understanding will soon be known.

Jesus's promise to send the Holy Spirit to reveal God's purposes is not limited to the disciples. At the conclusion of chapter 3, we studied how Paul also reiterated God's desire to impart deep truths to the early church. John 8:47 says, "He who is of God hears God's Words." Throughout God's Word, we learn how He desires to reveal Himself to His people.

Let us look at just a few of these scriptures.

> Call to me and I will answer you, and show you great and mighty things which you do not know. (Jeremiah 33:3)

Surely the Lord our God has shown us His glory and His greatness, and we have heard His voice from the midst of the fire. We have seen this day that God speaks with man; yet he still lives. (Deuteronomy 5:24)

He made known His ways to Moses, His acts to the children of Israel. (Psalm 103:7)

Hear, O Lord, when I cry with my voice! Have mercy also upon me, and answer me. When You said, "Seek My face," my heart said to You, "Your face, Lord, I will seek." (Psalm 27:7–8)

All the people saw the pillar of cloud standing at the tabernacle door, and all the people rose up and worshipped, each man in his tent door. So the Lord spoke to Moses face to face, as a man speaks to a friend. (Exodus 33:10–11a)

He who has My commandments and keeps them, it is he who loves Me. And he who loves Me will be loved by My Father, and I will love him and manifest Myself to Him. (John 14:21)

No longer do I call you servants, for a servant does not know what his master is doing; but I have called you friends, for all things that I heard from My Father I have made known to you. (John 15:15)

Faith comes by hearing, and hearing by the Word of God. (Romans 10:17)

Today, if you will hear His voice: Do not harden your hearts, as in the rebellion, and as in the day of trial in the wilderness. (Psalm 95:7–8; Hebrews 3:7–8)

In the first three chapters of Revelation, Jesus repeatedly warns the church, "He who has an ear, let him hear what the Spirit says to the churches."

God's ways emphasize His desire to reveal Himself so we fulfill His purpose. He has an eternal plan, and we all have roles to play in completing that plan. What we now fear, the difficulty we now face, and the faith to overcome are factors in that plan. Like the disciples, we may not see any correlation between present difficulty and God's plans. Yet Jesus makes a way for us to hear and understand all we need to know.

In the Old Testament, God spoke audibly through dreams and visions amid the fire, thunder, and lightning and even in a still, small voice. In the New Testament as well as today, God speaks through the power of the Holy Spirit in us. In this chapter, we will look more at conforming our minds to Christ so we posture ourselves to "hear" the Holy Spirit. We will also look at opportunities from the Old and New Testament God gave to increase our spiritual listening senses. As we discuss these, glean how this process prepares us to hear Him as well.

God reveals His will to His people. To hear Him, we must realize He desires to speak, and we must avail ourselves to Him. A heart hardened to God by fear, doubt, and unbelief will not comprehend what He reveals. Disobedience and failing to walk in holiness weakens our ability to hear. To strengthen the signal and to lessen the static interference, we must honestly assess the importance of trust, obedience, and holiness in our relationship with God. Jesus sent His Spirit to empower us. The Spirit lives within. If faith comes by hearing and if God desires to grow faith, doesn't it stand to reason that He will speak and provide the strength to surrender in trust, to obey, and to pursue holiness?

We need to understand who the Holy Spirit is. We need to understand His purpose. Read this illustration of the Trinity to help frame our understanding of how God makes Himself known.

> Imagine that I have the most wonderful thoughts and that if you only knew my thoughts, your life would be changed forever. What would I have to do? I would have to translate my thoughts into words. Then my words would be the exact representation of my thoughts. My words would be my thoughts in a different form. The essence of my words and my thoughts would be exactly the same, but my thought would now be in the form of my words.

It will take one more element for me to be able to get my thoughts across to you. It will take the breath of my mouth rushing over my vocal chords to form the voice that makes my words heard. My voice takes my word and makes them known to you.

Do you see how I speak *from* my thoughts, *through* my words, *by* my voice? Three actions in one.

Let my thoughts represent the Father, whose thoughts toward you are wonderful and precious according to Psalm 139:17–18; whose thoughts are higher than your thoughts according to Isaiah 55:8–9. The Father translated Himself into Word. Just as my thoughts are my words, so the Word was God. God the Father and God the Son are the same essence in different forms. The Thought was now in the form of the Word (John 1:1–2, 14). The Word is the exact representation of the Thought (Hebrews 1:3). The Word makes the Thought known (John 1:18).

Now the third element: the Spirit. The Greek word *pneuma* translated "Spirit" is also translated "breath." The Breath of God's Mouth is a picture of the Holy Spirit throughout the Old Testament. Just as my breath creates the voice that delivers my words, the Spirit takes Jesus and makes Him known to you. (John 16:15). *From* the Father, *through* the Son, *by* the Spirit.[21]

Do you believe God speaks to you? Are you willing to hear Him? Do you make time to listen? In 1 Samuel 3, we read about Samuel's instruction for hearing God. God was speaking to Samuel, yet Samuel initially did not know who was speaking. The priest Eli taught Samuel how to posture himself to hear God.

---

[21] Jennifer Kennedy Dean, *Live a Praying Life: Open Your Life to God's power and Provision* (Birmingham, AL: New Hope, 2003), 114.

Read 1 Samuel 3:1–21. When the Lord called Samuel in verse 4, how did Samuel respond?

Samuel availed himself to the voice, but who did he believe it to be?

How does verse 1 describe Samuel's relationship to the Lord?

How does verse 7 describe Samuel's knowledge of the Lord?

Reread verses 1, 19–21 and summarize your understanding of God's desire to make His Word known to His people.

What response did Eli give Samuel to say to the Lord?

What was Samuel's initial response to God's Word?

Samuel had to learn how to hear and serve God. Samuel had been trained to serve Eli the priest. Now, God would equip Samuel for more than serving humanity. Samuel was sensitive to the instruction of the priest, but this was merely training to make him sensitive to God. It took Eli three times to realize what was happening to Samuel. Despite Eli's shortcomings, he did not try to circumvent or interfere with God's desire to commune with Samuel personally. Instead, he properly and wisely taught Samuel how to surrender and avail himself to God's voice. Samuel moves beyond service for God to understand his need and God's desire for intimate communion. "Samuel grew and the Lord was with him," states verse 19. Because of this intimacy, God "let none of his words fall to the ground."

Samuel's early life is another illustration of commitment to service absent intimate communion with God. When Samuel was a toddler, his mother gave him to the Lord for priestly service to live with Eli and train in the temple. While Samuel spent his early years serving in a religious environment, he did not understand how to listen and talk intimately to God.

This parallels our Christian growth. When we first become a Christian, we are eager to serve and please God. Too often, we find ourselves so busy serving God that we do not realize our need to listen to Him. We may find ourselves busy yet powerless to live obediently. With the advent of modern technologies, our resources even in the church have become so vast that a dependence on the personal direction of the Holy Spirit is not always apparent or necessary to function; someone else may have done that for us. In our efforts to streamline and facilitate service, we may unintentionally underemphasize the need to spend time listening for God's specific direction individually. What we have intended as a corporate aid may cause us to overlook the need for personal reliance on the Holy Spirit.

We, like Samuel, must realize God is speaking and how He personally speaks to each of us.[22] We too must learn how to respond to Him. God speaks because He wants us to know Him. He speaks to reveal understanding of His will and ways. Though we may not audibly hear God, we can hear Him in our fully surrendered hearts and minds. The remainder of this chapter helps identify obstacles to hearing and teaches how we posture our inner, spiritual self to hear. We want to expand our ability to distinguish the voice of God from our own desires or that of the deceiver.

We hear God by the Word revealed to us by the Holy Spirit, and we have access to His Word from many sources.

- the written Word or Bible—personal reading, sermons, studies, testimonies, and godly counsel—2 Timothy 3:16–17
- worship—adoration as well as psalms, hymns, and spiritual songs—Colossians 3:15–16

---

[22] The scope of this study includes the foundational manner and ways in which God fellowships with us today. There are denominational differences in interpretations and understandings regarding manners in which God presently reveals Himself that are outside the scope of this study. This study is not an attempt to refute or clarify these discussions. Our focus is to fuel the desire and to facilitate a deeper need for a more intimate fellowship with God.

- meditation—a Christ-focused reflection on the Word—Romans 12:1–2
- prayer—the leading of the Spirit to focus our spirits and will in verbal response to the Word and will of God—Jeremiah 29:11–13
- faithful obedience—postures us to "hear" and "see" His power—Hebrews 11:8–19, 11:32–35 (and Judges 6, the example of Gideon we have studied)

All these are avenues God uses to reveal Himself and His will. However, it is important to realize we can be doing some or all of the above and still ignore or fail to recognize the voice of God. Just like Samuel, our role as obedient servants can overpower His voice calling us into deeper communion and intimacy. Our obedient service is necessary training. However, He lives in us and wants us to know and hear Him.

All the above should be a priority with God but not mechanically or legalistically because it is the "right" thing to do. These should be more than activities to check off our daily spiritual to-do list. God designed these as avenues or entry points to reveal His presence and power. In 1 Samuel 3:10, we learn that God came and stood and called "as at other times." How many times had the fullness of God been in Samuel's presence but he failed to recognize it? How many times do we fail to recognize Him? We can be encouraged by the faithfulness of God to persevere as we learn to listen.

Learning to listen is a process. Hearing God occurs through a progressive walk with Him. As we obediently engage in Christian services, we should do so with the expectation of meeting God. I love the old hymn, "In the Garden," which gives witness to the blessing of intimacy with God.

> I come to the garden alone, while the dew is still on the roses.
> And the voice I hear falling on mine ear, the Son of God discloses.
> And He walks with me, and He talks with me,
> and He tells me I am His own.
> And the joy we share as we tarry there, none other has ever known.

The holy, sovereign, God of heaven and earth wants to meet and talk privately with you and me!

Quiet times with God focus our attention to hear and recognize Him throughout the day. God speaks to our hearts while we worship, pray, read His Word, and meditate on His Word and as we fellowship with other Christians. Each of these activities is an entry point that allows God to focus our cluttered minds and self-centered hearts on Him. When God begins to gain our focus, we find that He speaks to us any time of the day or night and during any type of routine activity and daily responsibility. Like Samuel, we progressively learn to posture ourselves to hear God. This understanding encourages perseverance as we learn to hear, and it should fuel worship of the God who patiently waits on us to recognize Him in our midst.

Our goal in responding to God is to remain focused on Him and His purposes. He can speak to us throughout our day regardless of our activities if we expectantly ask Him to. John 16:24 says, "Until now you have asked nothing in My name. Ask, and you will receive, that your joy may be full." Jesus lived on earth in continual communication with His Father. He modeled how God empowers us to live. If we desire God to make Himself known to us, we must ask and avail ourselves to Him.

Pray, "Speak, Father, for your servant hears." Be prepared to listen and respond in the way He leads even if it also causes us to fear.

Can you recall times when you know you have "heard" from God—a time He gave very specific direction, instructions, comfort, or rebuke?

How did He make it known to you (i.e., reading His Word, a Bible study, sermon, testimony, worship, prayer, meditation, other Christians, etc.)?

Did you immediately recognize it was Him, or did understanding come later?

Reflect on a significant or specific time God spoke to you. Ask Him to reveal a bigger picture of His character through that situation. What

new aspect of Him was He revealing, or what of His goodness was He reminding you of?

When God revealed Himself, did it increase your fear of the situation or of Him? Why or why not?

When God spoke, was your *faith* in Him increased? If so, describe how.

If you had a revelation or instruction from God that caused you to be more fearful of the situation, ask God to reveal any unbelief or lack of understanding. Ask Him to open the eyes of your heart and focus you to hear His truth, will, and way for that situation. Allow Him to give you a heart sensitive to what the Spirit is saying.

If you are not sure you have heard Him, ask Him to make Himself known to you in a personal way and be sensitive to how He gently, quietly, and often very subtly responds. Realize that recognition He has spoken may not always be instantaneous.

Journal what He eventually reveals.

> *Therefore Eli said to Samuel, "Go, lie down; and it shall be, if He calls you, that you must say, 'Speak, Lord for Your servant hears.'" So Samuel went and lay down in his place. Then the Lord came and stood and called as at other times, "Samuel! Samuel!" And Samuel answered, "Speak, for Your servant hears."*
> —1 Samuel 3:9–10

Set Your Mind to Hear

Begin with worship, meditation, and prayer.

> The Sovereign Lord has given me an instructed tongue, to know the word that sustains the weary. He wakens me morning by morning, wakens my ear to listen like one being taught. The Sovereign Lord has opened my ears, and I have not been rebellious; I have not drawn back. (Isaiah 50:4–5)

> "Holy Father, help me listen clearly to You. Reveal the areas of my life that strive against hearing You. Fill me with Your peace so my mind is focused on You."

As with the whole of Christian life, God is our source of strength and power even for responding to Him. He speaks; He gives us a desire to listen; He postures us to listen. Yet as we witnessed with Samuel, God is always the gentleman who draws us close to Him without demanding our response though He deeply desires it. In the above passage, Isaiah states that he "has not drawn back," he has not rebelliously backed away from God's invitation. We still have responsibility to respond to Him. We must listen and surrender to His instruction.

In 2 Timothy 1:7, we read, "For God has not given us a spirit of fear, but of power, love and a sound mind." Note the distinction made in this verse—the source of destructive fear is not God, who is the giver of power, love, and a sound mind. If Satan is successful at capturing our thought life, he is successful at undermining every aspect of our being. For this reason, 1 Corinthians 2:16 tells us Christians have the mind of Christ.

I think the order of God's gifts in this verse is providential. God gives power, love, and a sound mind. God-given power enhances our capacity to love and know love, which stabilizes our minds on healthy, not fearful, thoughts. By attacking our thought life, Satan attempts to undermine God's gift of a sound mind. If we succumb to his attacks, fearful thoughts will cause us to minimize or disregard God's love for us. We will question God's leading and faithfulness. As we are separated mentally from the awareness of His love for us, His power in us diminishes until we regain mental focus. The following reveals this contrast between God's provision and Satan's attacks.

SATAN ATTACKS	GOD PROVIDES
SOUND MIND	POWER
LOVE	LOVE
POWER	SOUND MIND

Satan attacks the soundness of our minds and thus reduces our awareness of God's love and power. Because of this attack, Romans 8:38–39 offers a truth to remind ourselves and Satan of.

> For I am persuaded that neither death nor life, nor angels nor principalities nor powers, nor things present nor things to come, nor height nor depth, nor any other created thing, shall be able to separate us from the love of God which is in Christ Jesus our Lord.

No created thing or power can separate us from the love of God! Because Satan is persistent with his attacks, we will continue to look at ways to overcome them with a mind rightly focused on God's truth, power, and love.

Jesus modeled how to live with power, love, and a sound mind. Jesus remained in constant, prayerful communication with His Father. God was the source of Jesus's power, love, and focus through prayer. But once again, the disciples reveal the typical way we often respond to God's invitation to pray and listen that opens the door for destructive fear to clutter our minds from understanding spiritual realities through the physical visibilities.

As Jesus prepares to face the brutality of the cross, He goes away to pray, to surrender His thoughts and temptations, to focus on God's love for humanity and to receive the empowerment to be a vessel for that love. Once again, Jesus takes only the three closest disciples with Him.

Read Mark 14:32–42. How many times did Jesus leave His seclusion of prayer to urge the disciples to pray?

From verses 34–36 and Matthew 26:36–39, describe the difficulty of Jesus's struggle.

What seemed to be the source of the disciples' hindrance to pray? (vv. 38, 40).

From Mark 14:38, why does Jesus say they need to pray?

Jesus is facing His most difficult challenge as the Son of Man and the required obedience to fulfill God's will. He has taken those closest to Him for support and for their own empowerment and understanding. Unlike Samuel, the disciples did not realize the importance of listening and responding to God. While Jesus reveals this is to fulfill prophecy (Mark 14:27), it illustrates the contrast between a proper response and blind confusion to God's invitation to speak with Him. The disciples would learn from this experience in Gethsemane, but the present situation leaves them fearful, unprepared, and ill equipped for the difficulty at hand. Jesus promised to bring to their remembrance all these happenings, and through revelations of the Holy Spirit, the understanding granted would mature their faith and prepare them for the future (John 16).

A lack of understanding, physical fatigue, and the familiarity or routine of Jesus's presence hinders the disciples' response to Jesus's admonition to pray. Christ acknowledges their spirit is willing but their flesh is weak. Nevertheless, He urges them to pray.

As Jesus's successful time of prayer demonstrates, hearing God empowers one to face even the most extreme difficulty and remain focused on God's purposes so clearly that it changes the world. God wants us to hear Him because He knows the blessing it provides and the impact it has in our sphere of influence.

We have discussed how the Holy Spirit dwells in us to reveal the deep things of God. We have also discussed the danger of a hardened heart to prevent understanding of His Word. Even when hearts are receptive to God, we must also surrender our thought life to Him as Jesus modeled in Gethsemane.

Read Romans 12:1–2. Why must our minds be renewed?

Read Isaiah 26:3–4. What happens to the one whose mind is set on God?

Read 2 Corinthians 10:3–7. What must be brought into captivity and obedience to Christ?

Our every thought must be aligned with God. How did Christ endure the difficulties of His persecution and crucifixion? In the Garden of Gethsemane, He struggled to bring every thought captive in obedience to God's will. The intensity of this struggle resulted in his sweating great drops of blood until He was able to proclaim, "Nevertheless, not My will, but Thine be done."

In John 14:16–21, Jesus explains the power God grants His followers through His victory. Take a moment to comprehend this marvelous truth: Jesus's victorious power over sin, over thoughts, lives in us through the power of the Holy Spirit!

We are not left alone in this world to accomplish God's will in our strength or in our Flesh (John 14:18). In 2 Corinthians 10:3, Paul states that we may walk in the Flesh (meaning we struggle to surrender our desires to the Spirit) yet we do not war according to the Flesh. God gives the power to conquer a thought life that is not holy and not in accordance with an obedient surrender to Him. Because Jesus sent the Holy Spirit to indwell us and to reveal the deep things of God, we have the power to surrender thought. This surrender and resulting empowerment gives us the mind of Christ (1 Corinthians 2:16).

Christ is the head of the church body, symbolic of a physical being. The mind is the primary source for the senses of sight, hearing, taste, touch, and smell, which prompt automatic responses by the body. The brain directs the functions of the body; the body does not strive against it. Likewise, Christ is the Head of the church body. Christ, filled with the Holy Spirit, is the spiritual core that influences the church body. We are to have the mind of Christ. Relying on Christ's mind, the church body, by design, is compelled to respond to Its leading. Christ's mind is our source for spiritually seeing, hearing, and tasting the truths God reveals. Power. Love. Sound Mind.

Let us look at scripture warning of the dangers when the mind is not focused on God.

> And do not seek what you should eat or what you should drink, nor have an anxious mind (anxious mind). (Luke 12:29)

> Be of the same mind toward one another. Do not set your mind on high things, but associate with the humble. Do not be wise in your own opinion (prideful or self-righteous mind). (Romans 12:16)

> For consider Him who endured such hostility from sinners against Himself, lest you become weary and discouraged in your souls [mind] (discouraged, despairing mind). (Hebrews 12:3)

> Now, brethren, concerning the coming of our Lord Jesus Christ and our gathering together to Him, we ask you, not to be soon shaken in mind or troubled, either by spirit or by word or by letter (deceived mind). (2 Thessalonians 2:1–2)

> But I see another law in my members, warring against the law of my mind, and bringing me into captivity to the law of sin which is in my members. ... For those who live according to the flesh set their minds on the things of the flesh, but those who live according to the Spirit, the things of the Spirit. For to be carnally minded is death, but to

be spiritually minded is life and peace ... So then, those who are in the flesh cannot please God (flesh-focused or rebellious mind). (Romans 7:23, 8:5–6, 8)

Anxiousness, self-righteousness, deceitfulness, despair, rebelliousness, and shortsightedness cause us to fear what is or what may be. This mental focus leads us to respond in ways contrary to God's will. Appearances consume us to the point of tuning out God's perspective.

In chapter 1, we discussed the power of presumption to fuel fear. In this passage in 2 Corinthians 10:7, Paul asks, "Do you look at things according to the outward appearance?" Even when our spirit is willing to hear and respond to God, our flesh may be weak. Unrecognized and unconfessed fear, doubt, and pride clutters our minds with presumptions that distort recognition of truth; this is what happened to the disciples in the Garden of Gethsemane.

In 2 Corinthians 10:5, we are told to cast down arguments, strongholds (such as fear and doubt), and every "high thing" (or prideful thing) that opposes the knowledge of God. Looking at situations from outward appearances fuels presumptuous thought. Listen to what God's Word says about human wisdom.

> For it is written, "I will destroy the wisdom of the wise, and bring to nothing the understanding of the prudent." Where is the wise? Where is the scribe? Where is the disputer of this age? Has not God made foolish the wisdom of this world? ... Because the foolishness of God is wiser than men, and the weakness of God is stronger than men ... For you see your calling, brethren, that not many wise according to the flesh, not many mighty, not many noble, are called. But God has chosen the foolish things of the world to put to shame the wise, and God has chosen the weak things of the world to put to shame the things which are mighty. (1 Corinthians 1:19–20, 25–27)

When my husband and I began to experience marital issues, Satan attacked my thought life in many ways. Satan greatly fueled fear and doubt to undermine strength and the hope to persevere through difficult times. I knew we were not experiencing God's plan for marital intimacy, and questioned whether we would attain it again. Though I knew of marital difficulties experienced by other Christians, I began to believe that our struggles were singularly unique. Those who know my husband and me from youth and our courtship may be surprised by this confession. This is how destructive Satan's schemes can be. I convinced myself I was a failure as a wife and as a child of God. My thoughts were hopeless, full of despair, full of failure, and most of all full of fear for the future. Satan's attacks on my thoughts separated me from my husband's love, and God's love. Hurt built a barrier that blocked the love my husband did show (a "wall of protection"), as my thought life made me focus on what was missing more than what was provided. Guilt separated me from God's love, which would have eased fear and fueled peace to refocus my thoughts on truth.

Thankfully, God brought resources and people in our marriage to refocus trust in Him. This gave the ability to persevere as He began giving His wisdom for marriage. Since that time, I have heard many accounts of similar false truths plaguing the minds of Christians. When the divorce rate among professing Christians is almost as high as non-Christians, it is evident that our minds are focused on the appearances of circumstances rather than on God's wisdom, power, and love.

From the evidence of physical visibilities, it can appear love is forever gone from the marriage. Constant conflict, neglect, and an unwillingness to care anymore are very convincing evidences that the marriage is lost. All intimacy, unity, and attraction may be absent from the relationship, but all may not be lost as we will continue to explore. God has wisdom for restoring marriages, renewing intimacy, and rebuilding the family.

The world (and too many Christians) will say, "Divorce and move on with your life. God wants you to be happy." Too often, divorce only exchanges one set of problems for another especially when children are involved. Divorce when it is in disobedience to God's Word is not the straight and narrow path to happiness. With God, there is hope for restoration. God forgives and heals, but the consequences of divorce too often are painful obstacles to peace and rest.

If you are praying about divorce, be careful that you are praying with a pure and holy heart and in accordance with God's Word regarding it. In the midst of hopelessness and despair, it is easy to pray for our desires instead of

God's will. Where marriage difficulty and tension exists, our minds have a natural tendency to focus on the hurt and recurring problems. Our prayers must first surrender this clouded mind before clear discernment of God's will is understood.

A desire for happiness should not supersede obedience to the marital covenant. Seek God's wisdom. Do not be deceived by the outward appearances or your and your spouse's feelings and desires. Begin by setting your mind on God's will, and then surrender as a vessel of intercession for your spouse. God gives the desire and strength to fulfill His will, power, and love to endure and overcome. Stop focusing on what you can see and feel and listen to God. Call to Him, and He will show you great and mighty things *you do not know* that will strengthen your marriage. Things may not change immediately, but feelings and emotions are cyclical. Give God time to work in your hearts and marriage. Honoring Him through your marriage is the most lasting path to contentment.

God opens ears to hear His will, but do not fear what He says. Do not be rebellious; do not draw back out of fear, doubt, or pride. When we come to the point of saying, "I can't live like this anymore," we are at the prime place where God can reveal His power for His glory. He never intended us to find bliss apart from Him. Allow Him to transform your desires for marriage into His desires. He knows we need Him and is saying, "Dear one, I have a better way; allow Me to show you how to have the intimacy and fulfillment you so desperately need."

Follow the example of Christ and persevere in prayer until you can honestly confess, "Not my will but thine be done." Take up your cross daily and follow Him. Resurrection in the Spirit follows crucifixion of the Flesh. Taking up the cross is not a sentence for perpetual pain but the way to receive God's power for deliverance and restoration!

Refer to the scriptures above warning us about the dangers of a mind not focused on God.

Using this as a guide only, ask God to reveal the below thoughts existing now in your mind that diminish His peace and rest. Beside the applicable items, respond to what God reveals. Respond to thoughts or burdens not listed. Express any anger, frustration, or disappointment to God.

Allow Him to help you honestly face where you are and then lead you where He desires you to be!

Anxiousness—I am anxious about:

Self-Righteousness—I struggle with pride and/or a spiritual ego in the following ways/areas:

Discouragement—The following drains hope, frustrates, and depresses me:

Deceit—I struggle to acknowledge to myself or others when I hurt or cause hurt. I struggle to be transparent about my weakness for fear of rejection. I need to please people, so I tell them what they want to hear whether it is true or not:

Self-focused thoughts:

Rebellious thoughts:

Read Philippians 4:6–7, Isaiah 26:3, Romans 8:6, Psalm 85:8, and 1 Corinthians 7:10–15. What is the blessing from God repeatedly promised in these verses to a mind surrendered to the Spirit of God?

Prayer of Restoration and Trust
"Father, thank You for revealing thoughts that are preventing me from hearing You. Thank You for the power to tear down and remove the obstacles to the truth I need. Thank You for replacing falsehoods with Your wisdom and understanding. Thank You for filling my mind with Your peace."

Focused to Hear

Begin with worship, meditation, and prayer.

> Cast all your cares upon Him, for He cares for you. Be sober, be vigilant, because your adversary the devil walks about like a roaring lion, seeking whom he may devour. Resist him steadfast in your faith, knowing that the same sufferings are experienced by your brotherhood in the world. But may the God of all grace, who called us to His eternal glory by Christ Jesus, after you have suffered a while, perfect establish strengthen, and settle you. (1 Peter 5:7–10)

> "Lord, help me comprehend the need to release my burdens to You. Allow me to realize the harm of holding onto burdens and how this clouds my ability to listen to Your still, small voice. Teach me how to release the focus of my mind so I may walk in Your grace."

The first verse of the passage above is familiar to most. We often sing worship choruses encouraging us to cast our cares on Him. But this passage goes beyond exhorting us to relinquish worry by also teaching why we need to cast all of our cares and promising hope when we do.

A cluttered mind prevents hearing God clearly. Gideon did not receive specific instructions regarding God's will until God filled his heart with peace. The disciples did not resume teaching about Christ until the fear from Christ's death was replaced by peace and empowerment from the Holy Spirit even though their physical safety was not secure.

As burdens are cast, God settles hearts even when the burden remains. When filled with His peace, hearts are focused to hear Him reveal specifics.

Surrendering burdens is often difficult. The trouble is usually not in recognizing the need to cast them but in doing so. Too often, we are overwhelmed especially when others imply that casting means we forget them completely or that they are immediately resolved when cast. At times, I feel as if I have boomerang burdens. I cast them, but they keep coming back with no apparent hope or victory in sight.

When I reflect on the word *cast*, I think of casting with a rod and reel. Without taking this parallel to extremes, there are many similarities between casting with a rod and reel and casting our burdens. The rod remains in your hand when the line is cast into the water. One of the benefits of cast fishing is the ability to put the lure where you want it to go, a move you could not accomplish with pole fishing (where the line and lure remain very near and still). The lure attracts a prized fish, the next meal, or something to throw (give) back. The cast must be successful for the line and lure to secure a fish. Without a proper cast, the only thing caught is yourself or those unfortunates nearby!

There is never a guarantee we will catch fish on our first casts. Likewise, when we cast burdens to God, the burden is often not removed immediately. Just as the rod remains in our hands, the source of the burden may remain, but with the cast, we are now distanced from the hook.

The lure Satan uses to cause pain now may secure God's goodness but only when cast away. Skillful casts will result in a catch; poor casts may result in the lure getting snagged on someone or something. The properly cast hook no longer is a source of harm to the one who holds the rod, the burden. Instead, it is an instrument to receive a blessing. As we cast the burden into the Living Water (into His sea of mercy and grace), we express desire to receive God's purpose. It is an act of faith and trust that God eventually uses the burden to bring something good (Romans 8:28).

Cast your burdens and catch a blessing! The fish, the prize we seek to receive, should not necessarily be the removal of the burden but God's purpose for it. It may be a blessing testifying to God's greatness. It may be nourishment to survive until there is future need. It may also be a gracious gift of God that by sharing it with others we give it back to Him.

Sometimes, problems are resolved with the initial cast. However, before God's blessing is received, there may be a need to repeatedly cast and for much silent, patient waiting. But the prospect of receiving the blessing should motivate perseverance. The need for repeated casting is not due to the inadequacy or inability of God but perhaps to Satan's persistency to torment us until we catch God's provision. We must continue to resist him; we must wait for the right conditions to catch the blessing. In the interim, we improve our casting skills and develop an appreciation for the experience. The wait deepens intimacy with God.

The difficulty in casting can also come from a refusal to learn how to fish. Without a rod and reel, without a burden, there is no equipment for casting. With no line to cast, no lure, there is great difficulty—for most of us, great impossibility—in catching fish. Likewise, we would not experience the joy of knowing God more fully without perceiving our need to cast our burdens. Without a burden to cast, we would fail to receive and learn some aspect of His goodness.

Writing this study has been difficult at times because Satan wants us to remain captive to fear. God continues reinforcing these truths in my own life. About halfway through writing this study, I became very discouraged about its pace and progress. Fear of failure and rejection began to consume my thoughts and cloud my focus on God's promises. Satan tormented me with fear, but God gave me the opportunity to live what I taught. However, that knowledge did not alleviate my frustration. I cast this burden to the Lord, but no immediate peace came. Satan, the roaring lion, continued his attacks until God's blessing finally came one night at prayer meeting.

Reading from Psalm 34, the pastor spoke about fear and our need to cry out to God (cast our burdens) to allow a fear of the Lord to overcome fear of everything else. There were many things he spoke of that only God and my husband knew I battled then. God revealed His intimate love for me through the pastor's words. God was speaking to me through familiar truths and reminded me of His love, concern, and presence in the middle of my need in a personal way. The mere topic and words spoken by the pastor at that time revealed to me that God had heard my cry.

Nothing about my situation changed. This study was not miraculously completed. Yet in casting my burden, my fears, I found God's intimate comfort and peace. Had I not faced such a great need, the pastor's message still would have been true but not have had such a personal impact. Without that burden of fear and without casting it to God, I would not have seen and heard God's goodness on such a personal level. By voicing my need—a need God already knew I had—I heard His response through the pastor's words. The peace God gave me empowered me to trust Him and persevere. I was renewed and strengthened to fight the doubts and fears Satan used to divert my focus on God's purpose.

What we fail to cast consumes our thoughts and emotions and clouds our view of what God accomplishes through turmoil. This diminishes sensitivity to hear God. It prevents viewing circumstances or others' actions through God's truth. We have already learned of God's faithfulness that causes us to listen. However, refusal to relinquish burdens traps them in the recorder of our minds to be replayed; that leaves us easy prey to the prowling lion. From the passage above, we should be warned, reassured, and motivated to stand against the darkness we face. Satan caused Eve and Adam to *willingly* trade God's goodness for lives of pain and sin.

God may or may not allow immediate deliverance, but He gives hope, comfort, and peace when we are willing to cry out and listen to Him. I heard a pastor once give an admonishment for surrendering anger that hurt and disappointment bring: "Don't nurse it, don't rehearse it. Disburse it to God, and let God reverse it!" Moreover, I would add, "purse" His deliverance. Patiently wait for and receive with joy the provision God eventually grants when burdens are given to him.

Beloved of God, you may have begun to question where the power of God is for your circumstance. Dear one, God is working *in* your circumstance. There is a purpose for your difficulty, and there is an end of it. Allow God to minister to you personally through the remainder of this study. Persevere in prayer. Pray for understanding His purposes and what He wants you to learn about Him. What He completes in the spiritual realm is for your good and His glory.

Casting cares means to:

- confess our frustrations and needs to God honestly,
- confess our dependence on Him to empower or deliver us, and
- wait hopefully and obediently for His provision.

Confess the Frustration

We completed an exercise to cleanse our minds of the natural tendencies in response to fear. This is the necessary first step in learning how to cast cares upon Jesus. We must be honest with Him and ourselves about our emotions and destructive thoughts. Voicing them in prayer helps us realize how difficulty affects our minds and emotions. We must learn to do this immediately as these defeating thoughts and feelings arise. The longer we wait to cast, the more time Satan intensifies their hold over our hearts as we mentally rehash, repeat, and meditate on them. The longer we hold onto them, the more they become the only "truth" we believe.

We can confess our frustrations to God quietly and quickly even in the middle of other activities. Gideon's people lived in caves partly due to a refusal to confess their rebellion and rely on God. The Angel of the Lord came to Gideon as he worked; that allowed him to vent (cast) his cares and gradually opened his understanding in the process.

Depend on God

After confessing cares, depend on God's power. Unless we realize we need God, we may find ourselves like the disciples informing God how to solve our problems. Scripture studied reveals how He wants to reveal Himself and His power in a way we may not expect or initially understand. He wants to demonstrate the truth of His Word. We may experience some level of peace after confession and be tempted with this newfound strength to run out and try to fix the situation. Be careful to discern that this is God's wisdom, not Satan's distraction. Do not settle for what is good; be resolved to wait for God's best. Test it with prayer, fasting, and His Word before acting. God's ways will glorify Him, not us. In fishing, too quickly reeling in the line can cause us to lose a fish. Our actions should align with His will *and* His ways.

Wait Hopefully

Confessing dependence on Him postures us to wait patiently for Him to act on our behalf. This is the final active step to cast our cares. During this time, we may have to repeat the first two steps to insure against Satan's further attacks. Satan wants us to feel hopeless, discouraged, and defeated. If we become exhausted dealing with these boomerang burdens, try intercession. Begin to intercede on behalf of people experiencing similar difficulties. It is not necessary we know who they are or their specific needs; just trust they are somewhere in the fellowship of believers. When we allow the Holy Spirit to mold prayers of intercession through our needs, Satan flees. Satan eventually ends his attacks when we use them as fuel for power praying! We *will* find rest from burdens. God is working perhaps unseen and unnoticed to perfect, establish, and strengthen us.

Peter subtly implies in verse 9 that we may not always be successful in fully relinquishing our burdens to the Lord. Consequently, our cluttered minds and battered emotions are vulnerable to Satan's attacks. When this happens, we are exhorted to "resist Him." Peter encourages us in the midst of fear and worry to be strong in faith and trust God to deliver us through this difficulty. He reminds us that suffering, our difficulty, is not unique but is common to others.

How do you describe the tone of verse 10?

What characteristic does Peter use to describe God?

What does Peter remind us we are called to?

How would you paraphrase Peter's reference to suffering in verse 10?

This verse gives us great hope for victory. Peter reminds us that God is a God of grace. God's mercy withholds punishment we deserve for sin. God extends grace when He grants blessing we do not deserve. While calling attention to the difficulty we will experience, Peter reminds us that God, who grants blessings we do not deserve, is using our situation for His glory, and our blessing! Peter reminds us that by casting our cares on Him and resisting the devil, we become vessels of this grace and mercy to others.

Peter also reminds us we are called to Christ's glory. Life's difficulties have purposes beyond our present needs and desires; sometimes, they are eternal, not immediate purposes. Just as the disciples struggled to understand God's bigger plan, fear overwhelms our thoughts and leaves us blind to Christ's understanding and revelations that grow faith. While we are focused on the here and now, God is working on kingdom plans that affect us today but also have far-reaching results beyond what we can fathom.

Peter continues in verse 10 by saying, "after you have suffered a while." Peter does not say "when" or "if" we suffer but "after" we suffer. Even if it is limited to the mental struggle between faith and fear, God's will or our own, God's goodness or Satan's deceit, suffering will happen. When it occurs, remain focused in faith for God only allows it for a while. Praise God, the difficulties we face will end! Nevertheless, God has a timetable for deliverance; God's timing ensures it glorifies Him and draws us closer to Him when we surrender to Him in its midst (remember Gideon's example). Let us not delay His provision by a prideful or stubborn refusal to trust and surrender to Him!

Finally, Peter concludes verse 10 with "the rest of the story." He reveals the blessings and goodness of God that come through casting burdens. The God of all grace "perfects, establishes, strengthens, and settles" us. Reflect on the grace God gives: He perfects you! He establishes you! He strengthens you! And mostly, He settles you!

Dear Beloved, allow the comfort and hope of this verse cradle you in the loving arms of your heavenly Father. God wants to perfect your life in ways far greater than any you have desired or imagined for yourself. Ephesians 1:20–21 says,

> Now, to Him who is able to do exceedingly abundantly above all that we ask or think, according to the power that works in us, to Him be glory in the church by Christ Jesus throughout all ages, world without end. Amen.

Journal what God speaks to your heart regarding His desire to perfect you.

God wants to establish you! Your physical and emotional security comes from the root of faith God has established and wants to grow in you. 2 Thessalonians 3:3 says, "But the Lord is faithful, who will establish you and guard you from the evil one."

Journal what God speaks to your heart regarding His desire to establish you.

God wants to strengthen you. The power to fight the battle of faith over fear comes through the knowledge of God's deep love for you. His Word tells you that perfect love casts out fear. He knows your situation. He has the love you seek. His love is power and strength. Meditate on Paul's prayer in Ephesians 3:16–19, allowing the Spirit to pray it for you. He prays that Christ would

> grant you, according to the riches of His glory, to be strengthened with might through His Spirit in the inner man, that Christ may dwell in your hearts through faith, that you, being rooted and grounded in love, may be able to comprehend with all the saints what is the width and length and depth and height—to know the love of Christ which passes knowledge, that you may be filled with all the fullness of God.

Journal what God speaks to your heart regarding His desire to strengthen you.

The final promise of God is to "settle" us. God grants us the peace that passes all understanding. He gives us rest.

> Come to me all you who labor and are heavy laden, and I will give you rest. Take My yoke upon you and learn from Me, for I am gentle and lowly in heart, and you will find rest for your souls. For My yoke is easy and My burden is light. (Matthew 11:28–30)

Learn from Christ how to respond to your situation and find His rest. He says He will be gentle and lowly in heart in his guidance of you. Allow His example to mold your response to others who cause you to worry and fear. Describe your willingness to surrender to this process God uses to settle you.

> *I sought the Lord and He heard me, and delivered me from all my fears. They looked to Him and were radiant, and their faces were not ashamed. This poor man cried out, and the Lord heard him, and saved him out of all his troubles. The angel of the Lord encamps all around those who fear Him, and delivers them.*
> —Psalm 34:4–7

Hearing Empowers Holiness

Begin with worship, meditation, and prayer.

> I will hear what God the Lord will speak, for He will speak peace to His people and to His saints; but let them not turn back to folly, surely His salvation is near to those who fear Him, that glory may dwell in our land. (Psalm 85:8–9)

> "Lord, I recognize my need to be holy. I need Your strength to surrender to the cross and to crucify my old patterns for living. I confess this process causes me to fear. Strengthen my faith to hear and trust You, amen."

God is holy; He is free of all moral evil. He is moral perfection. To commune in fellowship with Him requires purity in heart and a blameless, holy nature. Because we have all sinned and fallen short of the glory of God, only Christ living within us provides the way to fellowship with Him. However, God calls us to holiness as well. What we have learned of God and His Word reveals that we can trust Him to provide a path for holiness.

Holiness for us means to be set apart, separated from the world and self and remaining pure for God's purpose. It means our continual surrender to the power of the Holy Spirit living in us. The Spirit fuels the continual dying to sin and self so God can reveal His glory through us. Ephesians 4:17–24 admonishes us to hear God and be taught by Him so we live holy lives. This passage also reiterates the importance of renewing our minds and aligning them with the will of God.

> This I say, therefore, and testify in the Lord, that you should no longer walk as the rest of the Gentiles walk, in the futility of their mind, having their understanding darkened, being alienated from the life of God, because of the ignorance that is in them, because of the hardening of their heart; who, being past feeling, have given themselves over to licentiousness, to work all uncleanness with greediness. But you have not so learned Christ, if indeed you have heard Him and have been taught by Him, as the truth is in Jesus: that you put off, concerning your former conduct, the old man which grows corrupt according to the deceitful lusts, and be renewed in the spirit of your mind, and that you put on the new man which was created according to God, in righteousness and true holiness.

This passage reiterates that a mind not focused on God blinds understanding, causes ignorance that alienates the Spirit, and hardens hearts. However, when we hear God, we are empowered to put away the old man, be renewed in our minds, and put on the new man. (This passage reiterates the pattern of hearing the Word, following His will, and receiving His power). Holiness is revealed when we focus on God's purposes, not our own agenda or desires. In 1 Peter 1:13–15, Peter says,

> Therefore gird up the loins of your mind, be sober, and rest your hope fully upon the grace that is to be brought to you at the revelation of Jesus Christ; as obedient children, not conforming yourselves to the former lusts, as in your ignorance; but as He who called you is holy, you also be holy in all your conduct, because it is written, "Be holy, for I am holy."

Holiness occurs through humble surrender to hear God. These passages emphasize the need to set aside ignorance and the desires of the Flesh or self to be holy. In this passage, Peter admonishes us to "gird up the loins of your mind." He exhorts us to gather and restrain any hindrance or distraction in our minds so we are set on holiness. This instruction teaches a mental posture so we have the mind of Christ (1 Corinthians 2:16). Those professing Christianity should live visibly set apart from the ungodly conduct of the world. This lifestyle of holiness should draw the desperate and hungry to God, not push them farther away. Andrew Murray stated about a century ago,

> The revival we need is the revival of holiness, in which the consecration of the whole being is to the service of Christ. For this there will be needed a new style of preaching—in which the promises of God to dwell in His people, and to sanctify them for Himself, will take a place which they do not now have.[23]

In August 2003, a terrible summer storm hit our city early one morning. While I was in my family room, an incredibly loud clasp of thunder shook the house. Shortly afterward, lightning hit which caused my house to strongly rattle and vibrate. I glimpsed a flash of red-orange light from a back window. I was certain lightning had struck something but was not sure what. We had five large oak trees in front and on the side of our home and four tall pines on the other side. Given the direction of the light, I believed (hoped) it had hit a taller pine tree, not one of the oaks. To our dismay, two days later, my husband discovered the damage to our prettiest, largest live oak. I was devastated. This was a new home to us, and I had envisioned many things to do in the yard with this tree as the focal point.

Initially, we were not sure the extent of the damage but given the sights and sounds of the strike, it was hard to be optimistic. As we began to research lightning strikes, our hope further diminished. When lightning strikes a tree, the heat is so intense it steams the heart of the tree causing all moisture to evaporate. If lightning penetrates the perimeter or reaches the roots, there is little hope for long-term survival. Even when there appears to be minimal external damage, it is possible the tree will die very slowly sometimes over years.

In our case, lightning indeed struck the tree to the ground and penetrated

---

[23] Andrew Murray and Leona F. Choy, *The State of the Church* (Fort Washington, PA: Christian Literature Crusade, 1983), 68.

it. There was only a two- or three-inch-wide strip of bark removed, but in the following year, almost all of the bark buckled and fell off the forty-year-old tree. All the branches leafed out in the spring, but in the intense heat of the summer, the two branches taking the direct hit lost all their leaves.

There have been many ways God revealed Himself through this incident, but there is one lesson in particular I share here. God used this to bring to my remembrance[24] His saving power that causes us to "put away the old man" to live a holy life. It helps us understand how this process improves the landscape of life to empower holiness.

God reveals His glory through lightning that testifies to His power. Just like the flash of light in the lightning strike on my tree, when God's gift of salvation is received, there is often a quick, tremendous flash of light in our lives testifying to His power to save and change us. This transformation is often visible and felt by those in our sphere of acquaintances.

When the light and strength of salvation reach us, God's redeeming power consumes the penalty for sin. Guilt evaporates. The power of God comes into us. Instantly, we become His children. He puts His Spirit in us forever changing our infrastructure. The old life once relied upon for survival dies though we may not fully comprehend all that means at the time, even though it may not be outwardly visible.

However, a new process of growth is also taking place slowly. As we grow in the Spirit, we are in a process of dying to the Flesh. We die or learn to put away the former parts of us that His power consumed. For the Christian to grow, death to sin, self, and Flesh is required. In John 12:24, Jesus says, "Unless a grain of wheat falls into the ground and dies, it remains alone; but if it dies, it produces much grain." The life of Christ is a picture of life coming from death. The visible effects of this process may in some cases be more instantaneous than others. For some, the effects are gradually revealed.

Before the power of the lightning penetrated the tree, my tree was beautiful. I had great plans for it. It brought shade and served a good purpose. Is this not how we often look at ourselves? It is hard to die to ourselves, our desires, and what we perceive as safe, comfortable, enjoyable, and good. We may sometimes dread the thought of losing any of that

---

[24] He conformed my thoughts to the truth of His Word.

former life until we grasp the blessing of God's plan for new life. Our old lives often may have been very good, possibly even very moral or religious, but are we living touched by the power of God? Are we willing to die to our definitions of what is beautiful? Are we framing our viewpoint based on what we physically see or the transformation in the unseen?

While there may be initial changes visible in us as Christians, we must continually cast aside Flesh, our own desires and will so the fullness of God's power is revealed through us. This means to surrender even those attributes that appear good and worthy as mentioned in the last chapter. Sometimes, that process is painfully ugly and disturbing. It hurts to have part of us stripped away. God often uses the heat of summer, the trials of life, to begin severely stripping away what is not of Him, even those good, beautiful parts. Are you fighting this process? Are you still trying to salvage what needs to be removed for your best welfare?

Someone we consulted about removing the tree believed it could be saved even while acknowledging there would be virtually no bark on the trunk and many major limbs would have to be removed. What a frightful thought! The tree wasn't pretty any longer; it would detract from the landscape and the value of our property if it remained. The sick and dying tree needed complete transformation. I had to trust God to bring something new from this occurrence.

With the tree removed, our concerns for its impact on our house's foundation would be alleviated. My sister, a horticulturist, helped me design the front landscape. As much as we dreaded it, we had it removed. The risk of leaving a decaying tree close to the house in an area prone to tornadoes and hurricanes was too great. It can never again be the same. We must allow God to bring something new to the landscape by removing what is a great source of harm and decay.

Today, there is a large, kidney-shaped flowerbed where the oak tree stood. Many family and friends have commented that the removal of the oak has enhanced the beauty of the yard, not taken away from it. "It was meant to be," they exclaim. Several neighbors across the street are able to enjoy the year-round flowers from their windows.

Six months after the tree was removed, our area was hit extremely hard by Hurricane Rita and Ike a couple of years later. I am confident this tree would not have survived either. Our home was miraculously one of the few on our block that managed to survive without a tree falling on or through it.

We Christians should embrace what God allows in our lives to put away the old man and to put on the new man, to empower us to live holy lives set apart for His purpose. Our bodies are houses for Christ. What parts of your home or its landscape is the power of God penetrating and asking you to put away? What needs to be removed so He can replace it with something more beautiful? Any attempts to salvage or cling to the old can never recreate past pleasures and only delays the future beauty God brings in its place. What we fight to cling to will endanger us when the storms of life hit.

When we put on the new man, when we surrender to walk with Him in holiness, we are prepared to weather these storms. The world may take one outward look at this spiritual process and find it very disturbing and foolish. Just like my tree expert, often others entice us to save what is dying though it may greatly distort all beauty and health in the process. They and sometimes we cannot envision the long-term plan of God to bring something beautiful from what appears contrary to contentment.

Desires to cling to past beauty prohibit us from receiving future beauty, though different, it still brings great joy. Other "experts" may tempt us to resist God's removal of the old and its replacement with something greater. "Therefore, if anyone is in Christ, he is a new creation; old things have passed away; behold, all things have become new" (2 Corinthians 5:17).

It has been several years since the landscape changed drastically. We have lost five more trees, which casts more light on the garden. The need to refine the garden is never-ending. Though the work is difficult and sometimes costly, it enhances its beauty. However, in some areas, weed control has become a more challenging dilemma particularly where the weeds begin to grow up through small shrubs and perennials instead of around them. In this instance, mass use of weed killers is not always an option for it would kill the plants we are nurturing. The only way to remove these weeds without destroying the entire plant is to pull them out one by one. As I gently remove them, I am careful to remove the entire weed, not just the portion above the surface. If the root remains, the source for the weed's growth remains and will allow it to spread more rapidly.

As Christians pursuing holiness, this same process is necessary to deal with sin. If we desire intimacy with God, we must pursue a Spirit-centered life instead of a self-centered life. There is not an easy or healthy way to remove all sin in one mass effort. Instead, we must deal with sin one by one daily and persistently as it pushes through the surface to reveal its presence, distort beauty, and damage health. Unaddressed, sin will grow and put others next to us at harm. Instead of growing a faith tree able to provide shelter to others, we risk the health of others nearby by nourishing sin.

It is often easier to recognize and deal with the visible effect of sin on the surface than it is to deal with its roots. In Psalm 32, David models how to deal effectively with sin's multilayers. David confesses his sin with Bathsheba at every level: the transgression (the act of adultery or sin of the body), the sin (lust or sin in his mind), and the iniquity (the rebellion from God's law or will or sin in his heart). David aptly describes how a failure to repent takes a toll on our total being, but he also shares the benefit repentance ensures the body, mind, and soul.

David bears witness to the importance of an honest confession of sin from the surface to the core of our being. Charles Spurgeon describes this process as the Trinity of heaven conquering the trinity of sin. The trinity of sin reveals that transgressions or sins of the body are not isolated. Sins of the body are the consequence of sins of the mind, which are the consequence of iniquity in the heart. Failure to confess and repent at the core of our hearts keeps us trapped in cycles of sin of the mind and body. God's Spirit convicts and empowers repentance. God desires repentance for the healing, freedom, and restoration it provides. The below diagram summarizes this process.

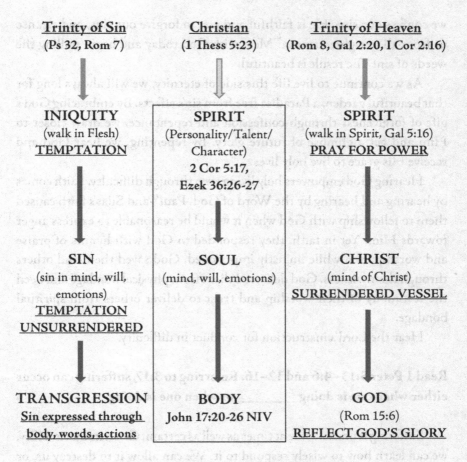

Like pulling difficult weeds, the burden of dealing with sin may seem so overwhelming that we avoid it all together, but a refusal to deal with sin only brings more destruction, not life or beauty (Romans 6:23). We may fear the process for we may dread getting rid of the dying tree we once viewed as beautiful. When fear of rejection or failure exists, one may find it difficult to fully embrace sin's depths or roots and thus fail to embrace complete healing and restoration. God's yoke is easy and His burden is light so come and find rest. Burying sin's effects, failing to confess its depth, hinders our relationship with God and affects our intimate relationships with family and friends.

Until God calls us home, our willingness to repent will always bring blessing while we are still on earth. In 1 John 1:8–9, we read, "If we say that we have no sin, we deceive ourselves, and the truth is not in us. But if we confess our sins, He is faithful and just to forgive our sins, and cleanse us from all unrighteousness." Meet with God today and begin pulling the weeds of sin! The result is beautiful.

As we continue to live life this side of eternity, we will always long for that beautiful garden, a Paradise free from sin's effects. By embracing God's gift of forgiveness through confession and repentance, we draw closer to Him and get a glimpse of future glory. By repenting, we hear God and receive His grace to live holy lives.

Hearing God empowers holy living even through difficulty. Faith comes by hearing and hearing by the Word of God. Paul's and Silas's faith caused them to fellowship with God when it would be reasonable to express anger towards Him. Yet in faith, they responded to God with hymns of praise and worship even while unjustly imprisoned. God saved them and others through their witness. God delivered them from physical bondage and used the testimony of their worship and trust to deliver others from spiritual bondage.

Hear the Lord's instruction for conduct in difficulty.

Read 1 Peter 3:13–4:6 and 12–16. Referring to 3:17, suffering can occur either when one is doing _____ or when one is doing _____.

Suffering is unavoidable at times as well as certain. Given its inevitability, we can learn how to wisely respond to it. We can allow it to destroy us, or we can grow through it. Whenever we experience internal or outward difficulties, we should ask God to reveal what part of the old self He desires to put away. Even when suffering comes from doing good, there is generally some aspect of our Flesh that surfaces, most often in the way we respond to the situation. Remain willing for God to reveal what that is and allow Him to guide you into holiness.

In verse 4:1, what are we in the flesh (our physical being) to be armed with?

According to verse 4:1, what does the Man who has suffered in the flesh cease?

From 4:2–3, why do we need to have the mind of Christ?

In verse 4:16, what is to be our conduct in suffering?

Read Hebrews 5:7–14. What did Jesus learn through suffering?

What did His learned obedience through suffering accomplish?

When I think of Jesus as the Son of God, it is hard for me to recognize His need to learn obedience to be perfected. I tend to dwell on Him as the already perfected deity, not the Son of Man who must experience and suffer in the flesh. Jesus's suffering caused Him to learn obedience. His obedience over temptation perfected and empowered Him. This victorious power lives in each child of God. Remember Galatians 2:20: "I am crucified with Christ, therefore I no longer live, but Jesus Christ now lives in me." We are to have this same mind of Christ, a mind that accepts the path even through the suffering God allows. We have His assurance that it will empower us to live victoriously over sin. Suffering causes one to put away the old man and to live as a new man in Christ. Suffering empowers us to overcome sin to live obediently!

What makes obedience to this exhortation hard? Describe the difficulty of dying to Flesh when responding to conflict and suffering.

How would you describe the difference between walking in holiness and having self-righteousness? What is the main, necessary attribute that distinguishes the two?

Why is a glorifying conduct important to us? (1 Pet 4:17).

We, God's people, are to live holy lives. We should communicate to a lost world that the power of God is sufficient to strengthen marriages, raise children who desire to please and honor Him, and positively influence relationships with others in society. What stability and hope for healthy marriages are we modeling to the world? What difference are we allowing God to make in our lives? What of His wisdom do we seek when we enter dating and marriage relationships? What of His wisdom do we seek and wait for when we encounter tough marital problems? How are we willing to suffer through and seek deliverance from hurt and disappointment to allow God to perfect and settle us as we remain faithful to God and faithful to our marriages? How do we seek understanding that would empower willing obedience?

Our path may be difficult. It requires endurance and perseverance when we want to quit. But Christ, who has also suffered victoriously in the Flesh, lives in us. Suffering brings victory over sin; it drives us to depend on the power of God when we would otherwise live self-sufficiently. God desires to change life's landscape drastically and create something more beautiful than we can conceive. God speaks to us. He gives hope. He gives strength.

Is your faith focused to recognize Him in the middle of the storm? Do you doubt who He is even when He reveals His power? Set your mind to hear Him!

Ask God to reveal or remind you of a difficult situation He has already worked for His good. Give Him praise for what He speaks to your heart. Allow His past faithfulness fuel trust in His present greatness. This same faithfulness and goodness is working presently though perhaps unseen and unfelt in your difficulty. God never changes. "God is good all the time! All the time, God is good!" Rejoice today in His goodness! Walk in His holiness!

'Twas grace that taught my heart to fear, and grace my fears relieved.
How precious did that grace appear the hour I first believed.
Through many dangers, toils, and snares, I have already come.
'Twas grace that brought us safe thus far, and grace will lead us home.
The Lord has promised good to me. His Word my hope secures.
He will my shield and portion be as long as life endures.[25]

Hear What the Spirit Says

Begin with worship, meditation, and prayer.

> Behold, I stand at the door and knock. If anyone hears My voice and opens the door, I will come in to him and dine with him, and he with Me. To him who overcomes I will grant to sit with Me on My throne, as I also overcame and sat down with My Father on His throne. He who has an ear, let him hear what the Spirit says to the churches. (Revelation 3:20–22)

"Blessed Jesus, grant sensitivity to the areas of my life I refuse to open to You. Reveal today what is needed to have the fullness of Your presence. Focus my heart on Your goodness and grace so I will overcome my fear of opening the door."

This passage from Revelation is a familiar one often quoted when encouraging the lost to respond to Christ's invitation of salvation. However, this passage comes toward the conclusion of Christ's warnings to the seven churches. The picture this text paints in its full context is of Christ standing at the door of His chosen ones–those who have already committed to follow Him, yet have shut Him out.

Prayer is too often one critical area of our relationship with God in

---

[25] From the hymn "Amazing Grace"

which we do more talking than listening. It is easy to shut Christ and His will out of our lives if we treat prayer as a means only to get things from God. Prayer is the tool for making our requests known to Him, but God's Word also tells us He knows what we need even before we ask (Matthew 6:8). As we will discuss in this section, prayer is not necessary for informing God of our needs but for recognizing Him amid expression of our need. By bringing our needs to God in prayer, He is more glorified when we recognize His provision. Trust in Him is deepened. It enables us to know Him more.

As children enter the toddler years, their mothers generally know what their children need before they ask. A child may point to a cup and grunt, but until the mother practices saying the word *drink*, she may temporarily withhold the child's provision long enough for him to practice forming a new word. Her delay is for the child's best interest. The mother wants the child to learn how to speak. His thirst becomes an entry point for another provision—his perhaps unrecognized need to form intelligible sounds. As the child adds words to his vocabulary, he is able to express himself and function in this world. The child learns to trust his mother to provide for his need and develops an affectionate relationship with her through that provision. As he learns to communicate with her, he is also equipped to communicate with others.

God wants us to hear Him so we know how to ask specifically for what He has to give. Since He already knows what we need, it is reasonable to assume there is a greater purpose in His instructions to ask. He wants to conform our desires to His will. We may ask for milk to quench our thirst, yet the provision He has may be meat to feed a looming hunger. As revealed in His Word, His provision exceeds what we ask, but to recognize that provision, we must view His eternal perspective. When we fear His provision, we close the door to fellowship. The very provision we seek waits outside the door of our hearts. Fear, doubt, and unbelief keep us from opening the door to that understanding.

God also wants to expand our ability to relate and communicate with Him so we know how to reveal Him to others. He teaches how to commune with Him beyond grunts, groans, and cries for help sometimes by delaying His provision. As He delays and we persevere in prayer, we are more likely to recognize His power and goodness when the provision comes.

Just as a loving mother does not ignore her thirsty child, we can trust

God's faithfulness to provide for us as well. Romans 8:26 teaches that the Spirit always intercedes for us even when we do not know how to pray. Yet this merciful provision should not be an excuse for failing to develop a deeper prayer relationship. Do not miss the opportunity to fellowship with God through prayer.

His ways for teaching us are uniquely individual. At the risk of taking this illustration too far, God knows the word we need to learn to repeat in response to our current need as well as what equips us to function in the next step of growth. That is why we need God's *rhema*, His Living Word. By seeking those deep things of God, our prayer life is enriched and we are better prepared to recognize His provision. We know God provides for our thirst, but how He gives that provision from Christ will be personal.

We have mentioned our need to spiritually hear and see God. We need to recognize the spiritual organs and senses God requires to know, hear, and understand Him. There are four major components to spiritual senses that posture us to gain His eternal perspective:

- surrendering to God—yielding our hearts and minds to the Spirit
- hearing God—listening to the will and ways of God as the Holy Spirit reveals through His Word
- responding to God—voicing in agreement the will of God and obediently acting as He leads
- waiting on God—patiently watching for God's power and glory to be revealed (briefly discussed in chapter 5)

We may struggle in our prayer life in quality or quantity, but God knows what we need. He may sometimes withhold His provision long enough to conform our prayers to His. He waits for our surrender. James 4:3 states, "You ask and do not receive, because you ask amiss, that you may spend it on your own pleasures." As we allow Him to develop our communion with Him in prayer, we become more like Him. Psalm 37:4 says, "Delight yourself in the Lord, and He shall give you the desires of your heart." God molds our hearts and aligns our desires with His provision when we seek Him.

God initiates fellowship. Christ is knocking on the door of our hearts and minds and waiting for our eager welcome. The verses from Revelation reveal what we have previously noted about God's character. He extends an invitation for intimate communion, but He does not demand or force it to happen: "*If* anyone hears My voice." To hear, we have to listen. Too often, our greatest problem is that we fail to listen. We may have an intense prayer life or a busy schedule of church service, but if we are always talking to God and are busy *for* Him, we are missing the critical element of our relationship: listening to and waiting on Him to reveal Himself and His will (remember Martha and Mary).

Too often in Christian living, we perhaps unconsciously have the attitude, "Don't call me—I'll call you" toward God. This is an attitude of self-sufficiency that subtly says, "I need God only when *I* think I need God." Even the most earnest followers can fall into this attitude when they allow a desire to please or prove themselves to God more than recognizing a need for His fellowship. Christ is pleading with us, "he who has an ear," he who desires to listen to God in humility and reverence, "let him hear what the Spirit says."

We settle for so little of God in prayer when we view it as one-way communication. It is not that Christ through the Spirit is not there; it is that we are not tuning our senses to His presence. True prayer is a *response* to God, an agreement with His will. To respond, we must hear. When we experience answered prayer, the source of that prayer is God's will. Prayer does not originate with our words, ideas, or good intentions but with revelations of God's will to our spirit from His Spirit.

If the answered prayer we experience is limited to things we think originated with us that God graciously provided, our understanding of the purpose of prayer is misguided. We cannot be the source of answered prayer for the glory is not ours to receive. The source of answered prayer is God, for the glory is for God as Jesus testified and demonstrated. In John 14–16, Jesus repeatedly promises the sending of the Holy Spirit as the way to receive God's plans, purposes, and provisions. Power praying happens when we are vessels for the Spirit of God to author God's will through prayer.

Christ asks, "Do I have your undivided attention? Can you hear Me now? Are you focused on what *I* am saying? Are you ready to be still and know I am God? Are you ready to learn how to voice in prayer what I have waiting to give through fellowship? Do you hear Me knocking on the door? Do you realize My presence?"

While Romans 8:26 says the Spirit intercedes even when we don't know what or how to pray, God desires our witness of His work. That witness empowers trust, fellowship, and strengthened faith. Christ requests full access to our hearts and minds so He may reveal the heart of God's desires because He loves us and wants us to know Him. He chooses to partner with us to fulfill on earth what is ordained in heaven (John 17, Matthew 18:18–20). God does not need us to complete His will, but He chose us to participate in its completion. This partnership provides opportunity to know His goodness. This truth is absolutely wonderful ... amazing ... humbling ... motivating!

There is joy in close fellowship Christ longs to bring. It is easy to conceptualize when the provision or path is visibly good, but when it is not, we may find ourselves less joyful and more reluctant to partner in prayer for its completion. In these circumstances, we can again look to Jesus's example from John 17 and learn from His interceding goodness and blessings voiced just prior to His abuse and crucifixion.

Jesus reiterates in John 15:15, "No longer do I call you servants, for a servant does not know what his master is doing; but I have called you friends, for all things that I heard from My Father I have made known to you." Servants are required to commit themselves to work. A friend, however, enjoys relationship, a mutual sharing between two people who care for one another. This relationship takes us beyond performing a specific task and allows us to learn the ways of God, who desires fellowship. Christ is our friend who wants to come in the door of our lives and help us hear and understand God's provision.

"To him who overcomes," Jesus proclaims. Hearing goes beyond the ability to hear physically or spiritually; it implies that hearing so penetrates the heart and soul of a man that he is compelled to respond. To hear means to remain humble and teachable before the Lord. He is not expecting us to live holy lives on our own but in fellowship with Him by His power. We never outgrow our need for Christ. Spiritual maturity means realizing a greater need for God, not more independence. Our lifetime is insufficient to learn all there is of God. As Paul says, now I see through a glass darkly, but then I will see Him face to face. Until God calls us to heaven, we never outgrow our need of Him or exhaust knowledge of Him. As we respond to His invitation for fellowship, He continues to teach more about Himself.

During a home-renovation project, homeowners have to let the carpenter in or they will not realize their plans. Likewise, God has a plan for our life. When we chose Him as Savior, we signed off to the renovation work He wants accomplished. Now that we are His children, He wants to transform us into the image of His Son, the Master Carpenter. Jesus is knocking on the door of believers' hearts to complete God's work and ensure God's plans are followed. Yet He desires to accomplish more than work. He deeply desires intimate fellowship. He desires us to participate in the completion of God's plan. He wants us to know Him more fully and wonderfully through this process. But we must open the door!

In Revelation, Jesus reveals how the church has deviated from God's plan. He gives opportunity to adjust willingly to Him. "He who has an ear, let him hear!" Andrew Murray very succinctly summarizes the sin of the churches in Revelation 2–3 as follows.

> In Ephesus, it was a lack of LOVE. The constraining love of Christ was no longer found. In Pergamos, it was a lack of TRUTH. They had forsaken the inspired Word, tolerated the teaching of error. In Sardis it was a lack of LIFE. They had a name of being alive, but were dead. In Laodicea it was a lack of FIRE. The baptism of the Spirit and of fire was no longer known.[26]

In Thyatira, it was complacency resulting in a lack of holiness. Evil was tolerated in the form of idolatry and sexual immorality through the teaching of Jezebel. Christ praised Smyrna and Philadelphia as churches seeking and following the heart of God.

We shut Christ out of our lives,

- by failing to reveal His love,
- by forsaking His truth,
- by living lives of righteous pretense professing to be a Christian while living a lifestyle of our own choosing in and outside church,

---

[26] Andrew Murray and Leona F. Choy, "Repent," in *The State of the Church* (Fort Washington, PA: Christian Literature Crusade, 1983), 95.

- by serving in our own strength and not recognizing our need for the Holy Spirit,
- by allowing religious doctrine, routine, and tradition to become more important to us than relationship with Him and others, and
- by refusing to live holy lives separate from religious traditions, worldly religions, and beliefs.

We are to follow no religion or doctrine other than the Word of God.

What areas of your life or ministry are you shutting Christ out of in an attempt to accomplish what is good in your own strength? Circle all that apply.

- **relationship with God**
- **prayer**
- **worship**
- **study of the Word**
- **fellowship**
- **stewardship**
- **ministry/service**
- **marriage/relationships**
- **parenting**
- **career**
- **other**

Too often, one of the difficulties for seasoned Christians is a willingness to accept the Flesh and sin that remains in their hearts. Christians who have a deep desire to please God sometimes also have such a fear of failing Him that it makes recognition of the Flesh and confession of sin difficult.

Perhaps the difficulty you face results from failing to embrace this truth. God refines those He loves so they more fully glorify Him. We repeatedly refer to 1 John 1:6–9 in this study as it reveals the dichotomy of our human nature that needs to be aligned with God.

> If we say that we have fellowship with Him, and walk in darkness, we lie and do not practice the truth. But if we

walk in the light as He is in the light, we have fellowship with one another, and the blood of Jesus Christ His Son cleanses us from all sin. If we say that we have no sin, we deceive ourselves, and the truth is not in us. If we confess our sins, He is faithful and just to forgive us our sins and to cleanse us from all unrighteousness.

Given the above answers, what does the Spirit say is missing? As you circle *all* that apply, pray each as an expression of surrender and invitation for Christ to come through the door of your mind and empower you with more of Him.

- I need a selfless Love for Him and/or others. In order to give His love, I need to realize the depth of His unconditional, relentless love for me.
- I need His truth regarding where I am or where He wants to lead me.
- I need to accept more fully the truth and relevancy of His Word.
- I need to rely earnestly on His power, not my own wisdom and intellect. I need knowledge of His Word to become power and life.
- I need to embrace that apart from Him, I can do nothing successfully or for His glory
- I need a greater passion to seek His face, to pursue His favor.
- I need a greater sensitivity to the Spirit so I may abide in Him, not my Flesh.
- I need to understand how I quench or grieve the flow of His Spirit.
- I need purity in heart, mind, and body.
- I need greater surrender to the Trinity of heaven so I confess the trinity of sin of my body, mind, and soul and embrace peaceful restoration!

Hear what the Spirit says, and open the door to the fullness of Christ. Do not allow fear of failure or insecurity to prevent you from honestly facing what He reveals. Rest in the flood of His power in your life as you open your heart to understand further His plan and purpose.

For I know the plans I have for you, says the Lord. Plans to prosper you, not to harm you. Plans to give you a hope and a future. Then you will call to Me and pray to Me, and I will listen. You will seek Me and find Me when you search for Me with all your heart.
—Jeremiah 29:11–13

Growing Faith 4

"This is My Beloved Son, Hear Him!"

At the end of chapter 2, we discussed the miracle of the feeding of the five thousand and the second instance of Jesus calming the sea for the disciples. We learned how the disciples struggled with doubt, fear, and unbelief until Jesus and Peter climbed in the boat instantly calming the sea. We begin by discussing the second opportunity for the disciples to exercise faith in feeding the multitudes. Remember also from the Growing Faith 3 discussion the preparation of Jesus's teachings and miracles to lay the foundation for understanding His power over sin. Let us see Jesus continue to build upon this foundation of faith by reading Mark 8:1–13.

> In those days, the multitude being very great and having nothing to eat, Jesus called His disciples to Him and said to them, "I have compassion on the multitude, because they have now continued with Me three days and have nothing to eat. And if I send them away hungry to their own houses, they will faint on the way; for some of them have come from afar." Then His disciples answered Him, "How can one satisfy these people with bread here in the wilderness?" He asked them, "How many loaves do you have?" And they said, "Seven." So He commanded the multitude to sit down on the ground. And He took the seven loaves and gave thanks, broke [them] and gave [them] to His disciples to set before [them]; and they set [them] before the multitude. They also had a few small fish; and having blessed them, He said to set them also before them. So they ate and were filled, and they took up seven large baskets of leftover fragments. Now those who had eaten were about four thousand. And He sent them away, immediately got into the boat with His disciples, and came to the region of Dalmanutha. Then the Pharisees came out and began to dispute with Him, seeking from Him a sign from heaven, testing Him. But He sighed deeply

in His spirit, and said, "Why does this generation seek a sign? Assuredly, I say to you, no sign shall be given to this generation." And He left them, and getting into the boat again, departed to the other side. (Mark 8:1–13 NKJV)

This time, Jesus raises the need to feed the people who have not eaten for three days. When He expresses His compassionate concern to the disciples, they once again respond by focusing on the impossibility of man to make adequate provision. "How can one satisfy these people with bread here in the wilderness?" From our perspective, this seems an incredibly strange response given that they just recently witnessed the feeding of the five thousand, the walking on the water and many other miracles. Compare Jesus's statement in verse 3 to the disciples' initial statement in the previous account in Mark 6:36. In Mark 6, the disciples came to Jesus urging Him to send them away from the deserted place for food. In this second account, Jesus seemingly preempts a similar response by the disciples by disregarding this as an option: "If I send them away they will faint on the way." He seems to preempt all their arguments that would hinder belief and expectation in the power of God. It appears that Jesus provides hints to encourage them to finally look beyond themselves to embrace the power of God.

The disciples question is very interesting. "How can one satisfy these people with bread here in the wilderness?" Is this a rhetorical question, or are they truly uncertain? They know the historical provision of manna for ancient Israel in the wilderness and have seen God's Son miraculously answer this question just recently. Given our perspective, their unbelief is unbelievable! Were they perhaps attempting to refer to spiritual hunger using physical needs to illustrate? After the first miracle of the five loaves and two fish, the multitudes seeking Christ grew in number and relentlessly pursued Him and His miraculous power. Since the desire for Christ's ministry expanded, could they be asking how only "one" man could satisfy a growing spiritual hunger for the Bread of Life?

The disciples have not demonstrated spiritual understanding to suggest such philosophical insight. Ironically, their question is very appropriate for what Jesus ultimately reveals. This seemingly ill-stated question again sets the stage for Jesus to reveal the One who truly can satisfy the hunger of this people physically and spiritually. However, their hearts are still not focused to receive spiritual understanding. They ask, but rhetorically, not expecting a response.

Can this also be said of us? How often do we ask the questions that God wants to answer yet remain unprepared to discern His provision? In posing the right question, circumstances may overshadow any expectation of receiving God's answer. How many of our questions are more rhetorical than sincere? Do we also underestimate God's willingness to answer questions that we do not believe can be answered? How often do we recognize that He may be the one who placed the question in our minds to fuel expectations of a demonstration of His power?

Let us look at how Jesus reacts and what follows this miracle. There are seven loaves of bread available. Whom do we know Jesus to be? He is the Bread of heaven, the Bread of Life, the One in whom we are perfected as God's children. Given that the Old Testament repeatedly gives witness to God's attention and concern with details, it is easy to believe that the numerical references to seven here are not coincidence. The timing of this miracle and its sequence following Jesus's previous teachings about sin is evidence of God's sovereign concern for building on the foundation of faith.

In the previous miracle of the five loaves and two fish, we learned Christ attempted to teach the disciples that God would provide in the ministry He has called them to fulfill. As such, twelve baskets, the same as the number of disciples, remained from that miracle. He reassured them individually of His continual presence. Since then, they have also begun to realize Jesus is truly the Son of God. By the time this second feeding miracle occurs, the disciples have learned the above truths and more. But understanding Jesus as the cleanser and deliverer from sin is not understood yet by His followers. In Mark 7, we read how Jesus begins to reveal His power to cleanse from within, to bring life to the soul, and to provide more than outward cleansing. This second miracle of feeding the crowds now builds on the foundation for this understanding.

The disciples gathered seven loaves and brought them to Jesus for His blessing. Once everyone was fed, seven large baskets remained. They witnessed seven loaves feed about four thousand people and seven full baskets remain. The number seven is used throughout God's Word as a symbol of God's perfection and completion. Seven loaves are broken and dispersed to feed the multitudes, yet more of the bread, not less, remains. What remains is perfection multiplied in abundance.

Jesus subtly responds to the disciples' question "How can one satisfy all this hunger" with "I AM The One, The Perfect One, The Bread of Heaven, the Bread of Life." Jesus, the Bread of Life, would be broken on the cross. His blood would be poured out to satisfy our need to be filled with Him. His brokenness and death did not diminish His perfection; it completed it. Yet His sacrifice was not for the Jews only but for all people and for all time. When Christ, the Bread of Life, is shared with others, all know more of His abundance. Christ, God's love, is in no way diminished. Instead, the kingdom of God expands, is multiplied in abundance, and completed! Truly, this is a powerful spiritual principle that reveals the fullness of Jesus's purpose on earth and prepares the disciples to see the eternal benefit of the physical brutality they will soon witness with His crucifixion.

Notice again that God's ways reveal more of Himself, His power, and His will by revealing current truths and future spiritual plans through the provision of a present physical need. This is a pattern of His ways He continues with us, but we must be willing to hear with spiritual ears and see with spiritual eyes of faith.

In this interchange, Jesus used physical need to illustrate a spiritual principle, yet the disciples still do not grasp the analogy. After the feeding of the five thousand, Christ already revealed himself as the Bread of heaven (see John 6:25–59). However, John 6:60–63 reveals that the disciples believed this to be a hard saying that no one could understand. He previously told them He was the Bread of heaven. Then He gave them further teachings and miracles to reveal Himself as the Bread of life. But their focus remains limited by physical needs. This is evident immediately following when Jesus cautions them to beware of the leaven of the Pharisees as recorded in Mark. The disciples fail to understand His meaning; they suppose He is referring to their failure to bring bread. Listen to Jesus's frustrated response.

> "Why do you reason because you have no bread? Do you not yet perceive nor understand? Is your heart still hardened? Having eyes, do you not see? And having ears, do you not hear? And do you not remember? When I broke the five loaves for the five thousand, how many baskets full of fragments did you take up?" They said to Him, "Twelve." "And when I broke the seven for the four thousand, how

many large baskets full of fragments did you take up?" And they said, "Seven." So he said to them, "How is it you do not understand?" (Mark 8:17-21).

Marveling at the misguided focus of His disciples, Jesus does not attempt to clarify His saying about the leaven of the Pharisees. The disciples do not demonstrate hearts ready for or sensitive to spiritual discernment. Once again, they focus only on the physical, literal meaning of Jesus's words without comprehending the spiritual parallel. Christ recalls His great faithfulness to provide for the hungry to shed light on the foolish confusion over their misguided understanding.

Following this miracle and discussion, Jesus gives the disciples opportunity to testify who He is. Peter responds by confessing Jesus is the Christ. Given their understanding of who He is, Jesus begins to prepare them for the suffering He will endure. However, this is too much for Peter to tolerate. While Jesus speaks openly of His coming suffering, Peter calls Him aside and begins to rebuke the One he has just professed to be the Christ: "Far be it from You, Lord; this shall not happen to You" (Matthew 16:22). While Peter has been sensitive to revelation of the Spirit regarding who Christ is, complete surrender to understanding is still lacking. As quickly as Peter is sensitive to the Spirit of God, fear consumes him, fueling fleshly reactions that further fuels rebuke from Jesus.

Then in Mark 9, Jesus takes Peter, James, and John up on a high mountain by themselves and is transfigured before them.

> His clothes became shining, exceedingly white, like snow, such as no launderer on earth can whiten them. And Elijah appeared to them with Moses, and they were talking with Jesus. Then Peter answered and said to Jesus, "Rabbi, it is good for us to be here; and let us make three tabernacles: one for You, one for Moses, and one for Elijah"—*because he did not know what to say, for they were greatly afraid.* And a cloud came and overshadowed them; and a voice came out of the cloud, saying, "This is My beloved Son. Hear Him! Suddenly, when they had looked around, they saw no one anymore, but only Jesus with themselves. Now as

they came down from the mountain, He commanded them that they should tell no one the things they had seen, till the Son of Man had risen from the dead. So they kept this word to themselves, questioning what the rising from the dead meant." (Mark 9:3–10 NKJV; emphasis added)

This encounter with Jesus on the Mount of Transfiguration is a pivotal point in Jesus's equipping the disciples. To grasp why this word from God is so important, let us recap what has transpired between Jesus and the disciples up to this point.

We looked repeatedly at Jesus's continual admonishments to surrender the hardness of the disciples' hearts so they may hear and understand His teachings and grasp the purpose behind His power. We repeatedly see how the disciples are blinded by fear and unbelief despite the miraculous experience of His power. Ever since the discussion between Jesus and the Jews regarding the need for inner cleansing, we see the miracles and teachings take on a stronger message. Jesus shifts His focus from merely revealing His power as the Son of God to help all perceive that He is the One who cleanses sin. We know from our study that the disciples have been given the understanding to grasp this teaching, but they struggle to perceive it. Jesus attempts to reinforce this truth to prepare the disciples for His coming crucifixion and resurrection that will complete His cleansing of all sin.

Given the extreme difficulty Jesus knows is ahead and the testing of their faith that coincides, the disciples need this teaching to help sustain their faith. The Spirit will bring to their remembrance these occurrences when they are fully ready to understand. After Jesus reveals the importance to seek inner versus outward cleansing, He further reiterates Himself to be the Bread of heaven, the One who will satisfy and sustain life eternally. Then, He gives the disciples opportunity to reveal understanding by asking who they perceive Him to be. They recognize Him as the Son of God, but they do not want to listen to Jesus's words or recall from prophetic scripture the suffering that Jesus and they will have to endure to establish His kingdom.

As the three chosen ones witness Jesus's transfiguration, God's voice from heaven proclaims, "This is My beloved Son, Hear Him!" This is a very holy moment. Peter, James, and John are greatly afraid. They feel the need to worship. However, they are so overwhelmed by the presence of the most revered Moses and Elijah and the glory of Jesus that they lose focus on the proper form for worship.

Even in this holy moment, it is hard not to parallel this situation to common family interludes. This situation makes me think of times when I would give my older son instructions for the younger. Often, the younger refused to accept the authority I gave the older. Until I intervened and said, "*I told him to tell you,*" he was hesitant to accept my word through my messenger.

Mark 8:14–21 reveals Jesus's escalating frustration with the disciples' inability to understand. Afterward, just when Peter correctly testifies who Jesus is, Peter unknowingly tempts Him not to allow the preordained suffering. Given that Jesus must experience all you and I experience, imagine the temptation fueled by Peter's words to fear His crucifixion and the temptation to escape it. Jesus gives evidence of temptation by rebuking Peter as an instrument of Satan. Now, on this mountain, with the glory of God radiating the body of Christ and with the witness of Moses and Elijah, God said to Peter, James, and John, "Hear Him." God is saying, "This *is* My beloved Son! I have sent Him to you! Hear what I have given him to speak!" It's as if God the Father warns His younger children not to argue with His older Son but to hear His words, believe what He says, and do what He asks, for "I told Him to tell you … Hear Him!" My own parental experience echoes in my mind: "Don't make me come down here again!"

From this point through Jesus's crucifixion, there are very few instances recorded by Mark in which Jesus chastises the disciples for failing to "hear and understand" when teaching in parables. One example follows immediately after this transfiguration when He expresses disdain over the lack of faith to drive out demons by the disciples left behind. The other does not occur until after Jesus's resurrection in Mark 16:14. While Jesus continues to tell them of things to come and while He is aware that their understanding is not complete, there seems to be a change in the environment of these discussions. The repeated warnings previously recorded by Mark take a softer form of exhortation instead of a stern, frustrated correction as He encourages them to pursue understanding.

Imagine the changed hearts and strengthened faith that probably occurred in Peter, James, and John. Most likely, God humbled and refocused their attention after this phenomenal experience. Given this occurrence, it is not surprising that the nature of their future discussions takes on a more eternally focused tone. It is also understandable why the disciples in the future are more cautious to express a lack of understanding to Jesus Himself but rather discuss their confusion among themselves.

I can imagine Peter, James, and John cautioning the others not to present their misunderstandings to Jesus. No doubt this experience instilled a fear and awe of Jesus as the Son of God, who they now understand to be more than their teacher and close companion. They seem more slow to speak and react and more alert to hear if only in a physical, not a spiritual, sense.

Imagine the reassurance this transfiguration gave Jesus. This miraculous radiance is but a shadow of His former and future glory to be restored when He takes the right hand of God's throne. While Jesus remained in continual fellowship with God through fasting, worship, and prayer, His fellowship with His Father is not what it once was. This is a brief fellowship with God in the presence of the three disciples. The disciples are given an earthly glimpse of heavenly things to come. Despite their sincere dedication, complete understanding is lacking. This experience gives Jesus third-party validation to who He truly is in the presence of His closest followers.

No doubt it was also an encouragement to the Son of Man who in all points must be tempted as you and I. While we do not know what Jesus discussed with Moses and Elijah, it is reasonable to assume that Jesus had to gain strength on the mountain with His Father and with the two wise prophets of God who have also experienced a path of suffering. The following change we read in scripture between Jesus and the disciples support this theory. Jesus needs this restoration and renewal to withstand what He will soon endure. God empowered His Son to fulfill His purpose.

Once again, Christ models God's truth. God does not expect us to fulfill His will in our own strength but puts His power in us to obey. To receive this power, Jesus slipped away from the skeptics and critics to draw near to God. God's power came in the moments of mountaintop intimacy. He takes His closest (though still misguided) allies for moral support. This experience also served to strengthen the understanding of His protégés. They hear God. After this witness of power, they will less likely be vessels of temptation to Jesus.

While we may not experience such a miraculous demonstration of God's glory and power, we can be reassured that God uses needs, sufferings, and blessings to draw our attention to Him. He still has a measure of power for our purpose and empowerment though different from Jesus. He draws us into that safe place to reveal this power in and through us. We may not have the benefit of the physical presence of Jesus, but we have His Spirit. Just like the disciples, it may take many situations for us to fully recognize our need to focus on God and His power in our midst. We must learn to hear Him. Blessed is he who quickly responds!

God wants us to learn how to hear Him for there is great importance to what He has to reveal. If God is going to great lengths to get our attention, we can be certain He has a provision of understanding He is preparing us to receive. We can learn from the disciples the need to hear and understand the spiritual parallel behind the situation we face. First, we must realize our need surpasses the physical, the earthly. Second, through our vented proclamations and rhetorical questions, we must realize there are answers to those questions God longs to reveal. God has an eternal, spiritual purpose for it. Imbedded in that purpose is His desire for us to learn more about His power and to prepare us for His future will and path. He brings to our remembrance what He has spoken when He has prepared our hearts for understanding. He is strengthening faith!

"Behold I stand at the door and knock."

Toward the end of our study, we delve deeper into scriptures for marital strength and accountability. Before we have that discussion, let us listen to the healing God has for those who have experienced divorce. Behold, Christ stands at the door and knocks! Hear Him!

The following is an excerpt from a September 25, 2012 article in *The Gospel Coalition* called *FactChecker: Divorce Rate Among Christians*, by Glenn T. Stanton.[27]

---

[27] https://www.thegospelcoalition.org/article/factchecker-divorce-rate-among-christians.

Professor Bradley Wright, a sociologist at the University of Connecticut, explains from his analysis of people who identify as Christians but rarely attend church, that 60 percent of these have been divorced. Of those who attend church regularly, 38 percent have been divorced.[1]

Other data from additional sociologists of family and religion suggest a substantial marital stability divide between those who take their faith seriously and those who do not.

W. Bradford Wilcox, a leading sociologist at the University of Virginia and director of the National Marriage Project, finds from his own analysis that "active conservative Protestants" who regularly attend church are 35 percent *less likely to divorce* compared to those who have no affiliation. Nominally attending conservative Protestants are 20 percent *more likely* to divorce, compared to secular Americans.[2]

[1] Bradley R. E. Wright, *Christians Are Hate-Filled Hypocrites... and Other Lies You've Been Told*, (Minneapolis, MN: Bethany House, 2010), p. 133.

[2] W. Bradford Wilcox and Elizabeth Williamson, "The Cultural Contradictions of Mainline Family Ideology and Practice," in *American Religions and the Family*, edited by Don S. Browning and David A. Clairmont (New York: Columbia University Press, 2007) p. 50.

The divorce rate for professing Christians is 60 percent, which is comparable to the national average. However, there is a "substantial marital divide between those who take their faith seriously and those who do not."

For the divorced Christian reading this, you are more than a statistic. Your experience is real. Nevertheless, it is important for us to see the benefit and power God has for the marriage relationship grounded in faith over fear. Regardless of the reason for your divorce, it is clear that your life has been affected personally by the curse of living in a fallen, sinful world outside God's design. Regardless of the reason, despite who left whom, sin and hardness of hearts have dealt devastating, difficult consequences in the deepest, most intimate aspects of your life. God sees. God understands. God comforts. God embraces you. Rest in His love.

You may struggle to question the applicability of this study so far to the broken marriage. It may be difficult to comprehend how Christ can sympathize with your pain since He never married let alone walked the path of divorce on earth. One may ask, "How could He possibly have walked the path victoriously to offer me hope when He never married or had children in a broken marriage? His path was not the same. He cannot understand."

In the Old Testament, God repeatedly uses the marriage covenant to describe the nation of Israel's relationship with Him. In Hosea, God reveals the depth of His unconditional love to pursue those who have chosen a life of sexual immorality outside the covenant relationship, the *spiritual marriage* between God and His people. The New Testament refers to Christ as the Groom and the church as the bride. In heaven, there will be a Marriage Supper of the Lamb (Christ) with those whose names are in the Book of Life.

As studied in Revelation 3, Christ stands at the door of the church that shut Him out—those who have moved away from living in a right relationship with their Groom. As these scriptures reveal, Christ has felt the sense of abandonment, rejection, shame, betrayal, and grief associated with intimate separation. In this study, we have also looked at the frustration of Christ with His followers, the founders and leaders of the future church to whom Christ is intimately and spiritually bound. One of these followers delivered Christ into the hands of those who crucified Him. Yet Christ never forsakes the church but lays His life down for it willingly, though its members are sinners and undeserving of this sacrifice.

Christ grieves for this brokenness and longs to restore it. To understand Christ's empathy for your situation requires you to look at divorce and God's restoration for it through the spiritual realities buried in the earthly visibilities. I pray this study is helping you navigate through this process for restoration unique to your situation.

Reflect on our discussion of Matthew 13. Recall what scriptures reveal about the by-product of understanding: healing and restoration! Christ knows how the sin nature and the schemes of Satan infiltrate His sheep and short-circuit His design for marriage. Christ prepared the way for us to hear Him and gain this understanding as well. Hardness of hearts causes us to lose the power of understanding, but faith causes us to hear and understand!

God guides us to understand sin and its effects on marriage so we find healing and restoration to Him. Fear, grief, disappointment, and guilt through divorce are obstacles to hearing God. God has answers to your questions. God has a path for leading you through the grief, solitude, and social separation that often comes with divorce. Self-doubt and condemnation associated with regrets and what-ifs serve no purpose to heal. Healing only comes from hearing God's truth and comfort. Condemnation brings guilt, torment, and isolation from God; conviction brings repentance, peace, and intimacy with God.

I feel inadequate to provide words of consolation for your unique situation. But God is more than adequate and more than willing to meet you in quiet solitude and wrap you in His tender, loving embrace. He stands at the door waiting.

Listen to the lament and confession of David as an encouragement to find the path for healing through any situation; remember that David committed adultery, conspiracy, and murder to conceal the sin he should have confessed. Hopefully, your experience has not been the result of so much violence. Not all divorces are the result of adultery, but even when these most intimate violations have occurred, there is healing and restoration. Through David's example, trust God has a plan of restoration for you as well.

> Have mercy upon me, O God, According to Your lovingkindness; According to the multitude of Your tender mercies, Blot out my transgressions. Wash me thoroughly from my iniquity, And cleanse me from my sin. For I acknowledge my transgressions, And my sin is always before me. Against You, You only, have I sinned, And done this evil in Your sight—That You may be found just when You speak, And blameless when You judge. Behold, I was brought forth in iniquity, And in sin my mother conceived me. Behold, You desire truth in the inward parts, And in the hidden part You will make me to know wisdom. Purge

me with hyssop, and I shall be clean; Wash me, and I shall be whiter than snow. Make me hear joy and gladness, That the bones You have broken may rejoice. Hide Your face from my sins, And blot out all my iniquities. Create in me a clean heart, O God, And renew a steadfast spirit within me. Do not cast me away from Your presence, And do not take Your Holy Spirit from me. Restore to me the joy of Your salvation, And uphold me by Your generous Spirit. Then I will teach transgressors Your ways, And sinners shall be converted to You ... O Lord, open my lips, And my mouth shall show forth Your praise. For You do not desire sacrifice, or else I would give it; You do not delight in burnt offering. The sacrifices of God are a broken spirit, A broken and a contrite heart—These, O God, You will not despise. (Psalm 51:1–19)

Do not allow the schemes of Satan or the follies of the Flesh cause you to lose the power of understanding! Cling to the provision of healing and restoration available to those who seek it! Christ stands at the door and knocks. He wants to come in and nurture the seed of faith growing in your heart to dispel your fear, relieve your pain, cleanse your shame, and heal your hurt and grief. Confess your need for Him!

If you initiated divorce with or without biblical grounds, do not let fear keep you on a path of destruction. You may have left your spouse for the "true" love of your life, or out of exhaustion with the way your marriage was, or both. Your response to real difficulty may be based on earthly, not spiritual realities. Fear perpetuates fear and blinds us to receiving God's way of deliverance and restoration. Confess your need of Him!

If your spouse left, resulting in an unwanted divorce, bring your feelings of rejection, betrayal, hurt, and grief to God. Open the door and let Christ meet with you in the midst of your pain and grief. Receive His comfort. Receive His peace. In this rest, allow Him to bring understanding for restoration of your heart and possibly restoration of the marriage even after divorce.

You may have divorced many years ago and already found healing and restoration. Allow this faith strengthening to shelter others in difficulty.

Perhaps it is your children. Perhaps it is friends or coworkers. Allow others to benefit from the wisdom and understanding God provided. Remember how God used David's, Peter's, and Paul's strengthened faith to further His kingdom. Give glory to God for His faithfulness, love, and grace.

Open the door and fellowship with your heavenly Counselor. Allow this healing to make you wise and strong in faith in present relationships. God is the God of grace. God is a redeeming God. God never rejects the humble and contrite heart.

Let anyone who has ears to hear, hear Him!

⇜ Chapter 5 ⇝

The Power of Understanding

*The Spirit of the lord shall rest upon Him, The Spirit of
wisdom and of understanding, The Spirit of counsel and might,
The Spirit of knowledge and of the fear of the Lord.*
—Isaiah 11:2

Hear and Understand

Begin with worship, meditation, and prayer.

> Hear my children, the instruction of a father, and give attention to know understanding; for I give you good doctrine; do not forsake my law. (Proverbs 4:1–2)

> "Lord, give me the desire to understand the power of understanding. Teach me how to be sensitive to the ways You reveal Yourself to me. Help me further identify the tools of Satan that prevent the growth of faith."

What is understanding? As we will explore further, it is not the ability to be all-knowing or a bargaining chip to use with God: "God help me to understand _____ so I can be on my way." It is not the ability to predict the future. Understanding allows us to discern God's past or present work in a way that empowers future recognition of Him.

The Bible speaks of a peace that surpasses understanding. This peace is received through worship and prayer; it is an intimacy that focuses our hearts and minds on God, not the problem (Philippians 4:6–7). Worship and prayer draws us to God and God to us. In His presence, God's consuming love overpowers the problem. The peace that surpasses understanding is a peace that defies explanation or reason. It does not say that this peace replaces or substitutes for understanding, but that God's peace is superior to it. (Recall the peace imparted to Gideon and how it was given amid unchanged circumstances. It was received when Gideon realized God's will and presence.)

Philippians 4:6–7 subtly reveals that understanding is not complete and all knowing. If we had eternal knowledge of all things, we would see how God works all things for our good and His glory and therefore would not be anxious. But we don't always have this level of understanding this side of heaven, so we need God's sustaining peace—the peace that passes understanding. It calms us when there is no understanding of the difficulty, pain, or hurt. This verse implies that some understanding is revealed, but it falls short of what we want and seek. Since we cannot comprehend all God's ways or reasons for difficulty, God instead provides peace. It is not a consolation; it is superior because it comes from an awareness of His presence in our circumstance.

So what is the role of understanding in life, and why does the Bible tell us to seek it above knowledge and wisdom, if all we need is God's peace (Proverbs 4:7)? Though often incomplete, is understanding a catalyst for receiving peace?

I recently came across a quote, "God does not ask us to understand; He asks us to serve and obey." This statement is intended to focus on the importance of trusting and obeying even when understanding is lacking, and for remaining humble before God. But I want to break this statement down in light of our study on understanding. Unwavering commitment to God's purpose is admirable and can accomplish much to further God's kingdom. God certainly searches for hearts loyal to His purposes (2 Chronicles 16:9). But His Word also instructs us to seek understanding (Proverbs 4).

As we explore, understanding who God is empowers trust and

obedience. We typically define or limit understanding to knowledge of God's purpose for difficult circumstances, not to the God who works those circumstances to achieve an eternal purpose. Our focus typically is on how understanding relates to self, not how it pertains to God or His ways. Recall from chapter 2 how Jesus attempted to expand the disciples' understanding of who He was as Christ though His form was that of man. The key point was comprehending *God* in their midst and *God's* plan and purpose.

When faced with a difficult need, the disciples typically looked to their own resources, not God, as the solution for the problem. They did not understand God's ability to provide through Jesus or through them, or the extent God would reveal His power on earth. Likewise, God pursues relationship with us to progressively reveal His fullness. As we come to understand who He is, our trust in Him deepens and faith grows. Faith comes by hearing the Word of God. Knowledge, wisdom, and understanding of the Word—of who God is—grows faith. Obedience is a product of this understanding. In the remainder of this study, we present scripture to reveal that a deepening of service and obedience is the result of deepening understanding and intimacy with God. This is the example Jesus modeled for us as the Son of Man.

For the sake of argument, follow this line of reasoning: if we are to serve or trust and obey when there is no understanding as quoted above, what motivates us to trust and obey? Is it self-effort or determination? Is this what God asks us to give—the best of our Flesh? Or does God ask us to surrender Flesh and allow His Spirit to live through us (Luke 9:23; Galatians 2:20)? Wouldn't a level of understanding be required to surrender Flesh, our desires? We typically don't deviate from self easily.

Do we trust and obey because God said so? If so, what is the motivation for pleasing God? A fear of the Lord? His love for us? Is it because of our knowledge that God is the I Am? If we serve and obey because of who we know God to be and want to please Him, aren't we obeying because we understand who God is and not just engaging in dutiful or blind obedience? Understanding who God is, though perhaps not His purposes, empowers obedience.

Do you typically trust someone you do not know? Would you do what a stranger commanded you to do? While there may be a general level of trust in human decency, for the most part, you would not allow a stranger to impact your life on a personal, intimate level or give you instructions to blindly follow. The stranger would at least need some level of revealed authority such as that of a doctor, a paramedic, or a teacher. Trust but verify. To trust strangers, you must first understand their motivations. You will want to first comprehend that their purpose or intentions are for good. You want to know who they are or who vouches for their credibility. You want to understand them. We have already laid the foundation for understanding—the importance of knowing and hearing God.

The above makes the point that whether we consciously think about it or not, there is always a level of understanding present in trust and obedience. In this chapter, we will continue to look at scripture revealing the role of understanding to fuel faith. We will learn why we should seek understanding even when the Prince of Peace lives in our hearts. The question this study explores is whether God intends to expand that understanding. If so, how and to what extent can we gain understanding? We have already explored how fear, doubt, and unbelief limit it.

In practice and perception, when the word *understanding* has been used by Christians or the church, it is implied one refers to full, complete knowledge of all things, but this is contrary to scripture. The Bible reveals that there is a secret and a revealed will of God, but there is no specific parameter given for the revealed will.

Deuteronomy 29:29 says, "The secret things belong to the Lord our God, but those things which are revealed belong to us and to our children forever, that we may do all the words of this law." There is a secret will of God that we will never know this side of heaven, but there is a revealed will of God we are to seek because it instructs how to "do all the words of this law." The problem we generally have in receiving understanding is that we become so focused on trying to understand the secret will (that we cannot know) that we fail to seek the revealed will. We may focus our hearts on receiving that one significant revelation to such a degree that we fail to recognize those small things until God gets our attention. Satan can use the pursuit for the secret will to make us doubt God's concern for us, doubt His willingness to reveal Himself, fear what He may do, and disbelieve or distrust what He is doing. To seek God's revealed will and to receive that understanding is to be empowered to trust what He is doing, even if we cannot understand His secret will.

We have to look at many scriptures to outline the parameters for understanding. God reveals to us what is necessary to fulfill our purpose. Are we willing to hear with understanding? Do we realize it as an available provision? Are we seeking it? Is the motivation of our hearts aligned with God's purpose or our own?

Randy Templeton, my husband's uncle, once shared this insight.

> Spiritual maturity breaks down into three phases, each characterized by a phrase (refer to 1 John 2:12–14)
>
> 1. childhood (has belief, a seed of faith)—Christ *with* me;
>
> 2. adolescent (seed of faith takes root and grows)—Christ *in* me; and,
>
> 3. father (faith of a mustard "tree")—Christ AS me.[28]
>
> The child has acquired knowledge of God's justification (knowledge of purity before God, received from forgiveness of sin, "just-as-if-I never sinned"). The adolescent has internalized the knowledge to make it wisdom, and that wisdom connects him to the power of God (to empower godly living). The father in the faith has meditated on wisdom and it has matured into understanding, knowing God's ways. He or she is the person God trusts with His secrets[29] and whom God trusts to act on His behalf.[30]

Reflect on how the above also parallels what we reviewed about spiritual maturity in Judges 6. The surrendered servant models Christ as me, the

---

[28] Notice the last phase states Christ AS me, not Me as Christ. Pride, self-righteousness, or discouragement and weaknesses often cause us to distort the latter phase and project self and Flesh as the prominent person in the equation even after living victoriously with Christ in me. Remember how quickly Peter stumbled, and remember what we learned was missing in Peter—greater dependence on God's power.

[29] Daniel 2:28–29, 47; Job 11:16; 2 Chronicles 16:19; John 16:13.

[30] Credited to Norman Grubb, parentheticals added by this author.

deliverer Christ in me, and those in need of restoration or growth reveal Christ with me, the seed of faith that is beginning to grow.

Understanding is spiritual revelation received by those maturing in Christ. The topical index of the NKJV defines understanding as "knowing things in their right relationship." Understanding is to see circumstances with an eternal perspective, or seeing spiritual realities through earthly visibilities. Knowledge gains truth. Wisdom empowers the application of truth. When we read, listen to, or memorize God's Word, we gain knowledge of it. As we learn to apply this knowledge of His Word through life's circumstances, we exercise wisdom. Understanding is to realize the eternal perspective and spiritual purpose in accordance with God's *revealed* will. It is to become aware of how God's presence works spiritual purposes through life's circumstances. It is to recognize and experience knowledge and wisdom of God's ways.

The disciples repeatedly struggled to discern spiritual parallels behind physical situations. When Christ taught the disciples, understanding usually meant to comprehend the Word He preached and the miracles (power) He performed recognizing they served a greater purpose than the obvious. Understanding would allow the disciples to learn what the provision (the teaching or the miracles) taught them about God—His immediate plan, character, love, and ways to fulfill the eternal purpose.

The passages studied reveal three elements necessary to gain understanding—in order to see spiritually, there must be: *knowledge of His Word, a recognition of His power, and discerning wisdom from His Spirit.* It is the Word, power, and Spirit that provides knowledge, wisdom, and understanding. Reflect on this in regards to what was stated about hearing the Trinity: from the Father, Son, and Spirit, through their Word, Spirit, and power, we receive knowledge, wisdom, and understanding.

The lessons in this chapter repeatedly look at these levels of revelation—Word, Spirit, power/knowledge, wisdom, and understanding. The following illustration correlates these levels of revelation with our progressive spiritual maturity outlined above.

1 JOHN 2:12–14

CHILDHOOD →	ADOLESCENCE →	FATHER
KNOWLEDGE	WISDOM	UNDERSTANDING
TRUTH	TRUST	EMPOWERMENT
RECOGNIZE	SURRENDER	OBEDIENCE
FLESH	TO SPIRIT	
HEAR	**TRUST**	**REVEAL**
HIS WORD	**HIS SPIRIT**	**HIS POWER**
	(to reveal His Will & Ways)	Lk 4:1–14, Jn 17

Note from the diagram above that a response to God is required at all stages to mature to the next. The attributes denoted at each stage refer to a significant maturing of that attribute.

Isaiah 11 prophesies Christ's coming to earth in the form of man. God would empower Jesus as the Son of Man with a measure of empowerment necessary to fulfill God's purpose. Isaiah 11 defines that spiritual power, and included in it is the Spirit of understanding. Since Christ came to model all things for us, we can conclude that God likewise empowers us with a measure of empowerment necessary to fulfill God's purpose (Ephesians 4:7).

Embedded in that empowerment is a level of understanding, a revealed will necessary to trust and obey. This is not a one-size-fits-all measure of understanding. It is first and foremost in accordance with God's design (Romans 12:3). It is not an all-knowing power. It is not having complete knowledge of the entirety of God's purposes (1 Corinthians 13:12). It also is not automatically imparted always. While there can be divine revelation anytime as God wills, most of the time, understanding must be sought (Matthew 6:33, 7:7; Psalm 37:4; Proverbs 4:7). Hearts have to be prepared and trustworthy to receive understanding as we shall see. To begin this discussion, let us look at the provision of understanding God granted Jesus remembering that Jesus modeled for us and experienced all that God may ask of us.

Through Isaiah's prophecy of Jesus, we learn the seven spiritual attributes needed to fulfill His purpose. One of those is a Spirit of understanding.

> There shall come forth a Rod from the stem of Jesse, And a Branch shall grow out of his roots. The Spirit of the Lord shall rest upon Him, The Spirit of wisdom and understanding, The Spirit of counsel and might, The Spirit of knowledge and of the fear of the Lord. His delight [is] in the fear of the Lord, And He shall not judge by the sight of His eyes, Nor decide by the hearing of His ears; But with righteousness He shall judge the poor, And decide with equity for the meek of the earth; He shall strike the earth with the rod of His mouth, And with the breath of His lips He shall slay the wicked. Righteousness shall be the belt of His loins, And faithfulness the belt of His waist. (Isaiah 11:1–5)

Isaiah prophesies the coming Messiah. In verse 2, we read of God's fullness granted His Son. He is empowered with the Holy Spirit of the Lord, the spirit of wisdom, the spirit of understanding, the spirit of counsel, the spirit of might, the spirit of knowledge, and the fear of the Lord. Even for our Savior and King, we see God's specific gift of knowledge, wisdom, and specifically understanding, the provision we typically minimize, distort, or overlook altogether. But as Jesus demonstrates through the parable of the sower, it is a gift necessary to fully receive all other revelation. Understanding goes beyond knowledge and wisdom. The Hebrew meaning for wisdom in this verse is wise skill. The Hebrew meaning for understanding is discernment.

Wisdom is the God-empowered skill to apply knowledge; understanding is the God-revealed discernment of His eternal perspective or purpose.

Based on the use of the word understanding in the Old Testament, we learn there are three different levels or degrees of understanding that God imparts. In Exodus 31:3 and 35:31, God granted understanding or intelligence. To Daniel in 5:11–12, God granted understanding, or insight. As mentioned in Isaiah 11:2, the understanding given Christ is discernment, or spiritual perspective. This level of understanding is also the one referred to repeatedly throughout Job. Job reveals Christ by foreshadowing the understanding Christ is given, and further, to foreshadow God's will for Christ to reveal measures of understanding.

While each of these is an obvious gift of God, the level of understanding this study admonishes us to receive is primarily that of spiritual discernment, the eternal perspective and focus God imparts through the indwelling power of the Holy Spirit. It is remaining in that uninterrupted, unquenched, and ungrieved flow of the Spirit.

As stated above, understanding is not all knowledge of all things. Understanding who God is (His fullness) is even more important than gaining understanding of His eternal purpose. Understanding His fullness leads to revelation of His purpose. Our pursuit of God helps us find peace that surpasses understanding. Ephesians 4 encourages us to pursue understanding so that we reach our fullness in Christ.

When we recall Job's request for understanding, we are reminded of his desire to comprehend God's purpose for his situation. Job was a righteous, obedient man. We know God allowed Satan to test Job. This level of understanding sought was part of God's secret will. However, there was a level of understanding God provided Job that resulted in a greater fear of the Lord. Job came to know the Lord more as a result of this affliction by Satan. Job wanted understanding of his pain; instead, God gave Job greater understanding of God. Even through this terrible difficulty Satan intended for harm, God revealed His goodness to Job. But it was available only through Job's fear of God. From Isaiah 11 above, we learn that Jesus also was given "knowledge and a fear of the Lord." Why would God's Son need to be given a fear of the Lord? Listen to what Matthew Henry says about the correlation of understanding (discernment) to a fear of the Lord.

> By this it will appear that we have the Spirit of God, if we have spiritual senses exercised, and are of quick understanding in the fear of the lord. Those have divine illumination that know their duty and know how to go about it. Therefore Jesus Christ had the spirit without measure, that he might perfectly understand his undertaking; and he did so, as appears not only in the admirable answers he gave to all that questioned with him, which proved him to be of quick understanding in the fear of the Lord, but in the management of his whole undertaking. He has settled the great affair of religion so unexpectedly well (so as effectually

to secure both God's honour and man's happiness) that, it must be owned, he thoroughly understood it.[31]

The first sentence of this quote is worth repeating: "By this it will appear that we have the Spirit of God, if we have spiritual senses exercised, and are of quick understanding in the fear of the lord." When we exercise spiritual senses, we demonstrate a fear of or reverence for the Lord. We give testimony to the Spirit of God in us, His Spirit of understanding. God may bestow gifted intelligence. God may grant a supernatural ministry. But for God to grant discernment, a spiritual, eternal, perspective of the kingdom of God, there must be a fear of the Lord. There must be a reverent willingness to realize our nothingness before God and man to remain in the flow of a spirit of understanding. A fear of the Lord keeps us in a posture of humility, keeping in check pride and self-exaltation potentially fueled when we receive revelation and understanding. Fear of the Lord exalts God above self.

Jesus also reveals God's provision of understanding through the parable of the sower, the foundation that prepared the disciples for Jesus's entire ministry. While this may not be the first parable Jesus gave, it occurs early in His ministry and built His followers' faith. It reveals what is necessary for a true, fruitful conversion from a life of sin, that is, outwardly hearing God's Word and receiving it in our hearts through understanding.

Read Mark 4:1–20. As you answer the questions that follow, consider this passage as a guide to help us identify what prohibits and what nourishes spiritual maturity.

In verse 13, what does Jesus say is the result of failing to understand this parable?

---

[31] Matthew Henry, "Commentary on Isaiah 11," in *Matthew Henry Commentary on the Whole Bible*, Blue Letter Bible, May 4, 2005, http://www.blueletterbible.org/Comm/mhc/Isa/Isa011.html.

Why is understanding this parable so critical? What is the key emphasis of this parable?

In verse 14, what does the sower sow?

Read the same parable in Matthew 13:1–23.

From both gospels but particularly Matthew's, we learn that hearing alone is not enough. Understanding is the nourishment that takes what we hear (the seed or Word of God) and grows it into a fruitful harvest. Examine this fundamental truth about understanding: We may hear God's Word, but Satan, tribulations, persecutions, cares of this world (busyness), and the deceitfulness of riches prevent the Word sown in our hearts from taking root and producing fruit. We may hear enough to gain information or knowledge, but without understanding, we lack the wisdom to comprehend eternal truth and we fail to progress from babes, to adolescents, to people of mature faith.

Have you ever bought a potted plant with the intention of transplanting it somewhere in your yard? Generally speaking, plants that are not transplanted quickly in a larger pot with better soil, or in well-fertilized ground, die sooner than necessary. Most soils in purchased potted plants do not have a healthy portion of rich dirt to sustain long-term health. This prevents the plant from holding moisture around the roots. When a healthy plant is transplanted in its natural climate, there is sudden growth due to its being in richer soil and greater access to moisture from the earth. As long as the ground is watered and fertilized, the plant thrives. By adding natural fertilizers like peat moss, compost, cottonseed meal, or bone meal, we replenish nutrients and stimulate plant growth. Such plants require less maintenance than do potted plants, and their beauty is often superior.

Hearing and understanding cultivates good ground. God plants His seed of faith in the soil of our hearts, but unless the soil is well maintained with understanding, faith will not grow. Understanding is like the fertilizer used to enrich plant health. Understanding applies God's Word, His Spirit, and presence into circumstances that nourish the heart and stimulate faith. When grounded in rich soil with adequate sources of light and water, faith's seed has better access to the spiritual nutrients to make it flourish.

Christ told us what happens to the mustard seed. When this smallest of seeds is full grown—when it has taken root in fertile soil—it becomes much greater than a small herb. In Matthew's parable, failing to have fertile ground to nurture and grow the Word of God causes us to stumble, to fall by the wayside, to become unfruitful. In Matthew 13:23, Christ says, "But he who received seed on the good ground is he who *hears the word and understands it*, who indeed bears fruit and produces: some a hundredfold, some sixty, some thirty" (emphasis added).

The Holy Spirit is our source for understanding. Christians are *sealed* with the Holy Spirit (Ephesians 4:30). As children sealed with His Spirit, we are empowered to relate to God in intimate fellowship. Often without our conscious awareness, the Spirit works to guide and convict to reveal truths of God's Word. But the *filling* of the Holy Spirit is God's power at work in and through our lives. Unlike the one-time sealing of the Holy Spirit at salvation, the filling of the Holy Spirit should occur continually throughout our walk with God as we surrender to Him. The filling of the Holy Spirit occurs when we seek and invite God's presence consciously. Galatians 3–5 gives warning against beginning Christian faith in the Spirit only to surrender to live in the Flesh. We are urged to "walk in the Spirit" (Galatians 5:16) so that we do not carry out the desires of the Flesh. We grieve or quench the filling of the Spirit through sin or disobedience but remain sealed by it. To walk in the Spirit is to surrender to the continual filling of the Spirit. The parable of the sower identifies general obstacles that quench or grieve this filling.[32]

Matthew 13:19–23 details the obstacles to the seed taking root and producing fruit (the consequences of not understanding). In the space following each verse below, describe how these obstacles past or present may have prevented understanding in your daily relationship with God. Where applicable, express your need of God.

---

[32] Again, I highly recommend *The Sensitivity of the Spirit* by R. T. Kendall as an excellent, exhaustive, and empowering study of this subject.

Verse 19—failing to understand results in the wicked one snatching away what was sown. How has Satan thwarted the Word God gives for application? How does he prevent, interrupt, or invade quiet time? How does he minimize your prayer life? Does he interfere with reverent worship? Does he make you feel too inadequate or disinterested in or fearful of obedience?

Verse 21—tribulation and persecution causes us to stumble. When persecuted, ridiculed, or mistrusted for your beliefs, how have you responded? Do you allow this tribulation to permanently halt the work of God in your life? How are you allowing God to be revealed through your response to those who persecute you? Are you willing to persevere with a trust in the promises of God above the opinions of men?

Verse 22—cares of this world and deceitfulness of riches choke the Word causing unfruitfulness. When life's circumstances are difficult, do you respond as if God has abandoned you or as if God has no power to deliver you through the difficulty? Is your pursuit of material things and earthly comforts interfering with God's plan for your life?

You may be thinking, "There is a big difference between the disciples and me. I already have the Holy Spirit living in me to give understanding, and the disciples did not at the time this instruction is given."[33] While this may be true, it still does not negate our need to surrender doubt, unbelief, and fear. The ploys of Satan and our actions in the Flesh quench the filling (the fellowship or partnership) of the Holy Spirit. With the Spirit quenched

---

[33] Though the disciples did not yet have the indwelling Holy Spirit, it does not mean they were without revelation from God prior to Pentecost. There still was opportunity for God to reveal understanding. For example, when Jesus asks the disciples, "Who do you say that I am," and Peter replies, "You are the Son of the Living God," Jesus responds by saying that only God could have revealed that to him. Peter, absent the indwelling Spirit, received understanding, a revelation from God. Peter was a disciple who pursued understanding Jesus and service for God.

or even grieved with disobedience, the power of understanding diminishes until we repent.

The disciples' lack of understanding did not hinder God's power, but it did affect both their expectation and celebration of it. When they failed to understand, their expectations of what God would do did not increase. When later faced with similar situations, this lack of understanding left them ill equipped to trust God's miraculous provision in almost identical circumstances. It was not a lack of understanding the situation that was crippling; it was the lack of understanding God's fullness in it.

We also may fail to realize our need for understanding or the extent of God's gift of it; this can cause our lives to remain blinded by unbelief. Without hearing Him and perceiving a need to understand, how will we be prepared to accept the new and unfamiliar presence of His goodness in ways we have not yet experienced? How can we expect to rise above our traditions, our familiarity with His ways, and our present knowledge of Him to learn more about the vastness of His almighty character? How limited or dulled will our mirrored reflection of Him then be to a world desperate to see what He has to reveal? Can we honestly say we already understand the fullness of God?

In Mark 7, we read about Jesus healing the deaf and mute man by spitting on his hands and touching the man's ear and tongue to restore senses. A short time later, after the miracle of the seven loaves, Jesus similarly heals a blind man by actually spitting on the blind man's eyes and then touching them. In Mark 8:23–25, Jesus asks, "'Do you see anything?' And he looked up and said, 'I see men, for I see them like trees, walking around.' Then again He laid His hands on his eyes; and he looked intently and was restored and began to see everything clearly."

The Greek word *diablepo* used in Mark 8:25 means to "see everything clearly." In this verse, it describes the clarity of sight Jesus further gave the man. The same Greek word is used in Matthew and Luke's account of Jesus warning those who judge to first get the log out of their eyes before removing specks from others' eyes (see Matthew 7:5 and Luke 6:42). Jesus speaks metaphorically in this warning, and the sight encouraged is that of understanding, to see clearly, to comprehend with spiritual discernment God's perspective of all sin. Jesus conversed with the blind man, altering and continuing His touch until the man could fully see. This miracle (power) gives witness to Jesus's prior warning on the speck (Word) to reveal that Jesus was the way to "see clearly," to understand with spiritual sight (His will). He communes with us as a friend to ensure we understand God. The pattern of God's ways in His Word is to provide clear understanding.

Think about people who have a fear of flying. Because of this fear, they miss an opportunity to see firsthand the awesome beauty of God's world. Granted, there are many places they could go without flying, but it would take longer and require greater effort. Similarly, we may feel content with our experience and knowledge of God. We in fact may have experienced great blessings and received His goodness and wise leading in many ways. But there is more to experience when we allow Him to open understanding and grow faith.

Do not fear how He chooses to reveal Himself. God is the same yesterday, today, and tomorrow. The God of yesterday as seen in His Word wanted to reveal Himself. We need to be willing to see Him clearly today to prepare us for tomorrow. We must be opened to learn how understanding is a catalyst for that revelation.

God progressively reveals His understanding for our situation. Let me share this personal illustration of the parable of the sower.

I was given a small hibiscus plant by a guest. It was only about eight inches high, but it had one bloom opened and a bud soon to open. It looked pretty in my kitchen, so I decided to leave it there for a short while before I transplanted it in the yard. But it stayed by the sink and under the cabinet lighting for a year! Each time I worked at my kitchen sink, I was reminded it needed to be watered. Because of my busyness, it stayed inside through spring, summer, fall, and winter. Leaves would die and new leaves grew in their place, but the plant never again bloomed, and it didn't grow. Water was the only real nourishment it received. The light was artificial and insufficient. The soil became depleted of nutrients. It had no fertilizer, no stimulator, no replenishment to nurture a healthy root system.

Could this be a picture of your relationship with God? Are you rooted in church yet settling for substitutes for what He has to give? Are you exposing yourself to God's Word but failing to seek His provision of understanding? Are you being fed solely by the fruit of others' study, others' service, or others' worship? That may help sustain you, but it is probably insufficient to overcome Satan's schemes, tribulation, and persecutions.

God is your greatest source for the strength necessary to overcome fear. You may be busy at home, work, and church, but busyness for God is not as nurturing as feeding on His presence. You need the Living Water, the light of God's Son personally, not indirectly revealing Himself to you as the Word of God keeps you rooted mightily in His will.

Jesus told the disciples in Mark 4:12 that failing to understand the parable of the sower would result in their lack of understanding everything else. This lesson is therefore critical for laying the foundation of faith. If we do not set aside time necessary for God to cultivate what He speaks to us, we will never live victoriously over fear. The tug-of-war will be intense and exhaustive. Our busyness chokes the Word and becomes unfruitful.

After progressing from the stage of Christ *with* me to Christ *in* me, it often may become more difficult to mature to the state of Christ *as* me. Satan intensifies his attacks to prevent faith from maturing to this level. The reasons are many, but a most critical reason is to halt intercession: power praying the will and purposes of God beyond our own need. Too often, we stay so busy with concerns of life or the busyness of Christian service that this level of intercession is minimized if not hindered altogether. As we train spiritual senses to intercede, we are further empowered with understanding to discern how to navigate personal difficulty or decisions, which are often the self-focused sources of hindering intercession.

God has a specific path for each of us. There are things He wants us to learn and discover about Him unique to our life and purpose; they are ours alone to discover. We may hear His truth, but is it falling on good ground? Have we made cultivating our hearts and minds a priority? What are we doing to ensure the soil, our hearts, remains a fertile place for His Word to grow? God longs for us to fully mature into our beautiful purpose.

For we are His workmanship, created in Christ Jesus for good works, which God prepared beforehand that we should walk in them.
—Ephesians 2:10

For it is God who works in you both to will and to do for His good pleasure. Do all things without murmuring and disputing, that you may become blameless and harmless, children of God without fault in the midst of a crooked and perverse generation, among whom you shine

> as lights in the world, holding fast the word of life, so that I may rejoice in the day of Christ that I have not run in vain or labored in vain.
> —Philippians 2:13–16

Prepared for Understanding

Begin with worship, meditation, and prayer.

> He who disdains instruction despises his own soul, but he who heeds reproof gets understanding. The fear of the Lord is the instruction of wisdom, and before honor is humility. (Proverbs 15:32–33)

> "Lord, help me learn how to maintain fertile ground for my faith to grow. Teach me how to posture myself to receive understanding. Teach me how to recognize Your path for peace and hope even in great difficulty."

Opening our spiritual eyes and ears to understanding is more difficult than simply opening our eyes and ears to process sights and sounds. Instead, we must open our hearts and minds to receive the seen and unseen things of God. But even this becomes difficult to accomplish when we attempt it in the Flesh or with human reasoning.

In the prior section, we discussed the Word–spirit–power formula for understanding, for growing faith. The majority of this chapter unfolds God's provision of understanding, but we begin by looking at our role in this partnership. We have mentioned the following responses that nurture the filling of the Holy Spirit, who develops our spiritual sensitivities. We want to look at these more deeply.

1. hearing the Word—trusting and obeying God,
2. remembering His Word and His promises, and
3. recognizing His power—a growing knowledge of who God is and an ever-increasing expectation of what He will do.

Hear to Trust and Obey

Previously, we discussed how God makes a way for us to know Him, His deep truths, and His revealed will. We also discussed the difficulty in trusting someone we don't know. When we accept Christ as Savior, we commit our lives to Him. We commit to trust and obey. Just as an infant responds to a loving parent or caregiver with trust, we trust God. As our Creator, He comprehends what is needed for trust. To trust God requires faith that He acts on our behalf and has good intentions for us even when circumstances appear contrary. Part of growing in faith is to understand that God's guidelines and leading are for protection, not depravity. The struggle to believe this is foundational to sin's origin.

Adam and Eve knew God intimately but failed to trust God's purposes. Instead of trusting God, they trusted Satan's lie and disobeyed. God made himself real to Adam and Eve, but for them to trust and obey His limitations would require faith that He was acting on their behalf. Satan undermined faith by fueling doubt in God's protective restriction. Satan tempted them to believe God kept them from experiencing greater goodness. Thus, they failed to trust God. They relied on their limited understanding distorted by Satan.

Faith fuels trust. A growing faith in God provides spiritual sight, so trust is not always completely blind. Proverbs 3:5–7 says, "Trust in the Lord with all your heart, and *lean not on your own understanding. In all ways, acknowledge Him, and He will direct your paths. Do not be wise in your own eyes*; Fear the Lord and depart from evil" (emphasis added). This admonishes us to trust God and put away our own understanding and, through faith, lean on God's understanding to receive His direction. It does not say to trust blindly; it encourages us to seek God ways above self. When hearts are fully surrendered to the Spirit of God in us, we receive God's measure of understanding to empower trust. Draw near to God so His presence also empowers you to trust even those secret things that remain hidden. As you draw near, rest assured that this deepening faith will also empower greater trust.

2 Chronicles 16:9 says, "for the eyes of the Lord run to and fro throughout the whole earth, to show Himself strong on behalf of those whose heart is loyal to Him." Just as faith fuels trust, trust fuels obedience. Obedience prepares our hearts to understand further. God gave a gift of

understanding to Solomon, but He admonished Solomon to keep His ways and walk in His commandments. God seeks those who seek Him, those who are willing to remain loyal to His purposes. Listen to this prayer in Psalm 119, which models a humbled heart surrendered to receive understanding. Notice the important elements to understanding we have identified—the need of the Word, a fear of the Lord, a teachable spirit, and a request for understanding—all of which empower obedience.

> Teach me, O Lord, the way of Your statutes, and I shall keep it to the end. Give me understanding, and I shall keep your law; indeed, I shall observe it with my whole heart. Make me walk in the path of Your commandments, for I delight in it. Incline my heart to Your testimonies, and not to covetousness. Turn away my eyes from looking at worthless things, and revive me in Your way. Establish Your word to Your servant, who is devoted to fearing You. (Psalm 119:33–38)

Let's look at other scriptures correlating obedience with understanding. Summarize this correlation in each verse below.

Deuteronomy 4:5–6

Psalm 111:10

Proverbs 14:29

Isaiah 11:2–5

Job 28:28

Jeremiah 4:22

Those who are obedient are adorned with understanding. Those who have understanding observe the commandments and instructions of the Lord. The psalmist in the above passage says, "Give me understanding, and I shall keep your law." The psalmist recognizes the empowerment to obey that understanding gives. Since understanding serves an important role in empowering obedience, we must be aware of Satan's schemes to preempt understanding (as he did with Adam and Eve), even when we have surrendered hardened hearts.

Sometimes in spiritual infancy, we are eager to trust and obey though we may seek to do so in our own strength. As our own strength grows weary, Satan and Flesh often cause us to promote self above God's leading. Obedience postures us to receive further understanding because it keeps us in unbroken fellowship with the power of the Holy Spirit.

Through the Spirit, God reveals spiritual realities in physical visibilities. When there is willingness to obey, God uses what we see, hear, and experience in the earthly realm to understand His truths in the spiritual realm. Judges 6 reveals this pattern with Gideon's response and obedience to God. Through worship—surrender, trust, and fear of God—God revealed Gideon's next step. Gideon's obedience postures him to experience more of God's power, provision, and instruction. Obedience proves Gideon's trustworthiness and reveals God's faithfulness and power.

Remembrance of His Word and Promises

Let us study how Jesus helped the disciples see the goodness of God in the presence of devastating news. Jesus cultivated understanding to grow the disciples' faith.

Read John 14:25–29. In verse 27, what does Christ leave with the disciples?

What does He tell them not to be?

In verse 28, how does Christ say they should respond if they fully understood?

Read John 16:1–7. After describing great persecutions and afflictions that the disciples must face in the future, how do they respond? (v. 6).

In the middle of great uncertainty, affliction, and trouble, Christ tells the disciples He is giving them peace. We know Jesus gives peace that passes understanding. It is His peace, the peace the Father gives His Son, who is soon to be brutally beaten, crucified, rejected, mocked, and killed. It is an unshakeable peace. But this is not the first time Jesus revealed Himself as peace.

Let us return to the early miracles Jesus performed in the presence of His disciples. Given the above discourse, we can now better understand Jesus's desire for the disciples to trust Him as their source of peace during this early miracle. He was preparing them to recognize and receive a future provision while meeting a current need.

Read Mark 3:35–41. What command does Jesus issue in verse 39?

At the time Jesus prepares the disciples for His crucifixion, they most likely are not thinking of this early moment with Jesus and the power demonstrated in their presence on the stormy sea. They may hear His admonition to receive peace, but understandably, they are too focused on present circumstances to remember past provisions. Even if the disciples recalled the past power of Jesus, they do not recognize the necessity to rely on it in this dilemma. After all, one may rationalize, the situations are different. What does *that* provision have to do with *this* news? This is true if we observe these differing scenarios with only physical comparisons, but if we look at the spiritual parallel, there are significant similarities.

At the beginning of His ministry and now near the end, Jesus demonstrates His power to grant peace. Providing for the disciples' safety in a storm was merely the vehicle to teach them about God's power in Jesus. Jesus first demonstrates this ability through physical uncertainty and now, as their relationship deepens, in spiritual uncertainty (very much influenced by the physical). Christ models for us how to have peace in these times; He is the peace that lives in us. Circumstances may be different, and their fear, doubt, and unbelief still exist, but so does the lasting peace of Christ. Repeatedly throughout His ministry, Jesus emphasizes the need for peace in the midst of uncertainty. Remember our early discussion of Philippians 4:6–7: "Be anxious for nothing, but in everything by prayer and supplication, with thanksgiving, let your requests be made known to God; *and the peace of God, which surpasses all understanding, will guard your hearts and minds* through Christ Jesus" (emphasis added).

In our quest for understanding especially in the midst of great difficulty, we are continually admonished to receive peace so our hearts and minds will be guarded against fear, doubt, and unbelief, so we are positioned to thwart Satan's schemes, and so we are postured to receive understanding and rest. He promises peace that passes understanding that cannot be physically comprehended or explained. It is a peace that overshadows the still-present turmoil.[34]

Fear and anxiety blind understanding and cause a focus on the physical crisis more than God's eternal purpose. Long before this present sorrow, Jesus gave them the opportunity to prepare for today. In the past, He demonstrated His power to bring peace over physical hardship. His provision met their immediate need, but it was also preparation for future events. The situations may be different, but there is constancy in the nature and provision of Christ. It was God's will that the disciples learned to trust the fullness of God's power in Jesus.

We are no different from the disciples when difficulty surfaces. Though we may instinctively know of God's power and peace and may fully acknowledge His past faithfulness, too often we allow current distresses to keep us from calling out for and relying on that power. Perhaps we refuse to accept the way He chooses to reveal His power, and Satan may convince us this situation is hopeless. We may unconsciously feel too unworthy, too undeserving, of God's intervening power. Satan clutters our minds with the vastness of the mountain so that we forget the indwelling power that can cause this mountain to become a plain (Zechariah 4:6–7).

As Philippians 4:6 says, we must choose not to be anxious so we do not forget God's past provisions. This principle is crucial to prepare

---

[34] This level of peace has been demonstrated to us by Gideon, Daniel and his friends, Christ, and Paul.

understanding. God's past personal faithfulness could be the source of understanding His provision for a current personal prayer.

Let's look at one more instance, this time in the Old Testament, in which God spoke comfort in the middle of chaos. Begin by looking at God's prophecy of judgment to fall on His people in Jeremiah 25:8–11 and 27–33. Briefly summarize God's judgment.

Read Jeremiah 29:4–14. Summarize the tone of God's instruction in verses 4–6.

Read Jeremiah 29:10–14. Summarize God's plan of restoration.

God released fierce judgment on His people as punishment for their sins. Jerusalem and Solomon's temple are being destroyed. Many are killed. Survivors are carried from the Promised Land (their home for 500 years) into Babylonian captivity. Yet in the middle of this horrible devastation, God also reveals His plan for restoration. (Notice how this plan generally parallels that of Judges 6; learn God's ways!)

In 29:7, what does God tell His troubled, hopeless people to seek?

Sometimes, we remain so absorbed with the severity of our need that it is necessary to have physical witness to comprehend spiritual truths. Later, the Spirit may bring to our remembrance revelations not previously understood and grant further understanding. This teaches us that God often has to prepare the way for understanding. Sometimes, it is a matter of preparing us to receive or endure what He must reveal. Sometimes, it is a process of preparing or completing circumstances that are vehicles for understanding. God uses this delay to align our hearts to His and prepare us to receive His provision.

As I walked with God during my mother's illness and death; God strengthened faith. A short time after my mom's death, I was diagnosed with a benign liver cyst. After many unsuccessful attempts to have it removed, it was determined that I should have laser surgery at a major medical center by one of the leading specialists on laser surgery. As the surgeons preoperatively finished reviewing the surgical procedures, God brought Proverbs 3:5–6 to my mind: "Trust in the Lord with all your heart and lean not on your own understanding." Mentally reciting this verse and praying it for the doctors were my last thoughts before the procedure.

What was supposed to have been a twenty-four-hour outpatient surgery turned into a very painful and difficult three-day hospital stay. The amount of postoperative pain and the inability to gain relief from it is indescribable. I came out of the procedure with swollen, discolored eyes and multiple bruises where tubes and needles had been. Furthermore, a few months later, the cyst returned larger than before. I was informed by other specialists that this type of surgery would never have been a permanent treatment for my condition. Instead, I needed the left lobe of my liver removed. I was very concerned about the risks of this procedure and the pain and recovery. From the beginning, I was told this would require at least one week in the hospital. I could expect more pain in and out of the hospital than the previous surgery entailed, along with longer recuperation at home.

My mind and emotions were flooded with what ifs, regrets, and concerns. How could I possibly endure more pain over a longer time? Why did I have the other procedure? I asked God to give me rest instead of fear and anxiety. The Spirit led me to read Psalm 91. As I read this passage, peace flooded my soul. In reassurance, I knew that my situation was in God's hands and that His angels had charge over me (v. 11).

Through that passage, I believed the Lord reassured His plan and purpose for my life beyond this illness. As I rested in this peace, God brought the experience of praying Proverbs 3 prior to the first surgery to my mind. It was as if He spoke assurance to my heart that the verse had not been intended for *that surgery* alone but to *prepare me for what He knew was ahead*. When God birthed that Word in me prior to the first surgery, He knew that I would endure difficulty and that subsequent surgery would happen. God's provision for the first surgery was also preparation and comfort for the future surgery. This provision of peace came through the remembrance of His prior word.

The God who desired to calm and prepare His disciples moves to calm and prepare us. The Spirit moves in us to remember His Word and promises.

Recognition of His Power

Tunnel vision prevents understanding and limits recognition of God's power at work around us. It locks us into a goal that may or may not be the goal God intends. Even when the goal is godly, tunnel vision can cause us to ignore God's ways for its completion. For example, our faith is to grow from a seed to a tree, but the goal of the tree is not just to grow for the sake of becoming taller or beautiful, but to provide shelter and protection for others. We should always allow God to expand spiritual vision so we can better glimpse His eternal plan. As learned in Mark's gospel, God uses all aspects of our relationship and interaction with Him as an entry point to reveal Himself and His power. As faith grows, as we learn how to receive understanding, we begin to see how individual experiences, teachings, prayers, meditations, worship, etc. all reveal God's provision for present and future needs. As we learn to recognize this faithful, sovereign design of God, our understanding and expectations of what He accomplishes increase. Our hearts, minds, and even physical senses surrender to comprehend His power at work.

Billy Graham said, "I can't see the wind, but I can see the effects of the wind." We also feel the wind. God provides, protects, heals, and directs through the Holy Spirit. We see the effects of His power though we may not see Him. We may sense the nearness of His presence. During these revelations of His power, understanding postures us to know Him more fully and to further discern His purpose for the demonstration of His power.

My mother died of colon cancer in November 1999. We knew shortly after her diagnosis that her condition was terminal, and yet my family prayed for her physical healing. After only a few months of praying, I had a strong understanding in my heart that God would not heal her physically in the way we wanted. Yet there was still a level of emotional and spiritual healing God burdened me to intercede for, but understanding of why and specifically for what did not come to me until much later. Had I become embittered or angry at God during the revealing of His will, my understanding may not have been as complete. My prayers of intercession would have been hindered by my anger. Since my prayers kept me focused on a need though it was not fully understood, they prepared me to look for God's provision. The need caused me to seek God and watch for His power. It caused me to expect a deeper understanding of His goodness I did not realize was available.

At the end of this chapter, I will share more about God's power that was revealed to my family prior to my mother's death. For now, let me say the goodness and power He gave us exceeded expectation. God answered our prayers but in a different way than we thought possible.

When God grants understanding, sometimes, His provision may not be what we hoped for; but the goodness He bestows will be more than we could imagine even during great times of grief. He aligns the desires of our hearts to agree with His. His desires and plans ultimately reveal His goodness.

As we learned from Judges 6 and Jeremiah 29, even when difficulty results because of rebellion and disobedience, God issues instructions for finding peace and hope! Beloved, this should greatly encourage you today! God grants understanding in the middle of the most devastating circumstances and confusion. God grants peace and hope even when the difficulty we experience is the consequence of our own actions. Even when we are the most undeserving, He redeems and restores. This is true in reference to salvation and for transformation into the image of Christ "from glory to glory" (2 Corinthians 3:17–18) as we learn to surrender to Christ *as* me. In the middle of devastation and chaos, God tells His people to pray for and embrace the peace in this land of exile "for in its peace you will have peace." Peaceful hearts and minds prepare us to receive God's clear direction.

God's Word reveals His ways for restoration. He promises to respond with healing and restoration to those who have understanding (Matthew 13:15). Even in the middle of our darkest night, God offers comfort. We need not become so consumed with our situation that we miss His provision. It may very well come in some form of past faithfulness, a time of preparation for trusting Him today. That is why it is so important to specifically praise God for His past personal faithfulness during our present need. That is why it is important to learn to recognize His power and presence through His provisions. This gives Him opportunity to "bring to our remembrance" what may be a present source of faith and strength. Let us apply this truth.

Is there an aspect of your life not as settled as you believe it should be? Your marriage or other close relationship, your physical home, your job, a ministry, your health, etc.?

Can you recall a situation in which God gave peace? What did that provision teach you about God, and how may He being using that experience to focus your heart today? What scripture did He give or reveal at that time?

Ask God to reveal how He would have you receive peace in the area that is not as settled as you know He intends. Journal what He reveals to serve as a reminder of His will and promise of peace.

He who dwells in the secret place of the Most High Shall abide under the shadow of the Almighty. I will say of the Lord, "He is my refuge and my fortress; My God, in Him I will trust." Surely He shall deliver you from the snare of the fowler And from the perilous pestilence. He shall cover you with His feathers, And under His wings you shall take refuge; His truth shall be your shield and buckler. You shall not be afraid of the terror by night, Nor of the arrow that flies by day, Nor of the pestilence that walks in darkness, Nor of the destruction that lays waste at noonday. A thousand may fall at your side, And ten thousand at your right hand; But it shall not come near you. Only with your eyes shall you look, And see the reward of the wicked. Because you have made the Lord, who is my refuge, Even the Most High, your dwelling place, No evil shall befall you, Nor shall any plague come near your dwelling; For He shall give His angels charge over you, To keep you in all your ways. In their hands they shall bear you up, Lest you dash your foot against a stone. You shall tread upon the lion and the cobra, The young lion and the serpent you shall trample underfoot. "Because he has set his love upon Me, therefore I will deliver him; I will set him on high, because he has known My name. He shall call upon Me, and I will answer him; I [will be] with him in trouble; I will deliver him and honor him. With long life I will satisfy him, And show him My salvation."

—Psalm 91:1–16 NKJV

The Gift of Understanding

Begin with worship, meditation, and prayer.

> Therefore give to Your servant an understanding heart to judge Your people that I may discern between good and evil. For who is able to judge this great people of Yours? And the speech pleased the Lord, that Solomon asked this thing. Then God said to him: "Because you have asked this thing, and have not asked riches for yourself, nor have asked the life of your enemies, but have asked for yourself understanding to discern justice, behold I have done according to your word; see, I have given you a wise and understanding heart, so that there has not been anyone like you before you, nor shall any like you arise after you. And I have also given you what you have not asked: both riches and honor, so that there shall not be anyone like you among the kings all your days. So if you walk in My ways, to keep My statutes and My commandments, as your father David walked, then I will lengthen your days." (1 Kings 3:9–15)
>
> "Lord, help me more fully understand the power of understanding. Give me wisdom and understanding of Your Word so I may know You more. Help me recognize You through the circumstances of this day."

In the above passage, we read of the remarkable gift of understanding given to Solomon. Solomon's request for understanding pleased the Lord so much that God gave him more than asked. God bestowed on Solomon a provision of understanding; it is clear from other scriptures we have studied that God wants us also to receive understanding.

In chapter 2, we briefly discussed the power of understanding and learned God responds with healing and restoration when we receive the understanding available. By looking at other Old and New Testament references where God gives or grants understanding, we can better understand His desire to bestow it. By each reference, summarize the phrase that speaks of this gift.

Exodus 31:3

Exodus 36:1

1 Chronicles 22:12

Proverbs 2:6

1 John 5:20

Note from these passages that God granted wisdom *and* understanding necessary to fulfill His will. As learned previously, they are not the same, but most references mentioning wisdom also mention understanding inferring that they are not mutually exclusive. In this lesson's meditation passage, note that Solomon asked for an understanding heart, but God granted a *wise and understanding* heart. Gaining understanding is a progressive knowledge of the things of God. Its first prerequisite is knowledge of God's Word; the second is the wisdom to obey and apply the Word. But even with these prerequisites, there is still the need to seek understanding.

As we learn from Solomon, understanding did not just happen. Solomon recognized his need for it and asked God to grant it.[35] Scripture repeatedly speaks of our need to seek it also. Understanding is spoken of at least 249 times in the Bible, and 60 of those mentioned are in Proverbs. More than any other book, Proverbs encourages us to seek understanding. Solomon gives many admonitions to seek it; he reminds us it is a gift. We do not gain wisdom and understanding by our merits and intellect (which are in themselves gifts of God). God is the giver of understanding, and those who delight in pursuing righteous living must seek it. Summarize the phrase from each verse exhorting us to seek understanding.

---

[35] Ecclesiastes is a book that reveals the understanding—the eternal perspective of life—that Solomon eventually gained through his dependence and obedience to God as well as his failures.

Proverbs 2:2–9

Proverbs 3:13

Proverbs 4:1

Proverbs 4:5

Proverbs 4:7

Solomon places a specific emphasis in Proverbs 4:7 on seeking understanding even more than wisdom. "In all your getting get understanding" further reveals the importance of this level of revelation and empowerment. As seen earlier through the phases of Christian maturity, our goal should be to reach that place of maturity of Christ as me. Understanding is needed to empower that level of surrender. With understanding comes a revived and renewed energy to trust and obey. Shortly, we will learn how understanding quickly cleared away confusion, disappointment, and fatigue in the men on the road to Emmaus. Too often we realize that faith and understanding are necessary to come to know Christ, but we may discount the importance of their role to mature us in Christ, relying instead on self-effort. With understanding, spiritual discernment, we are postured to comprehend how God is working in our lives and in those around us. It postures us to make wiser decisions in all aspects, and it empowers the strength to follow God's will.

God wants us to understand His revealed will. We must realize our need to seek it and be sensitive to the moving of His presence. But some may be hesitant about their ability to understand the deeper truths of God especially in light of verses and passages that seem to contradict the above. Let's look at several of these.

> Have you not known? Have you not heard? The everlasting God, the Lord, The Creator of the ends of the earth, neither faints nor is weary. There is no searching of His understanding. (Isaiah 40:28)

"There is no searching of His understanding." At first glance, this verse may seem a discouragement to gain understanding. It implies an inability to perceive the things of God. But to fully understand this verse requires looking at the context in which it is given. Previously in verse 27, Isaiah quotes the grumbling Israelites: "My way is hidden from the Lord, and my just claim is passed over by my God." They *presume* the God of Creation is inadequate to discern and understand their need; "My way is hidden from Him," they cry. Isaiah promptly responds by reminding them who God is—the everlasting God, the Lord, the Creator. Isaiah responds by reminding them they cannot presume God has no understanding of their plight. "There is no searching of His understanding" describes the vastness of God's understanding, which is unending. This verse does not imply there should be no seeking of it but rather a focusing on its greatness.

> Oh, the depth of the riches both of the wisdom and knowledge of God! How unsearchable are His judgments and His ways past finding out! "For who has known the mind of the Lord? Or who has become His counselor? Or who has first given to Him and it shall be repaid to Him." (Romans 11:33–35)

We are reminded in this verse about the vastness and depth of God's wisdom. Paul says, "His ways are past finding out. For who has known the mind of the Lord." Like Isaiah, Paul is referencing the vast, unending ways and mind of God. This whole passage is made following mention of God's will to harden the hearts of the Jews so His will for Christ to bring salvation to Gentiles and Jews may be fulfilled. Paul is saying there are ways and purposes of God we will never comprehend (His secret will and ways). Paul's caution regarding God's ways is to guard against predicting or presuming the path God's will may take through its completion. It is a warning against presuming to know God's mind.

This passage is not a discouragement from seeking to have the mind of Christ as we have studied in 1 Corinthians 2. God gives us the mind of Christ, who reveals the will and ways of our Father. We cannot presume or predict the ways God fulfills His will, but we study His past ways so we can recognize Him as He works. We have already discussed the need to caution against presuming how God will move just because He has done so in the past. To do so could result in dependence on a method, program, or tradition more than God. We must have sensitivity to the present leading of the Spirit. Listen to commentator Matthew Henry's insight on this passage.

> The judgments of his mouth, and the way of our duty, blessed be God, are plain and easy, it is a high-way; but the judgments of his hands, and the ways of his providence, are dark and mysterious, which therefore we must not pry into, but silently adore and acquiesce in ... *O the depth!—Past finding out, anexichniastoi—cannot be traced*. God leaves no prints nor footsteps behind him, does not make a path to shine after him; but his paths of providence are new every morning. He does not go the same way so often as to make a track of it ... *For who hath known the mind of the Lord? And yet there he adds, But we have the mind of Christ*, which intimates that through Christ, true believers who have his Spirit, know so much of the mind of God as is necessary to their happiness. He that knew the mind of the Lord has declared him, John 1:18. And so, though we know not the mind of the Lord, yet, if we have the mind of Christ, we have enough. *The secret of the Lord is with those that fear him*, Psalm 25:14.[36]

We should not allow the vastness of God's fullness deter us from seeking that portion which He wills to impart. We, like the Gentile woman, should cry out to feast on the crumbs that fall from the table. Yet we also have those promising words that Jesus proclaims in John 15, "No longer do I call you servants ... but friends ... and I reveal what the Father says." He reveals what is necessary to empower obedience and deepen our relationship with Him. We should ask God to reveal how He would have us respond to His ways. We should study God's Word so we can recognize His ways, the

---

[36] Matthew Henry, "Commentary on Romans 11," in *Matthew Henry Commentary on the Whole Bible*, Blue Letter Bible, May 6, 2005, http://www.blueletterbible.org/Comm/mhc/Rom/Rom011.html.

path He would have us follow to gain understanding of how to respond in obedience to Him (Deuteronomy 29:29). Paul's caution merely guides us in a path of humble surrender.

To conclude from this one verse that there is danger in learning about God's will or ways would be to disregard God's desire throughout the Word to make Himself known to His children. This verse teaches the danger of postulating the purposes of God as the three "friends" of Job attempted to explain the secret will of God. In Job 28:12–28, Job also speaks of the vastness of the wisdom and understanding of God. He first mentions what does not give wisdom and understanding only to conclude in verse 28 with explanation of its source, "And to man He said, 'Behold, the fear of the Lord, that is wisdom, and to depart from evil is understanding.'" Job sought understanding for the afflictions he endured, but eventually, even he became despondent when understanding wasn't given. Listen to his lament in Job 30:25–28.

> Have I not wept for him who was in trouble? Has not my soul grieved for the poor? But when I looked for good, evil came to me; and when I waited for light, then came darkness. My heart is in turmoil and cannot rest; days of affliction confront me. I go about mourning, but not in the sun; I stand up in the congregation and cry out for help.

God did not grant Job specific answers to his questions, but in Job 38–41, God does respond to Job's cry with a reminder of God's power, sovereignty, and wisdom. Listen to Job's following response to God in Job 42:2–3, 5–6.

> I know that You can do everything, and that no purpose of Yours can be withheld from You. You asked, "Who is this who hides counsel without knowledge?" Therefore I have uttered what I did not understand, Things too wonderful for me, which I did not know ... I have heard of You by the hearing of the ear, but now my eye sees You. Therefore I abhor myself and repent in dust and ashes.

Job was not allowed to learn the secret will of God. However, God's reminder and revelation of His almighty character humbled Job and postured him in a fear of the Lord allowing him to experience the goodness of God. After this humbled, repentant response to God, the Lord gave Job twice as much as he had before his affliction.

God created the eagle with a protective sensitivity to an approaching storm. When the eagle senses bad weather, it flies to the highest mountain point possible. As the storm currents approach, the eagle leaves the security of the mountain allowing the currents to propel him above the storm. Until the storms passes, the eagle soars in the sky viewing the storm below. The eagle is given the security of viewing the storm from a higher, safer perspective.

We may discern an approaching storm in our life, but too often, we want to cling to that mountaintop experience from our past. It is a place where we have experienced the goodness of God. Why would we want to leave? Think about which is worse: choosing to face the early storm head-on to propel us to safety or facing the full effects of the storm? Storms are one of life's inevitable certainties, but they don't always have to force us into the valley (where flash floods can take us out in an instant). During these times, God wants us to fly into the early approaching storm currents so the understanding He reveals propels us upward to see the storm from His perspective. The mountaintop experience is critical for our faith because it is this highest point from which God wants to propel us even higher to safety when the storm approaches. It poses a threat only when we try to cling to it longer than necessary.

Too many times, we become discouraged by the valley experience that seems to follow too closely our tender moment with God. Could it be that we failed to be sensitive to the warning signs of the approaching storm so God could move us to safety? Difficulty does not have to be a valley experience; it can be the propelling current to see things from a different perspective if we remain sensitive to God.

Have you ever become discouraged in seeking understanding?

Could you perhaps unknowingly be seeking God's secret will instead of His revealed will?

Is Satan discouraging you?

Are you struggling to trust God? Are you doubting God's ability or willingness to work in you through your situation?

Is there a mountaintop experience you may be in danger of clinging to? Are you focusing more on God or the experience?

Is God giving you signs of an approaching storm? If you are already in the storm, are there signs you can now see but perhaps missed early on?

Regardless of what you are in the midst of, how is God drawing you to a place nearer to Him to expand your perspective of His purpose?

Record any revelations God has been speaking.

What comfort and security is He giving you through these revelations?

What comfort and security do you need? Write it as a prayer to God.

For this cause everyone who is godly shall pray to You in a time when You may be found; surely in a flood of great waters they shall not come near him. You are my hiding place; you shall preserve me from trouble; you shall surround me with songs of deliverance.
—Psalm 32:6–7

God's Presence Opens Understanding

Begin with worship, meditation, and prayer.

> And He opened their understanding, that they might comprehend the scriptures. (Luke 24:45)
>
> "Lord, grant me sensitivity to understand what You speak to me. Help me understand the greater purpose. Help me discern how this understanding teaches more about You."

In Luke 24:45, the Greek meanings for "open" as well as "understanding" refer to the opening of one's mind, soul, and intellect to proper reasoning, judgment, and wisdom.[37] This verse occurs during a discourse between Christ and the disciples after His resurrection. Previously in the chapter, He appeared to the women at the tomb, Peter, two disciples on the road to Emmaus, and now, He appears to all eleven of the disciples. While the women at the tomb remembered the prophetic teachings of Christ and understood, the disciples are still confused.

While on the road to Emmaus, several of Christ' followers review and discuss the events since His crucifixion. They are perplexed and confused. In Luke 24:21, they say, "We were hoping that it was He who was going to redeem Israel. Indeed, besides all this, today is the third day since these things happened." Now, hopes are dashed. Jesus has been dead three days;

---

[37] "Open"—to open one's soul, i.e., to rouse in one the faculty of understanding or the desire of learning, Blue Letter Bible, dictionary and word Search for *dianoigo* (Strong's 1272), Blue Letter Bible, 1996–2002, August 1, 2005, http://www.blueletterbible.org/cgi-bin/words.pl?word=1272&page=1.
"Understanding"—the mind, comprising alike the faculties of perceiving and understanding and those of feeling, judging, determining a) the intellectual faculty, the understanding b) reason in the narrower sense, as the capacity for spiritual truth, the higher powers of the soul, the faculty of perceiving divine things, of recognizing goodness and of hating evil c) the power of considering and judging soberly, calmly and impartially Blue Letter Bible, dictionary and word search for *nous* (Strong's 3563), Blue Letter Bible, 1996–2002, August 1, 2005, http://www.blueletterbible.org/cgi-bin/words.pl?word=3563&page=1.

the stench of death had set in with finality. They are not recalling that Jesus raised Lazarus after four days; they are not yet recalling teachings on the resurrection of Christ. They are not learning God's ways. Jesus's path for redemption is in fact almost complete but they do not grasp this truth. In their confusion, in their attempt to mentally process and understand, the answers are present before them. Jesus, the Christ, is Himself in their company, but their recognition of Him has been restrained (v. 16).

Let's discuss further what happened as He appeared to those on the road to Emmaus and unfolded the truth of prophecy.

> And beginning at Moses and all the Prophets, He expounded to them in all Scriptures the things concerning Himself. Then they drew near to the village where they were going, and He indicated that He would have gone further. But they constrained Him, saying, "Abide with us, for it is toward evening, and the day is far spent." And He went in to stay with them. Now it came to pass, as He sat at the table with them, that He took bread, blessed and broke it, and gave it to them. Then their eyes were opened and they knew Him; and He vanished from their sight. And they said to one another, "Did not our heart burn within us while He talked with us on the road, and while He opened the Scriptures to us?" (Luke 24:27–32)
>
> **"And beginning at Moses and all the Prophets, He expounded to them in all Scriptures the things concerning Himself."**

Christ prepares their understanding by illuminating the truth of God's Word. (Faith comes by hearing and hearing by the Word of God.) These believers in Christ are confused by God's ways. They have a seed of faith but are consumed with disappointment, doubt, confusion, presumptions, and fear. Let us see how Christ once again reveals His *Word*, presence (*will*) and *power* to grow faith. He begins by increasing the sensitivity of their spiritual senses. With the Word fresh in their minds and hearts, they are postured to recognize the truth of it in their midst.

Notice what part of scripture Jesus reveals. He spans God's Word past to present. He does more than focus on what He imparted to them recently prior to His crucifixion. He unfolds the truth of God's entire Word, which reveals the truth He wants them to understand. All of God's Word points to the Christ. God always uses the Word to reveal Himself, His will, and His way.

> **"Then they drew near to the village where they were going, and He indicated that He would have gone further. But they constrained Him, saying, 'Abide with us, for it is toward evening, and the day is far spent.'"**

They already had plans when Christ meets them and travels along. "They drew near to where they were going." Christ would have continued in the journey and in the Word, but *they constrained Him*. He did not force His way but continued with them in their plans. They still didn't grasp fully the presence of Christ in their midst, but the Word shared fueled their desire for Him to remain in their presence.

How many times do we consciously or even inadvertently constrain Christ? Are we too overwhelmed to bear any more intense revelation? How often are we overwhelmed with physical, mental, or emotional exhaustion that we have no strength to continue perhaps unaware of the blessing of doing so? We carry on with routines, even religious routines, not anticipating our need to modify them for Christ's presence that reveals further truths. God just significantly fulfilled His will through Christ. Jesus was in their midst to reveal these purposes. But the day was far spent, and they were too overwhelmed to bear any more of the same old routine of the day. They needed rest.

The disciples reveal our need to ask Christ to remain with us for rest and nourishment. They reveal how doing so can posture us to receive further blessing. Christ is faithful and patient as we learn to be sensitive to His nearness and counsel.

> **"And He went in to stay with them."**

Too often, we may fail to ask Jesus to stay, for we, unlike the disciples, may be certain of His presence. Perhaps we are too intimidated and fearful about what He may say in our midst. Perhaps we fail to invite Him because we presume He has many more important things to do than spend a few quiet moments with us. Perhaps we are too exhausted (or maybe even ashamed) to perceive ourselves worthy company. Perhaps we are fearful of what the fellowship will include and are concerned about how others perceive it.

These excuses could have been used by the disciples had they perceived who this Person was. Perhaps this is why Jesus comes to us in our blindness when we least believe His presence a possible provision. If we recognized Him, would we be willing to be at ease in our fellowship with Him? His ways reveal the desire to meet with us as we are without any pretense or guard over our hearts and minds. He wants to journey with us. He wants to rest with us. He wants to talk with us as our Friend, not as a Master (John 15:15). Remember the example of the Angel of the Lord who visited Gideon as he was—a fearful, hiding, insecure man with a weak seed of faith surrounded by a rebellious people.

The disciples' hopes are completely dashed. They cannot conceive any possible way for Jesus to be so near, yet He is! His priority is to give them the understanding they seek. He accepts their invitation. He stayed with them until their physical needs were no longer an obstacle to receive His spiritual provision.

I believe in this passage, Jesus's presence to His followers is much like the Holy Spirit is with us. The Holy Spirit is often near and we do not realize it. We go to God in prayer consumed with our physical need while the Spirit is there to reveal a greater spiritual need. God knows what we need—the physical and the spiritual—before we ask. He abides with us until the physical need is no longer a barrier to our recognizing His presence. What a motivator this should be to increase our spiritual sensitivities and to relieve anxiety.

The Spirit causes us to remember God's Word through reading scripture, through worship songs, through a word of encouragement, through prayer, or through a memory of God's personal faithfulness. We also should invite the Spirit to remain so in fellowship we may gain revelation of God at work in our midst. We should not fear His presence or His fellowship. We should realize He is near to provide understanding.

I have learned when a worship song, hymn, verse, or passage is stuck in my mind it is God trying to draw my attention to His presence. Sometimes, the message is one of intercession God uses to fuel prayer. Sometimes, it is a song of protection from spiritual warfare and pending spiritual attacks. Sometimes, it is to reveal the next step of His ways for completing His will. Sometimes, it just a reminder I need to be still and know He is God. A need to just rest in His presence and receive His love and strengthening. I have learned to follow Samuel's example and say, "Speak, Lord, for your servant is listening." This postures me to hear and see God's leading more clearly. It postures me to awaken spiritual sensitivity to see God's provision through the prayer He birthed through the song. He grows my faith through His Word, by His presence, and through His revealed power.

"Now it came to pass, as He sat at the table with them, that He took bread, blessed and broke it, and gave it to them. Then their eyes were opened and they knew Him."

Jesus blessed their provisions and served *them*. They were hungry, tired, bewildered, confused, and afraid. Their need was great. Yet Jesus was there in the middle of their need helping provide and bless what was necessary to sustain. "Come to Me all you who are weary and heavy laden and I will give you rest" (Matthew 11:28). This provision is far less than all He offers, but it is the necessary avenue for greater understanding (see Luke 24:35).

Reflect more on the significance Jesus's presence reveals about His concern and care. Jesus could have already revealed to them who He was long before now. Verse 16 tells us that their eyes had been restrained so that they would not know Him. He tarried with them, inquiring about their troubles. Does this sound familiar? Isn't this similar to the interchange between Gideon and the Angel of the Lord? Isn't this how God is with you and me? God brings us to the place of searching, pondering, rehashing events, and meets us there to help us sort out our troubles. He allows us to voice the problems, to consider the impossibility of His promise to be fulfilled given the realities at hand. This can occur through conversations with others or in silent meditation. The conversation continues as we perhaps are unaware of the presence of His Spirit.

He didn't rush into their situation just to drop a wonderful, overwhelming piece of news to grant understanding and then leave. He *slowly* prepared their understanding with His secret presence. He journeyed with them in their difficulty, revealing His Word along the way. He blessed and served their need. He fellowshipped as a friend. He was not a commanding master.

The desire for relationship reiterated throughout God's Word is witnessed in this passage. We are reminded that He is our Source for every need and is always meeting that need even when we fail to physically recognize His hand in it. While we may have the knowledge that God is always near, present, and working, we take for granted those opportunities when He may reveal Himself, His power, in a more comprehensible way. He exhorts us to grow in faith and trust the unseen. However, He continually seeks to strengthen faith with the awareness of His presence as with Gideon and the disciples.

I wonder what specifically triggered that moment of understanding. Could it have been His prayer or the way He served the bread? Was there a familiarity with either that brought to their remembrance many previous experiences with their Lord—or perhaps that Last Supper forever etched in their memory? They spent over three years with Jesus learning His ways, mannerisms, and personality as they observed His manner of praying. Could His present behavior reveal what they had attentively witnessed? His countenance has changed, but the unchanged heart of their Teacher is slowly unveiled to reveal the greatness of their Lord and Savior.

God desires for us to learn His ways not so that we learn to predict His manner and settle into a comfortable religious routine, but so we can recognize His presence, Word, and power at work in our lives. God attributes ancient Israel's rebellion as failure to learn His ways and failing to know Him more. The more we come to know God when we are fully aware of His presence, the more we learn to recognize Him at work when His presence seems an impossibility.

What happened when their eyes opened? They knew Him. They recognized God in their company. Hope became evident, real, and tangible. Their understanding of Christ and of God's plan and purpose for their recent experiences deepened. This Person and the circumstances experienced in their everyday routine of life took on greater significance to their spiritual growth. They were aware of God's presence and power in their midst.

> "And He vanished from their sight. And they said to one another, 'Did not our heart burn within us while He talked with us on the road, and while He opened the Scriptures to us?'"

Christ vanished as soon as they had understanding. How fleeting are those sometimes overwhelming revelations of the power of God yet how lasting and life changing they are. There was no further time for questioning, at least now; no time for resting in this presence. After the fact, after receiving understanding, they reflected on recent events and understood how their hearts bore witness to what their minds and physical senses failed to process because of their anxiousness. They were recognizing how the presence of Christ affected them on every level, which gives them a sensitivity to recognize Him in the future.

Prior to opening understanding, Christ recited God's Word. Remembrance of God's promises in His Word was vital to receive understanding. Knowledge of the Word revealed its truth in their midst. Understanding gave them more than knowledge by opening their spiritual eyes to see what physical senses overlooked. This spiritual sight would forever strengthen faith.

When their understanding was restrained, they were graced with His presence, His instruction of the word, and His blessing and service. Once understanding was opened, His presence vanished, but joy, hope, peace, and physical restoration filled them. (This is consistent with Gideon's experience.) What more could we ask of our God? We should not allow frustration from a lack of understanding obscure the blessed presence of our Lord, nor should we grieve for His presence when He grants a measure of understanding to sustain us until the next encounter with His goodness. We are never without His provision.

Remember how exhausted the disciples were? Remember how they urged Jesus to rest when He would have continued? Let's read how understanding affected them.

> So they rose up that very hour and returned to Jerusalem, and found the eleven and those who were with them gathered together, saying, "The Lord is risen indeed, and

has appeared to Simon!" And they told about the things that had happened on the road, and how He was known to them in the breaking of the bread. Now as they said these things, Jesus Himself stood in the midst of them, and said to them, "Peace to you." But they were terrified and frightened, and supposed they had seen a spirit. (Luke 24:33–37)

They rose up *that very hour*. No longer were they concerned with continuing their plans. No longer were they too exhausted to travel further. Understanding fueled great empowerment. It changed their agenda. It renewed their hopes. It strengthened their exhausted bodies. It encouraged their spirits. It strengthened their faith. It created desire to share this news with others who were distraught and defeated. *Understanding empowered them to obediently respond to the plans and purposes of God!*

This news is uncontainable. Who do they want to tell? Their fellow servants who they know are looking for this answer. Those they know will benefit the most from this news. Yet how did those looking for hope respond? With unbelief, doubt, and fear! Their hearts were hardened to perceive truth from one another. Only Jesus could break through that hardness to reveal truth, and even that took quite a bit of evidence before their understanding opened.

They had good reason for their fear, doubt, and unbelief. Remember how the disciples had dispersed in the Garden of Gethsemane, how Peter had denied not only following but also knowing Him, and how the Jewish leaders unjustly tried, brutally tortured, and crucified their beloved Prophet? Added to this confusion was the missing body. The Jews had been suspicious of the disciples plotting to steal His body resulting in the guarded tomb. They even attempted to frame the disciples for stealing His body (Matthew 28:11–15).

Now the body *is* missing but not as a result of the disciples' actions. What if this is truly Jesus and the Jews find them together? Wouldn't that prove the disciples have stolen Jesus's body? How would they explain Him alive? Given the sequence of events, it is easy to comprehend their fear, confusion, and disbelief. Understanding their turmoil, Jesus instantly appears in the midst of them proclaiming, once again, peace.

The disciples respond to His presence with fear and terror supposing they had seen a spirit. Mark 16:14 says of this appearance, "Afterward He appeared to the eleven as they sat at the table; and He rebuked their unbelief and hardness of heart, because they did not believe those who had seen Him after He had risen."

This verse describes their fear and unbelief as they are once again shocked by His presence and power. Had the disciples not had the two experiences on the storm-tossed sea, I can't imagine them physically withstanding such horrified amazement. In this postcrucifixion storm of controversy, the disciples *still* do not expect a miraculous provision of resurrected peace. He gives them the opportunity to touch and feel His body and scars, and He eats with them as further witness to being the resurrected Jesus, not merely a spirit.

Are you often shocked by, or afraid of, His presence and power more than trusting of it? Only Jesus can break through the hardness of our hearts. Yet, we should faithfully and obediently respond to the power of understanding God grants and share Him with others. Hearts can be hardened to salvation, but as we see in this study, they are also often hardened to growing the faith planted in our hearts. We cannot be discouraged by believers who fail to heed our testimony or ministry; we must trust Christ to validate our witness in His time and way. They are rejecting the truth of God, not us, which leaves them longer in fear, doubt, unrest, and turmoil.

The best witness is to remain focused on how God is leading you. Allow them to see the peace of God in you. Becoming distracted from His purposes by their lack of understanding empowers their unbelief and doubt by keeping your own heart and mind in distress. This is definitely easier said than done. Just as the disciples struggled in faith, so do we. Yet God is more faithful than the skeptics; He is more loving and patient in helping us fulfill His plan.

Read the following words of Matthew Henry on this passage as recorded in Luke.

> By an immediate present work upon their minds, of which they themselves could not but be sensible, he gave them to apprehend the true intent and meaning of the Old Testament prophecies of Christ, and to see them all fulfilled in him: *Then opened he their understanding, that they might understand the scriptures,* v. 45. In his discourse

with the two disciples he took the veil from off the text, by *opening* the scriptures; here he took the veil from off the heart, *by opening the mind.* Observe here, [1.] That Jesus Christ by his Spirit operates on the minds of men, on the minds of all that are his. He has access to our spirits, and can immediately influence them. It is observable how he did now after his resurrection give a *specimen* of those two great operations of *his Spirit* upon the *spirits of* men, his enlightening the intellectual faculties with a divine light, when he opened the understandings of his disciples, and his invigorating the active powers with a divine heat, when he made their hearts burn within them. [2.] Even good men need to have their *understandings opened;* for though they are not *darkness,* as they were by nature, yet in many things they are *in the dark.* David prays, *Open mine eyes. Give me understanding.* And Paul, who knows so much of Christ, sees his need to learn more. [3.] Christ's way of working faith in the soul, and gaining the throne there, is by *opening the understanding* to discern the evidence of those things that are to be believed. Thus he comes into the soul by *the door,* while Satan, as a thief and a robber, climbs up some other way. [4.] The design of opening the understanding is *that we may understand the scriptures;* not that we may be *wise above what is written,* but that we may be *wiser in what is written,* and may be made *wise to salvation* by it. The Spirit in the word and the Spirit in the heart say the same thing. Christ's scholars never learn *above their Bibles* in this world; but they need to be learning still more and more *out of their Bibles,* and to grow more *ready* and *mighty* in the scriptures. That we may have right thoughts of Christ, and have our mistakes concerning him rectified, there needs no more than to be made to understand the scriptures.[38]

---

[38] Matthew Henry, "Commentary on Luke 24," in *Matthew Henry Commentary on the Whole Bible,* Blue Letter Bible, August 1, 2005, http://www.blueletterbible.org/Comm/mhc/Luk/Luk024.html.

How many times do we allow disappointment, fear, and doubt cloud revelations before us, the testimony of others, and the witness of our own eyes? Though our hearts and spirits may burn with conviction of truth, we still may lack complete understanding. Christ is faithful to persevere until we receive what He makes a way to reveal when we invite His presence to remain and are sensitive to His Spirit. Remember Revelation 3:20: "Behold, I stand at the door and knock. If anyone hears, he will open the door, and I will come in and dine with him." This is an expression of Christ's desire for intimacy that will impart understanding of God. *He waits for us to open the door.* Too many try to live the Christian life with self-effort, with the door closed to Christ. While there may be knowledge of God's Word, understanding and power is absent in the way we live.

Open the eyes of your heart to see hope in your midst! This passage should encourage us to remain alert and sensitive to God's presence and power. God is near! God unveils His Word and reveals the truth of it in all life. Our recognition of His presence may be a brief glimpse of His eternal purpose, but it will be what we need to strengthen our faith to conquer fear for the moment.

God wants to prepare understanding, which may require removing obstacles. When we are faced with a need that causes us to fear, we generally go through the five basics for questioning: what, when, were, why, and how. Sometimes, we consciously voice these in prayer or just cry out in dire need knowing God is aware of our frustration. Our questions, our need for understanding, may sound something like these.

God, *why* is this happening to me?
How in the world am I going to get through this?
God, *what* will You do to help me?
Where is the deliverance I need?
When will this ever end?

Granted, our prayers may not always be this self-focused, but if we are honest, most of us can testify to feeling and thinking this way during some crisis. Too many times, the questioning begins with the why. Often, our need to know why consumes our focus and blinds us to the still, small voice in our midst there to answer many of the other questions. Just like Gideon and the disciples, He may be walking in the presence of our circumstance—in the middle of our questions and confusion—unveiling the scriptures that give answers. But perhaps our confusion or pain is so intense that we can't process what He reveals though our hearts burn in the presence of His Spirit.

Perhaps unconsciously, we have the mind-set that to know why is to gain complete understanding. When that question of the secret will remains unanswered, we may even give up seeking God and any wisdom. Because we fail to understand why, we may believe there is no understanding to receive. We may unintentionally close the door to the understanding available. We may fail to invite Jesus to linger with us, to come in and dine with us.

Understanding is more than a one-time revelation of significant details. God's Word says, "My ways are higher than your ways, My thoughts are higher than your thoughts" (Isaiah 55:8). God's ways and purposes are beyond our comprehension. Like the disciples, we are often not ready to fully comprehend everything God wants to reveal at the first instance we ask. But God gives us a desire to seek the understanding He has to reveal. However, that understanding will be revealed gradually. It is revealed as we take time to fellowship with Christ, rest in His presence, and welcome the revealing of His Word as we allow the Spirit to pray over us (Romans 8:26).

Understanding is not having all your questions answered. It is learning how to experience God's presence and power in the midst of unanswered questions and receive His perspective of the circumstance.

There are two basic criteria for receiving understanding. First, according to His sovereign plan, God chooses what He reveals, when He reveals it, to whom He reveals it, and how He reveals it. Remember what He said to Moses when he asked to see God's glory: "I will be gracious to whom I will be gracious, and I will have compassion on whom I will have compassion" (Exodus 33:19b). But His sovereign power over understanding does not negate our need to ask for it. We can rely on the Spirit to stir in us a hunger for the understanding God wills to impart.

This brings us to the second criterion: we must seek understanding with the proper motive. When the desire of our heart is to understand so we more fully know His desires, know Him, experience Him, and learn to recognize Him, we are postured in humility to receive what God may graciously reveal. Generally speaking, when this is our focus, we have a fear and trust in Him that empowers us to persevere and endure the difficulty. There still may be some level of physical or emotional distress, but there is a willingness to trust even when it is hard to discern His presence or purpose in our situation.

If, however, we ask "Why?" out of bitterness and anger, we are not approaching God with humility and a reverent fear of His wisdom. Our bitterness and anger grieves the Holy Spirit, which blocks understanding. We should always be honest with God about our emotions and frustrations, but our honesty should propel us to confess them as well (as Gideon exemplifies). If we allow God to settle us, to fill us with His peace and trust even without receiving understanding, we allow Him to prepare our hearts to recognize Him. We have to be willing to say, "Not my will, but Thine be done" even when our hearts seem to break with hurt, disappointment, or uncertainty.

The New Testament gives an example of the secret will of God. Look up Mark 13:32. What does this verse tell us about Jesus's understanding of His Second Coming?

This passage teaches us that there is a secret will of the Father that at times not even the Son Himself knows. If there are significant parts of God's will that even Christ cannot know, surely we can accept there are things we cannot know. However, Jesus has repeatedly taught us that the revealed will of the Father Jesus makes known to us. In chapter 3, we discussed God's provision through the Holy Spirit to reveal the mind of Christ to the spiritual man. We have also looked at several passages from John that indicate Jesus's promise of the Holy Spirit to bring understanding of God's will. This refers to the revealed will of the Father. Remember particularly John 15:15: "for all things that I heard from My Father I have made known to you." What does Jesus make known to us? *All* things Jesus hears from the Father will be revealed. John 16:13–14 echoes this teaching as Jesus states that the Holy Spirit also does not speak on His own authority, *but what He hears, He will speak.* God, in His sovereignty, reveals understanding through the Son by the power of the Holy Spirit. Job 32:8 says, "But there is a spirit in man, and the breath of the Almighty gives him understanding." The

Hebrew term used for *understanding* in this verse refers to a discernment revealed by the Spirit of God.

The Bible is the basis for us to understand the revealed will of God. Our need to study His Word to know Him and to learn more of His character has been repeatedly affirmed throughout this study. The Holy Spirit may speak to our minds or hearts to grant us the wisdom to apply and fulfill God's will. However, without knowledge of the Word, it becomes more difficult, even impossible, for us to recognize the voice of the Spirit.

How are you cultivating time in your prayer life to hear God's revealed will? Are you opening the door when Christ knocks, desiring Him to come in and fellowship? If not, what causes the hesitation?

Journal what He reveals and remain sensitive to how He brings this will to pass. Recording these helps bring to your remembrance His revelations even if much time passes before they are fulfilled or understood. He wants you to know Him more fully. God's revelations serve to prepare or protect you mentally, physically, emotionally, and spiritually for the path ahead. As you gain understanding, realize that He is using this experience to reveal more of who He is as your loving Father.

> *He who gets wisdom loves his own soul; He who*
> *keeps understanding will find good.*
> —Proverbs 19:8

> *Get wisdom! Get understanding! Do not forget, nor turn away from the words of my mouth. Do not forsake her, and she will preserve you; Love her, and she will keep you. Wisdom is the principal thing; Therefore get wisdom. And in all your getting, get understanding. Exalt her, and she will promote you; she will bring you honor, when you embrace her. She will place on your head an ornament of grace; A crown of glory she will deliver to you.*
> —Proverbs 4:5–9

JANELLE TEMPLETON

Understanding God's Ways

Begin with worship, meditation, and prayer.

> Show me Your ways, O Lord, Teach me Your paths. Lead me in Your truth and teach me, for You are the God of my salvation; on You I wait all the day. (Psalm 24:4–5)
>
> "Lord, help me understand the importance of learning Your ways for revealing Yourself and Your will. Teach me how to recognize You in the midst of challenges. Help me distinguish between Your will and Your ways so I may know You more."

As we use the phrase *His ways*, we refer to the path God uses to reveal and complete His will for our life and circumstance and how that path leads to eternal purposes and God's glory. He has a way for His will to be completed. We should seek understanding that way. We need to position ourselves to receive what He reveals.

God's ways are also the pattern for revealing His love. As mentioned, His ways are unique for every situation and person, but there are basic, unchanging similarities as well. God's character is constant. As we study the pattern of His ways in the Word, we learn something more about the vastness that helps us identify His unique pattern. As we study God's Word and read of His past promises, it teaches us about His unchanging character and love. We learn about His mercy, grace, justice, and protection. We see His disappointment and discipline for sin.

As we continue fellowship with Him, we become more adept at applying His guidelines for what we currently face. While we cannot predict the pattern of His ways or grasp His numerous, unending ways, we can posture ourselves to seek and recognize them as they unfold to complete His will.

Understanding God's ways is especially important in positions of leadership or authority. Regardless of our vocation, we should aspire to mature to that place of Christ as me—the surrendered servant—so that our faith is a guide to others in our sphere of influence. Understanding God's ways is an important part of that growth.

While there is sometimes an implied exhortation to seek God's ways, often, very little distinction is made between knowing His will and His ways. As we have seen in Mark, the disciples finally realized Jesus was the Son of God revealing Himself as King. Peter's bold defense of Christ in the Garden along with James and John's vying for positions by Christ's throne are two examples of how the disciples understood God's will without understanding His ways. They failed to recognize where His kingship would be established as well as what would need to occur for its establishment.

God's ways serve three primary purposes. First, they set in motion events that ultimately result in His completed will (for an example from the Gospels, to establish Christ's heavenly reign as King). Second, God's ways use each event, each progression toward His completed will, to prepare His children to understand and receive that will (for example, as a building block for the disciples' faith). Third, it stretches our knowledge and experience of God's power to understand specific truths. Jesus taught God's Word and demonstrated the teachings with miraculous revelation of the power and glory of God (for example, by deepening the disciples understanding of who Christ is as the Son of God).

To recap, God's ways teach us: the path for completing His will, how He uses this path to grow faith, and how His power fuels deeper understanding of Him.

We see these purposes of God's ways through the Gospels, and David's prayer above also emphasizes these objectives. First, David boldly asks, "Show me Your ways." David's expression of his need for this level of understanding goes beyond seeking God's will, to understand His ways. Like Gideon, David reveals how God strengthens faith through obstacles, adversity, failure, triumph, disappointment, and worship. David worshipped God from his early days with his harp and composition of psalms. David's life and prayers reveal the important distinction of seeking God's ways, and the impact of personal prayer and worship when both are fervent and when they are deficient.

How many times do we pray, "Lord reveal Your will for …?" What I believe we desire is God's *specific* direction. By voicing this prayer, we certainly express a desire, a need, to obediently follow God. However, too often, our mental focus is on discerning God's ultimate result chiefly because we want to be done and move beyond. But we, like the disciples, may not yet be prepared to fully comprehend that ultimate plan. God's will may require a delayed versus an immediate provision. Often, there is a portion of His will already in motion that we are poised to receive but perhaps don't initially recognize.

David models for us how we become prepared. As we see in David's example, he teaches us a more appropriate way to approach the what, when, where, why, and how questions. In this prayer, David does not expect God to completely rid him of this situation. Instead, he seeks wisdom and understanding from God on how He would have him respond through it. (You will also note in this particular plea that David is not concerned about asking why.)

"Show me Your ways, O Lord"

To help us recognize God's completed will more clearly, David models for us a much more specific prayer by asking, "Show me Your ways." It expresses humble dependence on God. The prayer begins with the confession: "I need to know *Your* ways, Lord. Not my own desires, not my own good plans." It is an acknowledgment that we have no good plans except to understand the ways of God. David's life was in danger when this prayer was voiced. David knew God's will was for him to reign as king. While the security of this kingship could be questioned given his circumstances, David appears to remain confident in God's ultimate will yet is desperate to understand how God would have him respond. This prayer confesses contentment with accepting God's purpose for today's preparation. "I want to follow Your ways, Your purposes for today" even though God's path appears to move David further from his purpose. David does not allow the physical danger to overshadow the promises of God. His faith remains focused on spiritual truths, not earthly visibilities, and the guidance necessary to obey them.

"Teach me Your path"

His next request continues to reveal his desire to know how to respond as he prays, "Teach me *Your* path." David has acknowledged his need to understand God's ways, and now he asks how he should specifically respond to what God reveals. "God, I must know what I should do today and how and when." Often, conflict and uncertainty arise as we surrender to God's will. Even when we have understanding of what, Satan wants to halt surrender as we seek to respond. Therefore, knowing how and when to respond during these difficulties is critical for victory. Sometimes, the path is difficult. When we have waited on God's revelation, God gives us confidence even in the midst of difficulty. This assurance deepens faith and trust that God has a higher purpose that He is revealing. When faith is not focused on God's purpose, we become consumed by circumstances, causing us to respond in our Flesh rather than our spirit.

The disciples gave another example of understanding God's will yet not His ways. The disciples were healing and performing miracles among the multitudes but could not heal a demon-possessed young man. When they later sought understanding of what they had done wrong, Jesus replied, "This kind can only go out by much prayer and fasting." They generally knew what to do; they knew the spirit needed to be called out of the child, but they did not comprehend how it could be accomplished. Their action was correct but their preparation was lacking. The method and approach to healing that had previously been effective would not work in this situation. They had faith to perform other miracles, but Jesus stated this healing required *much* prayer and fasting.

In Matthew's account, Jesus stated that the disciples could not cast out the demons because of their lack of faith, which comes from hearing the Word of God. Prayer and fasting postures us to hear and understand God's Word, thus increasing faith. An increase in prayer and fasting would not increase the power of God, but would increase their expectation of what that power could accomplish. It would partner with God to gain victory in the spiritual realm and release His will on earth through a focus on God's specific Word for that situation. It would posture and prepare them to understand and embrace God's power once revealed. It would deepen their dependence on God and thus strengthen the partnership. It would further give glory to His power that surpasses the strength of man.

How many times do we find ourselves in a similar situation? How many times is prayer used to seek cursory blessing of approval for *our actions* instead of the consecrated source for divine power? When we pray for approval of our request, how is our expectation or knowledge of God stretched? We do not acknowledge a greater power but merely confirm what we know. This does not posture us to allow God to expand faith but merely to rely on what we have. Failing to realize the role of prayer and fasting can leave us ill equipped to understand God's ways. We may understand what needs to be done, but understanding how to fulfill His way may require an expression of faith we have not yet experienced.

In performing this miracle, Christ also says to the disciples that faith only the size of a mustard seed is necessary. They are not relying on the power of God through that seed of faith but on their knowledge and experience. God intends that faith, that smallest of all seeds, is to *grow* into a tree. Our faith grows as our knowledge and expectation of God grows as we hear and understand Him. The growth comes with the consecrated desire to pray, fast, and worship Him. These are our avenues for knowing Him and expanding understanding of who He is, what He can do, and most of all, what He will do. Prayer and fasting keeps us focused and attentive to learning *God's* path.

"Lead me in Your truth and teach me"

David's prayer continually deepens. With each line of this prayer, we see David more specifically ask for understanding and direction. Each request reveals a resolve to focus on God until his prayer is answered. Why would it be necessary to emphasize a need to comprehend God's truth, to emphatically state it this way? David has already expressed a strong desire to know God's will and way; that implies a desire for God's truth. David continues His plea by explicitly requesting understanding of truth.

Perhaps David realizes that presumptions and Satan's attacks can distort God's truth. David reveals the need to focus on spiritual realities beyond the physical visibilities. He surrenders to God's leading and says, "Teach me." With this request, David expresses a desire for God to open understanding so faith becomes sight, so trust is not blind. Could he perhaps recognize the danger of responding from an earthly, human perspective that sometimes results from blind trust?[39] He seems to implore God to grant clear, decisive

---

[39] By definition, trust infers a willingness to obey without complete understanding. When the term "blind trust" is used, refer to previous discussion of how one can come to a deeper understanding of God that propels trust, even when understanding of circumstances is incomplete.

direction for surrender. David models what Christ asks of the church in Revelation: "Open the door so that I may come in." David expresses his desire to learn from God through fellowship, not just to be a recipient of God's provision. David models the need to relinquish our understanding of the natural man to receive understanding of God's truth: "Lead me in YOUR truth God, not my limited, presumptuous understandings."

God's Word says that the heart is deceitful above all things. His Word reiterates the importance of guarding our mind against the schemes of Satan. David's request to be led in God's truth models how to guard our hearts and minds in Christ Jesus.

When we, like David, steadfastly resolve to seek God's leading and allow Him to teach His truth, we surrender to learn the ways of God. David expresses a need for knowledge of truth and the wisdom to apply it—"Teach me." God stated that the rebelliousness of Israel in the Old Testament happened when they failed to learn God's ways. We need not blindly surrender to God's leading. He seeks our obedience but reveals how we can learn more about Him in the midst of obedience. We should be attentive to recognize how our path to obedience can reveal the pattern of God's ways.

As we have seen through Jesus's discourse with the disciples, He often reveals greater power to His leaders before revealing it to the masses. I have experienced this in ministry. Even when there is unity of purpose among the team, team leaders may have differing levels of understanding of God's ways. There can be agreement on the ultimate ministry goal, but some leaders may miss God's presence and power accomplishing that same purpose in the lives of leadership.

While this difference in understanding may not thwart the fulfillment of God's ways for the masses, it can fuel discord, mistrust, doubt, and skepticism among the leaders. Some can miss what Jesus is doing in others and therefore not trust their discernment or fail to support how God is specifically moving them to lead.

Recall Jesus walking on the storm-tossed sea toward the disciples gripped in fear. Only Peter gained a level of understanding about Jesus that fueled his faith and trust to step out of the boat. Recall how the disciples could not accept mentally or spiritually what they had witnessed. It wasn't an issue of seeing, but understanding—a failure to discern what God did through Peter's faith. Peter and the other disciples demonstrated a desire for Jesus to "lead me in Your truth," but only Peter said, "Teach me" on a personal level. Peter's bold trust empowered him to walk on water. As he continued to trust, he walked. As he feared or doubted, he began to sink. The remaining disciples were in the boat all headed the same direction, but were paralyzed with fear and confusion. They witnessed Jesus's power, but only Peter trusted it and found peace on the stormy sea. Jesus brought peace to the sea, but peace was delayed to those who doubted.

This study exhorts us to realize obstacles preventing surrender. I urge those of you in ministry leadership to remain sensitive to this process in the spiritual lives of team leaders as well. Some may serve with understanding of God's ways though they may not be able to articulate it. Others may not even perceive their need for this level of understanding. Therefore, when you witness Jesus's presence and power working a new truth in a team member, affirm this to the entire team. Testify to the Lord's goodness in ways that overshadows envy, mistrust, and frustration Satan fuels through these differences in experience. As a leader, give outward, third-party credibility for how God is working in that fellow leader to advance His purpose for the team (just as Joash gives to Gideon in Judges 6). Direct the glory to God to help the team remain kingdom focused and poised to expect God's power revealed through each leader. When possible, be the catalyst for all of the team leaders to experience peace.

"You are the God of my salvation"

David reiterates His absolute dependency on God. He reveals a heart devoted to exalting God above his strengths. He relinquishes desire to rush ahead in his own abilities and commits to wait on God as long as necessary even while in great physical danger.

David is the anointed king; he is called to a position of authority and importance. David is a mighty warrior; he has established a standard of military excellence. In the eyes of the majority of the kingdom and God, David is greatly loved; he has found favor in the sight of God and man. However, His understanding of how to respond to his situation does not rely on these skills and accomplishments. He is seeking deliverance from God alone and is content to wait on God's timing even at great risk to his life and kingship.

God may grant us great gifts, talents, positions, and even recognition, but it is *His* understanding, power, we need. David teaches us to: focus on God's purpose above a threat or inconvenience to our *position*, focus on God's purpose above the adequacy or inadequacy of our *performance*, and focus on God's purpose above our *perception* by others positively or negatively.

David is not willing to trust his well-being to his very commendable strengths and abilities. He casts aside fear of imminent danger to trust and wait on God's provision. He knows God's faithfulness and is not willing to minimize faith in God for earthly accomplishments. He demonstrates a contentment to wait on God to reveal how he should respond. He is willing to obey God and entrust the consequences to Him. "'It is not by might, not by power, but by My Spirit' says the Lord" (Zechariah 4:6).

"On You I wait all the day"

We are a society of instant gratification. We look for ways to streamline every aspect of our lives so we can cram more activities into our already hectic schedules. We don't like to wait for anything. However, one of the virtues of waiting for things is a deeper appreciation of them when we receive them. We invest emotionally and relationally in the process of waiting and thus more greatly cherish, care for, and protect what we have sacrificed to gain.

This is not limited to material things; it is applicable to relationships as well. Newlyweds who had been committed to premarital purity can testify to this virtue. Anyone who has struggled to have children can testify to this. It should not seem odd therefore that our relationship with God be any different. Since God desires us to know Him more fully and to value our relationship more dearly, it shouldn't surprise us that He would orchestrate waiting on Him into our prayers, provisions, and difficulties. Let these words of Andrew Murray encourage you to wait on God.

> [In the Christian life] there may be much praying with very little waiting on God. In praying, we are often occupied with ourselves, with our own needs, and with our own efforts in the presentation of them. In waiting on God [in prayer], the first thought is of the God upon whom we wait.

We enter His presence and feel we need just to be quiet, so that He, as God, can overshadow us with Himself. God longs to reveal Himself, to fill us with Himself. Waiting on God gives Him time to come to us in His own way and divine power ... Dear Christian, begin to see that waiting is not one among a number of Christian virtues, to be thought of from time to time. But, it expresses that disposition that lies at the very root of the Christian life. It gives higher value and a new power to our prayers and worship, to our faith and surrender, because it links us, in unalterable dependence, to God Himself. And it gives us the unbroken enjoyment of the goodness of God Himself.[40]

David models how we are to wait on God in prayer. As we invite the Spirit to unveil God's revealed will, we are empowered to pray in agreement to it. Voicing this revealed will in prayer postures us to see God's power at work through the provision. It prepares us for the provision. It allows us to see God's ways unfold through His provision, giving glory to Him and strengthening faith over fear. God often allows circumstances greater than what our wisdom and understanding can resolve. His past equipping may be insufficient for our present need. He wants us to know Him more. He wants us to receive His provision for today. We need to recognize our need to wait, seek His understanding, and allow Him to teach us His ways.

Indicate an issue in your life in which God is asking you to wait.

Describe any temptations to rely on your own abilities to accelerate the provision.

Describe what new aspects of His goodness He is revealing during this process of waiting.

---

[40] "Waiting On God," *Andrew Murray Collected Works on Prayer*, n.p.: Whitaker House, 2013.

Let's recap the ways that destructive fear brings chaos in our lives and hinders faith.

- Fear fuels doubt, unbelief, presumption, paranoia, insecurity, all distorting truth.
- Fear fuels self-protection, not God-dependence.
- Fear clouds the ability to see God's presence and hear His voice in our midst.
- Fear fuels further disobedience and distance from God.

God is always working in the midst of fear though we may not clearly or fully see Him at first. Let's recap what we have learned about His ways to break through the barriers of fear.

- He meets us where we are even in the middle of self-destruction or self-pity.
- He speaks to us as the person He intends us to become, not the one defined by our weaknesses, sins, or failures.
- He expands knowledge of who He is as God through His Word.
- He teaches a specific truth through His Word that is unveiled through life's experiences (which may be through difficulty or fear) by a revelation of His power and presence.
- He grants progressive understanding of His presence and power.
- He continues this process until we receive the understanding He longs to give and what we have learned to seek.

As Proverbs 4:7 urges, we must seek wisdom in life, but in all our getting, we are to get understanding. God desires we receive the measure of understanding available. Learning God's ways postures us to receive it.

Growing Faith 5

Unity and the Power of Understanding

> *Brethren, do not be children in understanding; however, in*
> *malice be babes, but in understanding be mature.*
> —1 Corinthians 14:20

> *God looks down from heaven upon the children of men, to*
> *see if there are any who understand, who seek God.*
> —Psalm 53:2

> *A Song of Ascents Of David. Behold, how good and how*
> *pleasant it is for brethren to dwell together in unity!*
> —Psalm 133:1

Understanding is a by-product of unity with God. Unity, agreement with God, happens when we accept His will and surrender to His ways—when we trust in who God is. It is aligning our hearts with the heart of God. It is the willingness to say, "Not my will, but Thine be done." In this section, we look at the effect of unity personally as well as corporately.

Personal understanding is an important element for church unity. In a body of people, there are many different spiritual gifts, talents, and opinions. When we perceive the need to seek understanding personally and corporately, God gives a broader perspective of these differences. As we surrender to Him, He molds our differences through the Spirit into agreement. Where discord exists, it may be due to the strengths of our Flesh (even good Flesh) failing to yield to the Spirit's move in others as well as ourselves.

Jesus stressed and modeled the need to lay aside our strengths and rights to serve others. It is easy to become confident and focused on our personal purpose to the neglect of discerning what God is doing in the church as a whole, and how our revelation fits into others' purposes. Understanding is a progressive revelation as we focus on God above self and as God prepares us or the provision.

Shortly, we will look at scripture that reveals how unity can be without understanding. This type of agreement does not result in surrender to God's will. Even if it is the fulfillment of good intentions God uses for His glory, it is not a direct seeking of or surrender to His heart's desires. Let's first look at an example of understanding and corporate unity birthed after disobeying God's ways.

Through King Cyrus, those Jews willing to return to Jerusalem from captivity left Babylon to begin rebuilding their city and temple. Upon their return, God warned them to remain set apart, not to intermarry with the foreigners who had since occupied their homeland. They failed to heed God's warning, and that sin combined with disputes among the foreign inhabitants prolonged their task of rebuilding the temple and wall around Jerusalem. They agreed with God's will to return to Jerusalem, but they did not surrender to following His ways. This failure to follow His ways greatly interrupted completion of His will. Through the consequence of their sin, God gave them a hunger for understanding.

In Nehemiah 8, we see the people gather at the gate of the completed wall to hear the Word of God. Most Jews were dependent on the priests to read and teach them the Law. Many did not have a copy of the written Word, and the Holy Spirit was not indwelling them to give understanding from within. Here we find a focused hunger to seek and hear God.

Read Nehemiah 8:1–18.

The people gathered as one man, asking Ezra to read the Law. The congregation eagerly pursued understanding God's Word. This passage reveals many things about the corporate power of understanding. (This power is also available to us individually when we respond to God the way the congregation responded.) As the chapter unfolds, we learn that the people gathered were those "who could hear with understanding." The Hebrew word used for *understanding* in this chapter is *biyn*, "to separate mentally, to attend, consider, and distinguish."[41] Those who gathered did so in unity. They eagerly desired to hear from God with understanding. Their

---

[41] Blue Letter Bible, dictionary and word search for *biyn* (Strong's 0995), Blue Letter Bible, 1996–2002, February 8, 2005, http://www.blueletterbible.org/cgi-bin/words.pl?word=0995&page=1.

minds were renewed and focused on allowing God's Word to penetrate their hearts. Given where they had been, what they had been through, and how they had rebelled, this was an important growth marker. They recognized their need for God's Word. They were hungry for it. Their focus was no longer on the difficulties of their task or their disobedience. Their minds had been renewed to seek and focus on God's spiritual truths in corporate agreement.

Had the Jews not been through their previous difficulty, it is unlikely they would have perceived their need to understand. They did hear, they did understand, and God did faithfully respond to their understanding with healing and restoration (recall Matthew 13:14–15). Their willingness to seek God with understanding hearts resulted in:

- unity with God's purpose and His people (vv. 1–3)
- humility before God (vv. 4–6)
- worship of God (vv. 7–8)
- confession of Sin (vv. 9–10)
- joy (vv. 11–12)
- obedience (vv. 13–18)

There is great significance in grasping the power of unity to further understanding. Agreeing with God's purpose even when we lack complete knowledge of it is necessary to receive further understanding. The Jews' humility and spiritual hunger resulted in intimate communion with God and His people and eventually brought a more specific understanding of God's desires.

God does not reveal His deep truths to casual observers. Jesus spoke in parables so the Word of God would be protected from those who opposed God's purposes. But a provision of understanding is granted to those who seek it. It is not automatically received by Christians; they are charged with pursuing it. God trusts revelation and understanding to those who are committed to following His will, those whose hearts are in unity with His. Remember what 2 Chronicles 16:9 says: "For the eyes of the Lord run to and fro throughout the whole earth, to show Himself strong on behalf of those whose heart is loyal to Him."

Our nation is at a critical junction spiritually. For the first time in my adult life, the discord between opposing ideologies is uncharacteristically high. To listen to the news and read social media one would not recognize unity in our nation, only unity among segmented groups at odds with one another. Moments that typically would call for respect of our nation's character and heritage have only seen greater division. In many ways our spiritual condition parallels Israel's period of rebellion prior to and during its Babylonian captivity.

Christians and Christian leaders have been praying many years for revival in this country which leads me to conclude it is a provision God is preparing. Just as God led those Jews "willing to return from captivity" to rebuild Jerusalem, I discern God is calling Christians in this nation to be a catalyst for revival, restoration, and unity in America. I pray God uses this study to restore us and strengthen faith so that we see God at work even through our nation's division.

Unity with God is the key.

Genesis 11:1–9 is an instance where unity resulted in great power yet was absent God's will. Through this scripture, we observe the power and danger of unity acting apart from God. In Genesis 11:6, God describes the people as "one" with one language. He says that the strength of unity is so powerful that nothing they purpose to do will be withheld from them. God preempts their human plans by confusing speech that preempted hearing and understanding.

Through this occurrence, God teaches much about the great power of unity. We learn spiritual truths from this earthly event. God is teaching that unity from any source is an unstoppable force absent His intervention. God's response reveals that the power of unity is so great that anything agreed upon by a body of people is possible. If unity among humans for even ungodly purposes is this powerful, can you begin to appreciate a deeper understanding of unity with the almighty God? Can you grasp why Jesus says that it only takes mustard seed faith to move mountains?

Let us refresh our memory with familiar verses (emphasis added).

> So Jesus said to them, "Because of your unbelief; assuredly I say to you, *if you have faith as a mustard seed*, you will say to this mountain, 'Move from here to there,' and it will move; and *nothing will be impossible* for you." (Matthew 17:20)

With men this is impossible, but *with God all things are possible.* (Matthew 19:26)

If you ask *anything in My name* [unity with Christ], I will do it. (John 14:14)

I am the vine, you are the branches, He who abides in Me, and I in him, bears much fruit; for *without Me you can do nothing.* (John 15:5)

You did not choose Me, but I chose you and appointed you that you should go and bear fruit, and that your fruit should remain, that *whatever you ask the Father in My name He may give you.* (John 15:16)

Again, I say to you that if two of you agree on earth concerning anything that they ask, it will be done for them by My Father in heaven. (John 15:16)

Comprehending unity's power should encourage us to draw closer to God. But it should also give rise for caution and reflection before we rush ahead with what we perceive to be the right direction. We should seek God's will above the consensus of men. As we learn from Nehemiah 8, a consensus is powerful when seeking God. Understanding means knowing things in their right, godly, relationship and recognizing the eternal perspective.

However, human understanding and wisdom, as we have also learned, is foolishness to God. The majority consensus in Numbers 13 was to kill Caleb and Joshua to avoid the risks of taking possession of the Promised Land. The consensus in Judges 6 was to kill Gideon in retaliation for destroying idolatrous altars and rebuilding the altars of Jehovah. In the Exodus, the consensus, which included Aaron the future high priest, was to build a graven image to worship instead of waiting on God's direction. Daniel's friends were sentenced to the fiery furnace because of their failure to worship the king, yet their lives were spared because of their unity and devotion to God. In each of these situations, there was at least one person, one leader, who understood the will of God and had the courage to steadfastly proclaim it despite the general consensus.

This sets the example that leaders have the responsibility to seek understanding of God's will and ways as well as help others also understand. Leaders should learn to be sensitive to hardened hearts in the church and seek God's guidance regarding moving forward. A godly leader in humble unity with God's purposes should discern the pride, doubt, fear, and unbelief that blind understanding. However, this discernment must first be applied to your own heart so there is certainty of the direction God is leading. Prayer, fasting, worship, and the Word of God are the prerequisites for this discernment process.

Ask God to reveal a past situation where you may have been part of a consensus that did not act according to God's ways. Ask Him to give you a broader perspective of that situation so you may identify or recognize His grace in that circumstance.

Reflect on situations where He has called you to be the leader with the courage to speak His truth against opposition. How did you respond? What was the result, and what did it teach you about Him?

Acts 2:1–13 records the filling of the Holy Spirit at Pentecost that Jesus promised repeatedly. What happened at Pentecost is the opposite of what happened in Genesis 11 above. People of every tribe, nation, and tongue were gathered "in one accord." (These many languages resulted from God confusing the one language of the ungodly, self-exalting unity in Genesis 11 generations before.) As the "divided tongues of fire" descended on them filling them with the Holy Spirit, they began to speak in languages unknown to them yet clearly understood by all. Even though there may be disunity with God adversely effecting us, God has a plan for redemption and restoration!

With God, even what is divided can be understood and brought into a spirit of unity—when all involved are willing to surrender to Him. We must lay aside our plans, agendas, insights, gifts, experiences, traditions, preferences, fears, and presumptions to receive God's plan. It means approaching the situation with a focus on Him, yielding hardened hearts of unbelief. God, who is unchanging in character, often requires us to move in different methods and directions so we stay more dependent on Him than on a method.

The people in Acts gathered expectantly awaiting the coming of the Holy Spirit promised by Christ. However, do you suppose any one present anticipated exactly how God would send His Spirit? Typical of any unexpected, unfamiliar display of God's power, there were skeptics and cynics who tried to attribute what was happening to anything other than God's power. But as Peter began to reveal God's Word, the prophecy foretold of old, about three thousand who "gladly received" understanding, were converted that day. The power of God's Spirit revealed, coupled with understanding of His Word, fueled a lasting empowerment of the body of Christ.

Is this not also what we have seen throughout Christ's ministry? In equipping the disciples as well as ministering to the multitudes, His Word demonstrated and illuminated by God's power revealed the glory and will of God. This reveals a consistent pattern of the general way God speaks to His people in the Bible and today. His will and ways are coupled with the Word and the power of the Spirit. If we desire understanding, we too must surrender ourselves to a study of God's Word and recognize His power as demonstration of the Word. (The disciples had their understanding "opened" before Pentecost resulting in the ability to recognize the Holy Spirit's power; see John 20:22 and Luke 24:45.)

The unity we exhort the church to seek is recognition of the movement of God. His power grants unity among a diversity of gifts, talents, personalities, and opinions. God can, and often will, give corporate revelation of how He specifically wants His people to move (as witnessed repeatedly in the Old Testament). However, even among New Testament Christians living with the indwelling Holy Spirit, some will have hearts hardened to recognize the Spirit's movement. Instead, there may be reliance on self, traditions, or experiences in similar situations. Some attempt to misinterpret, pervert, or misuse the Spirit's move for selfish reasons. Some ignore or dismiss revelations of the Spirit's power.

While God's past ways can certainly be a guide, it should be recognized that this may not be His current way. *His ways will not contradict who He is in scripture.* Understanding His fullness is important for recognizing

Him presently. Discerning sensitivity to the lack of understanding is also required as well as consecrated prayer for God to bring unity.

A responsibility of leadership is the sensitivity to when and how God would have them proceed to not disobey or hinder His will or way. As with the disciples, some team members may not be able to understand this move until after God's will is completed. Moses, Caleb, and Joshua risked proceeding with God's way when the majority would have killed them for it (absent God's intervention). While your life may not be physically in danger in similar situations, you may risk your reputation and your credibility among some.

Have you ever been in a service where God's presence is clearly moving yet someone says or does something intentionally or unintentionally that quenches the movement? Often, what is said or done draws attention to a person (either a strength or weakness) distracting from the Spirit's move. Sometimes, it is done by interjecting humor in an otherwise serious moment.

Growing up as a pastor's daughter, I was privy to conversations among leaders that revealed fear of God's Spirit moving corporately. Sometimes there was concern that things were getting too spiritually intense that it would make the church body—or the unchurched, "unenlightened" guests—uncomfortable. Sometimes, leaders perceive the need for God's Spirit to be veiled just as Moses needed to veil his face before the frightened Israelites (because of fear, doubt, or unbelief). But 2 Corinthians 3:17–18 reveals that where the Spirit of the Lord is, there is freedom; there is no need for the veil for the Spirit gives understanding.

We have also seen scriptures where God for His purpose restrains understanding. Given this as a way of God, is it right to fear that someone may not understand a move of God? Can we not trust the Spirit to provide or withhold understanding according to His will? Surrender to God's leading is more unifying in the church than fear of the Spirit's leading. Leaders have the responsibility to equip the body to embrace God's presence, not fear it. Satan wants us to fear the result of God's Spirit at work for he knows Its power. God wants us to pursue and embrace It for He knows Its power. As we mature in our relationship with God, we will not fear His nearness or presence or how others may judge us because of it.

Leaders have the burden to model this surrender to God's Spirit in a corporate gathering. Leaders must guard against their fear of the Spirit's movement. It is important for leaders to seek God's purpose for His presence. An appropriate response is to surrender in corporate prayer at that moment of His presence. God more than man understands the complex mix of varying spiritual maturities in the corporate meeting. Fear God, not the rejection, spiritual immaturity, or complaint of man. Trust God to work. People need to know that God is real, that God is a personal God. Trust, don't fear, how He reveals Himself corporately. We can trust the wisdom of His ways.

Unity with God's purpose, not with the agendas of man, is necessary to ensure a lasting inheritance. Let us look at 1 Corinthians 3:10–16.

> According to the grace of God which was given to me, as a wise master builder I have laid the foundation, and another builds on it. For no other foundation can anyone lay than that which is laid, which is Jesus Christ. Now if anyone builds on this foundation with gold, silver, precious stones, wood, hay, straw, each one's work will become manifest; for the Day will declare it, because it will be revealed by fire; and the fire will test each one's work, of what sort it is. If anyone's work is burned, he will suffer loss; but he himself will be saved, yet so as through fire. Do you not know that you are the temple of God and that the Spirit of God dwells in you?

Note that this passage refers to heavenly rewards, not the eternal security of the believer, for he "himself will be saved." Every Christian may work to advance the kingdom of God, but only those whose works build with gold, silver, and precious stones receive lasting rewards. To build with gold, silver, and precious stones is to receive and teach the Word of God in its purity and entirety without corrupting or distorting its meaning. It is to exalt God above self, to follow God's ways above ours. As this study reveals, this requires a heart free from fear and unbelief that would misunderstand or distort the Word in truth or deed.

Those who build with wood, hay, and stubble still build the kingdom but with no lasting reward. It is possible to be saved yet do good and worthy works for God in our Flesh, that is, with a heart failing to surrender to the indwelling Spirit. Matthew Henry expounds on this point.

> Others *build wood, hay, and stubble*, on this foundation; that is, though they adhere to the foundation, they depart from the mind of Christ in many particulars, substitute their own fancies and inventions in the room of his doctrines and institutions, and build upon the good foundation what will not abide the test when the day of trial shall come, and the fire must make it manifest, as wood, hay, and stubble, will not bear the trial by fire, but must be consumed in it. There is a time coming when a discovery will be made of what men have built on this foundation: *Every man's work shall be made manifest*, shall be laid open to view, to his own view and that of others. Some may, in the simplicity of their hearts, build wood and stubble on the good foundation, and know not, all the while, what they have been doing; but in the day of the Lord their own conduct shall appear to them in its proper light. Every man's work shall be made manifest to himself, and made manifest to others, both those that have been misled by him [Satan] and those that have escaped his errors. Now we may be mistaken in ourselves and others; but there is a day coming that will cure all our mistakes, and show us ourselves, and show us our actions in the true light, without covering or disguise.[42]

Those who serve in the Flesh and depart from the mind of Christ build with wood, hay, and stubble. While God may use these efforts to advance His kingdom, there is no lasting reward for the believer. We studied the importance of surrendering to the mind of Christ. With this surrender, there is no self-exaltation, self-effort, or self-protection. To further ensure

---

[42] Matthew Henry, "Commentary on 1 Corinthians 3," in *Matthew Henry Commentary on the Whole Bible*, Blue Letter Bible, August 24, 2005, http://www.blueletterbible.org/Comm/mhc/1Cr/1Cr003.html.

a lasting inheritance, we must surrender fear, doubt, and unbelief that produce a hardened heart. Hearts hardened to the recognition of God in our midst quench understanding of God's will and ways for building His kingdom with lasting rewards.

Because of unity's power, we can understand Satan's attempts to cause divisiveness in God's church. These schemes can be the root of destructive and divisive fear when the fear of failure takes root and strengthens among the body of believers and even more so among church leadership. Though the motive may be protection of the church, acting through the fear of failure blinds truth of God's ways for protecting in a way that edifies and unifies the body.

Peter failed to publicly acknowledge his relationship with Jesus. Saul of Tarsus failed to believe that Jesus was God's son—the same God he sought to exalt. Saul believed God needed his assistance to protect Judaism. This perceived need, a lack of understanding God's full plan, and fear of Christ's followers, fueled the persecution and murder of innocent Christians. Despite these failures, Christ interceded to restore unity with God for Peter and Saul (Paul). This unity brought greater understanding and empowerment to obey than they could perceive was necessary to fulfill their purpose.

Today, unity in God's church is compromised by numerous denominational beliefs that become the fuel for fear, doubt, and unbelief. There is even great discord within denominations. Unity does not come from merely tolerating one another's beliefs; it comes from understanding the greater purpose of God's will. It comes when we take eyes off denominations to see God working through one another's real or perceived weaknesses.

Jesus chastised the Pharisees for teaching as God's commands the traditions of men. Jesus was crucified by the Pharisees who rejected God in their midst. Doctrinal differences can cause similar divisions in the church today. Satan chokes the fruitfulness of the church as we busy ourselves with divisions. Just as the Holy Spirit united what was divided in regards to language at Pentecost, I pray for the day His Spirit greatly unites the divided in and among denominations. That certainly will be a day of great conversions as the glory of God will be lifted up. When there is unity, there is an unstoppable power. When there is unity with God, there is an overwhelming demonstration of His power and glory. We exhaust energy when we focus on divisions, ignoring what God's presence and power accomplishes to grow faith. Perhaps we are more concerned pushing among the crowds to see Jesus first, that we miss the opportunity to touch the hem of His garment.

We see the numbers and power of unity among other religions, agnostics, and atheists in this nation growing rapidly, but how are believers in Christ seeking such unity? We need to prepare for the coming of our Lord and Savior and the unity we will have as believers for eternity. I exhort the church of Christ to lay aside differences and focus on the common goal of building the kingdom of God.

We need devotion to a deeper understanding of God's Word as well as embracing the Holy Spirit to empower fulfillment of the Word. 1 Thessalonians 1:5 says, "For our gospel did not come to you in word only, but also in power, and in the Holy Spirit, and in much assurance." We receive the gospel in this way, and we also grow in faith, through the Word, power, and Spirit in much assurance.

Following the previous passage in 1 Corinthians 3 on heavenly rewards, Paul gives a caution to ministers of the gospel.

> Let no one deceive himself. If anyone among you seems to be wise in this age, let him become a fool that he may become wise. For the wisdom of this world is foolishness with God. For it is written, "He catches the wise in their own craftiness."
> The Lord knows the thoughts of the wise, that they are futile. Therefore let no one glory in men. (vv. 18–21)

Paul, once greatly deceived by his religiosity, cautions church leaders to be careful of the deceitful heart. Religious traditionalists believe in what God has accomplished in the past but fail to acknowledge how He is working presently. The deception witnessed in church leadership today comes in two basic ways: one by focusing on religious tradition or routine to the neglect of the Spirit's leading; and the second, by perverting God's word in part or its entirety to justify a doctrine of man. Will the church of God today recognize the hand of God to prepare the world for Christ's return? Will we in unity receive and rejoice in how He works through those of different but genuine denominations? To prepare, we must be willing to hear His Word and understand His power. We need to seek spiritual realities present in earthly visibilities.

Paul exhorts the church to build the kingdom with a reverent fear of God (not fear of persons within the church or in other denominations) and surrender to the power of Jesus Christ. Fear of God is lacking among many calling themselves ministers of the Gospel. Unity with God, humility before Him, worship of Him, confession, praise, and obedience result when we perceive our need for God and allow His power to transform hearts. Without this process, hearts continue to remain hardened dulling sensitivity to God's leading. We want to learn from the disciples how to trust and rely on God's provision when we find ourselves presented with a new need. We also have much to learn from Christ's example with the Jewish leadership crucifying Him. He demonstrated more compassion over their sin than He expressed in anger over their hardened hearts: "Forgive them Father, for they know not what they do."

Throughout this study, we have asked questions to help identify sources of fear in our lives. We have asked questions regarding understanding God's power to work through these circumstances. These introspective questions are intended to help trace God's ways for revealing His will and His power through His Word reiterated in our daily walk. These reflections and meditations serve to increase understanding God's spiritual purposes for physical visibilities causing fear, doubt, and unbelief. These questions serve to strengthen unity with, and trust of, God's leading.

To navigate from fear to faith, we need and should desire greater understanding of God and His ways. We need to understand His Word, surrender to His Spirit, and watch expectantly for His intervening power. We should have hearts open to receive spiritually what God reveals through the physical. We should seek to recognize and understand the ways of God in practical living.

If I have told you earthly things and you do not believe,
how will you believe if I tell you heavenly things.
—John 3:12

Make me understand the way of Your precepts, so shall I meditate on
Your wondrous works ... I have chosen the way of truth; Your judgments

> *I have laid before me. I cling to Your testimonies; O lord, do not put me to shame! I will run in the way of Your commandments, for You shall enlarge my heart. Teach me, O lord, the way of Your statutes, And I shall keep it to the end. Give me understanding, and I shall keep Your law; indeed I shall observe it with my whole heart. Make me walk in the path of Your commandments, for I delight in it.*
> —Psalm 119:27, 30–35

The Spirit of Understanding— We'll Understand It All By and By

God meets us where we are. He uses the trials and circumstances of life to posture us to receive His provision of understanding. He repeatedly put the disciples on a storm-tossed sea. The multitudes went hungry, but He had a provision of bread to satisfy. Each one of the many miracles and demonstrations of His power, those fulfillments of His Word, postured His followers to more fully perceive the spiritual purpose for His coming. His interaction, fellowship, and instruction prepared them for understanding.

God also met me while in fear. Yet before I could find deliverance from it, I had to fully face it just as Gideon did. Some of what I have shared in this study can frighten many in their pursuit of intimacy with God, but please persevere to hear the rest of the story. With or without God, we are certain to face things in this life we had rather not. With God, it is possible to survive stronger and wiser and be more at peace than without Him. The disciples' fear and unbelief did nothing to exempt them from difficulty; it kept them miserable in it.

Surrender to the Spirit of understanding postures one to recognize how God reveals His presence and power, something we desperately need in uncertain times. The following testimony gives witness that the God who revealed Himself miraculously in the Old and New Testament is a God who still desires to reveal His power and presence to His children today. He is the real thing—still! Through and since this significant life event, God brought to my remembrance circumstances that fueled my need to understand the power of understanding. These have been some of the most difficult times of my relationship with Him and my life, but they have also fueled some of the most intimate revelations of His goodness and power. We may fear circumstances, but He wants us to fear Him. He prepares us to receive His goodness—even through what we fear.

In this study, we have discussed the process God used with Gideon and the disciples to grow their faith from fear. This partial testimony gives a current example of this process in the pattern of my life. Only now can I trace the process of His ways. Before I share the details, let me illuminate my pattern more succinctly. First, He led me into a study of fear, reinforcing the truth that He is not the author of fear but the nurturer of faith (His Word). He led me to pray for these truths for myself, my family, and particularly my mom. Second, He gave opportunity for me to take that knowledge—that He is not the author of fear—and apply that truth as wisdom. I had to face fear to be delivered from it (His will). Third, through a difficult but eventual surrender to His agenda, not my own, God gave tremendous understanding and peace. God revealed His presence and His power at work (His power). God strengthened faith.

Before my mother died of cancer, God graciously granted the desires of her faithful heart as He prepared her to willingly go to heaven. Several months after her diagnosis, God revealed that her illness was terminal and that her physical healing was not His plan despite our prayers for healing. However, God also gave me a heavy burden to pray for her to find freedom from fear, more than just a fear of dying though I did not know specifically what that meant. Later into her illness, I studied *Breaking Free—Making Liberty in Christ a Reality* by Beth Moore. God used that in my life, and it became a prayer guide as I interceded for my mom and the fear I believed troubled her.

My mother was a great woman of faith. Her favorite hymn was "Trust and Obey." She had a remarkable gifting of grace, of faith, and of joy through any circumstance, and she definitely was a woman of prayer who feared the Lord. She was a sacrificial servant with a childlike faith—ever loving, hopeful, and gracious. She loved the fellowship of family and friends. She loved life, and she never met a stranger. She could travel anywhere in the world and meet someone she knew or find a mutual acquaintance. Throughout her illness, she communicated her desire for us to remain joyful at the end and to remember her full of life and joy. In her humorous way, we were warned repeatedly not to stand around her bed watching her die. She was careful to take care of so many details so we would not have to face things in our grief after she passed.

A few things beyond the obvious concerned her. She did not like heavy doses of morphine for pain. Because of the many stories heard over the years of people who hallucinated near death, I believe she feared losing her dignity. For most of her fourteen months of illness, she remained relatively active and self-sufficient given her condition. Only her last month was constantly difficult, and even at that, only one week was severe. But I can honestly say Mother was a woman of grace throughout her illness who gave great glory to God for the strength with which she faced her difficulty and embraced death.

It was at the beginning of that particularly severe week that we knew the end was near. My sister called on a Sunday morning to say Mom was slipping in and out of consciousness and they were calling all of us home. My father asked, "Is this it, Betty? Are you dying?" My quick-witted mother, having learned after forty-five years of marriage how to respond, said, "Well, I don't know, J. I've never died before!" Words that though humorously stated would prove somewhat prophetic.

Three of her five daughters and son arrived by early afternoon. My sisters along with our dad and mom's mother gathered around her hospice bed at our family farm to exchange good-byes. Mother was trying to hold on to life and consciousness until my brother and oldest sister could join us. As we stood there crying, reflecting, and praying silently, we saw Mom's eyes open wide and slowly stop to glare at each one of us around her bed. We realized we were "standing around her bed, watching her die." Wanting to respect her wishes but not wanting to leave, I asked if we could sing hymns. She nodded. We sang her favorites. These were hymns we shared as a family over the years from the old *Heavenly Highways* hymnal. We chose hymns that reminded us of hope in Christ and of the blessings of heaven. Periodically, Mom would regain consciousness enough to harmonize.

My brother and sister arrived later in the evening with their chance to say goodbye, but she did not die that day. Over the following week she deteriorated rapidly each day. By Wednesday, it was very difficult to understand why God did not take her. I even began to get angry because Mother looked so tormented. While we adequately managed her pain, she did not look peaceful. Her organs were shutting down. Large lumps appeared all over her body. Her face was distorted, and her mouth was drawn like that of a stroke victim's. She was so weak that she had no control over body movement, and she couldn't really speak. She periodically would grunt or groan or say a few words too quickly and inaudibly to recognize. Her breathing was shallow, and her color was ashen.

Each time hospice indicated she was probably in her final hours, we would gather around the bed and say our good-byes, telling her it was all right to go home to the Lord. We sang hymns for hours until we had no strength to sing. The singing calmed us as much as her; it helped us to focus on God's eternal purpose for going home.

That particular Wednesday became my own crucifixion moment. It was difficult for me to release Mom to God not just because I wanted her with us but also because of the prayer burden God gave. I firmly believed it was for some purpose that Mother would reveal before she died. But she could no longer speak, and she appeared to be in much discomfort and torment. I had no hope of seeing my prayers answered this side of heaven. I could not understand why God had given me such an intense burden to pray with the belief of seeing them answered only for it to end that way. Neither was this the way of death she prayed for. I had to surrender all of this to God and willingly trust that my prayers and hers would be answered even if we had to wait until the other side of glory to understand. It was not an easy surrender, but it eventually came.

This process of deterioration, good-byes, and singing continued for a week. Each morning, after hours of singing the night before, she would strengthen momentarily in some small way. By evening, with her condition once again severe, the process of good-byes and worship repeated. Then Sunday morning, a week later, my dad awoke us all at 5:30. Believing Mother had died, we were overwhelmed by what we witnessed. She was sitting up in bed with a glass of Coke in one hand and water in the other. There were no lumps on her body. Her face was completely normal. She was talking and had full but weakened use of her body.

She said, "I've been up with your dad since four this morning. I wanted to talk to him and then to all of you. I asked him to pour a glass of Coke so as I talk with you, I will sip and finish it." And she did. "This is my sign to you that I know what I'm saying. I'm not hallucinating. This is 'the real thing.' I am so grateful that God allowed me to come back and tell you all these things before I die. I have been through all the phases of death, and I have no more fear! It is so wonderful there! I don't see how anyone could reject Him."

"Mom, are you in pain?" we asked as she clutched her stomach.

"No, I'm in a spirit of prayer. Praise you, Jesus! All the songs you sang to me this week were written years and years ago, but they were written for this time and purpose. God has allowed me to see how all the things in my life are to be used for His glory." Mother's favorite life verse was Romans 8:28. "God has given me the peace that passes all understanding. I know this is difficult for you to understand right now, but you will understand by and by."

So many things filled my heart as I heard those words. Awe. Thankfulness. God had answered so many prayers of so many. She said, "I have no more fear!" There are no words to adequately express my gratitude for God's gracious and miraculous answer to prayer for her. We knew by faith that God would give understanding of her life in glory. Never did we imagine He would allow her to have that peace on earth, let alone to share that joy with her family. Knowing the heart of His child, God graciously allowed Mother to share eternal blessings with her family from her own resurrected voice of praise!

The physical change in her condition was miraculous to the point we wondered if God was completely healing her. God removed her fears I didn't fully understand but nevertheless interceded for. When we believed Mother to be in torment, God actually spiritually renewed her soul and partly her body. Later, a friend reminded me of 2 Corinthians 4:16–18 (NIV).

> Therefore do not lose heart! Though outwardly we are wasting away, inwardly we are being renewed day by day. For these light and momentary trials are achieving for us an eternal glory that outweighs them all. So we focus not on what is seen, but on what is unseen. For what is seen is temporal, but what is unseen is eternal.

While we focused on what we could see and became discouraged, God led us to focus on His unseen purpose as we sang hymns in worship to intercede for spiritual realities. But our comfort and understanding was not immediate. In fact, we did not even consciously seek it initially. Without fully comprehending, we were experiencing Romans 8:26: "Likewise the Spirit helps us in our weakness. For we know not what we should pray for, but the Spirit intercedes for us with groaning which cannot be uttered." Worship focused us on the spiritual realities more than the physical visibilities. As we worshipped through grief, the Spirit interceded for Mother and renewed her spiritually, and ultimately physically strengthened her dying body.

Just as the worship of Paul and Silas brought power to release them from prison, worship brought power to mother and released her from life's trials and the regrets, fears, and pain of death! Yes, even from the pain and agony of the dying process, for Mother did not die that day. She would be with us one more week! It was a week of joy and laughter, and fellowship. She had an incomprehensible level of spiritual understanding and insight. It was as if God pulled back the curtain of glory for revelation of spiritual realities, but also brought joy and fellowship with her family still on earth. We reduced her pain medication for she had less pain the final week. This was the week of Thanksgiving, which is always the primary time of year our family gathers. That day, Mother had us dress her. She came to the table, blessed our family meal, and ate with us though she had not eaten food in more than a week.

God allowed our family to experience the blessing of heaven in a remarkable way through her testimony and our experiences of that final week. By removing her fears and allowing her to share with her family the goodness He gives to all in glory, God relieved the heaviness of our grief and gave us joy even before Mom died. He removed the sting of death and revealed His peace to her and miraculously to us. It's as if God slowed down the process of death so we could glimpse with our physical eyes what happens when He calls His children home.

Through the phases of death, the body decays while the spirit is renewed. The essence of who we are is strengthened and with the final breath is instantly transformed. What we as observers of those dying see is contrary to what happens in the spiritual realm. God truly gives comfort in the middle of chaos, life in the face of death.

God allowed faith to become sight. While we knew Mother would gain understanding of her life in heaven, we didn't expect to hear the blessing from her own voice of praise. In a small but miraculous way, she took us with her to the throne of God to receive more of His goodness than we could imagine. She never again returned to the tormented physical state she had lived in for a week. She died very peacefully on Sunday noon after Thanksgiving with no one standing around her bed. The church of her youth, wedding, and memorial service sang as the choir special in the hour of her death, "This World Is Not My Home."

When Mom said to us, "You'll understand it all by and by," there was a prompting in my heart leading me to know she was not speaking only of future, eternal knowledge. Even then, I believed there was understanding God would give prior to a reunion in glory. God brought to my remembrance one of the hymns referencing His truth. The second verse gives a testimony of Mother's witness throughout her life and death, and a reminder of God's promise through her words to us.

> Faithful till death said our Loving Master, just a few days to labor and wait. Toils of the road will then seem as nothing, as we sweep through that beautiful gate. Farther along we'll know all about it. Farther along we'll understand why. Cheer up my brother, live in the sun shine, we'll understand it all by and by.[43]

Farther along, we'll understand by and by. God gradually opens the eyes of the heart to understanding. There are levels of understanding we can receive on earth, but one day, we will gain full understanding of God's purposes. We have an eternal hope and joy for the difficulties we experience. We had prayed for a miracle of healing, but as we focused on the Healer in worship, God gave healing in a way different from what we had originally desired. His provision gave us more of Him than we knew to ask for. We prayed for our mother's life, but He graciously revealed personally the power of His life. We prayed and worshipped without expecting such a provision. Mom obediently and willingly surrendered to leave this world and family she loved to live with her God. One of the visions she shared the final week

---

[43] From the hymn "Farther Along."

was of her "sitting at the throne of God, holding the hand of Jesus," the Blessed Savior, the Author of grace, the Source of understanding!

We'll understand it all by and by! Oh the blessed goodness of our heavenly Father who knows what we need even before we ask! He knows we need understanding to strengthen faith and has made a provision for it. Yet He wants us to ask. He may ask us to wait because He wants us to faithfully persevere until we are emptied of the limited focus of this world. He jealously desires for us to be filled completely, adequately, and sufficiently with Him! Oh what greatness comes from the God jealous for our love! He is the Real Thing! He is worth seeking!

> Tempted and tried we're oft made to wonder. Why it should be thus all the day long, while there are others living about us, never molested though in the wrong. Farther along we'll know all about it. Farther along we'll understand why. Cheer up my brother, live in the sunshine. We'll understand it all by and by. When we see Jesus coming in glory, when He comes from His home in the sky; Then we shall meet Him in that bright mansion, We'll understand it all by and by![44]

---

[44] Ibid.

⊰ Chapter 6 ⊱

The Faith of a "Mustard Tree"

The kingdom of heaven is like a mustard seed, which a man took
and sowed in his field, which indeed is the least of all the seeds; but
when it is grown it is greater than the herbs and becomes a tree.
—Matthew 13:31–32

The Seed of Faith—His Word

Begin with worship, meditation, and prayer.

> But without faith it is impossible to please Him, for he who comes to God must believe that He is, and that His is a rewarder of those who diligently seek Him. (Hebrews 11:6)

> "Lord, thank You for revealing Your desire for my faith to mature beyond that small seed Christ planted. Continue teaching me how to prepare my heart so it will mature and bear fruit according to Your will."

Without faith, it is impossible to please God and live victoriously over fear. Faith is not merely the seed needed for salvation; it is an ever-increasing power that fuels our ability to relate to God, to trust Him, and to empower surrender. This final chapter of *From Fear to Faith* revisits what Gideon unfolded about God's ways. We want to review how the revelation of His Word, His will, and His power matures faith.

Regardless of where you are in your personal journey, I pray this study has reiterated that we need God to reveal Himself. I hope it has renewed your confidence that He will, and that you are more equipped to overcome the obstacles to hear, understand, and see Him with spiritual eyes. I hope this need is a prayer that intensifies or renews in your faith journey. If you have already reached the Christ as me stage of growth, I pray this study perhaps highlights the ways God nurtured your faith to this level. If you were reminded of the obstacles Satan uses to undermine faith, I pray the Spirit will use this remembrance to nurture someone else still on that journey.

In this chapter, we further explore how God as faith's author and finisher grows faith's seed into a tree of life.

1. His Word—faith comes by hearing the word—Romans 10:17.
2. His will—we are His workmanship created for a purpose that we should walk in it—Ephesians 2:10.
3. His power—God works in us to will and to do His will—Philippians 2:13, 2 Thessalonians 1:11.

It is impossible to trust and obey God without faith because faith is believing in the promises of God, the truth of God, which empowers trust and obedience. When we lose sight of His promises, understanding truth is distorted and we take matters into our own hands to manufacture a desired outcome. Think of how Abraham and Sarah went down this path initially with Ishmael. God rewards those who seek Him with greater faith, greater power to trust, and greater power to obey. Jesus told the disciples that they need faith only the size of a mustard seed to fulfill the miraculous (Matthew 17:20). We are not admonished to stay a seed but to be a planting of the Lord in fertile ground that reaps a harvest in due season. A small seed of faith demonstrates the power of God, but God has a plan for the seed of faith to grow. He is the author and finisher of faith.

In John 14:12, Jesus tells the disciples that they will do the works He has done and that His going away to the Father will empower them to do greater works. The seed of faith is in them, but the filling of the Holy Spirit will empower their faith to mature. Their faith will strengthen to conquer fear and unbelief as their understanding is opened. Let's summarize this promise of Christ: The Word lives in us (John 14:13–20). The Holy Spirit gives understanding of the indwelling Word (John 14:21–26). Faith comes from hearing the Living Word (Romans 10:17). He brings to our remembrance the truths of His Word as they are unveiled in the circumstances of life (John 14:26–29). As He opens understanding, this deepening of faith empowers surrender to His will (Philippians 2:13) to trust and to obey.

Christ told the disciples they needed only little faith, but when He opened their understanding prior to His final ascension, their faith strengthened greatly. They returned to Jerusalem with great joy praising and worshipping God continually in the temple (Luke 24:52–54). This empowered response was a great witness to the power of strengthened faith over fear. These were the closet followers who fled the garden in great fear during Jesus's arrest. They returned to the temple amid those who had crucified their Lord. Their fear was vanquished. No longer was their safety and position of great importance. They were willing to risk all to posture themselves to receive what Christ promised to send. In great faith and trust, they praised and worshipped God with joy eagerly anticipating the fulfillment of Christ's promise of the Holy Spirit.

Through the parable of the seed that grows into a tree, Jesus reveals both the blessing of faith as well as the power of God. While this teaching intends to encourage us to believe and hope in the power of God, too often today, it is used as a crutch that hinders perceiving a need for God to strengthen faith. We may rationalize, "If I need only a tiny bit to know God's power, why should I seek more?" Somehow unconsciously, we too often view this verse as the most we can hope for, a standard measure for mature faith, that is, faith as small as a mustard seed. Perhaps we also fail to seek more faith for we fear what God plans to accomplish through it. Faith is a living, moving, growing seed of God. It is not intended to stay a small seed buried under the topsoil of life. It is intended to break open, respond to the warmth of the Son, be nourished by the Living Water, and grow into a viable, strong tree. This growth produces a harvest for the kingdom of God. It provides shelter to others. It is life, health, happiness for us.

If you have ever planted vegetable or flower seeds, you can understand the anticipation and excitement of watching the buried seed finally begin to produce a shoot. When you see it wilt, you water it. When you see weeds grow up around it, you remove them. The growth process is now above ground where you can evaluate its progress and anticipate the bloom or the harvest. There is excitement and frustration when the weather—the major influencer completely out of our control—effects its growth positively or negatively. Just as a gardener has to learn to work with or in spite of weather conditions, the Christian has to learn to work with God or in spite of self and Satan to nurture faith to its maturity.

Through the examples of Gideon and the disciples, scripture reveals God's intent for the faith process to be observed, anticipated, and celebrated. This spiritual sight equips us to know how to join with God, overcome Satan, and surrender self so that faith matures. Jesus gave the disciples opportunities to express their faith and see their weaknesses so they would know how to further recognize and respond to the Word that grows faith. While God is the author and finisher of faith, He wants us to see this process so we recognize His care to make us flourish. He desires our fellowship in the journey.

When we witness God's power, we are awed by His greatness and grace. His power is a blessing, a reassuring comfort that is humbling. However, whatever miraculous power of God we have experienced is little compared to the fullness of God. Because of His greatness, it often takes very little of God's power to settle, appease, awe, and impress us. Our expectations are often not very high maybe because we feel unworthy of or guilty about asking for too much. We are content to settle for little faith because we expect only a little power. While we may not consciously say or think this, our unwillingness to surrender to grow faith is evidence of the true attitude of our hearts. It is easy to take what little we already have and get busy building the kingdom for God. All the while, Christ is knocking on the door of our hearts waiting to give so much more than we settle for.

God planted the seed, the Word, in our hearts. "Faith comes by hearing, and hearing by the Word of God." When we hear God, we hear His promises, ways, will, and love revealed through His Word to make faith grow. We have to draw near to God to hear Him and learn what His promises are. The Greek term for "word" is *rhema*, the Living Word. It is

God's present-speaking voice. Through the Holy Spirit, His Word gives application and instruction for our present needs and situations. God's Word always accomplishes His will, but through the Holy Spirit, through the Living Word, He reveals how we are to respond. This understanding and communication with Him strengthens faith, keeps us postured in humility, and keeps us focused on recognizing His hand at work, empowering trust to wait on Him. It causes us to remain kingdom focused instead of trusting earthly visibilities.

In the last chapter, I mentioned how God used my favorite life verse, Proverbs 3:5–6, to prepare me for a liver resection. God planted that verse in my heart many years earlier as a significant passage. It was only in the last few years of my mother's life that I truly realized the significance of Romans 8:28 as her life verse. Some years after her death and after my liver resection, I came across the Bible my parents gave to me on my thirteenth birthday. It was not my working Bible that I marked up or wrote in but my special Bible that I preserved except for very few notations. In the blank pages were two verses noted when I was young: Proverbs 3:5–6 and Romans 8:28.

Years before, these two life-altering events happened (my mother's miraculous passing and my own blessings of healing and comfort). God planted His seed that would sustain me and reveal His personal presence and concern with what grieved me. These popular verses were a personal *rhema* for a specific need. God opened understanding to allow me to see His ways working throughout many years and experiences. When God brought to my remembrance praying Proverbs 3 prior to the first surgery, the word God had already used to comfort and prepare me many times before became my *rhema* for that moment. God appropriated the same word in a new situation so I experienced Him in a more personal way. As He opened understanding, I heard God, and faith was strengthened. Nothing about my situation changed. I still had many concerns. Yet I heard God and was reassured of His hand over my life. By bringing this to my remembrance, understanding empowered trust through the second surgery.

The meaning of the verse did not change to fit the current need, but the new application caused it to be more meaningful. As I continually gave Him my burden of fear, He reassured me I was on His path, not to have any regrets, to trust Him, and not lean on my own understanding about the pain. As the surgery drew near, God repeatedly used people to unknowingly quote this verse to reinforce His presence. God also repeatedly used others to reassure me that His angels had charge over me (Psalm 91:11) without their awareness of the hungry prayer voiced in the midst of my need or the comfort God already provided through Psalm 91. My prayer asked God for comfort that could come only from supernatural intervention.

The liver resection went very well. The recovery time in the hospital was shorter than anticipated and was less painful than my previous experience. Also, God answered my prayer to experience His comfort and presence in a very personal way. I believe God supernaturally intervened to put me on a particular floor with particular nurses who were outside the norm. The surgery was performed the day after Christmas, and because of overcrowding in the hospital, I spent the week of recovery on the orthopedic floor. The nurses who cared for me that week were Joy, Blessing, Peace, Paul, Christine, and Mary! I was convinced that these names had to be Christmas code names designed to bring cheer to patients during the holidays. However, I was repeatedly reassured (because I repeatedly asked) that these were their actual names. As they weaned me from an epidural to oral pain medication, Comfort was my nightly nurse the final two nights of my stay. I know I was placed on the orthopedic floor with these specific nurses as my caregivers by God's design. This blessing was His continued reassurance that my life was in His hands. God in fact had put His angels in charge over me. He allowed me to experience in the practical, physical realm what He previously reassured was accomplished in the spiritual realm. (His power revealed.) He strengthened my faith to conquer fear and graciously allowed my faith to become sight. By allowing me to see His goodness in a tangible sense, my faith and worship increased.

While I am sure I do not yet have complete understanding of God's purpose for this in my life, I know that this experience, this strengthening of my faith, was necessary for what I would soon face. In the months that followed, I encountered one of the most difficult times of persecution as His child that I have experienced to date. Had my faith not been strengthened so mightily and personally, His purposes could have been quenched by the doubt, fear, and unbelief that tried to consume me. His personal goodness served as a continual reminder that He was in control despite how out of control circumstances seemed.

God wants us to know His truth, but He further intends for His truth to become life. God also demonstrated this principle through the miraculous provision of manna while the children of Israel roamed the wilderness. Let's learn more about the ways of God to meet with us in the midst of a great need and teach us how to know His Word as Life.

Read Exodus 16:4–36.

When faced with hunger in the wilderness, how did the Israelites respond?

In verse 8, who does Moses say they are grumbling against?

How does God respond to their grumbling? (v. 11).

Based on verses 16–17, how much did each person gather?

For how long did God provide the manna? (v. 39).

While Israel wandered in the wilderness forty years, God supplied them with manna daily. Except for the extra provision they were to store for the Sabbath, they were not to accumulate manna for future use. They gathered only according to their present need. Manna, the bread of heaven, was provided through God's spoken word. His provision was available and waiting before they awoke each morning. For God's provision to become nourishment for their bodies, they were required to gather and prepare it each day. They had no way to farm, no storage mechanisms, and no food preservation techniques that could assist them to self-sufficiently provide food. They were completely dependent on the faithful Word of God. When they chose to partake of the provision from His Word, it became life and health to their bodies.

In the middle of doing household chores one day when my children were toddlers, this fleeting but significant prayer was voiced in my heart: "Lord, I need to return to Your word." In retrospect, I probably said it more to myself than to God, but I know it was a desire God wanted fulfilled. Through a series of following events, I found an insatiable hunger to study His Word to a degree I had never before experienced in my relationship with Him.

It wasn't until years later that He brought to my remembrance this fleeting prayer. When this prayer was voiced, I was in my own wilderness in some respect for God began removing any semblance of security in my life. We had moved to a new city, and our first child was an infant. My husband and I had always wanted me to stay home with our children. While I loved being with our son, I found the adjustment from a professional career as a CPA to a stay-at-home mom difficult. (Yet when I went back to work in their preteen years, I struggled with guilt and regret.) My husband made a significant career change after completing law school. His focus shifted from his law education to establishing a new career, and that put more strain on our relationship. Our move to a new city initially removed us from the fellowship and accountability of exhorting brothers and sisters in Christ.

A career, a husband, and godly friends were no longer available sources for strength. God was drawing me into a greater realization of Him as my primary Source. But with the busyness of motherhood, even though my need was great, I had not turned to His Word to the degree I should have. I was very involved in church, and my prayer life and worship of Him was a vital part. I even participated in Bible study. While God personally spoke and ministered to me in each of these venues, He had specific things for me in His Word He could give to me only directly, not through another source. As I responded to His invitation, I embarked on a very significant and life-changing journey with God. Though subsequent circumstances were often very difficult, I had the reassurance and presence of God. I have been able to persevere and endure because of the way His Word became power and life.

Some of you may feel as if you are in an emotional or spiritual wilderness, a barren place void of all that is good and pleasant. While in the wilderness, we are not settled as we should be and find it difficult to know peace and rest. (In a sense, we are all in a wilderness physically speaking because the beauty of this earth is not anything like the Promised Land of heaven that awaits us.) But God has given His Word, His bread of heaven to nourish us until we are settled in the Promised Land of heaven. Our responsibility is to come to Him each day to receive that provision. He does not give complete understanding, but He does supply what we presently need and can comprehend. By hearing, we receive, and by understanding, the Word is prepared for daily consumption. By faith, we take in His Word and come to know it as life.

2 Timothy 3:16–17 reiterates this truth: "All Scripture is given by inspiration of God, and is profitable for doctrine, for reproof, for correction, for instruction in righteousness, that the man of God may be complete, thoroughly equipped for every good work." God wants us to know His Word. He wants it to dwell in us. As we read and study God's Word, we are postured to more fully recognize the Word living in us and that is at work in the situations we face.

Is there someone you are continually "grumbling" to about your need?

Is that someone God?

Are you willing to confess this grumbling as a lack of willingness to trust where God has you right now?

What Word, what *rhema*, is God giving for your present need?

Will you come before God and humbly confess your need to Him, with no strings attached?

Confess your willingness to gather and prepare daily the provision He has waiting.

With man, it is impossible, but with God, all things are possible. God repeatedly provides food for His children when they have no means or hope of getting it soon. His provision waits for us. We must not allow our belief, our desires in what He *can do* become our focus. Focus faith on God to trust what He *will do*.

We recognize that the body can survive without food longer than it can survive without water. Our bodies are over 70 percent water; it is a most vital element for our survival. Taking this knowledge of our physical need into consideration, reflect on the spiritual parallel of God's Word. God nourishes with food and sustains with water.

> Jesus said to them, "I tell you the truth, it is not Moses who has given you the bread from heaven, but it is my Father who gives you the true bread from heaven. For the Bread of God is He who comes down from heaven and gives life to the world ... I am the Bread of Life. He who comes to Me will never go hungry, and he who believes in Me will never be thirsty." (John 6:32–33, 35)

He who comes to Christ never hungers. More important, he who believes in Christ is never thirsty. We came to God for salvation, but how are we believing in His power at work to grow faith? The Word feeds our hunger and quenches thirst. "Taste and see that the Lord is good; blessed is the man who trusts in Him!" (Psalm 34:8). "Whoever drinks of the water that I shall give him will never thirst. But the water that I shall give him will become in him a fountain of water springing up into everlasting life" (John 4:14). We need the Living Water to sustain and grow faith and to overcome our thirst. Don't just come to Him; have faith in Him!

Faith that Believes—His Will

Begin with worship, meditation, and prayer.

> And not being weak in faith ... He did not waiver at the promise of God through unbelief, but was strengthened in faith, giving glory to God, and being fully convinced that what He had promised He was also able to perform. And therefore, it was accounted to him for righteousness. (Romans 4:19-22)

> "Lord, help me recognize when I am tempted to prioritize belief in a desired outcome above faith and trust in You. Strengthen me to persevere until Your provision is complete. Help me recognize Your power as I surrender to wait on You. May You be high and lifted up as I walk in faith."

"For we are His workmanship, created in Christ Jesus for good works, which God prepared beforehand that we should walk in them" (Ephesians 2:10). We were created for a purpose. We were created for good works that we should walk in them. God has a plan for our life—His will—that He longs to reveal so we fulfill our destiny. As we have learned, worship plays an important role in understanding the specifics of God's will. This is important to align our will with God's. One of the weeds that can greatly choke faith is our will or our belief in a desired outcome. If our will, or what we mistakenly perceive to be God's will, doesn't materialize faith can be undermined. If the anticipation was great, faith can be shattered when we focus on the physical visibility more than the spiritual reality.

God's Word is the source of His will. To distinguish between our will and His, we can look to His Word for clarification as His will does not contradict His Word. Likewise, understanding His will helps us to embrace His power. There is the old saying, "*That* is something we just don't have to pray about;" we do not even consider a certain path or voice it in prayer because it contradicts God's Word and thus cannot be His will.

Since we need to discern God's will above our own desires, we will explore a few distinctions between belief and faith.[45] This is important because of the temptation to embrace our will once His Word is planted in our hearts. Because belief is an element of faith, it is easy to fall into the temptation of focusing more on a belief than on God. Enthused, energized, and motivated by revelations of His Word, Satan seeks to undermine revelation of His will, power, and ways for unfolding them. He attempted this with Jesus in the wilderness (Luke 4). His schemes are consistent. The disciples couldn't heal the demon-possessed child in Mark 9 because the lack of faith impeded needed prayer and fasting (Mark 9:29). In Mark 9:19, Jesus said, "O faithless generation, how long shall I be with you? How long shall I bear with you? Bring him to Me." Though God's will for healing was understood, the disciples failed to seek the power needed. They didn't go to God in prayer to the degree needed, so Jesus said, "Bring him to Me."

Hebrew 11:1 says, "Faith is the substance of things hoped for, evidence unseen." Faith is what fuels our desire to relate to God. This definition also insinuates that belief is a necessary ingredient for faith, a believing in things hoped for. But belief in and of itself is not faith. Too often, belief causes us to focus on the provision we seek instead of the Provider. In chapter 3, we discussed the importance of seeking God's face more than His hand and the example of Martha and Mary. Perhaps this was a faith lesson for what Martha and Mary would face in the near future with the death of Lazarus (see John 11). It was a lesson to seek God for more than His hand of provision. Despite Jesus telling them Lazarus's illness was not unto death but for God's glory, Lazarus died. Physical realities conflicted with Jesus's revelation. Martha had belief in Jesus's healing power; when she saw Him after her brother's death, she expressed frustration that He had failed to intervene with healing (John 11:21). This is belief, but Martha continued with an expression of faith in John 11:22: "But even now I know that whatever You ask of God, God will do." With this confession of faith, Jesus reassured her that Lazarus would rise.

In John 11 Martha finally has her own "Mary moment." Martha expresses her surrender to God above His hand of provision. Her expression

---

[45] In her study *Live a Praying Life*, Jennifer Kennedy Dean draws attention to the need for our faith to be more than mere belief. I suggest the reader consider this study, and subsequent works of Dean to more fully probe these distinctions.

of deep faith to Jesus proves she understands what Jesus has been trying to teach the disciples and the multitudes—that He is the Son of God with the power over life and death (John 11:23–27). That "whatever" (John 5:19, 11:22, 12:50, 15:14, 16:13, 23) Jesus asks of God, God will do. Even though she wasn't quite certain of the possibility for Lazarus to rise again, Martha expresses belief, hope, trust, and surrender to the Will of God—*whatever* God *will* do. Her focus is on the power and person of God not in a particular outcome. In John 11:41–43, Jesus's prayer expresses to God a validation for Martha's faith in a way that only she would recognize by asking for God's intervention. "Father, I thank You that You have heard Me. And I know that You always hear Me, *but because of the people standing by I said this*," (emphasis added). Jesus continues so that others may also have that opportunity to strengthen faith, "...that they may believe You sent Me... Lazarus, come forth!" *Whatever* Jesus asks, God will do!

Belief causes us to focus our prayers on receiving healing because we know God can heal. Our will may be for complete healing, but faith causes us to trust in the Healer and to worship Him whether or not we experience healing on earth. Faith also empowers us to wait on His provision of healing. Faith empowers us to trust in the perhaps unseen purpose for the condition. As repeatedly mentioned, faith causes us to believe what God *can do* and reaches beyond to trust in who He is and what He *will do*. Martha expressed all of these in John 11. God can unceasingly dispense blessings, but is that who He is? Is that what He will do in your life? In mine? Can faith dictate God's actions? Is that true faith, or is that belief and hope?

I heard the television testimony of a woman crippled by multiple sclerosis who had been confined to a wheelchair for fourteen years. Her husband was frustrated with her because she would not pray for God to heal her. She stated that she trusted God had a purpose for her condition, and though she did not specifically pray for healing, she had a peace that God would heal her in his time (her husband and others continually prayed for her). One Sunday morning at church during the middle of the sermon, she sensed God telling her to get out of her wheelchair and walk. She stood up carefully and slowly walked around the inside of the sanctuary three times while those present praised God for her healing. This is an example of faith in the Healer. Her heart was rightly postured to have faith in God, not an obsession with what she desired God to do. She had a steadfast resolve to trust the unseen purpose God had for her condition. Of course she desired healing, but that was not the focus of her faith. Who is God? He is a rewarder of those who diligently seek Him.

God allows tests of faith. As we are given the opportunity to trust in the unseen power of God, faith becomes sight. We see not always in a physical sense but with spiritual understanding when faith is exercised. We could see this stretching of faith as analogous to growing our seedling into a tree. God uses each test to propel us from that small seed into a strong tree. To prepare us more fully for these tests, we want to identify belief that is not faith as well as the proper role belief has in developing faith.

God begins His call of Abraham by saying, "I will make you into a great nation and I will bless you" (Genesis 12:2). God commands him to go to the land that "I will show you." Abraham does not know how God will fulfill this promise or where he is going, but he obeys.

Asserting our will or ways in prayer or action blinds understanding of circumstances. We remain at risk for attributing God's actions to Satan's or considering Satan's actions as God's will. This confusion robs us of the peace we often seek when asserting our will. Abraham had faith in God's will. Bearing a child with Hagar is indication, however, that Abraham did not always understand or follow God's ways. That decision did not result in peace for Abraham's household or future generations. Though there are far-reaching consequences from his (and often our) actions, God's promise would still be fulfilled. Abraham's disobedience did not change God's mind or plan for granting a son by his wife, Sarah. In Genesis 17:17, we see a more mature Abraham ask God for understanding of His ways. "Will a son be born to a man a hundred years old? Will Sarah bear a child at the age of ninety-nine? If only Ishmael [Hagar's son] might have your blessing!"

Abraham eventually sought understanding of God's promise, and God faithfully gave him an answer (see vv. 19–21). In Romans 4:18, Paul says that Abraham hoped against all hope. Yes, Abraham had fears, doubts, and misunderstandings ("against all hope"), yet he still hoped and trusted in the promises of God. Listen to what commentator Matthew Henry says about Abraham's faith.

> Though weak faith shall not be rejected, the bruised reed
> not broken, the smoking flax not quenched, yet strong faith

shall be commended and honoured. The strength of his faith appeared in the victory it won over his fears. And hereby he gave glory to God; for, as unbelief dishonours God by making him a liar (1 John 5:10), so faith honours God by setting to its seal that he is true, (John 3:33). Abraham's faith gave God the glory of his wisdom, power, holiness, goodness, and especially of his faithfulness, resting upon the word that he had spoken. Among men we say, "He that trusts another, gives him credit, and honours him by taking his word"; thus Abraham gave glory to God by trusting him. We never hear our Lord Jesus commending anything so much as great faith (Matthew 8:10 and 15:28): therefore God gives honour to faith, great faith, because faith, great faith, gives honour to God.[46]

The Romans 4 passage above says Abraham was "fully convinced that what He had promised He was also able to perform." Abraham's belief, Abraham's faith, rested in the desire of God's heart. Abraham's faith matured. Because Abraham grew to know God more, he knew God's heart or God's will. No longer was Abraham trying to manufacture a provision that fulfilled God's promise (as he did years earlier with Ishmael). Abraham was so firmly fixed on the promise of God, which he knows will not be fully realized until future generations, that he could trust God's current command. There is no evidence to empower Abraham's trust, only faith, a hope with evidence unseen. It matured as Abraham died to his own will to trust God. Abraham talked and fellowshipped with God, proving the faithfulness of God.

Faith trusts God's will without evidence, but faith also fuels expectation and recognition of God regardless of how He chooses to reveal Himself. It is knowing He is working even if there is no apparent provision. It goes beyond a willingness to hope when all physical realities appear hopeless to

---

[46] Matthew Henry, "Commentary on Romans 4," in *Matthew Henry Commentary on the Whole Bible*, Blue Letter Bible, February 9, 2005, http://www.blueletterbible.org/Comm/mhc/Rom/Rom004.html.

trusting Him if they remain so. To act in faith is to surrender to God and confess in prayer, "Not my will, but Thine be done."

The following distinction of prayer is perhaps the most freeing and empowering truth that we can apply to grow faith: prayer is not our will that is blessed or honored by God. Prayer is not us involving God. Exercising faith in prayer involves us in God's process for releasing His power and purpose. Answered prayer results from a response to the desire or need God birthed in our heart. (God knows what we need before we ask; Matthew 6:8.) Romans 8:26–27 reveals how the Spirit knows the will of God and is interceding for us even when we do not know how or what to pray. "Whatever" Jesus asks through the Spirit, God will do. The Spirit intercedes for us, and also reveals to us what and how to pray as we surrender to Him. For this reason, it is important to be still before we pray so we can provide opportunity for the Spirit to reveal the will of the Father. This reveals how there is also a spiritual purpose behind the physical need voiced in prayer. Embedded in that need (or perhaps the sole purpose of that need) is to draw close to God to experience more fully His personal love. We often take for granted God's desire to fellowship with us in all His works and ways. Through our response to Him, we are given opportunity to know Him more.[47]

Answered prayer is the result of our echoing and joining with the Spirit to pray the will of the Father. As long as we believe answered prayer begins with us, we risk inserting our will into the equation. We are at risk of incomplete surrender as a vessel for God's will. When faith fuels prayer in agreement with God, through Jesus's name, we are praying to be done on earth what is already accomplished in heaven. God's works are prepared

---

[47] Whether you believe New Testament miracles have ceased or continue today is irrelevant to realizing our need to learn from Christ's training of the disciples and their need to surrender unbelief. Today, we are in as great a need as the disciples were to surrender hardened hearts and allow faith to guide our lives and response to God's will. The teachings of Christ on this subject are therefore deemed in this study to be very relevant for today's Christians regardless of their belief in miraculous healings or to what extent God currently demonstrates His presence and power. Given either position, it is this author's belief that your relationship and experience of God will be enriched by allowing these teachings to mold how you communicate and respond to God in faith daily.

beforehand that we should walk in them. Prayer is preparation for that journey. As we voice God's will in prayer, we posture spiritual senses to recognize Him as the source of the provision. The Son of Man models this truth. He came not to do His will but the will of His Father who sent Him. Surrendered prayer was vital for His victory.[48]

Great Faith Gives Great Honor to God

The woman healed of the issue of blood also had more than belief; she too had faith. Her faith was not the source of healing power (God is); faith was merely the avenue through which God's power was revealed. The woman's faith joined with God's will to demonstrate His power. Her faith allowed the glory of God to be seen and experienced. Our belief cannot dictate God's actions. God acts according to His will, but faith allows us to experience the provision of His will.[49]

Expressions of faith are a way to publicly reveal desire for fellowship with God and to publicly reveal trust in who He is as God. In the passage above, Matthew Henry reminds us that God gives honor to great faith because great faith gives honor to Him. Great faith gives honor to God! As Jesus performed miraculous healings among the multitudes, what did He often ask prior to the healing? Do you have faith, or do you believe? Faith was not always necessary to receive God's healing, but the presence of faith results in the healed giving honor to God. Our sovereign God can, has, and will demonstrate His power without an apparent act of faith as we continue to discuss. Great faith gives honor to God because it testifies that without God's intervening provision, our situation is hopeless. Faith proclaims the truth that "with man it is impossible, but with God all things are possible."

As God is honored, He is welcomed as a greater power and presence in our lives. The door to knowing Him is more fully opened to communion and worship with Him both for the one of faith healed as well as the witnesses. The testimony of a great faith encourages others to strengthen

---

[48] S. D. Gordon's *Quiet Talks on Prayer* is an excellent discussion of prayer as the most important and necessary work for God's kingdom. It is the source of power for all service.

[49] Ibid.

their faith as well. The woman with the issue of blood had the faith to touch the hem of Jesus's garment. By the end of His ministry, we learn that multitudes pursued Jesus, and "as many as touched Him were made well." The great faith of this woman gave honor to God. Her act of faith was an example and inspiration for others to also pursue God's favor. As God was lifted up, the faith of others strengthened. Jesus also gave great honor to God as discussed in chapter 3. He did not come to receive His own glory but to glorify His Father.

Let's also look at what happened with the cleansing of the ten lepers as recorded in Luke 17 11–19.

> Now it happened as He went to Jerusalem that He passed through the midst of Samaria and Galilee. Then as He entered a certain village, there met Him ten men who were lepers, who stood afar off. And they lifted up [their] voices and said, "Jesus, Master, have mercy on us!" So when He saw [them], He said to them, "Go, show yourselves to the priests." And so it was that as they went, they were cleansed. And one of them, when he saw that he was healed, returned, and with a loud voice glorified God, and fell down on [his] face at His feet, giving Him thanks. And he was a Samaritan. So Jesus answered and said, "Were there not ten cleansed? But where [are] the nine? Were there not any found who returned to give glory to God except this foreigner?" And He said to him, "Arise, go your way. Your faith has made you well."

All ten lepers needed cleansing. They *all* appear to recognize Him as "Master." They *all* come to Jesus asking for His mercy, but not specifically requesting healing. By addressing Him as Master, there is an implied surrender to follow whatever command He gives. There is some small seed of faith that prompted their approach. Therefore, when Jesus tells them to go show themselves to the priest, they immediately obey.

When are they healed?

How many of them are healed?

One of the healed lepers returned to Jesus to do what?

What does Jesus say about this one who gives thanks?

When all ten lepers obeyed Jesus's command, they were healed immediately. The power of God cleansed the lepers who were Jews as well as the one who was a Samaritan. Only one, the Samaritan, returned to thank God.[50] Jesus distinguished the behavior of the Jews, those not confessing great faith, from that of the Samaritan.

The Samaritan gave great honor to God through his demonstration of faith, and as a result, Jesus gave great honor to him. Jesus recognized and acknowledges his faith. Jesus said to him, "Your faith has made you well." However, at the time that was said, the leper was already healed physically. We can see through the healing of the other nine that great faith was not necessary for them to be physically healed, only a seed of faith. God's power, through mercy, healed their disease. But these were Jews, God's chosen people, who failed to recognize and acknowledge the bestowed power of their Jehovah Rapha. Their bodies may have been healed, but there is no deepening of their relationship with God as their Savior, no cleansing of their souls.

However, the Samaritan, who was separated from fellowship and

---

[50] This causes me to wonder whom the Jews credited for their healing. Leprosy was believed to be a disease inflicted as the result of sin. Since they had obeyed the instruction of this healing Master, did they attribute healing to their obedience? Since priests were the ones to ceremonially rule or judge over lepers' cleansing, did they believe their healing was completed only with the priest's verification of their cleansing? Did they recognize that Jesus was in fact the instrument of their healing without realizing His power was given by their God?

worship of God by his birth, was told his faith had made him well. By the Samaritan's expression of faith, it is reasonable to conclude that Jesus spoke of a spiritual as well as a physical healing. Great faith was not required for the healing originally sought, but it was the avenue to receive the blessing of fellowship with God. The demonstration of faith brought healing on a level not recognized as necessary. If we do not have faith in the power of God, the expectation for it to be revealed, how likely are we to recognize Him as the Source when it is released? How greatly God is glorified when we express faith!

God can and will act without our active exercise of faith. Two other examples are the miracles of Jesus calming the sea twice for the disciples. In either instance, they did not expect Jesus to have such power and afterward could not fully believe what they had experienced. It was God's will for Jesus to calm the sea to unveil His power through Jesus and testify Jesus as the peace. The disciples were not seeking this will. Sure, they were concerned with their safety, but that is just it; they were concerned with their physical safety, not seeking God's will to comprehend spiritual truth in the face of danger. Our will versus His will. Fear focuses on our comfort; faith focuses on His purpose.

When we express, confess, or exercise faith publicly, we honor God. It is a form of worship that exalts the Almighty. We testify that God is the Source of hope. Perhaps this is why the power of God went out of Jesus to heal the woman when she touched Him. Perhaps as with the leper, God wanted to demonstrate the blessing of faith in action. Perhaps these were miracles to demonstrate the blessing of His repeated admonition to have faith. After she was healed, He gives witness that her faith healed her. God does not want us to take for granted His desire to commune with us when we exercise faith. Jesus asked those He healed if they had faith because great faith always gives great honor to and fellowship with God.

The disciples, all ten lepers, and the woman experienced the benefit of God's divine power, *but those who demonstrated faith received God's peace and spiritual restoration.*

The demonstration of faith (or lack of) reveals a contrast between the disciples' and the woman's state of rest after experiencing the power of God. When the disciples on the storm-tossed sea failed to exercise faith, they were left still fearful on a calm sea. Absent faith, their fear of the physical changed to fear of the spiritual. They did not experience a fear of God that led to understanding but a fear of the circumstance that resulted in confusion. On the other hand, the woman who exercised faith "felt in her body that she was freed from her suffering" (Mark 5:29 NIV). She was confident of what God had done (knowing what had happened to her says verse 33) and that He was her Source.

Though verse 33 says she feared, this refers to a reverent fear of Christ. Her understanding of the power of God resulted in a reverent fear of God. In verse 34, Christ gave verbal witness to the crowd what she received and understood through faith: "Daughter, your faith has healed you. *Go in peace and be freed from your suffering,*" (NIV, emphasis added). As Jesus honored her faith, He also granted peace.

Faith beyond Belief

In our lessons, we have made distinctions between faith and belief because in practice, we often minimize true faith while overemphasizing belief. In practical living, belief is often rooted in our limited understanding, our desires, our hopes, our will, whereas faith is rooted in God's truth, plan, and purpose.

However, it is important to recognize little distinction is made between them in God's Word. The word *believe* is used almost seventy times in the Gospels in the KJV. For each of these usages, the same Greek word is used—*pisteuo* (pist-yoo'-o) and is "used in the New Testament of the conviction and trust to which a man is impelled by a certain ... higher prerogative ... of soul, and to trust in Jesus or God ... in doing something: saving faith."[51] While we have discussed belief that falls short of genuine faith, the use of *belief* in the Gospels refers to a belief that propels faith. It is a belief in God, not just belief in a desired outcome or timing. As used in the Gospels, belief is a seed of trust.

The Greek word for faith in Matthew 21:21 is *pistis* (pis'-tis), which means a "conviction of the truth of anything, belief; in the New Testament,

---

[51] Blue Letter Bible, dictionary and word search for *pisteuo* (Strong's 4100), Blue Letter Bible, 1996–2002, February 9, 2005, http://www.blueletterbible.org/cgi-bin/words.pl?word=4100&page=1.

of a conviction or belief respecting man's relationship to God and divine things, generally with *the included idea of trust and holy fervour born of faith and joined with it*"[52] (emphasis added).

From the Greek terms used for both "believe" and "faith," this passage teaches that there is no distinction between belief and faith as used in the Gospels. Therefore, *believe* is synonymous with faith. Both are rooted in the surrender and obedience to the divine will of God. As used in the New Testament, belief has nothing to do with the desires of man that are somehow blessed or tolerated by God. Belief that is a function of faith steadfastly believes what God can do so that there is unwavering trust in what He will do. It is a trust that compels us to agree with God in prayer for His will to be accomplished and then obediently surrender to Him through its completion.

God is the source and focus of faith. To put faith in God is to move beyond believing in a desired outcome or looking to a particular method for the outcome to materialize. Prior proof and experience, however, can serve a purpose. It expands our expectations and understanding of God's faithfulness. It increases confidence to seek Him. It teaches trust in the faithfulness of God to act on our behalf. It causes us to know Him more fully. It empowers us to recognize His power in the middle of difficulty.

When belief is the extent of faith, it leaves us vulnerable to fear, doubt, and unbelief. Belief can be questioned, disputed, manipulated, and shattered, but faith cannot. In John 3:12, Jesus said, "If I have told you earthly things and you do not believe, how will you believe if I tell you heavenly things." This statement reveals how belief in things seen and heard is definitely a basis for the foundation for faith; however, in our human nature, we are tempted to presume this belief is faith.

The disciples presumed Christ had come to reign as an earthly king. Jesus's response in the garden demonstrated God could have accomplished what the disciples believed: "Or do you not think that I could pray to My Father and He would send a legion of angels." God can, but that is not His will for today. God's will eventually results in Christ reigning on earth and

---

[52] Blue Letter Bible, lexicon and Strong's Concordance search for 4102, Blue Letter Bible, 1996–2002, February 9, 2005, http://www.blueletterbible.org/cgi-bin/strongs.pl?strongs=4102&page=1.

in heaven, but that was not the purpose for God's will at that moment. However, what occurs presently is necessary to complete God's ultimate purpose. Therefore, the disciples' focus, and usually ours, is on the present, while God's is on the eternal.

I previously shared how God burdened me to intercede against fear in my mother's life. However, there was another desire of my heart even prior to that burden. With the "understanding received by and by," I now see how God aligned the desires of my heart with His will for my mom's final weeks and prepared spiritual senses to see the eternal realities through the physical visibilities.

Some months before we were even aware of her illness, I began to long for my relationship with her to go beyond what we shared. I had a good relationship with her. We enjoyed one another's company and did many things together. While she had a deep relationship with God and encouraged her children to have the same, I longed to share more on a spiritual level than we had. As I began to pray for this to happen, I had a peace in my heart that God would allow this deepening of our relationship. My hopes were dashed, though, when she became terminally ill. However, I was determined not to be hindered in my pursuit. I had a timeline in which to receive God's promise, but I was determined it would come. Of course, I brought this fact repeatedly before God in prayer (as if He needed to be informed). Unconsciously, I demanded God to fulfill what I was certain He had promised to give.

The more I hoped and tried for these moments with her, the more they seemed to evade me for one reason or another (my will). During that time, I began to ask God to reveal the obstacle. His response was to pray for deliverance from fear (His Word). While I had no absolute confirmation of specific ways fear was present, I nevertheless surrendered to pray. As mentioned, He led me to a Bible study that dealt with fear in my own heart as well as prompted intercession for her.

Perhaps you can more fully appreciate how frustrated and discouraged I was those final weeks when Mom could no longer speak. How were we to have what God had promised to give (His will)? I was very disappointed and angry. There was an aching in my heart I did not know how God would fill. But when Mother physically revived that Sunday morning and began to share the goodness of heaven—sharing the presence of God that filled her with peace—God answered my prayer (He revealed His power). God removed the longing in my heart and filled me to overflowing with His presence. God did not "take" Mother away, depriving me of the relationship I sought. Instead, He began to transform her life before us. "I have been through all the phases of death and have no more fear ... God's allowed me to see how all things in my life are to be used for His glory," she said. This transformation resulted in a far richer experience with her and God than I ever imagined possible while on earth.

I had faith in God's promise, but it was belief, presumptions, my will in God's way for fulfilling His promise that caused me frustration. Had God given the outcome I desired earlier in her illness (or even absent an illness), I believe it would have been more difficult to accept her eventual death. His provision gave me what I desired with her and allowed our family to see His goodness in ways we did not expect and in ways we would not have presumed to seek. God's provision met more than my selfish need. His provision comforted more than my heart, as it has also been a comfort to many.

Remember what we learned about the mustard seed that grows into a tree: "It grows large enough to provide shelter for the birds." Our faith growth results in a blessing to us, and it meets the needs of others. Mom's gift of deliverance and peace is experienced by all Christians as they leave this world and enter eternity. Her verbal witness of this transformation gives encouragement to loved ones on earth to cope with grief and loss. It is an encouragement to Christians terminally ill not to fear the phases of death. It helps those witnessing this process, often in helplessness and grief, see the renewal of spiritual life that happens when the physical body is decaying and dying. It grants sight to spiritual truths we accept by faith. At a time when we feel helpless to help our hurting loved ones and when we feel left all alone, it is a reminder of the presence and power of God very near and very real. It offers hope through the truth that all the pain and difficulties of life, the thorns of the flesh, the weaknesses, and the disappointments along with all the joys, blessings, and goodness will be used for God's glory by those who love God and are called according to His purpose! (Romans 8:28).

Often, what motivates us to pray is belief, a hope in what we know God can do. I believed God could heal my mother and give us a richer spiritual experience, but that provision was withheld. God transformed my belief into a deeper faith. Belief was the catalyst for something greater than I could imagine. It fueled my expectation of God, yet it took a fully surrendered faith to understand God's power.

When our heart pursues God, we glimpse His goodness. He is not the author of confusion and depravity; He continually gives more than we deserve and more than we can imagine. God is sovereign; His plans and purposes surpass the visible, physical needs and comforts of this earth. He is an eternal God fixed on our eternal blessing. Coming to understand that God can do anything is an important stage in the growth of faith. Increasing our expectations in the miraculous demonstration of God's power demonstrates that growth.

Can you recall a time when you had "belief" (limited faith—your will) in a desired outcome that failed to happen according to your desire?

Can you perhaps now see how the hand of God worked in that situation?

Have there been situations where God's divine power intervened despite your unwillingness to trust or acknowledge Him?

What can you learn from that situation or God's hand in it that might help you demonstrate faith in a present or future need?

> *Ever since I first heard of your strong faith in the Lord Jesus and your love for Christians everywhere, I have never stopped thanking God for you. I pray for you constantly, asking God, the glorious Father of our Lord Jesus Christ, to give you spiritual wisdom and understanding, so that you might grow in your knowledge of God. I pray that your hearts will be flooded with light so that you can understand the wonderful future he has promised to those he called. I want you to realize what a rich and glorious inheritance he has given to his people. I pray that you will begin to understand the incredible greatness of his power for us who believe him.*
> —Ephesians 1:15–19 NLT

JANELLE TEMPLETON

Faith That Surrenders—His Power

Begin with worship, meditation, and prayer.

> So let us stop going over the basics of Christianity again and again. Let us go on instead and become mature in our understanding. Surely we don't need to start all over again with the importance of turning away from evil deeds and placing our faith in God. (Hebrews 6:1 NLT)

> "Lord, help me honestly face my limitations. I need Your strength and hope to persevere. I open the door of my heart to trust You and Your power even when I see no solution for my need. Give me understanding so I may know Your way."

When we recognize and receive Christ's power, we are postured to withstand the doubts Satan uses to steal joy and peace. Christ gives abundant life, but the thief steals, kills, and destroys. Satan's temptations to doubt God's power may come against the mind or thought-life. However, it could also come through cynics or skeptics who have no faith or who have hardened hearts of unbelief. Satan *steals* hope, which *kills* trust, which *destroys* surrender to God whereas an expression of faith testifies to the work of God. It acknowledges and receives His blessing resulting in unshakeable peace and joy in the heart of the one who walks in faith. Faith defeats Satan's attempts to steal hope.

When are we most willing to embrace the power of God in our lives? When we have exhausted our efforts or other avenues and find ourselves helpless. We continue fighting the good fight, but most often in our own strength until we ultimately reach an impossibility. Perhaps it is in our marriage: "I can't keep living miserably trapped like this," we may say. Perhaps it is with a difficult child: "I don't know what else to do," we may cry. Perhaps it is in pleasing God: "There is no way I can live a holy, pure life!" Perhaps it is in our ministry for God: "I am too tired or overwhelmed to continue." Perhaps it is through a difficult situation: "I don't see any other way out." Perhaps it is through loneliness: "Does anyone love me?"

Think again about the disciples, Peter particularly. He was one of the inner three close to Jesus. He was the rock upon whom Christ would build the church. It would be well into a three-year ministry before the full reality of who Jesus was would be understood, yet Peter had the faith to trust and follow Jesus from the beginning. We have learned from previous study of Peter's denial that this was not the full measure of faith God intended for Peter. Let us read Luke's account of this prophecy of denial.

> And the Lord said, "Simon, Simon! Indeed, Satan has asked for you, that he may sift you as wheat. But I have prayed for you, that your faith should not fail; and when you have returned to Me, strengthen your brethren." But he said to Him, "Lord, I am ready to go with You, both to prison and to death." Then He said, "I tell you, Peter, the rooster will not crow this day before you will deny three times that you know Me." (Luke 22:31–34)

Even when Christ prophesied his denial, Peter refused to acknowledge it. Peter believed his strength, his current level of faith, his steadfast willingness to follow was sufficient. It wasn't until he denied Christ that Peter willingly acknowledged that "with man it is impossible" as he went out and wept bitterly.[53]

Jesus said that Satan asked permission to sift Peter as wheat. What Satan intended for harm, God used to separate the chaff from the wheat; to reveal the self-effort, the Flesh, the weakness of faith that needed strengthening. Christ prayed that his faith would not fail, and Christ knew it would strengthen from this test, even a test he appeared to fail. He instructed Peter to strengthen the others. How can someone who fails a test be in a position to strengthen others unless he himself recognizes the source of his strength? "When you return to Me," Christ said.

Peter did not become so discouraged and defeated by his weakness that it halted all future purpose. Finding the end of himself, Peter returned to Christ realizing the need of His power. From that point of view, there was not a failing but ultimately a great, necessary victory. Peter's faith was

---

[53] Remember also what Job said when he realized how little his faith had been: "Therefore I abhor myself, and I repent in sackcloth and ashes."

strengthened to empower him to surrender to the ultimate self-sacrifice. There were no more denials, only the power of God through him. Peter ultimately did follow Christ to prison and death but not without first coming to an end of his own strength and gifting to fully rely on the power of God.

Listen to what Andrew Murray wrote about the man who came to realize he could not please God on his own.

> At first, he fights against it [the truth that with man it is impossible]. Then, he submits to it, but reluctantly and in despair. At last, he accepts it willingly and rejoices in it. At the beginning of the Christian life, the young convert has no conception of this truth. He has been converted; he has the joy of the Lord in his heart; he begins to run the race and fight the battle. He is sure he can conquer, for he is earnest and honest, and God will help him. Yet, somehow, very soon he fails where he did not expect it, and sin gets the better of him. He is disappointed, but he thinks: "I was not cautious enough. I did not make my resolutions strong enough." And again he vows, and again he prays, and yet he fails. He thinks: "Am I not a redeemed man? Have I not the life of God within me?" And he thinks again: "Yes, and I have Christ to help me. I can live the holy life."
>
> At a later period, he comes to another state of mind. He begins to see such a life is impossible, but he does not accept it. There are multitudes of Christians who come to this point: "I cannot." They then think that God never expected them to do what they cannot do. If you tell them that God does expect it, it is a mystery to them. A good many Christians are living a low life—a life of failure and of sin—instead of rest and victory, because they began to say: "I cannot, it is impossible." And yet they do not understand it fully. So, under the impression, *I cannot*, they give way to despair. They will do their best, but they never expect to get on very far.[54]

---

[54] Andrew Murray, *Absolute Surrender: And Other Addresses* (Chicago: Moody, n.d.), 66–67.

When in despair we say, "I cannot," we are the most vulnerable to Satan's attacks of doubt, fear, unbelief, and discouragement. Satan encourages us to bathe in defeat, to dwell on our inadequacies, but this is the place for victory. This is the place for the cleansing of Flesh. This is the opportunity for His glory to be revealed. Instead of giving in to despair, we should clothe ourselves in trust, for with God all things are possible. We should confess to God, "my spirit is willing, but my flesh is weak. I need Your power to surrender."

Yet how many times are we willing to make this confession? How many times do we simply confess, "I cannot" and close even our spirit to the filling of His holy power to work in us? The thought of persevering anymore is unbearable because we have no strength left, and we harden our hearts to even asking for more strength. In exhaustion, we lose our desire to continue. We become hopeless perhaps because we are looking for an outcome that doesn't materialize. We have belief, a little faith, that God has faithfully rewarded, but we are unwilling to ask for more or perhaps fail to recognize the need to ask for more. We perhaps cry out for a desired outcome, but do we simply cry out for God? We are willing for a season to persevere on our own, but perhaps we are unwilling for God to expand faith and align our desires with His. We may fear this process or deny its necessity.

While living in the realm of "I cannot," Satan causes us to fear surrender and fear relinquishing our perceived control. It is perceived for as we witness through both scripture and personal experience, life eventually brings us through difficulty in which there is no control. Our attempts ultimately are futile. "There is a way that seems right to a man, but leads to destruction." To surrender is to confess, "but God can." It is to acknowledge what Jesus wanted the disciples to grasp—to look beyond ourselves for the power of God to work through us.

"With God it is possible, but what does this mean?" we ask. To answer that question, look up Philippians 2:13 and fill in the blanks: "For it is _____ who works in you both to _____ and _____ for His good pleasure."

Peter grew to will or desire to obey God. However, his young faith did not understand the power required *to do* God's will. He diligently tried to obey but in his own strength and with human understanding.

The Greek word used for *will* in this verse means to be resolved and determined, to love. At first glance, the interpretation is hard to grasp. To will is the same as to love? Recall scriptures studied about fear. Fear destroys surrender, but perfect love casts out fear. Those who fear have not been made perfect in love. Even the most steadfast, strong resolve to please and honor God is insufficient as Peter demonstrated. Even resolve and determination must come from the power of God's love in us that dispels fear, discouragement, and hopelessness.

God "works in you to will—to love." Love conquers all, but sometimes, we feel separated from God's love. Sometimes, failure and frustration seem unending. As Gideon thought, it seems God abandoned us. But God will also use this frustration to align our hearts with His so we may know the full depth of His love and demonstrate it. Remember the Lord's response to Gideon's frustration: "Go in this might of yours, have I not sent you." The place of discouragement and despair we feel and fear is the source of His delight not because of the difficulty it brings but for His abundant provision it prepares us to receive.

Discouragement stirs a hunger in us for the love of God and for His power. As Andrew Murray's teaching expounds, we need not shut the door with "I cannot" but continue with "He can." We should not give Satan power to keep our hearts focused on self-pity; nothing separates us from the love of God.

If you feel separated from God's love as Gideon did, what fear, insecurity, doubt, or sin is God waiting on you to confess and surrender? Perhaps part of the "I cannot" is the cycle of sin that has you trapped in undesired behavior or addictions. Have you confessed this sin at every level—the *transgression*, the *sin* of the mind, the *iniquity* in the heart? God knocks at the door, waiting for you where you are as you are. His love is an available provision. His love will heal and restore at the deepest level of confession (Psalm 32, 51).

The Greek term for "to do" means to put forth power. God works in you to put forth power for His good pleasure. When we are in love, we don't want to keep it a secret; we want to express and share it. We want others to know the joy of it. Likewise, when we embrace God's love, obedience is less difficult because love fuels the power to desire and obey. Absent God's love, we would become like the stubborn mule who must be guided sternly with the bit and bridle (Psalm 32:8). We must be willing to confess, "It is not my desire and power, but the power of God's love through me." "Not by might, not by power, but My Spirit, says the Lord" (Zechariah 4:6).

If we read Philippians 2:13 inserting the Greek meanings for "will" and "to do," it reads like this: "For it is God who works in you to be resolved to love and put forth power for His good pleasure." The New Living Translation captures this understanding: "For God is working in you, giving you the desire to obey him and the power to do what pleases him." God's love in us accomplishes His desires. With man, it is impossible, but with God, all things are possible.

Throughout Peter's interchanges in Jesus's ministry, we see his boldness, his courage, his devotion to serve God through any difficulty. This level of boldness (which is definitely a strength in service to Christ) also fueled an equally intense fear of failing God. It fueled pride that blinded him from seeing his fear. Admirably, Peter intensely desired to please God. However, this desire did more to fuel pride in his own ability than to help him realize the need for humble surrender to God's power.

God allowed Peter to face that fear in order to see the grip it had on his heart. Pride and fear of failing God prevented him from recognizing his need for what would ensure victory: complete dependency on the love and power of God. Power. Love. Sound mind.

Satan has a plan for undermining the effectiveness of every strength and gift God bestows. It is often difficult to recognize our need to surrender strengths when we know these are the gifts God granted us to serve Him. But remember that Jesus also had to temporarily lay aside His gifts as the Son of God to become the Son of Man. He willingly surrendered to God's power to work through Him. Remember how Jesus stated He had come to do His Father's will, not His own. In Luke 4, Satan tempted Christ, and later, Peter did also to circumvent God's ways for completing His will. These are temptations we also face. Without realizing our need to surrender to God the good He gives, we are left vulnerable to Satan's immediate and often very effective weapons of pride, fear, doubt, and unbelief. It could be said that Peter considered himself a pretty good man and servant of God prior to his denial (after all, he was the rock of the future church). Until faced with an "impossibility," he perceived no reason for further surrender, no reason for further growth of his faith, no reason to embrace God's fullness.

We also act very independently and self-sufficiently in our God-given gifts when we walk in the Flesh instead of the Spirit. If we fail to recognize the hardness of hearts to God's ways, we also may find ourselves serving God in self-righteousness like Peter, in blind confusion like all the disciples, or in prideful religious legalism like the Jews. We need to learn as Peter did that we *never* outgrow our need to nurture faith. We never outgrow the need for continual, total surrender. Peter's example should challenge us to realize our continual need to depend on God's power above our Flesh.

What circumstance, what relationship, what mission or ministry is God currently wanting to fuel with His power?

Given what the Spirit revealed in response to the above, voice Philippians 2:13 in prayer and journal how the Spirit leads you to respond: "Lord I surrender to Your loving grace that fills me with boldness, determination, and perseverance to fulfill Your will. Show me how to reveal Your goodness and Your love."

Ask God to reveal how He is growing faith in your life now (respond to any or all of the following as He reveals).

What are the gifts or strengths He has given to accomplish your service to Him?

Through prayer, surrender these gifts back to God moment by moment. Ask Him to reveal any ways you may be attempting to operate these gifts with your own power. Acknowledge your dependency on Him and His power by confessing, "Lord I can't, but You can." Continue in obedient response until He gives peaceful assurance of His empowerment. Describe the flesh (arrogance, insecurity, self-sufficiency, frustration, hopelessness, etc.) God wants surrendered.

I cannot ...

God is empowering me to surrender my desired outcome of

God is empowering me to demonstrate a trust in His will by

I leave you with exhortations of God to surrender to faith's growth.

> *That the genuineness of your faith, being much more precious than of gold that perishes, though it is tested by fire, may be found to praise, honor, and glory at the revelation of Jesus Christ.*
> —1 Peter 1:7

> *Looking unto Jesus the author and finisher of our faith; who for the joy that was set before him endured the cross, despising the shame, and has set down at the right hand of the throne of God.*
> —Hebrews 12:2

> *Dear brothers and sisters, we always thank God for you, as is right, for we are thankful that your faith is flourishing and you are all growing in love for each other.*
> —2 Thessalonians 1:3 NLT

> *For whatever is born of God overcomes the world. And this is the victory that has overcome the world—our faith.*
> —1 John 5:4

"Lord Jesus, You shed Your blood to conquer sin, to conquer the darkness of this world. It is in Your name and by Your blood that we command the spirit of discouragement, despair, and futility to flee. You filled us with Your power and with the ability to will and do for Your good pleasure. You have not given us a spirit of fear but of power and love and of a sound mind. You are our hope and peace. We trust You to complete the purpose You began in us. In Jesus's name, amen."

Faith that Obeys His Ways

Begin with worship, meditation, and prayer.

> Let us draw near with a true heart in full assurance of faith, having our hearts sprinkled from an evil conscience and our bodies washed with pure water. Let us hold fast the confession of our hope without wavering, for He who promised is faithful. And let us consider one another in order to stir up love and good works. (Hebrews 10:22–24)

> "Lord God, may Your promise of faithfulness empower me to remain faithful and obedient to You. As You strengthen my faith, strengthen my dependence on You in every aspect of my life. Give me a steadfast commitment to remain holy and devoted to the truth of Your Word."

"Let us consider one another in order to stir up love and good works." Could you currently benefit from this level of fellowship? Have you ever been in a situation or need where it seemed beyond reach?

When we feel alone, it is often hard to hold fast the confession of our hope without wavering. But He who promised is faithful! Even when "the fellowship of the brethren" misunderstands or belittles our need, there is One who is ever present and ever faithful.

Thus far in this chapter we discussed the importance of His Word, will, and power. As we mature in faith, these ways for fulfilling our purpose are more effortless and unconsciously experienced. His Word, will, and power fuel obedience. Obedience to God's leading sometimes fuels fear, but as faith grows, His presence empowers us to obey what He commands even in the face of fear. The faith of Hannah gives witness to this truth.

Read 1 Samuel 1. What was the initial desire of Hannah's heart? What was she praying for?

What was the response by her husband to her need?

How did her husband's other wife, Peninnah, react to Hannah's situation?

What was the initial response to her prayer by her priest, her minister?

Given these responses to her need by those closest to her, describe Hannah's continual consecration to prayer? (vv. 11–16).

Instead of sharing her burden, Hannah's husband encouraged her to be thankful for what God had already granted through his love for her. Peninnah belittled Hannah by drawing attention to Hannah's barrenness and flaunting her own fertility. The priest initially treated Hannah's brokenness and consecration to God as wickedness, perceiving her to be drunk. But Hannah persisted; she held fast to a faith in God to provide a son despite the "'encouragement' of the fellowship" to focus more on "physical visibilities."

Hannah desperately wanted a son, and God needed a prophet. Apparently, God saw in Hannah what others around her could not or would not. In that day, societal protocol treated the barren woman as one cursed by God, but God, as author and finisher of faith, knew the seed of faith in her and what was necessary for its growth. God saw her as a woman devoted to Him, a virtue necessary for the mother of His prophet. Hannah's faith in God fueled surrender to His will. Through Hannah's perseverance in prayer while her provision was delayed, her will was transformed into God's will.

Before Hannah even conceived, God empowered her to obey. God's Word tells us that Hannah gave Samuel to Eli after he was weaned. A limited understanding cannot comprehend how such a seemingly desperate woman could give away her long-awaited child especially at such a young age. Initially, this was not Hannah's prayer, for it was a while before she surrendered to this desire of God. But the devotion that God saw in Hannah eventually was revealed to all by her demonstration of trust. Without others' knowledge of her barrenness and their false conclusions or insensitive advice, would her deep faith have been as visible? Would there have been such a testimony to God's power?

A willing act of obedience postured Hannah in worship, not in bitterness, when her son was given to the Lord. While this outcome was different from Hannah's initial desire, God's provision birthed joy and worship in her heart. God did not just give her one child; He blessed her with seven (God's symbolic number of perfection). Through the delayed provision, God worked in Hannah to "love and put forth power for His good pleasure." James also exhorted us to comprehend how genuine faith fueled willing obedience.

> What use is it, my brethren, if someone says he has faith but he has no works? Can that faith save him? If a brother or sister is without clothing and in need of daily food, and one of you says to them, "Go in peace, be warmed and be filled," and yet you do not give them what is necessary for their body, what use is that? Even so faith, if it has no works, is dead, being by itself. But someone may well say, "You have faith and I have works; show me your faith without the works, and I will show you my faith by my works." You believe that God is one. You do well; the demons also believe, and shudder. But are you willing to recognize, you foolish fellow, that faith without works is useless? Was not Abraham our father justified by works when he offered up Isaac his son on the altar? You see that faith was working with his works, and as a result of the works, faith was perfected; and the Scripture was fulfilled which says, "and Abraham believed god, and it was reckoned to him as righteousness," and he was called the friend of God. You see that a man is justified by works

and not by faith alone. in the same way, was not Rahab the harlot also justified by works when she received the messengers and sent them out by another way? For just as the body without the spirit is dead, so also faith without works is dead. (James 2:14–26 NASB)

This passage reiterates that faith goes beyond belief to trust in the will and power of God. Faith fuels works but our works reveal faith, for works demonstrate fulfilling, persevering, or overcoming our ability to accomplish what is within our apparent strength to accomplish. We demonstrate faith as we consider one another in love and stir up good works to accomplish the impossible. Works testify to faith in the power of God.

The example of Hannah reveals how we can be surrounded by supposedly godly people who often fuel more discouragement than encouragement. We are to be a fellowship of faith encouragers. This example serves as opportunity for us to reflect on the role we play to fuel the faith of our brothers and sisters. As faith encouragers, we can inspire others to hope and surrender to God's power to overcome temptation and difficulty.

We stated earlier that this is true especially in regards to marriage. It is not enough to believe divorce is harmful to families and society. Faith without works is dead. Faith in God empowers the work of unconditional commitment to an imperfect person. As a fellowship of encouragers, we should encourage reliance on God in marriage difficulty. Yet we may fear the receptivity of encouragement where there is brokenness, hurt, and betrayal. We may lack the strength or tools to work toward marital restoration when we witness or experience turmoil. Perhaps only one spouse seeks God's path for restoration further fueling fear of constant relational unrest.

Though we know divorce is difficult on many levels, fear of continual turmoil can convince us that it is the only path to peace. Like the disciples, we may not anticipate the power of God to bring peace in *this* situation despite our knowledge of His abilities and despite our awareness of Him in our midst. Because of hardened hearts of unbelief, fear, and doubt, we may miss His power at work in our relational storm.

For the remainder of this section's study, we want to stir up love and good works in the area of marriage to inspire reliance on God's power to find restoration. As mentioned, this study is not intended to bring condemnation but to build faith. This requires recognizing areas where hearts are hardened by hurt and pain that quench God's power. As we look at further scripture on marriage, remain focused on God's love to bring hope and healing through the difficulties of marital strife and divorce. I pray we allow God's love to carry us high above the storm of pain, hurt, discontent, hopelessness, and confusion often present in marriage and in the wake of divorce. While this is intensely personal in our experience, let us take the time to see what is happening in the spiritual realm of earthly discontent.

The one relationship that should give us the most encouragement can often be the one that causes the most turmoil (as with Adam and Eve). We discussed how Satan greatly attacks the marriage relationship, which has the greatest potential to give witness to our relationship with Christ. As a result, marital commitment is impossible in our own strength and even more so when there is hurt, disappointment, or betrayal. We need God's power to remain faithful. "I can do all things through Christ who strengthens me," says Philippians 4:13. The Greek term for "do" in this verse actually means to prevail or endure.[55] To receive His power to prevail, we must seek Him with a whole heart empty of our will and preconceived ideas of God's ways. Since hurt weakens the desire to endure we want to focus discussion on spiritual not emotional realities. Let's return to Mark to discuss Christ's Word for marriage.

Read Mark 10:1–12. Why does Christ say that Moses allowed certificates of divorce?

Write how Christ describes the holy union of marriage.

What does Christ warn about the one-flesh union?

---

[55] G2480—ischyō— Strong's Greek Lexicon (NKJV), Blue Letter Bible, accessed September 17, 2016, https://www.blueletterbible.org//lang/lexicon/lexicon.cfm?Strongs=G2480&t=NKJV.

I once heard a long-married guest couple on *Focus on the Family* say that in today's society, we are no longer willing to die to self so that the marriage may live but instead are willing to end the marriage so that self may live.

Why is this happening? Jesus says that God allowed divorce in certain circumstances because of the hardness of our hearts. Hearts become hardened when unresolved marital strife fuels doubt of restoration. Hopelessness fuels fear of continual tension and emotional withdrawal. Failure to surrender this to God weakens our strength to work through difficulty and restore intimacy. To protect ourselves from further hurt and disappointment, we may seek to end the marriage, or long before the leaving, we may complacently and unconsciously undermine its chances. We build an emotional wall of protection attempting to minimize further pain. This results in drifting away from each other, and fueling of "irreconcilable differences."

Hardened hearts cause us to respond to unmet needs in ways that fail to value our marriage and fail to respect our spouses. Hardened hearts prevent repentance from our own actions or reactions that cause marital discord and keep us trapped in the Genesis 3 curse. Prolonged unmet needs not surrendered continually to God harm the marriage in two primary ways: by seeking to meet the need with someone outside the marriage either emotionally or sexually, or by creating an impenetrable emotional, spiritual, and physical barrier that prohibits the spouse access to the one-flesh partner.

Even if we remain faithful, too much time and energy on the worthy venues of work, children, church, or hobbies further strains the marriage. These efforts are necessary, but they slowly erode intimacy when they become the priority above nurturing or repairing our marriage.

The emotional wall with our spouse is a barrier to intimacy. Because frustrations of the marriage have built the wall, we perceive a relationship with someone different as the only way to feel again. This false perception becomes reality and leads us to act in ways contrary to God's ways. The reality we may acknowledge is the difficulty in meeting one another's needs. The reality we often fail to realize is that sometimes the need is the result of a deeper spiritual or emotional need that only God can fill. God's way may be for that provision to come from Him. An overwhelming need for intimacy clouds this truth. This truth also may be distorted to rationalize that God is more concerned with self than our marriages. Yet we expect another person, not God, to heal us. Mentally and emotionally, we separate what God joined together as a way to deal with the fear of being trapped by unending loneliness.

Our daily priorities can be a distraction from dealing with suppressed, unresolved issues. Similar to Judges 6, unresolved issues also become dens of captivity that make us feel safe but are not optimal or what God intends. Yet often they are the place of survival we embrace, possibly because we *do* want to remain committed but don't understand the right path for restoration.

Unresolved marital and personal issues halt or hinder intimacy of our one flesh. Dutiful Christians are able to function with the appearance of unity even when the marriage lacks intimacy. When we continue in this "den of captivity" just like Gideon's family, we lose hope of God's intervention though we know of His past faithfulness. The idols we build—be it another lover, money, possessions, hobbies, family, work, or addictions—become our passions. Too often, we blame God for His failure to intervene without realizing His delay may be the result of our need to repent. In stubbornness or blindness, we may fail to repent. Once we turn to things outside the marriage, we may further blame God, or our spouse, for giving us no other choice but to end the marriage to find the peace and happiness desired.

It is true that we cannot survive this way indefinitely, but God offers deliverance that is healthier than what we often force on our family. We have personal responsibility for what *we* do to strengthen marriage and how *we* respond to its difficulties. Hardened hearts toward our spouses and possibly God preempt understanding how we should respond to frustration and perceive truth.

Our entire study discusses how the most devoted followers of Christ struggled with hardened hearts. But more important, we have focused on the power of God to grow faith to release fear, doubt, and unbelief that fuels the hardness. Just as God was faithful to empower the disciples, God teaches us how to love and respect our spouse amid conflict and withdrawal when intimacy seems hopeless. To those who love God and are called according to His purpose, God will use all things—even great marital strife—for His good and our blessing.

Without faith, we cannot persevere through hurt to forgive so that God uses our growing faith as a refining tool in the lives of our spouses.

Without faith, we will not humble ourselves to confess our own contributions to marital difficulty and perceive our own need to repent so intimacy can be restored.

Without faith, it is impossible to please God and remain committed to marriage.

Without faith, without hope in the faithfulness of God when it isn't visible in our situation, we will not surrender to His power to restore what is lost.

Without faith at work in marriage, we will not seek and wait on God's timing for restoration for both marital and personal issues.

Without faith, we cannot return emotional hurt with grace ("forgiving seventy times seventy"). We will not receive from God the love and patience to wait on the other's repentance and restoration of intimacy.

How can faith sustain marriage? By empowering us to forgive and by empowering us to repent. By empowering understanding of spiritual realities in the physical visibilities as we surrender in prayer and worship. By empowering us to be vessels of grace even amid frustration and disappointment.

When we forgive, we remove the hurt of the offense away from present interaction with our spouses even though we don't forget the hurt. We choose not to allow the offense to become an obstacle to pursuing one-flesh intimacy. Just as God removes our sin as far away as the east is from the west, we are not to retaliate against or punish our spouses for the offense. Forgiveness offers the relationship grace and time for trust to be restored.

However, it takes *both* forgiveness and the offender's repentance to *fully* restore the intimacy broken by the offense. Genuine repentance goes beyond apologies to rebuild trust through changed behavior. This process requires continued forgiveness and repentance from both partners as our actions and reactions during this process are not usually perfect and full of grace. Just as one has to mature to repent, one also has to mature to forgive. God will empower both if one turns to Him. Let God mature faith to strengthen our marriages!

Too often, we attempt to take the other's refinement on personally, in our own selfish way and time, or in the heat of an argument. When in anger, hurt, and disrespect we attempt to punish or return the pain of an offense, we are not trusting God to work in our spouses in His way and time. We are not trusting God to strengthen wisdom, perseverance, patience, gentleness, long-suffering in one another. Absent this trust in God, we become unwilling to take further risk and fail to believe God will refine the behavior in our spouses (though we know He can).

Likewise, demanding our spouses' forgiveness absent our needed repentance of issues (marital or personal) intensifies division and pain. Intimacy is damaged further when one spouse attempts to win an argument against the other half of their one flesh. This self-inflicted pain is counterproductive to peace. Marital conflict needs resolution to build intimacy and not allow hurt and bitterness to fester. Conflict resolution comes with honesty with one's own contribution to the conflict and understanding of each other's perspective. Recall the trinity of sin from Psalm 32. Until one repents at every level of body, mind, and soul, intimacy is undermined.

Restoration is a process and one made easier when each spouse chooses to be a vessel of God's love even when feelings fuel different thoughts. Conflict resolution is productive through healthy discussion, not in heat of the moment argumentative or disrespectful judgments of each other. The demands of life make these moments harder to find. Draw near to God for He works in us both to love and to do His will.

Anabel and Bill Gillham are known for describing a spouse as God's heavenly, divine sandpaper. Marital conflict is used more than anything as the sandpaper of personal refinement. The weakness that constantly rubs, irritates, and makes a mess of things also provides a smooth, beautiful product in the end. God intends to use the friction Satan uses to destroy to refine both spouses and strengthen the family. Satan seeks to undermine this refinement by attacking the soundness of our minds and emotions through unresolved or recurring marital strife. The relentless turmoil undermines the feelings of love. A Righteous Brothers' song states, "You've lost that loving feeling, whoa that loving feeling; You've lost that loving feeling, now it's gone, gone, gone."

But love is not always lost. The *feeling* of love may be lost; the emotional high of new love will fade, but it is replaced with something deeper, richer, and tested that can be strengthened by overcoming strife. When either spouse allows his or her love of God to fuel strength to do the work of commitment, the feeling of love *will* eventually return.

Emotions are cyclical, but God's love is constant and deep. We are to be a vessel of *God's* love to our spouse. (Read Hebrews 10:22-39 and meditate on how this passage applies to marital restoration.) Too often, we are vessels of raw, untamed emotions inflamed by pride, self, hurt, rejection, or fear. As one flesh, to abandon the spouse in any way is to harm who we have become. Too often, we do not allow God the time to work in our own hearts to restore feelings of love, to teach us how to be that vessel of His love. And too often, we sit back and wait for God to wave His hand to fix the marriage.

God strengthens the marriage as He refines *you*. Remember that God did not deliver Gideon, but raised him up as the deliverer. God strengthens you when you embrace the width, depth, height, and security of His love.

You cannot change your spouse, but you can strengthen your relationship with God. Our correction and repentance is necessary to learn how to persevere and demonstrate patience, gentleness, long-suffering, and meekness. Too often, we demand the repentance of our spouses without a willingness to surrender to our own refinement. We should not allow our spouses' responses to this process of growth or lack of it dictate our obedience and surrender to God's power.

Read Mark 10:13–16. What does Jesus command about the little children?

Who was forbidding the little children from coming to Christ?

What example of the little children are we to follow?

Describe what you believe it means to receive the kingdom of God as a little child.

It is interesting, though perhaps not coincidental, that this instruction about how to treat children coming to Christ follows Jesus's exhortations to remain faithful to our marital commitment. *Those closest to Jesus were forbidding the children from coming to Him.*

Spiritual and emotional unfaithfulness in marriage sends a subtle message to our family, children, and society that the power of God is insufficient to overcome and reconcile difficulty. The desires and wishes of the parents to find some relief from the pain often creates greater pain for the children when, or even before, the marriage is ended.[56] What kind of witness is that to those we are most committed to protecting and loving? How greatly can this deter our children from coming to and relying on the power of God? Through God's grace, children may depend more on Him instead of pull away. Nevertheless, what children endure reveals how divorce cannot fully separate the two God joined together despite the most careful effort.

Many believe that children are resilient and are eventually able to get over divorce. If our children have such capabilities, then why as the more mature adult aren't we resilient in resolving marital issues? If children are mature enough to deal with the hurt inflicted on them, why can't their parents find the strength and tools to deal with their own issues (many from childhood) that often contribute to marital discontent? Too often, we expect of them what we fail to do to ensure our own growth. Judges 6–7 reveals how the dens of complacency blind us to our need for change.

The movie *Hope Floats* with Sandra Bullock has a poignant scene where her husband tells her he doesn't love her anymore and wants a divorce so that he can marry her former best friend. The scene concludes with him trying to drive away while their young daughter is desperately, in great anguish, trying to leave with him. At the end of the movie in a tender scene where mother and daughter are finding restoration beyond this abandonment, Bullock's character tells her daughter, "Momma always said childhood is what you spend the rest of your life getting over."

Family is the one place that is to be a safe refuge from the *rest* of life's difficulty, but often it is the catalyst for it. As parents, we have the responsibility to create a safe, secure, environment for the life God entrusts to our care. There are no perfect parents as we all deal with generational sins, weaknesses, scars, hurdles, and dysfunction that were part of the

---

[56] There are biblical grounds for divorce. There are also situations when you or the children are in physical danger that requires separation at a minimum. To reiterate: this admonition to remain faithful in marriage is intended for those who feel overwhelmed by their perceived irreconcilable differences, not for those whose safety is in danger.

fallen world shaping *our* lives since childhood. But we can seek to break that cycle. We can seek restoration today. We can grow in faith to provide greater emotional stability in our home than that of our origin. We can open the door to Christ's way for persevering through marital strife to restore intimacy and stability in the home.

If children can get over the pain of divorce, we can get over the pain, hurt, and discontent not only to resist divorce but to rebuild intimacy. We do not have the right as their caregivers to demand more of them than we ourselves are willing to give. What we force children to do outside of the marriage (deal with sin, betrayal, pain, and hurt), we should do in the marriage with our spouses (deal with sin, betrayal, pain, and hurt). As the parents, we are to model faith in the power of God to be greater than the difficulty we face.

When Jesus realized the harm to the children, He rebuked His disciples and said, "Do not forbid them from coming to Me." After warnings on divorce, Jesus encouraged all those who had just heard those warnings to have the faith of a child.

Is your marital situation deterring your children from seeking God? Is the turbulent home and unresolved issues causing your children to intercede in prayer for their parents? God meets with us where we are and as we are with a Word to empower faith over fear.

Whether there is constant conflict or emotional distance with our spouses or whether there has been divorce, God calls us to remain faithful as He is faithful to us in our sinful, undeserving nature. God does not want us to end what He has joined together be that in the form of a legal decree or by remaining faithfully trapped in a strained marriage, having a form of godliness but denying its power.

Jesus proclaimed the faith of a child as an example for all to follow. Those with the faith of a child will receive the kingdom of heaven. If *we* have the faith of a child, we will trust God to empower marital growth to the one He has joined us to. It is a faith that fuels hope and joy. It is a power (love) that bears all things. It is a faith that trusts and fears God more than it does the difficulty. Our entire study has focused on the need to embrace the growth of faith to its maturity and the blessings of doing so. A mature faith provides shelter for others but especially our children. What promise of empowerment to follow God's ways!

If you are experiencing the consequence of divorce not of your choosing, how you respond to this situation and to your spouse should be an example of trust and dependence on God for your children. Christ was betrayed to face the brutality of the cross but endured with grace, mercy, and forgiveness for those "who know not what they do." Don't allow fear and grief to quench God's Spirit in you. You cannot control your spouse's behavior, but you can be a source of godliness for the situation and particularly your children, to protect them from further harm or from being used as a weapon against each parent.

I encourage those who have divorced to seek how God would use your experiences to encourage others in their marital commitment. Also, allow God to reveal understanding needed to avoid difficulty in a present relationship. Be willing to examine your part in past mistakes. If you have experienced multiple divorces, there may still be unresolved issues imbedded in fear that God needs to heal. Without this healing, present or future relationships will also suffer and lack the desired intimacy.

As God heals you, remain sensitive to how He would have you impart these truths to your children as they are able to learn. Children of divorce often fear marriage for fear of divorce. Gain godly insights from your experience that better equip and prepare them to embrace healthy, godly relationships. Allow them to benefit from your experience so they become wise and whole prior to dating. Do not accept Satan's lie that once divorced, you have nothing to teach. Read Psalm 32 and 51 and see how David's repentance fuels an eagerness to encourage obedience in the lives of others. Repentance fuels wisdom and restoration! Embrace it!

For those contemplating divorce I encourage you to remain committed to your marriage. Seek God's power to fuel hope and perseverance. Pray for God to reveal practical ways to stir up love and good works towards your spouse. Listen and watch as He draws you to Christians who give godly counsel for improving marriages in practical ways. Increase spiritual sensitivity to God at work. Recognize the spiritual warfare that fuels the physical reality you face but avoid dwelling on them. Instead, surrender them to God and pray against Satan's schemes and seek how God would have you respond. Wait on Him to fuel greater intimacy *in your marriage*. It is not always instantly, divinely imparted. But the path to intimacy will continually be revealed through resources, through His Word, and by the power of His Spirit. Have faith in God to sustain you and your family. Jesus provides peace in chaos.

Even if you perceive the grass greener on the other side, it still needs mowing. My husband likes to add that it also needs fertilizing. *Any* relationship requires maintenance. If *your* grass doesn't look as green as it should, assume responsibility for tending it. Yes, God designed that both spouses bear this responsibility, but society and the church lack proper training for marriage enrichment. Satan uses life issues to deter learning and exhaust efforts even when resources are available. The lack of effort of one spouse should not negate your efforts. Someone needs to "mow, fertilize, and water" your marriage, so make that a priority. One day, your spouse may learn and then take on some of the burden as well. Every successful relationship requires the surrender of self, which is never easy, quick, or painless.

The difficulty of marriage and God's power to overcome is part of my own journey from fear to faith. I once believed that good Christians never struggled with difficulty unrelated to betrayal, abuse, or addictions—a truly genuine Christian would always have a good (easy) marriage. Because my marital issues were more subtle I initially believed lies that isolated and undermined faith in God to heal. For this reason, this message is for those who are in the midst of circumstances that may appear hopeless but where God is raising up a Gideon or a surrendered servant in the home to bring restoration.

Don't allow doubt, fear, hurt, and pain presume this restoration is out of reach. Don't allow Satan to plant seeds of division and failure that undermine faith. Do not focus on physical visibilities but spiritual realities. Reach out to God and ask Him to show you the path for healing. Fear intensifies when we are anxious about something happening or something not happening. Our reaction testifies to our trust in God's faithfulness to deliver us. Surrender to allow God to use you even amid hurt to be a vessel for reconciliation.

Do not fight your spouse; fight *for* your marriage. When conflict arises or hurt is inflicted, recognize the warfare fueling it and fight against that in prayer. Fight for the emotional security of your children and grandchildren. Find the courage and patience to pray together. Praying together is powerful. It communicates love for each other, trust in God, a sense of security and value, and intercession for your children. Praying together absent feelings of love demonstrates trust in God to heal and restore feelings.

When you pray with one another, it deters arguing. When you see the benefit of prayer, you are more motivated to resolve conflict when it occurs. Prayer brings the desired atmosphere of peace in the home despite the difficulties of life that are certain to happen. Prayer puts the focus on God above the power of self and the power of hurt. If your spouse won't pray with you, you pray and journal the prayers. Create a record of the intercession so God's answers will be prevalent to you both in the future.

Too many Christian marriages live in the reality of a Genesis 3 relationship, feeling the full frontal assault of Satan and sin on the marriage. We do not seek or perhaps even realize the attainability of the Ephesians 5 relationship. We live too much in the marital realm of "I cannot" or "With man it is impossible" without persevering to discover that with God, *all things are possible.*

We may come to the place of saying, "I just can't do this anymore" without realizing the need to confess that God can through us. "I can endure all things through Christ who strengthens me." Often, while we believe in God's greatness, we fail to surrender our weaknesses to God or fail to trust God to empower our spouses to do the same. Like Peter, God may bring us to that point of realizing greater dependence on Him beyond our valiant, admirable self-efforts, or even in the wake of our failures.

For two to become one requires self-sacrifice, a dying of one's self-focused interests and self-protection so they gain and add the interests and well-being of another. In a society that extols self-promotion, this concept can be disturbing to some and perceived weak to others. That viewpoint is short-sighted. You are not losing control but gaining power when two become one and are centered in God's love. "A cord of three is not easily broken." Recall our study on unity. Recall the power that comes from those joined in unity of purpose. Unity is an unstoppable power. Since God has called for marriage to be a bond of unity centered around Him, imagine the strength, power, and stability this brings to the family and society.

Dr. Willard Harley is a psychologist and author who shares the principle of the "joint policy of mutual agreement" in his marriage-enrichment books. Though secular in its definition, the policy defines what couples can do to bridge the gap between the curse (of Genesis 3) and marital intimacy to build unity (Ephesians 5). The policy states that couples should never make any major (or possibly minor) decisions without the "enthusiastic mutual consent of each other." In his more-recent book *He Wins, She Wins* (which can be read in a few hours), he discusses how to apply this principle in difficult situations where mutual agreement is harder to achieve.

Reflect on what is required to live in enthusiastic mutual agreement. Its spiritual truth runs deep. Under the effects of the curse, self is exalted. Self seeks protection. Self seeks its own identity. Ephesians 5 calls us in love to put the welfare of our spouses above self's need for justice, comfort, or happiness. It promotes the strength of two becoming one. Mutual agreement requires calm discussion of the need or decision. It requires consideration of the other person. It involves patience to allow God to work in and lead each other, not a ruling over the wife by dismissing her need or promoting self-interest. Not desperate, manipulative nagging of the husband for what is desired. It requires self-sacrifice in a way that promotes intimacy, not fuels duress or resentment—it requires *enthusiastic* agreement.

To reach mutual agreement may require the refinement of conflict-resolution skills. It requires understanding the perspectives and needs of your spouse. It requires facing what each other may fear or dread. It requires honest reflection as to whether your own behavior fuels those fears. It is learning to listen with understanding to the other's perspective, not to mount a defense to relieve your fear or promote your self-interest. Living with enthusiastic mutual agreement is a way to live the teachings of Ephesians 5.[57]

Dr. Harley's book *Love Busters* is an aid for conflict resolution as is *His Needs, Her Needs*. The former identifies five keys habits destructive to intimacy: dishonesty, angry outbursts (or in-bursts), selfish demands, disrespectful judgments, and annoying habits (including independent behavior). In *His Needs, Her Needs*, he identifies ten needs common to husbands and wives that fuel intimacy and help them identify what the most important needs are to the spouses.

To identify love busters, the spouses should identify their own habits

---

[57] *Love and Respect* by Dr. Emerson Eggerichs offers spiritual understanding and application of Ephesians 5, while *He Wins, She Wins* is more of a quick secular discussion of these spiritual truths with periodic biblical reference.

that undermine intimacy. However, each spouse should seek to understand the most important *needs of the other* so efforts can be focused on those above the ones they seek for themselves.

If your marriage is hurting or could use some rejuvenation, I recommend these books because they equip a couple with a vocabulary that builds intimacy while teaching how to minimize conflict. Half the battle of marriage is learning how to resolve issues without using inflammatory communication. While some marital issues require much more assistance, my husband and I have used this material to help strengthen couples on the brink of divorce. Its guidance enriched and strengthened our marriage through difficulty as well. The key to applying Harley's principles is to focus on what you can change about yourself.[58]

Encourage those in your sphere of influence to love, honor, and respect their spouses. Encourage them to remain faithful when all seems hopeless. Encourage them to recognize and embrace the power of God at work in their lives. The understanding He longs to give can bring healing and restoration. As you wait on God's timing, He will draw you close to Himself and pour His love in you. The joy of the Lord will be your strength!

When we follow Christ's example of surrender, we allow God to use us as vessels for His power to be demonstrated to our spouse and children. It will require us to lay aside our "rights," perhaps even our right for justice. Recall Christ's focus as the Son of Man; remember His continual relationship with the disciples even when they did not understand, even when they forsook Him. Once Christ resurrected, the disciples eventually understood. Likewise, in marriage we often must be willing to persevere even when our spouses have little understanding of the issues at hand or what is necessary to remedy the problems. Perhaps we deny the issues or forsake the marriage relationship in various ways. Nevertheless, God is working. We must be willing to look to the day of marital resurrection; we can learn from the

---

[58] When reading Harley's books, highlight was is important to you. Using the same book, have your spouse do the same with a different color highlighter. Discuss these highlighted portions as a way to learn what the other needs and to see where there is common ground and understanding. It is important not to engage in love busters while discussing the material. Seek to understand what love busters you possess, and ask God to help you minimize and overcome these destructive behaviors.

disciples' failures how to remain sensitive to the nearness of His presence and desire for restoration. He will give you a Word to sustain you today, but that same Word He also uses to bring greater blessings and power in the future.

Your marriage has value! Obedience to God in this holy relationship has tremendous potential to positively affect those near you. The strength, compassion, and grace you give in marriage are witnesses to those in your sphere of influence.[59]

A Tree of Life

Begin with worship, meditation, and prayer.

> The kingdom of heaven is like a mustard seed, which a man took and sowed in his field, which indeed is the least of all the seeds; but when it is grown, it is greater than the herbs and becomes a tree, so that the birds of the air come and nest in its branches. (Matthew 13:31–32)

> "Lord, thank you for growing my faith and as a result drawing me closer to You. Thank You, Father, for stretching me to reach beyond what I can see possible with such a small seed. Be glorified as my life matures to more fully reflect Christ."

At the time this parable was given, the mustard seed was known as the smallest of seeds that would grow to a large shrub or tree about the height of a horse and rider in semitropical climates and to the size of a large hedge in more-temperate climates. This verse is a parable about the early church. After Christ's resurrection, the church was small, but when Christ comes

---

[59] R. T. Kendall's book *The Thorn in the Flesh* has a chapter specifically dealing with a difficult marriage and how God will use that as a blessing for His glory. I also recommend his book *Total Forgiveness*, which inspires one to pursue forgiveness.

again, it will have grown to its full intended "height" as a source of shelter from the wickedness of the world, a refuge to those who find solace there.

As a child of God, you are part of the church. As your faith grows, you are strengthened and you also strengthen the body of Christ. Thus far, we have seen how faith compels us to worship, trust, surrender, and obey. Now, we gain understanding of the mature faith's purpose.

Many verses in this study refer to trees. As we revisit some of these scriptures and others, we glimpse how God repeatedly compares the purpose of mature faith to that of a sturdy, mature tree. We will also further understand how great faith prepares us for intercession.

Read each verse or passage and write in the space provided the description or characteristic of the tree.

Proverbs 3:13–18

Wisdom - tree of life

Isaiah 61:1–3

Oaks of righteousness

Psalm 1:1–3

Tree firmly planted by streams of water; yield fruit in season; leaf doesn't wither

Proverbs 11:30

Fruit of the righteous is a tree of life

Revelation 22:14

right to tree of life

What two significant trees did God place in the Garden of Eden? (Genesis 2:9).

tree of life   tree of knowledge of good & evil

Which of these were Adam and Eve warned not to eat the fruit of? (Genesis 2:16–17).

Knowledge of good & evil

Why was this tree the only one prohibited?

They would die if they ate from it

After Adam and Eve sinned, what did God say and do about the tree of life? (Genesis 3:22–24).

Cherubim & flaming sword to guard it

What promise does Christ give in Revelation 2:7?

to him who overcomes - grant to eat from tree of life

Describe the role of the tree of life in Revelation 22:2.

healing of nations & bearing fruit

God placed the tree of eternal life in the Garden of Eden; it symbolized the gift of eternal union between God and man. Adam and Eve in immortal innocence were not prohibited from eating its fruit.

The tree of knowledge of good and evil symbolized God's gift of free will to man. In His prohibition against eating of that tree, God gave man the choice to obey Him and protection from sin's consequences through obedience to His instruction.

Until sin entered man, there was no need for eternal life. It in fact already existed as there was no sickness or death and there was no separation from God spiritually. However, once man sinned, humanity needed deliverance from spiritual death. God intended Christ to redeem man and grant eternal life.[60] By sending Christ to earth, God once again provided a way for humanity to know Him. To eat from the tree of life would disturb God's divine plan for redemption and fellowship with humanity. Thus, the tree of life needed to be removed as another source of temptation before God's will could be finished. God has taken man out of the presence and reach of the tree of life until after the second coming of Christ.

As seen from earlier passages, God made us a planting of the Lord. As we mature in faith, we give witness to the tree of life. This description gives a mental picture of the steadfast, unshakeable righteousness Christ nurtures. We are to be examples of God's knowledge, wisdom, obedience, and holiness and be witnesses to what is currently unseen (the tree of life),

---

[60] Ephesians 1:3–7. Sin separated man from fellowship with God, which He desired. Eating of the tree of life may grant eternal life, but it would not bridge the separation from God only Christ can grant.

but will be revealed with the return of Christ the King. Then, all those who have heard and overcome will partake of the fruit of the tree of life planted by the river near the throne of God.

This understanding allows us to glimpse God's general, eternal plan for faith. Hopefully, this glimpse encourages us to more fully embrace its growth and encourage discovery of God's specific plans for faith. Our faith is important to God! Our maturing faith gives great witness to the righteousness of God and the eternal blessing we will someday receive. Hearing with understanding causes faith to mature: "Till we all come in the unity of the faith, and of the knowledge of the Son of God, unto a perfect man, unto the measure of the stature of the fullness of Christ" (Ephesians 4:13). As trees of life, as trees of righteousness, we are joined as the body of Christ in unity of purpose and glory to God. We are to pursue the faith of Christ as me.

Besides Christ, perhaps one of the greatest examples of this mighty faith we are given in God's Word is that of Daniel. Daniel and his three friends were among the children and nobles sent for by the Babylonian king when Judah was destroyed and its people taken into exile. King Nebuchadnezzar instructed his servants to bring him "young men in whom there was no blemish, but good-looking, gifted in all wisdom, possessing knowledge and quick to understand, who had ability to serve in the king's palace."

Even at a young age, Daniel could be characterized as one who understood the importance of not conforming to the world but renewing the mind so he could prove the good and acceptable will of God (refer to Romans 12:1–2).

> But Daniel purposed in his heart that he would not defile himself with the portion of the king's delicacies, nor with the wine which he drank; therefore he requested of the chief of the eunuchs that he might not defile himself. Now God had brought Daniel into the favor and good will of the chief of the eunuchs. (Daniel 1:8–9)

Daniel's commitment to honor God with his life and body resulted in God continually setting him apart as the strongest and healthiest young man. Daniel 1:17 tells us that God gave him and his friends knowledge, skill, and wisdom. He also gave Daniel understanding in all visions and dreams. Later in Daniel's life, we read that the men of the kingdom "could find no charge or fault, *because he was faithful*; nor was there any error or fault found in him" (Daniel 6:4; emphasis added).

Read the following scriptures and note the empowerment God gave this man of faith. These scriptures show us how God worked in Daniel's life both to will and do for God's good pleasure. The giftedness God imparted is summarized below.

- Daniel 1:19–20: Daniel received wisdom and understanding greater than that of the king's magicians and astrologers.
- Daniel 2:14: Daniel answered the king's captain with counsel and wisdom.
- Daniel 2:20–23: God gives wisdom to the wise and knowledge to those who have understanding. He gave Daniel wisdom and might.
- Daniel 2:28, 29, 47: There is a God in heaven who reveals secrets.
- Daniel 4:18: The Spirit of the Holy God is in you to give interpretations.
- Daniel 5:12–15: The Spirit of God is in him giving him understanding and excellent wisdom.
- Daniel 6:3: Daniel was distinguished because of the Spirit of God in him.

In Daniel 4:34–37, describe what God grants to King Nebuchadnezzar.

Daniel's steadfast faith had a tremendous effect on King Nebuchadnezzar, the godless enemy of Daniel and the kingdom of Judah. He destroyed the great temple built by Solomon. Jerusalem was destroyed. Survivors who had not fled had been brought to Babylon where they lived in the consequence of their rebellion.

Looking at this from an earthly perspective, Daniel is a good-looking, wise, up-and-coming young man in the kingdom of Judah, but he and his close, godly, friends are taken in the prime of their lives to be servants of this wild, pagan, evil king.

However, Daniel's devotion to God empowers him to endure the exile and faithfully serve the one who is the instrument of so much turmoil in his life. Daniel has not become embittered or angry at God regarding his circumstance. Instead, he chooses to be a vessel of God's power to an evil king, a king who is willing to at least show great respect for God.

In the above passage, we once again are reminded that God responds to understanding with healing and restoration. Through Daniel's reflection of God, the king has come to know who God is and seeks His favor.

The book of Daniel reveals the many high positions of authority granted him by the king because of his godly wisdom and understanding. In Daniel 6:10, we are given insight to the great devotion Daniel had to his God: "And in his upper room, with his windows open toward Jerusalem, he knelt down on his knees three times that day, and prayed and gave thanks before his God, as was his custom since early days."

Daniel is a man of faith and righteousness who as we read above was granted much wisdom and understanding. Throughout his exile, throughout conflict, throughout the many responsibilities of his appointed positions, Daniel remained a devoted servant of God. His time alone with God, his need to depend on God remained a priority "since his early days."

While it could be said that Daniel certainly made the most of his exile through his devotion to God, it seems he never lost sight of the fact that God's people were not where God intended. Daniel's method and place of prayer revealed a hope for God's restoration of His people. Through this man of understanding, God began to bring that restoration (notice the pattern of His ways similar to Gideon).

Read Daniel 9:2–4. Then read Jeremiah 29:10–14. What happened to Daniel when he read the prophecy of Jeremiah? (Daniel 9:2).

What did this understanding compel him to do? (vv. 3–4).

Read Daniel's prayer of confession and intercession in 5–19. From verse 13, describe the conviction Daniel's understanding gave.

When God granted understanding of His Word in regard to Daniel's own people, the level of prophetic revelation God gave was unprecedented.

Daniel proved himself trustworthy through His humble service. Through Daniel's understanding and faith, God revealed the first detailed prophesies of the end times.

Daniel received unsettling details of the future power and coming of our blessed King. (Keep in mind that Nebuchadnezzar's palace where Daniel served was one of the palaces overtaken by coalition forces against Saddam Hussein during the Iraq war. Think about God's ways of revealing His Word for present and future needs.) Daniel, an intercessor for the people of his time, was also used by God to receive prophecy and intercede for future events. Daniel's faith and willingness to seek understanding prepared his heart to be worthy to receive such revelation. Through adversity and trials, Daniel steadfastly focused on God.

This study reiterates how God gives opportunities through fearful circumstances—whatever they are, however difficult they are—to increase our understanding of Him. We have learned the need to surrender hearts hardened with doubt and unbelief so we may understand the deep things of God. God wants hearts devoted to Him into which He can pour His truth. God looks for intercessors He can trust to pray in agreement with His present or future will. Instead, Satan would have us captivated by fear and distracted by the concerns of life so we are too exhausted, angry, depressed, and frustrated to look beyond what is happening to ourselves in the moment. As well stated in *The Purpose Driven Life*, "It's not about you," as Daniel greatly models. God allows what we currently face and perhaps fear. He uses it for our blessing and His glory if we surrender our hearts and minds (thought lives) to Him!

Get a mental picture of a snow globe. When we remain enslaved to fear, we are no different from the figures in a snow globe. We live trapped in our own world of difficulty constantly shaken by the snares of Satan. Possibly, we experience moments of rest when God settles us, but to truly live in freedom seems beyond hope. We are trapped by circumstance.

To pursue understanding is to live beyond the bubble. It is to shatter the cocoon-like mind-set Satan uses as a trap to realize there is a bigger God and a bigger purpose and plan for our existence and even for our struggles. As long as Satan consumes our time and mental and emotional energy in this tug-of-war between fear and faith, we will not have the energy or focus to intercede for the kingdom of God. He wants our marriages because he wants to destroy the witness and stability it gives our children and our society. He wants to destroy the confidence that a mature faith brings because he wants to undermine the faith of future generations. Without a willingness to growth faith, we will not seek understanding or even realize it is a provision of God. Without understanding, we will not become powerful intercessors to agree in unity with God for His will to be revealed.

Satan's efforts to destroy intercession will not thwart the will of God. As seen through scripture, God generally finds one who is faithful to Him and willing to intercede for His purposes. Failure to understand and intercede will leave us ill prepared to withstand the evil that is prophesied to increase in the end times. Daniel successfully survived being a captive servant of the Babylonian king by remaining steadfastly focused on God and on understanding as God revealed His higher purposes. By seeking and agreeing with God for His will to be done and allowing that agreement to give him the confidence to trust God through any adversity.

Some in Babylon did not see Daniel as wise despite the repeated demonstrations of his godly wisdom. They set a trap for Daniel and his friends, knowing Daniel would not cease worship of God. Since Daniel could not be controlled by this mandate, he needed to be destroyed. But Daniel adhered to Proverbs 4:5–9: "And in all your getting, get understanding. Exalt her, and she will promote you; she will bring you honor, when you embrace her. She will place on your head an ornament of grace; A crown of glory she will deliver to you."

Daniel and his friends were delivered from their adversaries and the evil plots to destroy them. Daniel models the mature Christian faith, of Christ as me. He was a surrendered vessel to the power of God, a vessel of understanding in accordance with God's plans. Daniel's understanding did little to change the hardness of their hearts and their rebellion against God, but it did invoke enough of a fear of God that they halted persecution.

Like Daniel's adversaries, the world today generally does not view Christians as wise but as naïve. They see our stand for godly principles as intolerant and judgmental in arrogance and self-righteousness. Often, Christians fuel this criticism when they respond to ungodliness with ungodliness. As Daniel exemplified, seeking God's understanding for the current need empowers us to endure and remain steadfastly focused on

God. The danger for us is not to respond to this worldview in the Flesh but in the Spirit to both Christians and non-Christians.

When people are dangerously close to the edge of danger, do our actions to help actually push them over the cliff or pull them to safety? Understanding through faith (not out of fear) helps us discern the action that is helpful, not destructive. But even helpful actions may be confrontational as we shall soon study with Gideon. Gideon also teaches us how to become equipped to withstand the confrontation even in the direst circumstances.

Satan wants fear or any difficulty in life to enslave our emotions, minds, time, and our effect on the kingdom of God. God will use that same difficulty as a motivating force for us to seek Him. We need to go beyond hearing Him to understanding Him.

Jeremiah 29:10–14 is one of my favorite passages as it summarizes the essence of God's love and redemption. Daniel prayed for it to be experienced by his people. Following this intercession, God revealed the end-time captivity and destruction as well as the restoration and eternal deliverance that would follow through Christ's Second Coming. Through this passage, once again, we see the ways of God to reveal a truth for the moment as well as preparation for a future time. The passage also points to the salvation Christ offers, how we receive it, how God grows faith, and how we will embrace eternity. I have inserted God's ways identified in this study that are consistent with this prophecy.

> For thus says the Lord, After seventy years are completed at Babylon, I will visit you and perform My good word toward you, and cause you to return to this place. [His Word] For I know the thoughts that I think toward you, says the Lord, thoughts of peace and not of evil, to give you a future and a hope. [His will] Then you will call upon Me and go and pray to Me, and I will listen to you. And you will seek Me and find Me, when you search for Me with all your heart. [Empowered Surrender] I will be found by you, says the Lord, and I will bring you back from your captivity; I will gather you from all the nations and from all the places where I have driven you, says the Lord, and

I will bring you to the place from which I cause you to be carried away captive. [His power]

When will we call upon God and pray to Him? "Then!" When we comprehend His loving thoughts, actions, and plans for us even amid sin's consequences and difficulty! God's Word assures us that we will find Him when we search for Him with all our heart. Hearts filled with fear cannot find the fullness of God. Whether fear is a deep-seeded stronghold or arises to destroy understanding in a present circumstance or decision process, God provides deliverance from its effects.

God continually makes provision to deliver His people from physical bondage, from the bondage of sin, and from the captivity of fear—a fear of rejection, failure, futility. He will "cause us to return from this place" of fear, rebellion, complacency, doubt, or unbelief. He is standing at the door of His church knocking and waiting to be found by those who search with a whole heart. He has a provision of hope.

Dear Christian, I pray the Lord rules in your heart and grows your faith to gain victory over fear. As His presence and power compels worship, I pray you are a testimony of peace even in the middle of chaos. As you hear, obey, and know Him, receive the joy that comes from a heart delivered from unbelief!

Throughout this study, we have looked at how God desired to empower His servants' faith in victory over fear. We learned that God has a good, hopeful purpose for our future despite appearances of circumstances. He has an eternal purpose that far surpasses the comforts and conflicts of this world. He wants to help us survive today and equip us for tomorrow. We cannot be equipped without knowing Him, without realizing there is more of Him we do not yet know.

Learning how to hear, see, and understand the spiritual realities behind the physical visibilities empowers trust in God's ways and will. Too often, we desire God to shine a floodlight far down the road to our future. God promises only to be a light for our path (Psalm 119:105). However, we also know from His Word that according to His sovereign design, He will reveal understanding of future plans and events from His Word as we learn to focus on His purposes rather than our self-interest.

As mentioned, most Christians realize the need to seek His Word and will. Too often, though, as did the disciples, we fail to comprehend how any revelations of His power correlate with revelations of His Word and will. Perhaps we miss this correlation for we stubbornly refuse surrender.

Perhaps we fail to look beyond our preconceived ways for His will to be fulfilled. His power revealed may be subtle or miraculous, but it is not an isolated gift from God. It is intended to further teach us of His fullness and cause us to look beyond ourselves, beyond physical visibilities, for the ways His will is to be completed. Through Judges 6 and Mark's gospel, we are reassured of God's presence and power to reveal God's purpose and plan and the empowerment to fulfill His will. Do you hear and understand? Do you have spiritual eyes willing to see spiritual realities in the physical visibilities? As we echo this understanding in intercession and worship God, faith is strengthened.

I pray you have heard how God would have you draw nearer to Him through your circumstances. I pray God has helped identify His ways for finishing faith as a tree of life, as Christ as me. I pray your hunger is fueled to seek God's specific ways for understanding His Word, will, and power so you experience more of His goodness. I pray you will not settle for mustard-seed faith but will continually hunger for and surrender to its growth into a strong, viable shelter in this world. I pray you understand God's desire to do in and through fear more than you could ask or imagine.

Growing Faith 6
Sheltered by Faith

As we conclude this study, we return to Judges to finish the faith lessons of Gideon. As Gideon realized the gracious presence of the Lord, he was compelled to worship. As he worshipped, God's peace consumed him. He built an altar to the Lord as a lasting testimony of the peace God granted him before the battle with the enemy ever began.

Worship was the pivotal response necessary to begin the transformation from fear to faith. Worship gives honor, glory, respect, and reverence to God. Worship acknowledges who God is and whom we desire Him to be in our lives. Worship restores God to the throne of our hearts and invites His presence in intimate communion. Worship focuses the mind on spiritual truth so that we hear and understand Him. As God is lifted up, self and the ways of our Flesh diminish and give God's wisdom, strength, and understanding to grow faith.

Worship is communion with God that proclaims His Word and gives Him the opportunity to conform our desires to His. It is one way God propels us beyond belief in an outcome to have faith in His will and way. Many hymns we sing were written during great difficulty particularly after loss of close family; two examples are "It is Well with My Soul" and "Tis So Sweet to Trust in Jesus." The message of these hymns reveals a faith focused on God in the midst of unimaginable tragedy.

We worship God in many different ways. However, an expression of worship through songs and hymns reveres God and focuses the faith of the worshipper. Colossians 3:16–17 says,

> Let the word of Christ dwell in you richly in all wisdom, teaching and admonishing one another in psalms and hymns and spiritual songs, singing with grace in your hearts to the Lord. And whatever you do in word or deed, do all in the name of the Lord Jesus, giving thanks to God the Father through Him.

Faith comes from the Word of God. These verses admonish us to dwell on that Word by singing hymns and spiritual songs.[61] Worship of God puts the focus on Him, not on self. When the body of Christ worships in unity, it proclaims the Word of God. As we worship, we have the assurance of His presence because He inhabits the praise of His people (Psalm 22:3). This worship lifts the name of the Lord and postures us to receive His peace and specific instructions as we learn from Gideon.

Worship through praise is an expression of faith we can exercise at any time and in any circumstance. The power of God is released through worship to work in the situations of our lives. The previous testimony of my mother gives witness to this power as well as testifies to faith's blessings.

Gideon's worship demonstrated the focus of his heart on a fear of the Lord more than on a fear of his circumstances. The specific benefits Gideon received as He communed with God are important for us to identify. We have already discussed some of these and will continue exploring these benefits through the last part of the story. Through worship, through fellowship with God, growing faith shelters us by granting

- a peace that passes all understanding,
- a progressive understanding of God's purpose,
- an understanding of God's way for today, and
- an empowerment to obey.

After God had Gideon's undivided attention, He began giving specific instruction for His ways to fulfill Gideon's purpose.

> Now it came to pass *the same night* that the Lord said to him, "Take your father's young bull, the second bull of seven years old, and tear down the altar of Baal that your

---

[61] If you do not feel gifted to sing, do not discount your ability to worship God through song. This passage says to "sing as with grace in your hearts." Worship through song depends on your heart, not your voice. I know gifted singers who miss the blessing of true worship. I know many more who have no talent to sing yet are greatly empowered by joining their hearts and minds with the worship songs and music of others. Be concerned with surrendering your heart and opening your spiritual ears more than sounds of your voice!

father has, and cut down the wooden image that [is] beside it; and build an altar to the Lord your God on top of this rock in the proper arrangement, and take the second bull and offer a burnt sacrifice with the wood of the image which you shall cut down." So Gideon took ten men from among his servants and did as the Lord had said to him. But because he feared his father's household and the men of the city too much to do it by day, he did it by night. And when the men of the city arose early in the morning, there was the altar of Baal, torn down; and the wooden image that was beside it was cut down, and the second bull was being offered on the altar which had been built. So they said to one another, "Who has done this thing?" And when they had inquired and asked, they said, "Gideon the son of Joash has done this thing." Then the men of the city said to Joash, "Bring out your son, that he may die, because he has torn down the altar of Baal, and because he has cut down the wooden image that was beside it." But Joash said to all who stood against him, "Would you plead for Baal? Would you save him? Let the one who would plead for him be put to death by morning! If he is a god, let him plead for himself, because his altar has been torn down!" Therefore on that day he called him Jerubbaal, saying, "Let Baal plead against him, because he has torn down his altar." Then all the Midianites and Amalekites, the people of the East, gathered together; and they crossed over and encamped in the Valley of Jezreel. (Judges 6:25–33, emphasis added)

As Gideon worshipped God, he was humbled and filled with His peace. His heart was focused on the greatness of God. This posture is a stark contrast to Gideon's focus as he threshed wheat when he was consumed with fear and insecurity. God did not give any specific details of His plan until after Gideon's faith was focused. Then, having Gideon's full attention, God gave him the first instruction to prepare Israel for its deliverance. The same night God gave the instruction, Gideon obeyed even in the midst of fear. God sent Gideon into his father's household to destroy the worship of

Baal and restore the altar to God. Think for a moment about the significance of that command.

When you have something significant you need to accomplish, who is the first wave of support you seek? Generally, your family, those closest to you. Those who know and love you best, those in and outside your family who would be most likely to sacrifice their comfort to help you. However, God did not send Gideon with some great motivational speech to unite his family to defeat this band of mass robbers. Instead, Gideon was sent on a very dangerous mission.

Look at this instruction from an earthly viewpoint; it would seem to have been a very divisive and destructive mission. He was charged with destroying the focus of his family's trust. This was their tradition, their religious worship. These altars and gods were their presumed source of strength.

God instructed Gideon to take his father's bull (not one of his own) of *seven* years. The Israelites had been in judgment for seven years. This was a bull his father had managed to hide for that time. This bull had probably been a major source for producing other cattle to keep them nourished. But this offering also appropriately served as atonement for Israel's sin as it signified the period of penitence, the age and end of God's judgment.

God instructed Gideon to take the *second* bull. In spite of the extent and number of raids by their enemies, Joash had managed to hide at least two bulls. The fact that he had any bulls spoke to his wealth, and revealed why God instructed Gideon to use a bull for the burnt offering. According to the offering rituals, a burnt offering atones for sin. The use of a bull without blemish speaks to the wealth of those offering the sacrifice. Recall how Gideon described himself as the weakest of his father's household. This emphasizes His overwhelming task to make this sacrifice on behalf of his father's household.

Any of you who have tried to be godly witnesses in your family can understand the fear Gideon had to face to obey. He had to overcome fear of rejection, futility, and failure. Gideon obeyed, but He did so under the protection of night for his life certainly was endangered as he obediently took this stand against Baal.

From an eternal perspective, we understand that this mission was necessary to prepare the hearts of those who eventually helped Gideon.

God knew that his family needed more than a temporal motivational speech fueled by the passion of man to defeat this army. They needed more than an obligatory devotion to family. They needed a fear of the Lord to empower a lasting commitment to follow God's plan. They needed trust in their almighty God. For many years, that trust had been misplaced. They needed to take their eyes off temporal, earthly circumstances to be reminded of the eternal God.

Gideon's faithful obedience moved his father to repentance but aroused anger and hatred in the hearts of men in the city. They still had hearts hardened toward the move of God in their midst. Their world of security had been disturbed, and they wanted the responsible party murdered. They who tore down the altar of Jehovah and lived wanted to kill the one who tore down the altar of Baal!

Perhaps you have received similar responses or been the one to give it. Their attitude revealed a selfish double standard we also at times reveal. Though we receive grace for our sin, we demand justice or punishment for those we perceive to sin against us. Their actions were the result of sin, but Gideon's actions were in obedience to God. Their sin blinded understanding of this truth until someone else intervened. Joash, Gideon's father, interceded cleverly; he reminded others of how foolishly they had put their faith in a powerless god.

Just as Joash reminded them of their sin, their enemies arrived in preparation for another attack. God reminded them of their need to repent, and their need for physical deliverance was made all too real with their enemies' arrival. What else could they do but trust God? He had removed options. God cleared the way for the power of His deliverance.

Is God perhaps allowing a similar pattern of His ways in your life? Is He using delay in deliverance to teach you a greater need of Him? Is He exhausting self's attempts to compensate for or remedy difficulty? Are you sure you are not looking to something or someone besides God as your deliverer?

Gideon faithfully obeyed God's difficult command and as a result was postured to receive further empowerment. Filled with the Spirit, Gideon rallied support from surrounding tribes to build an army of 32,000 to face the Midianites. Though Gideon obediently responded to God, his faith was young. He struggled with doubt about God's willingness to use him as proclaimed. The size of God's army seemed great until it was compared to the vastness of the Midianites, the Amalekites, and the people from the East who were "innumerable as the locusts." Gideon was struggling with understanding God's ways for accomplishing His will. Physical visibilities threatened to overshadow spiritual realities. To overcome, he asked for reassurance that empowered obedience. God graciously gave Gideon not one but two signs as requested. Following this affirmation from God, Judges 7:1 reveals that Gideon and the army "rose early" and encamped near the Midianites. Once reassured of God's purpose, Gideon did not hesitate to obey.

The Angel of the Lord had told Gideon He would use him to defeat this numerous enemy as "one man." With the army of 32,000 gathered, God gave Gideon another instruction. God ensured that Israel did not claim the victory that God had ordained as its own. They have been living in rebellion to God. God's plan for deliverance from the Midianites would not interfere with their need for spiritual deliverance. God would prove it was not the power of Baal nor the might of men that would defeat the Midianites. Let's look at God's process for reducing the size of the army.

> Now therefore, proclaim in the hearing of the people, saying, "Whoever is fearful and afraid, let him turn and depart at once from Mount Gilead." And twenty-two thousand of the people returned, and ten thousand remained. And the Lord said to Gideon, "The people are still too many; bring them down to the water, and I will rest them for you there. Then it will be, that of whom I say to you, This one shall go with you, the same shall go with you; and of whomever I say to you, This one shall not go with you, the same shall not go." So he brought the people down to the water, and the Lord said to Gideon, "Everyone who laps from the water with his tongue, as a dog laps, you shall set apart by himself; likewise everyone who gets down on his knees to drink." And the number of those who lapped, putting their hand to their mouth, was three hundred men; but all the rest of the people got down on their knees to drink water. Then the Lord said to Gideon, "By the three

hundred men who lapped I will save you, and deliver the Midianites into your hand. Let all the other people go, every man to his place." (Judges 7:3–7)

Though God intended to deliver the Midianites to Gideon and his army, His process of elimination ensured that only those truly prepared and focused for battle remained. Two thirds of those gathered—22,000—were fearful and afraid. The presence of fear is an obstacle of faith. It stands to reason that God desired men of faith to lead a battle to be won by His hand.

Among the remaining 10,000, God appeared to be looking for those who had their senses trained and poised for battle. There were many who were willing, but only a few were actually prepared for battle. Those who got down on their knees to drink would have their heads down and facing the water. That was a vulnerable position that would increase their likelihood to be easily overtaken; this indicated they weren't remaining cautious.

Verse 6 describes those who lapped water as bringing their hand to their mouths. That method left them more prepared to take an offensive or defensive position. They were better positioned to be on guard and aware of their surroundings. It suggested a more alert military stance. God used those who lapped the water, only three hundred.

Notice how the 32,000 initially willing to deal with the enemy were reduced to just 300—1 percent. God told Gideon,

> And it happened that same night that the Lord said to him, "Arise, go down against the camp, for I have delivered it into your hand. But if you are afraid to go down, go down to the camp with Purah your servant, and you shall hear what they say; and afterward your hands shall be strengthened to go down against the camp." Then he went down with Purah his servant to the outpost of the armed men who were in the camp. Now the Midianites and Amalekites, and the people of the East, were lying in the valley as numerous as locusts; and their camels were without number, as the sand by the seashore in multitude. And when Gideon had come, there was man telling a dream to his companion. He said, "I have just had a dream; to my surprise; a loaf of

barley bread tumbled into the camp of Midian; it came to a tent and struck it so that it fell and overturned, and the tent collapsed." Then his companion answered and said, "This is nothing else but the sword of Gideon the son of Joash, a man of Israel; for into his hand God has delivered Midian and the whole camp." And so it was, when Gideon heard the telling of the dream and its interpretation, that he worshipped. He returned to the camp of Israel, and said, "Arise, for the Lord has delivered the camp of Midian into your hand." (Judges 7:9–15)

God gave Gideon instruction to proceed into the camp where he had delivered the enemy into his hand. The tense of this statement is interesting. It is past tense: "It has been delivered." God knew the heart of his deliverer. God understands that with the progressive revealing of His will, we need a progressive strengthening of faith. Considering how God just decreased the size of the army God gave Gideon the opportunity to strengthen that faith, but the instruction also caused him to face his fear.

God instructed him to go into the vast enemy camp accompanied by only one servant to overhear a conversation that would "afterward strengthen your hands to go down against the camp." God revealed His Word and will. His will placed Gideon in the position to receive power to obey. But it was likely his initial thoughts were not of reassurance as he described the vastness of the enemy through the dimness of the night in verse 12. The reported size of the enemy was consistent with that from Judges 6; they were as numerous as locusts, and God has reduced the 32,000 soldiers to 300.

Pause to reflect on what God was doing to strengthen Gideon's faith. He was sending him virtually unprotected (from a physical perspective) into this enormous enemy camp to hear a conversation that increased confidence to obey. Gideon, as one man, would in fact face this great army and be reassured of the victory "already delivered." By the time God gave instruction for an offensive stance, Gideon's fear and doubt were eradicated. He victoriously transformed Gideon from fear to faith as one man in the middle of the vast enemy.

That was when the true battle, the spiritual battle, was won. Through the confident obedience of this leader, God's will was accomplished. What a stark contrast to the fearful, angry, defeated man hiding in a winepress just a short time ago. Without a word of rebuke or condemnation for Gideon's fear, God empowered him to progressively face and surrender the fear of his circumstances!

As Gideon entered the camp, he overheard two Midianites in a conversation. One was sharing his dream; the other was interpreting it as their defeat by Gideon through the hand of God. God orchestrated the dream and its interpretation by these armed, godless robbers to strengthen the faith of His devoted servant-deliverer. (Notice how God can and will use godless men to deliver prophetic messages.)

Let us look at analogies revealed through Gideon's encounters. In Judges 6, the Angel of the Lord appeared to Gideon while he was threshing wheat that was to be made into bread. In this dream, the loaf of barley is interpreted to be the sword of Gideon, the weapon of Gideon, the strength of Gideon. We have previously discussed how the conversation with the Lord while Gideon was threshing wheat refocused his heart from fear to faith. The Angel proclaimed Gideon to be a mighty man of valor while he was hiding in a winepress. In this dream, the might of Gideon was compared to a loaf of wheat barley. What was once indicative of fear became a symbol of strength. The newly harvested wheat was prepared into a baked loaf of bread. (God did not keep the wheat in a seed-like state. It was planted, harvested, and prepared to be consumed for nourishment.) This gave witness that God had prepared Gideon by changing his fear into faith. Through the power of God, a weakness had become a strength.

In this dream, there was also the impossible conquering of the tent by a small tumbling loaf of barley. The interpreter acknowledged this was possible only because God was with Gideon (opposite to how Gideon felt abandoned by God earlier). While it is obvious that only God could have placed this interpretation in the mind of the companion, it is still amazing that he seemed to specifically know of Gideon, "the son of Joash, a man of Israel." Remember how Gideon said he was the least in his father's house, which was in the weakest clan. Yet this man, this outsider, this enemy, specifically stated who Gideon was and acknowledged the source of his great power. Obviously, word had spread among the enemy about the man who had gathered an army to come against them.

Once again, the humble heart of Gideon was revealed as this

conversation compelled him to worship. In the company of his tiny army facing a vast enemy and present in the midst of that enemy with only one servant, Gideon lost his fear; his faith was mightily strengthened. He immediately responded with worship and obedience.

When he returned to gather the men of Israel, he told them the Lord had delivered Midian "into your hand." He did not focus the spotlight on himself. With his own fear relinquished and faith strengthened, he offered the same confidence to this small number of faithful few by reassuring them the Lord had fought the battle for them.

Gideon demonstrated the influential power of a truly godly leader who gave liberally what had also been given to him—confidence in the Lord. Through the previous process of elimination, we know these remaining men were of strong faith as well as great physical endurance, yet Gideon sought to spiritually empower them further as he himself had been empowered. What an inspiration!

Armed with weapons, trumpets, torches, and pitchers, they divided into groups to surround the camp in the middle of the night. Given this divine tactic, we can better understand why God needed men of faith to follow His command. A mere three hundred were sent against hundreds of thousands. They had been told God had assured them victory, but they had to trust this promise with a willingness to risk their lives by scattering themselves (not banding together) among the enemy. They had to act on spiritual truth, not physical appearances.

With the sounding of the three hundred trumpets and the crashing of the pitchers, Gideon and his men instilled a fear of the Lord in the Midianites causing them to cry out and flee while the Israelites "stood in their place." The enemy, presuming the Israelites to be in their midst as well as confused by the dark hour and the noise, fell by the swords of their own companions. They believed they were surrounded by a vast army unaware that it was little more than three hundred men of God. Those remaining fled in confusion. Gideon and his men pursued them and gathered reinforcements in their pursuit, reclaiming the water wells inhabited by the enemy.

God graciously, progressively, patiently, and gently helped Gideon transform from a man of fear to a mighty man of faith. He fulfilled His promise to use Gideon to deliver his people from the enemy as numerous as locusts as if they were one man. The Midianites were not killed or driven out by the sword of Gideon or by the power of a mighty army; they were destroyed because *fear* had caused them to panic and turn on their own. After seven years of "successful thievery," after great arrogance and power, fear caused this destructive, overpowering mass of thieves to self-destruct when one man chose to be transformed.

Read through Judges 8 about the continual, steadfast strength of this mighty man of valor. With man, it is impossible, but with God, it is possible for faith to strengthen and conquer all fear. Through faith in God, it is possible to trust and obey even amid great danger.

Let us reflect on the pattern of God's ways and how Gideon's purpose pointed to Christ. God sent Christ to earth as Jesus in the form of man empowered to obey God's deliverance of sin. From all the Jews who served God, there were only twelve initially chosen as His disciples. Of those twelve, Jesus often took only Peter, James, and John with Him for certain miracles and for times of support. In the Garden of Gethsemane, though His three disciples were encouraged to pray, Jesus found Himself alone only with prayer with His Father to empower obedience at Calvary. Throughout those final moments, Jesus offered instruction about what was to come; He interceded so their faith would not fail and they would receive empowerment the way God had empowered Jesus. Then Jesus, the Bread of heaven, as one Man, faced the cross alone. As He died, even His Father turned away from the great sin that fell on Jesus. Jesus as one Man took on the vast sin of humanity—past, present, and future—to bring spiritual deliverance.

Is this not also what God may ask of us? We too may find ourselves in life alone and without the support of those who are expected to understand and give the most when facing difficulty. Whether in a family or single, though we may be surrounded by people in the workplace, ministry, or church, we may find ourselves drawn away by God or circumstance in solitude of purpose.

You find out who your real friends are when you go through difficulty. Sometimes, the difficulty may be something not even true friends can help you with. Our Flesh tendency is to fear, dread, and become discouraged by solitude and isolation. We can even become angry at God or others for the abandonment we perceive. As Gideon and Christ revealed, God is nearer than we often realize and is using the time of solitude to draw us nearer to

Him to fill us with His strength to fulfill our purpose. How did Gideon's small army defeat the vast enemy? With trumpets and swords. We too have the sword of God, the Word of God, and worship to fight against fear, to fight against the vast schemes of Satan.

When our story of Gideon began, we learned of the failure of God's people to fear and worship Him. When Gideon's purpose was complete, the people wanted to appoint Gideon and his son as their rulers. But that surrendered deliverer instead focused their faith and worship on their almighty God: "But Gideon said to them, 'I will not rule over you, nor shall my son rule over you; the Lord shall rule over you'" (Judges 8:23). Gideon's heart was revealed as a heart of a servant, not that of a ruler. Gideon had been called of God to refocus worship to Jehovah, not to rule the people.

The people's desire to promote him in such a way was not surprising, nor is it an uncommon response to God's revealed power today. God wanted to rule His people, but they begged him for a king, so God gave them Saul. The Israelites continued to place dependence on an earthly leader above the leadership of God, leading to hundreds of years of rebellion despite momentary revivals. But we are no different today. People look for leadership, and it is often necessary. Christians particularly want godly leadership. But human nature has a tendency to elevate the person or to worship his power instead of fear and worship the Source. Like the Israelites, how willing are we to look to mortal men when so much has already been given by our almighty Father! But whenever God demonstrates His power through a person, it is for the purpose of glorifying Him, of worshipping Him, of fearing Him.

We should learn from the humility and weakness of Gideon and his people. We may be God's instruments, but He is our power and strength. Gideon wisely refused to rule, but his attempt to create a memorial to the power of God eventually resulted in worship of the memorial instead of devotion to God. This idolatry and the resulting sin eventually brought ruin to his household. "Then Gideon made it into an ephod and set it up in his city, Ophrah. And all Israel played the harlot with it there. It became a snare to Gideon and to his house" (Judges 8:27). The very thing, idolatry, God used Gideon as a deliverer for became the future snare for his household. This is a sobering lesson for those God calls for ministry, even those with successful ministries such as Gideon's.

Before we presume we would never fall into such a snare, let us remember the disciples, Jesus's closest followers, who willingly sacrificed all to serve Him. Early in ministry, when their faith was young—when doubt, unbelief, and fear ruled them more than understanding did—they focused on what earthly position, authority, knowledge, and recognition they could gain by their devotion to the Son of Man. At the time, they did not fully understand the full purpose of Jesus as the Son of God. As we have discussed, they certainly did not understand what was involved in establishing His kingdom. As they pondered who would be the greatest among them, Jesus reminded them that the last would be first. He told them they had to be willing to take up their crosses and deny themselves daily.

Do you fully understand what is necessary for the coming kingdom? What calling has God placed on your life? How are you tempted to allow others to focus more on that calling than on the power of God in you? Are the memorials or testimonies of what God accomplished building an idol in your or others' hearts? Or are you a catalyst for lovingly, humbly, gently keeping others postured in a fear of God reflecting His peace? Are you willing to face fear of rejection, futility, and failure to follow Christ and receive all He has to offer? How willing are you to embrace the difficulty God uses to crucify Flesh, to cleanse sin, and to empower? As you read the below verses, contemplate how fear, doubt, and unbelief are roots of destructive behavior.

> But know this, that in the last days perilous times will come: For men will be lovers of themselves, lovers of money, boasters, proud, blasphemers, disobedient to parents, unthankful, unholy, unloving, unforgiving, slanderers, without self-control, brutal, despisers of good, traitors, headstrong, haughty, lovers of pleasure rather than lovers of God, having a form of godliness but denying its power. And from such people turn away! For of this sort are those who creep into households and make captives of gullible women loaded down with sins, led away by various lusts, always learning and never able to come to the knowledge of the truth. (2 Timothy 3:1–7)

Fear blocks understanding truth. But God has not given us a spirit of fear but of power, of love, and a sound mind. God has a great calling for your life! He who began a great work in you is also faithful to complete it! He planted the seed of faith in your heart, and He gives the understanding necessary to nurture its growth. He is maturing you into a tree of righteousness that brings great glory to Him and wonderful benefit to you. The sweet intimacy of His nearness overshadows any difficulty of your surroundings.

This study focused on the process God used to restore and grow Gideon's faith as well as that of the disciples. Repeatedly in His Word, God reminds us He is near. Our fear of Him, our recognition of His power, compels us to worship and surrender to His will.

Beloved, you are in the presence of the almighty God! Recognize Him and listen to His words of love and encouragement and His plan and purpose. He offers peace to settle your heart so you can receive His fullness. Embrace His power that is working to propel you from fear to faith!

In view of all this, make every effort to respond to God's promises. Supplement your faith with a generous provision of moral excellence, and moral excellence with knowledge, and knowledge with self-control, and self-control with patient endurance, and patient endurance with godliness, and godliness with brotherly affection, and brotherly affection with love for everyone. The more you grow like this, the more productive and useful you will be in your knowledge of our Lord Jesus Christ. But those who fail to develop in this way are shortsighted or blind, forgetting that they have been cleansed from their old sins. So, dear brothers and sisters, work hard to prove that you really are among those God has called and chosen. Do these things, and you will never fall away.
—2 Peter 1:5–10 NLT

Leaders' Answer Guide

Introduction

What keeps us from "moving mountains?"
Unbelief

How great must our faith be to have power over the impossible?
As small as a mustard seed

Describe what happens to the mustard seed that is planted.
It grows into a tree large enough to provide shelter for birds

Read Mark 4:35–41. In verse 40, how does Jesus describe the state of the disciples?
They are fearful and they have no faith.

Chapter 1: Exposing the Root of Fear

In Genesis 3:1–5, what truth did Satan say to Eve?
Your eyes will be opened and you will know both good and evil.

What truth did Satan distort, and what was an outright lie?
Distortion: you will not surely die. There is not a physical death but a spiritual death.
Lie: you will be like God. Satan appeals to Flesh, not faith.

From verse 5, what is the "fear of something withheld" that Satan implies God is keeping from Adam and Eve?

The knowledge of good and evil.

Chapter 1: The Danger of Doubt

Write Lamentations 3:22–25.

Through the Lord's mercies we are not consumed, Because His compassions fail not. They are new every morning; great is Your faithfulness, the Lord is my portion, says my soul, therefore I hope in Him! The Lord is good to those who wait for Him, to the soul who seeks Him.

Write Lamentations 3:40–41.

Let us search out and examine our ways, and turn back to the Lord; Let us lift our hearts and hands to God in heaven.

Write Lamentations 3:57–58.

You drew near on the day I called on You, and said, "Do not fear." O Lord, You have pleaded the case for my soul; You have redeemed my life.

Chapter 1: Fear Arouses Anger

Read and fill in the blanks from the Word of God in Ephesians 4:30–32 and 1 Peter 3:8–12.

And do not <u>grieve</u> the <u>Holy Spirit</u> of God, by whom you were sealed for the day of redemption. Let all <u>bitterness</u>, wrath, <u>anger</u>, clamor, and evil speaking be <u>put away</u> from you, with all malice. And be <u>kind</u> one to another, just as God in Christ <u>forgave</u> you.

Finally, all of you be of one mind, having <u>compassion</u> for one another; love as brothers, be <u>tenderhearted</u>, be courteous; not returning <u>evil</u> for <u>evil</u> or reviling for reviling, but on the contrary <u>blessing</u>, knowing that you were <u>called</u> to this, that you may <u>inherit</u> a blessing. For "He who would love life and see good day, let him <u>refrain</u> his <u>tongue</u> from evil, and his lips from speaking guile; let him turn away from evil and do good; let him seek <u>peace</u> and <u>pursue</u> it. For the <u>eyes</u> of the Lord are on the <u>righteous</u>, and his <u>ears</u> are <u>open</u> to their prayers; but the <u>face</u> of the Lord is <u>against</u> those who do evil."

Chapter 1: A Fear of the Lord

Look up the following scriptures and briefly summarize what caused a fear of the Lord, paying close attention to the importance of the presence of God in each passage. Meditate on the similarities.

Genesis 22:8–12
Unwavering obedience at great cost

Genesis 28:16–17
Revelation through dreams

Exodus 3:3–5
Power and presence of God in revelation of His will

Judges 6:21–23
Honor and acceptance of sacrifice of offering; the consuming power of God

Daniel 3:25–30
Protective power of God

Daniel 8:15–17
Prophetic revelation through the Angel's presence

Luke 1:11–13, 28–30
Presence of Angel to reveal God's will

1 Kings 18:37–3
Consuming power; acceptance of offering as in Judges 6

To whom did God demonstrate His power or reveal His presence in the above passages? List not the names but the characteristics or nature of their hearts.

The righteous, unrighteous, the humble, the doubting

Read Exodus 20:4–5 and 34:14. From these verses and the passages above, why do you think God wanted to reveal Himself?

So His people would know His will, plans, and purposes and be empowered and confident to fulfill them by partnering with or surrendering in their completion

Chapter 2: What is a Hardened Heart?

In each of these verses, what group of people did Jesus indicate had hardness of heart?

The disciples

In John 12:40 and Mark 3:5, what group of people had hardened hearts?

The Jewish leadership

Chapter 2: Why a Hardened Heart?

In Mark 4:35 who is in the boat with Jesus?

The disciples

In Mark 4:30–34, what does God teach us about who He is and what He is capable of doing?

He has given Jesus power over nature.

In Mark 5:1–20, what miracle does Jesus perform?

He casts evil spirits out of the man and into the swine.

Whose power does Jesus now exert authority over?

The demonic, spiritual realm

Jesus continues to reveal the power of God over all situations. In Mark 5:35, what was the attitude of Jairus's household?

Overcome with grief, frustration in Jesus's delay

How would you characterize their depth of faith and its effect or lack of on the eventual healing?

They have no hope in healing, unbelief in Jesus's ability to heal. This unbelief and lack of hope have no effect on the healing.

Did all of the disciples enter Jairus's household with Jesus? (v. 37).

No; only three

Describe your understanding of this leading.

It appears to be a necessary revelation of Jesus's power to deepen the three disciples' understanding of Jesus's ability that would strengthen their faith. It protects Jesus's ministry from further doubt, confusion, and misunderstanding.

Jesus and the disciples return to Nazareth where He teaches with great wisdom in the synagogues and performs some miracles. In Mark 6:2–4, what was the response to Jesus and His wisdom in Nazareth?

They are skeptical, prejudicial; they question His qualification and authority. However, they do not dispute the legitimacy of His miracles, His mighty works.

In verses 5–6, what reason does Jesus give for the lack of miracles?

Unbelief and the familiarity of His own community, relatives, and immediate family (His "house")

Chapter 2: Hardened to Understanding

In Matthew 13:15, what does God state would have happened if they had seen with their eyes, heard with their ears, and understood with their hearts?

They would repent and turn, resulting in healing and restoration.

Chapter 2: Hardened by Unbelief

In Matthew 17:14–21, why couldn't the disciples heal the epileptic child? (Note that this conversation happens right after Jesus's transfiguration, but the failure of the disciples occurred during the transfiguration.)
Unbelief

What does Christ say is necessary to bring healing in this situation?
Much prayer and fasting

In Matthew 15:10, how does Jesus begin His teaching of the multitude?
"Hear and understand"

Reread Mark 6:1–6. What limited Jesus's ministry in His hometown?
Unbelief

Read John 20:19–29. What evidence does Thomas need to see in order to believe?
Thomas had third-party validation from the rest of the disciples who had been shown Jesus's scars. Thomas, however, wanted to touch as well as see scars.

What evidence does Christ offer?
Jesus granted the proof Thomas requested, allowing him to place his finger into the scars on His hands and the scar on His side, saying, "Do not be unbelieving, but believing."

What does Christ say about seeing and believing in verse 29?
Do not limit belief to what can be verified by seeing.

Chapter 2: "I Believe, Help My Unbelief"

Read Matthew 10:5–11:1. Summarize Jesus's instructions in the parallel account from Mark 6:8–11.

To take nothing with them on the journey—no bag, no food, no money, or money belts

To wear sandals but do not put on two tunics

To stay only with those who are receptive of you, where you will have peace. If there is no peace, leave, and "shake the dust of your feet"; do not give the lack of receptivity any further thought or action. The fact that they rejected the disciples' ministry will be an action that God will hold them accountable for in the day of judgment.

What are Jesus's exhortations in Matthew 10:26–28, 31?

Not to fear. To boldly proclaim what He reveals. He exhorts them to fear God more than fearing anyone who could physically harm them. He gave them power over unclean spirits.

What do the disciples accomplish in Mark 6:12–13?

They cast out many demons and anointed and healed the sick.

In Mark 6:30–31, the disciples reunite with Christ. They report on their ministry efforts, and Jesus tells them to rest. The crowds, however, prevent rest. Describe the spiritual hunger of the crowd in Mark 6:33.

They saw where the boat was headed, ran from surrounding cities, and arrived before the boat.

As Jesus teaches, time passes. The spiritual hunger is overshadowed by a physical hunger.

In verse 35–36, how would you characterize what the disciples say to Jesus?

The day has been long, and it is almost night. They and the crowds are hungry and tired. The disciples have nothing to feed them and don't want to be troubled with trying to feed such a multitude. It is a daunting and impossible task from their perspective.

Reread and write Matthew 10:9–10.

"Provide neither gold nor silver nor copper in your money belts, nor bag for your journey, nor two tunics, nor sandals, nor staffs, for a worker is worthy of his food."

Chapter 3: To Know Christ as the Way

Read John 14:1–7. What does Jesus reveal as the key to knowing the Father? (vv. 6–7).

Recognizing that Jesus is the only way to know God. When we know Jesus, we will know God.

In John 14:8, how does the disciple Philip respond to these words of Christ?

He wants to see God as further verification of Jesus's words.

In John 14:9–12, what does Jesus indicate as the source for seeing the Father?

Looking at Jesus and the works of the Father He performs. He tells them He and the Father are one. To know and see Jesus is to know and see God.

Chapter 3: To Seek His Face

Read Luke 10:38–42. In Luke 10:40, what was Martha asking Jesus to do for her?

To use His influence to persuade Mary to assist Martha in preparing the meal for Jesus.

In Luke 10:42, what does Jesus say about Mary choosing to seek Him?

Mary has chosen the one "needed" thing of service—fellowship—that will not be taken away from her. (She was building a reward that would withstand the fire of judgment.)

In Psalm 27:4, what is the "one thing" David is seeking, and what does he hope to receive from this seeking?
To dwell in the house of the Lord all the days of his life so he can behold the beauty of Lord and gain His counsel.

In Psalm 27:8, what does David say that God commanded him to seek?
His face

In Psalm 27:9, what does David request God not to withhold from him?
His face

In Chronicles 7:14–15, what happens when we seek God's face?
We will be drawn to turn from our wicked ways. He will hear our prayers from heaven.

Before He tells us to seek His face, what does God mention we must do?
Humble ourselves and pray to Him.

How will God respond to someone seeking His face? (v. 15).
His eyes will be open and His ears will be attentive to the prayer made in that place.

In Psalm 24:1–6, what characteristics describe the generation that seeks God's face?
They have clean hands and a pure heart; they have not lifted their souls up to an idol nor sworn deceitfully.

In 1 Peter 3:12, what is God's response to those who do evil?
The Lord's face is against them.

Read Revelation 22:1–5. In John's vision of heaven, what is the blessing described in verse 4?
God's servants shall see His face.

From reading all the above passages and verses, do you believe seeking the face of God is the goal or a means to a goal?

To seek the face of God is to seek His fullness, which should be the goal of all we seek from God.

Read Exodus 33:12–23. In verse 13, why does Moses tell God he needs to know His way?

So that he may know Him and find grace in His sight.

After God assures Moses that His presence will go before him, what does Moses ask God to do in verse 18?

He asks God to show him His glory.

In the first half of verse 19, what glory does God promise to reveal to Moses?

All His goodness and to proclaim the name of the Lord before him.

In Exodus 33:11, how does it say Moses speaks with God?

Face to face as a man speaks to a friend.

Chapter 3: To Know His Glory

Read John 1:18, 14:1–7. What does Jesus say is the key to knowing the Father?

Knowing Jesus.

From John 14:5 and 8, describe the disciples' level of understanding of Jesus's words.

They are still thinking with a physical perspective; they are not grasping the spiritual, eternal perspective.

In John 6:38, whose will has Christ come to complete?

The will of Him who sent Christ, God.

Read John 1:1–5, 14. Describe the power given to Jesus, the Word.
He was with God; He is equal with God. When He became flesh, He was filled with grace and truth.

What did Jesus, the Word, have to do so we could know Him and thus God?
Become flesh.

In John 8:38, 49–50, 14:13, 17:1–5, whom did Jesus come to glorify—Himself, God, or man?
God His Father.

Read John 12:44–50. In verse 49–50, whose authority was Jesus exercising?
The authority of the Father who sent Him.

What command did God give Jesus?
What He should say and speak.

What command in John 12:50 does Jesus say God gave?
Everlasting life.

Philippians 2:8–11 and Ephesians 1:20–23 teach us about Jesus's power and authority as Lord being restored. What does this Ephesians passage say Jesus must do before that could happen?
Humble Himself in obedience even to the point of death.

Describe the power and position of Christ after His resurrection recorded in these verses.
God has highly exalted Him and given Him the name above all names so all will worship Him. God seated Him at His right hand in heaven giving (restoring) Him power over all things.

Chapter 3: Obstacles to Knowing God

Read Jesus's prophesy of Peter's denial in Mark 14:27–31. What is Peter's response?

Even if all are made to stumble, he will not. He says he will even follow Christ to death before he would stumble.

Now read the entirety of Peter's denial in Mark 14:66–72. From verse 71, describe Peter's emotional state and reaction.

He was angry and frustrated and fearful; he began to curse and swear.

Read Philippians 3:4–15. In verse 6, how does Paul describe his obedience to the law?

He was blameless and righteous according to it.

In Paul's righteousness of the law as Saul, what were his actions toward Christians?

He persecuted them violently even unto death.

From verses 8–11, how would you describe Paul's desire to pursue Christ?

He is willing to lose all things to gain the knowledge of Christ. He does not want his own righteousness from the law but from faith in God. He wants to know Him and the power of His resurrection. He is willing to endure the fellowship of Christ's sufferings so he too may experience God's resurrection power.

How are Paul's exhortations similar to the lesson learned by Peter discussed above?

They both realize the need for God's power to fully surrender to and follow Him in faith, not their own merits.

Fill in the blanks from verse 10.

"that I may ____know____ Him and the ____power____ of His resurrection, and the __fellowship__ of His sufferings, being ___conformed___ to His death, if, __by any means__, I may attain to the __resurrection__ of the dead."

In 2 Corinthians 12:8–10, what does Paul say is the benefit of accepting your weakness?
You may know the strength and power of God.

Read John 17. In verse 3, how does Jesus describe eternal life?
To know God is eternal life.

Chapter 3: Empowered to Know Him

Keeping in mind the influences mentioned above that also infiltrated the church, read 1 Corinthians 2:1–5 and briefly describe the contrast Paul makes between what has empowered him and what has not.
He does not consider himself to be skilled with great speech or wisdom, but instead comes only in the knowledge of Christ in weakness, fear, and trembling.

Why does Paul indicate this distinction to be important? (v. 5).
So that their faith would be in the power of God, not the wisdom of men

Read 1 Corinthians 2:11–12. From verse 11, who is the giver of wisdom and all things spiritually discerned?
The Spirit of God.

In verse 10, how has the Spirit come to know the deep things of God?
The Spirit has searched all things, even the deep things of God.

In verse 12, what does Paul give as the reason for the gift of the Spirit?
That we may know the things freely given to us by God

Read 1 Corinthians 2: 6–8. To whom does Paul speak the wisdom of God?
The mature

In 1 Corinthians 2:14–15, describe how the natural man responds to things of God.
He cannot receive the things of the Spirit for he perceives them as foolishness. He cannot know them for they are spiritually discerned.

In 1 Corinthians 3:1–3, how does Paul describe the level of spiritual maturity of the Church of Corinth?
They are remaining babes in Christ, as carnal Christians, still clinging to the ways and things of the flesh. They are unable to receive the deeper spiritual truths.

Read 1 Corinthians 2:16, then fill in the blank.
"…But <u>we</u> have the <u>mind</u> of <u>Christ.</u>"

Chapter 4: "Can You Hear Me Now?"

Read 1 Samuel 3:1–21. When the Lord called Samuel in verse 4, how did Samuel respond?
Here I am!

Samuel availed himself to the voice, but whose did he believe it to be?
Eli's

How does verse 1 describe Samuel's relationship to the Lord?
He ministered unto the Lord under Eli the priest; he was a servant in the tabernacle of God.

How does verse 7 describe Samuel's knowledge of the Lord?
"He did not yet know the Lord, and the word of the Lord had not yet been revealed to Him."

Reread verse 1, 19–21 and summarize your understanding of God's desire to make His Word known to His people.
Without the indwelling Holy Spirit, God used priests and prophets to reveal His Word. God raises up a prophet with hearing sensitivities to Him

and communication skills and who earns the respect and credibility with His people to make sure God's Word and will are understood.

What response did Eli give Samuel to say to the Lord?
Speak, Lord, for your servant hears.

What was Samuel's initial response to God's Word?
Fear

Chapter 4: Set Your Mind to Hear

Read Mark 14:32–42. How many times did Jesus leave His seclusion of prayer to urge the disciples to pray?
Three

From verses 34–36 and Matthew 26:36–39, describe the difficulty of Jesus's struggle.
His sorrow and distress were grace. He was greatly burdened by the pending circumstances and prayed for God to make another way if possible.

What seemed to be the source of the disciples' hindrance to pray? (vv. 38, 40).
There was a weakness in their flesh. Jesus warned against temptations and the inability to overcome without prayer.

In Mark 14:38, why does Jesus say they need to pray?
To receive the empowerment to withstand temptation and to grant discernment to recognize the enemy.

Read Romans 12:1–2. Why must our minds be renewed?
So we may prove what is the perfect and acceptable or pleasing will of God.

Read Isaiah 26:3–4. What happens to those whose minds are set on God?
They will be kept in perfect peace as a result of their trust in God.

Read 2 Corinthians 10:3–7. What must be brought into captivity and obedience to Christ?
Every thought.

Chapter 4: Focused to Hear

How would you describe the tone of verse 10?
Hopeful, optimistic, overcoming.

What characteristic does Peter use to describe God?
The God of grace

What does Peter remind us we are called to?
Christ's eternal glory

Paraphrase Peter's reference to suffering in verse 10.
It is imminent but temporary.

Chapter 4: Hearing Empowers Holiness

Read 1 Peter 3:13–4:6, 12–16. Referring to 3:17, suffering can occur either when one is doing ___good___, or when one is doing ___evil___

In verse 4:1, what are we, in the flesh (our physical being), to be armed with?
The same mind of Christ, who has suffered in the flesh.

According to verse 4:1, what does the Man who has suffered in the flesh cease?
Sin

From 4:2–3, why do we need to have the mind of Christ?
So we will no longer live in the flesh but in the will of God.

In verse 4:16, what is to be our conduct in suffering?
To not be ashamed and to glorify God.

Read Hebrews 5:7–14. What did Jesus learn through suffering?
Obedience

What did His learned obedience through suffering accomplish?
His perfection

What makes obedience to this exhortation hard? Describe the difficulty of dying to Flesh when responding to conflict and suffering.

The natural tendencies of our Flesh are to fight pain, difficulty, oppression, unpleasantness—to protect self physically, emotionally, and spiritually. Therefore, when conflict and suffering occur, our first instinct is not to understand what God may be teaching or refining in us through the difficulty but to reinforce a safe zone for self.

In conflict with another person, we typically don't focus on any shred of truth from the other person. We look to see the fault of our "opponent." We also look to the manner of conflict, or the erroneous, hurtful, untruth communicated.

In suffering, instead of first seeking God's purpose in it, we may blame God for allowing it or presumably failing to end it in our time frame.

We are refined and learn obedience when we seek the wisdom to know how to respond: to know when to walk away and find a place of peace (as Jesus instructed the disciples at times) or when as Jesus did, to embrace the cross and face the erroneous accusations, shame, disgrace, and difficulty that will result in a further crucifixion of the self to embrace and reflect more fully His Spirit within.

How do you describe the difference between walking in holiness and having self-righteousness? What is the main, necessary attribute that distinguishes the two?

Humility is the primary difference as self cannot be exalted when walking in holiness. Self is the focus in self-righteousness, presuming to know the full ways and will of God in a given situation.

Why is a glorifying conduct important to us? (1 Peter 4:17).
Because we will be held accountable in the judgment.

Chapter 5: Hear and Understand

Read Mark 4:1–20. As you answer the questions that follow, consider this passage as a guide to help us identify what prohibits and what nourishes spiritual maturity.

In verse 13, what does Jesus say is the result of failing to understand this parable?
They will be unable to understand all other parables.

Why is understanding this parable so critical? (What is the key emphasis of this parable?)
It reveals the way to grow in faith to find God's will. This parable teaches the importance of hearing the Word and understanding it. Without understanding, we will be unable to comprehend and apply God's truth.

In verse 14, what does the sower sow?
The Word

Chapter 5: Prepared for Understanding

Let's look at other scriptures correlating obedience with understanding. Summarize this correlation in each verse below.

Deuteronomy 4:5–6
To observe the commandments is wisdom and understanding.

Psalm 111:10
A good understanding have all those who do His commandments.

Proverbs 14:29
He who is slow to anger has great understanding.

Isaiah 11:2–5
Righteousness and faithfulness adorn the one with understanding.

Job 28:28
To depart from evil is understanding.

Jeremiah 4:22
Those who are foolish and still have no understanding are wise to do evil.

Read John 14:25–29. In verse 27, what does Christ leave the disciples?
Peace not as the world gives, but His peace.

What does He tell them not to be?
Troubled—do not be afraid

In verse 28, how does Christ say they should respond if they fully understood?
They would rejoice.

Read John 16:1–7. After describing great persecutions and afflictions that the disciples must face in the future, how do they respond? (v. 6).
Sorrow has filled their heart.

Read Mark 3:35–41. What command does Jesus issue in verse 39?
Peace, be still!

Let's look at one more instance, this time in the Old Testament, where God again spoke comfort in the middle of chaos. Begin first by looking at God's prophecy of judgment to fall on His people in Jeremiah 25:8–11, 27–33. Briefly summarize God's judgment.
God will utterly destroy Jerusalem and send families into captivity.

Read Jeremiah 29:4–14. Summarize the tone of God's instruction in verses 4–6.
God instructs them to carry on with the normal routines of life—building houses, marrying, having children, planting, and harvesting.

Read Jeremiah 29:10–14. Summarize God's plan of restoration.
He desires to bring hope and not evil. When their hearts are fully His, He will hear their prayers and restore them to the Promised Land.

In 29:7, what does God tell His troubled, hopeless, people to seek?
Peace in the city of captivity. Pray for peace.

Chapter 5: The Gift of Understanding

Exodus 31:3
He filled them with the Spirit of God in wisdom and understanding.

Exodus 36:1
In whom the Lord has put wisdom and understanding

1 Chronicles 22:12
May He give you wisdom and understanding.

Proverbs 2:6
From His mouth comes wisdom and understanding.

1 John 5:20
The Son of God has come and has given us an understanding so we may know Him.

Proverbs 2:2–9
Apply your heart to understanding; lift up your voice for understanding.

Proverbs 3:13
Happy is the man who gains understanding.

Proverbs 4:1
Give attention to know understanding.

Proverbs 4:5
Get wisdom! Get understanding!

Proverbs 4:7
And in all your getting get understanding!

Chapter 5: God's Presence Opens Understanding

The New Testament gives an example of the secret will of God. What does Mark 13:32 tell us about Jesus's understanding of His Second Coming?

Not even the Son of God knows the day and hour of His return, nor the Angels, only the Father.

Chapter 6: The Seed of Faith—His Word

Read Exodus 16:4–36. When faced with hunger in the wilderness, how did the Israelites respond?
They grumbled, complained to Moses and Aaron

In verse 8, who does Moses say they are grumbling against?
God

How does God respond to their grumbling? (v. 11).
His glory appears before them in a cloud, and He promises to give them bread.

From verses 16–17, how much did each person gather?
Only as much as each needed.

How long did God provide the provision of manna, and when did the provision end? (v. 39).
Forty years. It ended when they came to the Promised Land.

Chapter 6: Faith that Believes His Will

When are they healed?
As they leave to see the priest

How many of them are healed?
All ten

One of the healed lepers returned to Jesus to do what?
To praise and glorify God; to thank Jesus for his healing

What does Jesus say about this one who gives thanks?
Your faith has made you well.

Chapter 6: Faith that Surrenders His Power

"With God it is possible? What does this mean?" we ask. To answer that question, look up Philippians 2:13 and fill in the blanks.

"For it is __God__ who works in you both to __will__ and __to do__ for His good pleasure."

Chapter 6: Faith that Obeys His Ways

Read 1 Samuel 1. What was the initial desire of Hannah's heart—what was she praying for?
For God to end her barrenness and grant her a son

What was the response by her husband to her need?
He dismissed her desire stating that she needed just to be grateful for how deeply he loved and cared for her.

How did her husband's other wife, Peninnah, react to Hannah's situation?
She flaunted her fertility to grieve Hannah.

What was the initial response to her prayer by her priest, her minister?
The priest believed her consecrated prayers to be the ramblings of a drunken woman as her lips moved but her voice was silent.

Given these responses to her need by those closest to her, describe Hannah's continual consecration to prayer (vv. 11–16).

She persevered to pursue God's favor to bless her with a child. She ignored the insensitivities and misunderstanding of those closest to her that should have understood. Their lack of understanding caused her to depend more fully on God's comfort and will.

In Mark 10:1–12, why does Christ say that Moses allowed certificates of divorce?

Because of the hardness of our hearts.

Write how Christ describes the holy union of marriage.

Man and woman are no longer two individuals but become one flesh.

What does Christ warn about the one-flesh union?

What God has joined together, let no man separate.

Read Mark 10:13–16. What does Jesus command about the little children?

Do not forbid them from coming to Him.

Who was forbidding the little children from coming to Christ?

The disciples, the chosen followers of Christ.

What example of the little children are we to follow?

Their willingness to receive the kingdom of God.

Describe what you believe it means to receive the kingdom of God as a little child.

A willingness to trust. To remain hopeful, optimistic; to see the joy and good in things. To search for understanding, and to thirst for knowledge and wisdom. To remain teachable.

Chapter 6: The Tree of Life

Read each verse or passage and write in the space provided the description or characteristic of the tree.

Proverbs 3:13–18
   Understanding is a tree of life to those who take hold of it.

Isaiah 61:1–3
   Christ has come to make us trees of righteousness, a planting of the Lord.

Psalm 1:1–3
   Those who delight in the law of the Lord are like a thriving, fertile tree.

Proverbs 11:30
   Righteous living yields a tree of life.

Revelation 22:14
   Obedient believers will inherit the tree of life.

What two significant trees did God place in the Garden of Eden? (Genesis 2:9).
   The tree of life and the tree of the knowledge of good and evil.

Which of these were Adam and Eve warned not to eat the fruit of? (Genesis 2:16–17).
   The tree of the knowledge of good and evil.

Why was this tree the only one prohibited?
   By restricting its fruit, God gave man a free choice to follow Him. To choose to eat of it would be to choose to know evil; God was attempting to protect them from a physical and spiritual death.

After Adam and Eve sinned, what did God say and do about the tree of life? (Genesis 3:22–24).

God drove man away from the tree of life to prevent them from also eating its fruit. He caused cherubim and flaming swords to guard the tree of life. (Now that sin had entered the hearts of man, so did their need for eternal life. God had a plan for Christ to be the provision for eternal life; therefore, the tree of life needed protection. Knowing sin, Adam and Eve could not partake of this tree's fruit as that was not part of God's way for man to find eternal life.)

What promise does Christ give in Revelation 2:7?

Those who hear Him and overcome shall eat of the tree of life in the midst of the Paradise of God.

Describe the role of the tree of life in Revelation 22:2.

The tree of life bears twelve fruits, yielding fruit all year long. The leaves of the tree were for the healing of the nations.

Daniel 1:19–20

Wisdom and understanding greater than the king's magicians and astrologers

Daniel 2:14

Daniel answered the king's captain with counsel and wisdom.

Daniel 2:20–23

God gives wisdom to the wise and knowledge to those who have understanding. To Daniel, He gave wisdom and might.

Daniel 2:28, 29, 47

There is a God in heaven who reveals secrets.

Daniel 4:18

The Spirit of the Holy God is in you to give interpretations.

Daniel 5:12–15
The Spirit of God is in him, giving him understanding and excellent wisdom.

Daniel 6:3
Daniel is distinguished because of the Spirit of God in him.

In Daniel 4:34–37, describe what God grants to King Nebuchadnezzar.
Understanding and restoration

Read Daniel 9:2–4 and Jeremiah 29:10–14. What happened to Daniel when he read the prophecy of Jeremiah? (Daniel 9:2).
He received understanding regarding the length of the period of exile—seventy years.

What did this understanding compel him to do? (vv. 3–4).
Pray with great consecration to intercede on behalf of his people.

Read Daniel's prayer of confession and intercession in 5–19. From verse 13, describe the conviction Daniel's understanding gave.
He realizes their exile is the result of their sin, which they have still failed to confess.

CPSIA information can be obtained
at www.ICGtesting.com
Printed in the USA
LVHW100958090222
710679LV00024B/238